EX
Br

San.

* *from the same publishers*

Transforming Politics

Power and Resistance

Edited by

Paul Bagguley
Senior Lecturer in Sociology
University of Leeds

and

Jeff Hearn
Professorial Research Fellow
Faculty of Economic and Social Studies
University of Manchester

First published in Great Britain 1999 by
MACMILLAN PRESS LTD
Houndmills, Basingstoke, Hampshire RG21 6XS and London
Companies and representatives throughout the world

A catalogue record for this book is available from the British Library.

ISBN 0–333–74676–7 hardcover
ISBN 0–333–74677–5 paperback

 First published in the United States of America 1999 by
ST. MARTIN'S PRESS, INC.,
Scholarly and Reference Division,
175 Fifth Avenue, New York, N.Y. 10010

ISBN 0–312–22231–9

Library of Congress Cataloging-in-Publication Data
Transforming politics : power and resistance / edited by Paul
Bagguley, Jeff Hearn.
    p.   cm. — (Explorations in sociology)
Includes bibliographical references and index.
ISBN 0–312–22231–9 (cloth)
1. Social movements.   2. Social history—1970–   3. Social change.
4. Social movements—Great Britain.   5. Great Britain—Social
conditions—1945–   I. Bagguley, Paul.   II. Hearn, Jeff, 1947–
III. Series.
HM131.T673   1999
303.48'4—dc21   98–53540
                                                                         CIP

This book is printed on paper suitable for recycling and made from fully managed and
sustained forest sources.

10   9   8   7   6   5   4   3   2   1
08   07   06   05   04   03   02   01   00   99

Printed and bound in Great Britain by
Antony Rowe Ltd, Chippenham, Wiltshire

Contents

List of Tables

Acknowledgements

This volume comprises revised versions of papers originally presented at the British Sociological Association (BSA) Annual Conference, held on the theme of 'Power/Resistance' at the University of York, 7–10 April 1997. It is one of four volumes, all published by Macmillan Press in 1999, produced from the papers given at the conference. The companion volumes are: *Practising Identities: Power and Resistance*, edited by Sasha Roseneil and Julie Seymour; *Relating Intimacies: Power and Resistance*, edited by Julie Seymour and Paul Bagguley; and *Consuming Cultures*, edited by Jeff Hearn and Sasha Roseneil.

The conference was one of the largest ever held by the BSA. Approximately 333 papers were presented, thus making the task of selecting papers for publication particularly difficult. We would like to thank all conference participants for their patience whilst we read the papers; inevitably there were many papers that we would like to have included but were unable to in trying to make this and the other volumes into coherent collections. The contributors to this volume are particularly thanked for revising their papers so swiftly and efficiently in response to editorial comments and suggestions.

The conference theme of 'Power/Resistance' is both a long-established one throughout the history of sociology and one that has seen increased interest and re-evaluation in recent years. This sense of continuity and change was present throughout the conference. The four volumes bring together papers on major sub-themes that *emerged* from the conference. However, there were in addition many other concerns and issues that were debated at the conference, such as the growing amount of work on transnational, international and global issues. Even so, it is probably fair to say that with such a wide-ranging overall theme of power and resistance, these volumes give an indication of some of the preoccupations of sociology, particularly British sociology, in the late 1990s.

We are extremely grateful for all the work of the staff at the BSA office both in Durham and at the conference itself – Nicky Gibson, Judith Mudd, Jean Punton (until November 1996), and especially Nicola Boyne, who assisted the organising committee throughout in solving and resolving all sorts of interesting problems. We also thank the Conference Office and the Department of Sociology at York University for their advice and hospitality, and the student helpers at the conference for their invaluable assistance. Special thanks are due to Sarah Irwin, who was a member of the conference organising committee in its early stages, prior to the demands of motherhood. Our thanks are also offered to our colleagues at Leeds

University, Manchester University and Åbo Akademi University for their support and encouragement. Our conference co-organisers, Sasha Roseneil and Julie Seymour, were a joy to work with, and the overall shape of the four volumes and selection of the papers was decided collectively by all four of us. Finally, we would like to thank Valery Rose for her highly efficient copy-editing.

Notes on the Contributors

Paul Bagguley is Senior Lecturer in Sociology at the University of Leeds. His main interests are in the areas of the sociology of protest, social movements, economic sociology and urban studies. He has carried out extensive research on unemployment and social protest, anti-poll tax protest and new social movements. In the fields of economic sociology and urban studies he has concentrated on debates around post-fordism, labour flexibility and post-industrialism, economic restructuring and its impact on trades unions, political economy and local labour markets, and on gender segregation in employment. His main publications include *From Protest to Acquiescence? Political Movements of the Unemployed* (1991), and he is co-author of *Restructuring: Place, Class and Gender* (1990).

Colin Barker is Senior Lecturer in Sociology at the Manchester Metropolitan University. His main interests are in the sociology of social movements and revolution, and Marxist theories of capitalism and the state. His books include *Festival of the Oppressed: Solidarity, Reform and Revolution in Poland, 1980–1981* (1986) and *Revolutionary Rehearsals* (1987). He co-edited *The Development of British Capitalist Society: A Marxist Debate* (1988) and *To Make Another World: Studies in Protest and Collective Action* (1996). He convenes the annual conference on 'Alternative Futures and Popular Protest' in Manchester.

Cinnamon Bennett is a research student in the Centre for Regional Economic and Social Research at Sheffield Hallam University, completing a PhD on the development of state-sponsored equal opportunities policies in the UK. Her focus is on the emerging strategy of 'mainstreaming' gender equality, and its relation to past delivery practice. She is currently working on research, funded by the EC 4th Community Action Programme for Equal Opportunities. This project explores the experience of gender mainstreaming at different tiers of governance in three member states.

Laurence Cox is Director of the Centre for Research on Environment and Community at Waterford Institute of Technology, and he is completing a PhD on the sociology of counter cultures at Trinity College, Dublin. He is editor of the green-alternative magazine *An Caorthann* [*The Rowan Tree*].

John Drury has worked as a researcher at the University of Sussex and the Trust for the Study of Adolescence, Brighton. His research interests include crowd behaviour, social movements, identity and intergroup relations. He has carried out research on anti-poll tax and anti-roads demonstrations and on police–public interaction.

Brian Elliott is Professor of Sociology and Head of the Department of Anthropology and Sociology at the University of British Columbia in Vancouver, Canada. His recent research has focused on aspects of environmental sociology – on the roots of activism in different communities, on mobilisations around environmental health, and on countermovements opposing the 'greens'. Earlier interests, pursued over his many years with former colleagues in Edinburgh, include studies of the petite bourgeoisie, urban political economy, social movements and the New Right. With Frank Bechhofer he co-edited *The Petite Bourgeoisie: Studies of the Uneasy Stratum* (1981), and with David McCrone he co-authored *The City* (1982) and *Property and Power in a City* (1989). An edited volume on *Technology and Social Process* was published by Edinburgh University Press in 1988.

Max Farrar is a Sociology Lecturer in the School of Cultural Studies at Leeds Metropolitan University. His PhD research on the construction and deconstruction of 'community' in Chapeltown, Leeds, is currently under examination.

Jeff Hearn is Professorial Research Fellow in the Faculty of Economic and Social Studies, University of Manchester, UK; Visiting Professor in Sociology, Åbo Akademi University, Finland; and Visiting Professor in the Department of Sociology and Human Geography, University of Oslo, Norway. He has written extensively on social and political issues, including state formation and development, the politics of social policy, and sexual politics. His publications include *'Sex' at 'Work'* (1987; rev. edn, 1995), *The Gender of Oppression* (1987), *Men in the Public Eye* (1992), *The Violences of Men* (1998) and he has co-edited *The Sexuality of Organization* (1989), *Taking Child Abuse Seriously* (1990), *Men, Masculinities and Social Theory* (1990), *Violence and Gender Relations* (1986), *Men as Managers, Managers as Men* (1996) and *Men, Gender Divisions and Welfare* (1998).

Valerie Hey is a Senior Researcher in the academic group Culture, Communication and Societies at the Institute of Education, London University. Her most recent book was *The Company She Keeps: An Ethnography of Girls' Friendship* (1997). She has also contributed to a reappraisal of class, 'Northern Accent and Southern Comfort: Subjectivity and Social Class', in *Class Matters: Working-Class Women's Perspectives on Social Class*, edited by Pat Mahony and Christine Zmroczek (1997). She is interested in using feminist poststructuralism in her research and analysis. She is currently co-directing an Economic and Social Research Council study looking at the role of gender in classrooms with a focus on teachers' and students' different pedagogic practices. She is currently developing a critique of New Labour in terms of its positions on gender and class.

John Holmwood is Reader in Sociology and Director of the Graduate School in Social and Political Studies at the University of Edinburgh. His main research interests are in sociological theory, philosophy of the social sciences and social inequality and welfare. His main publications include *Explanation and Social Theory* (with A. Stewart), *Founding Sociology? Talcott Parsons and the Idea of General Theory,* and he is the editor of *Social Stratification*, vols I–III, and co-editor of *Constructing the New Consumer Society.*

Ian Law is Director of the Centre for Ethnicity and Racism Studies at the University of Leeds. He is the author of *Racism, Ethnicity and Social Policy* (1996), and co-author of *The Local Politics of Race* (1986). He is currently working on the changing patterns of white racism, cultural competence in public services and 'race' coverage in the news media.

Elizabeth Lawrence is Senior Lecturer in Sociology in the School of Health and Community Studies at Sheffield Hallam University and is attached to the Centre for Regional Economic and Social Research at Sheffield Hallam University. She is the author of *Gender and Trade Unions* (1994).

Ruth Levitas is Senior Lecturer in the Department of Sociology at the University of Bristol. She has written extensively on utopianism, on the history of socialist and feminist thought, and on contemporary politics from the New Right to New Labour, and on the use and abuse of official statistics. Her latest book is *The Inclusive Society? Social Exclusion and New Labour* (1998).

James White McAuley is Reader in the School of Human and Health Sciences at the University of Huddersfield. He is the author of *The Politics of Identity: A Loyalist Community in Belfast* (1994), and several papers on Ulster loyalism.

Wallace McNeish is in the Department of Sociology at the University of Glasgow.

Paul Reynolds is Senior Lecturer in Politics and Sociology in the Centre for Studies in the Social Sciences at Edge Hill University College. His current research interests are in political sociology and radical politics and resistance – particularly the politics of sexuality and the politics of the left – political economy and the applications of contemporary social and political thought.

Beth Simpson is in the Department of Anthropology and Sociology at the University of British Columbia, Canada.

Clifford Stott is Lecturer in Social Psychology in the School of Social and Health Sciences at the University of Abertay, Dundee. His research interests focus upon the role of inter-group relationships in the psychology of collective violence. He has recently published work on football 'hooliganism' and the policing of crowds, and is currently engaged in a research project funded by the Nuffield Foundation on football-related violence during the recent football World Cup Finals in France.

Nicholas Turner was a Research Assistant in the Centre for Regional Economic and Social Research at Sheffield Hallam University from 1997 to 1998.

1 Transforming Politics: Power and Resistance

Paul Bagguley and Jeff Hearn

Politics transform and can be transformed; transforming politics is the theme that runs through the contributions to this collection. Twenty-five years ago a book such as this might have been preoccupied with questions such as neo-marxist state theory, general theories of power, and analyses of political behaviour restricted to voting patterns. Much of this would probably have been preoccupied with class-based power and resistance. While questions of the relationship of politics, political transformation, power and resistance are of recurrent importance in most, perhaps all, societies, they have a special relevance within contemporary British society and contemporary sociological analysis. The social divisions and political questions that run through this book reflect the major changes to the social, intellectual and sociological landscapes that have occurred since the 1970s. These changes in turn show the intellectual and social impact of social movements, even though in recent years the peaks of mobilisation may have passed for the moment. Class is no longer *the* central 'independent variable' of British sociological analysis, and this is reflected in this collection where questions of gender, sexuality, ethnicity and the environment loom large. Often these are grouped together as questions of 'identity politics' or 'new social movements'. However, this collection is not limited to these dimensions.

The wide range of approaches and substantive foci in this collection reflects the broadening of what sociology perceives as political. This is also partly a matter of the impact of a wide range of social movements, as well as an intellectual change with a finer-grained appreciation of 'the social'. Many of the contributions below have strong sensitivity to the unpredictability of political change, its impact on those producing the changes, the development of social movements, the contingency of collective action and the contradictory character of state responses to political conflict. We have not sought to impose a theoretical or methodological uniformity on the collection, as that would not represent either the state of sociological debate, nor the contributions to the conference from which they are selected. However, in many

1

different ways the contributions do address such questions as 'Has politics been transformed, and is it transforming?' and 'In what ways is contemporary politics transforming (or not transforming) dominant power relations, and representing (or not representing) resistance?'

The book is organised into four parts, each concerned with a different form of transforming politics – the different ways in which politics has been transformed by social movements and other social forces. The first part contains chapters that largely deal with the transforming impact of social movements and protest on the participants, and with the 'internal life' of social movements themselves. Whilst the contributions in this first part often deal with the relationship between individuals and the movements, the second part focuses on the historical development of social movements themselves, their rise, fall or failure. Part III contains chapters that examine the transformation of the state, and specifically the impact of social movements on the state. In particular, what the contributions within this part share is a concern with the ways in which the state has incorporated the concerns of certain social movements into established bureaucratic power structures and agendas. Finally, Part IV brings together those contributions that discuss that relationship between political transformations and transformation in current intellectual debates.

Colin Barker's chapter examines the theorisation of how the experience of protest and social movements has had empowering effects on the participants. Whilst noting that authors as diverse as Durkheim, Zolberg and James C. Scott have described similar phenomena, their explanations have frequently been lacking due to their emphasis on the sudden structural changes that open up the possibilities of sudden outbursts of collective action. Barker argues that future research needs to focus more on the actions of the participants. Underlying the 'outburst' that people find so empowering are not only the 'hidden transcripts' of resistance described by Scott, but also hidden networks of opposition that help to reproduce a culture of critique. Active opposition may be absent due to a lack of widespread support, realistic recognition of the lack of opportunities or threat of fatally destructive repression. Such sudden expressions of active opposition require more than the mobilisation of hidden transcripts and networks. Often they are in response to either the actions of significant outsiders, such as the police, or some new innovatory action from within the movement. The impact of these sudden outbursts is often unpredictable, as individuals describe how they discovered in themselves new capacities for action, and the movements themselves redefine or re-articulate established and new grievances.

Clifford Stott and John Drury take a more social psychological approach to the questions broached in Barker's chapter, and develop some of these questions using empirical evidence. Developing the social identity model of crowd behaviour constructed by social psychologists, they examine the 'riot' that developed from the anti-poll tax demonstration in London in March 1990. Echoing Barker's suggestion about the role of significant outsiders such as the police in triggering sudden outbursts of collective active resistance, they examine how the actions of the police transformed the social identity of the crowd from one concerned with the demonstration of non-violent opposition to the poll tax, to one united in its support for violence in self-defence against the police. Stott and Drury's analysis concentrates upon events as they unfolded during one particular demonstration. Through this they are able to demonstrate empirically how the change in social identity took place in response to police actions, transforming individuals' willingness to act in response to perceptions of the changing balance of power between the crowd and the police. Rather like Barker they raise the intriguing question of the possible longer-term persistence of these relatively short-term transformations that appear on the surface at least to be specific to the particular protest events.

During the 1990s debates on the character of social movements have been reinvigorated in Britain by the emergence of various forms of direct action, often associated with environmental questions. Central to these debates have been the cultural dimensions of these protests, questions of reflexivity and self-identity, and the apparent forms of 'disorganisation' that characterise them. Laurence Cox's chapter engages directly with these theoretical debates using empirical material from Ireland. In analysing these cultural milieux of contemporary social movements, Cox considers the issues of autonomy and reflexivity to be central. Whilst many debates around these issues remain somewhat abstract, speculative and anecdotal, with little reference to sound empirical evidence, Cox's study shows how social movement milieux are sources not only of individual changes, but also broader cultural change. He suggests that movement milieux are reflexive lifeworlds where local rationalities are developed and may be generalised to the wider society.

Wallace McNeish's contribution is a study of probably the most widely known of British direct action social protests in the 1990s: the anti-roads movement. He theorises the development of this movement through an application of Habermas' concept of 'lifeworld colonisation'. Resistance to the encroachment of technical logics and instrumental rationalities are exemplified in the anti-roads movement. Although often combining quite diverse social groups, such as local 'respectable' middle-class opponents to particular road schemes and younger 'full-time' activists who move around from one particular anti-road campaign to another, the movement as a whole has shown a surprising willingness to take 'unconventional' forms of action and preparedness to break the law. Rather like the suggestion in Barker's and Stott and Drury's papers (that conflict with the forces of law and order produces a radicalising effect), McNeish argues that legal and policy developments such as the Criminal Justice Act have had a radicalising effect on anti-roads protest.

If the chapters in Part I are primarily concerned with the emergence of social movements and their impact on participants, the chapters in part II are concerned with the impact of resistance and other responses to social movements, and the movements' subsequent evolution, and possible fragmentation and decline. In the first contribution to this part Max Farrar analyses the rise and fall of urban mobilisations in Chapeltown, Leeds, from the 1970s to the 1990s. He provides a sociological explanation of the decline and fragmentation of anti-racist and ethnic movements since the 1980s. Characterising these mobilisations as instances of urban social movements as theorised by Manuel Castells, he argues that their decline can be explained through the hegemonic incorporation of these movements into 'routine' legitimate politics, broader social processes of individualisation undermining the 'collective ethic' of the movements, and processes of ethnic segmentation within the provision of urban services. These processes have been associated with mainstream political discourses of corporatism, equal opportunities and ethnic particularism. Farrar's discussion can be usefully read in connection with Ian Law's and Elizabeth Lawrence and Nicholas Turner's chapters in Part III.

In the next chapter in Part II James McAuley tackles the daunting topic of Ulster unionism – daunting not just due to the complexity and fractiousness of Ulster unionist politics, but also because of the rapidly changing political situation in the North of Ireland. Challenging the dominant over-simplified view of unionism as an ossified social movement, McAuley documents its fluidity and factionalisation in the face of the peace process of the 1990s. Ulster unionists constructed a political tradition in defence of Protestant interests against the perceived threat of Irish nationalism. Recent changes within Ulster unionism have developed in response to the peace process which is perceived to be a threat to the unionists' core British identity. In analysing these developments McAuley utilises the 'framing' theoretical approach of Snow *et al*. In this way he seeks to analyse how Ulster unionists have sought to re-present their 'ultra-British' political identities.

Beth Simpson and Brian Elliott's chapter concerns the bases of resistance to environmental mobilisation in the British Columbia region of Canada. Despite widespread evidence of environmental problems the locality of their case study showed considerable resistance to attempts at mobilisation around environmental issues. Central to the basis of this resistance is the role of certain religious institutions. Within their case study district they show how distinct self-contained religious and ethnic collectivities have developed. These create structural divisions that make it difficult for community-wide environmental mobilisation to take place. Furthermore, they show how a strong pro-business political ideology among the dominant religious and ethnic groups can lead to a perception of environmentalism as an attack on their economic and social success. They argue that it is these features of the local political culture that blocked the development of local environmental protest.

The third part of the collection concerns state responses to social movements, and in particular the ways in which various state institutions have attempted to respond to the agendas of 'new social movements'. In Chapter 9 Cinnamon Bennett considers the longer-term outcomes of one of the most significant developments in British feminism during the 1980s – the emergence of women's committees in local government. The main remit of these committees was to focus upon the pursuit of equal opportunities for women at the level of the local state. In addition, as the later chapter by Elizabeth Lawrence and Nicholas Turner also makes clear, this feminist presence within local government was a means of representing social movements within the state. Using Connell's theoretical framework, she analyses the changing structures and practices of the gender order in her case study of local authority. This framework enables Bennett to identify the structure of men's domination and the practices that sustained them, as well as the feminist practices that challenged them. Her chapter is valuable for the ways in which she documents the effects of managerial reforms and the 'mainstreaming' of equal opportunities during the 1990s (a process analogous to some of the processes of incorporation of Black political movements analysed by Max Farrar in Chapter 6). These changes have largely abolished separate administrative structures for women's issues, leading to a sense of de-radicalisation and the erosion of the influence of feminist politics in the British local state.

The next chapter, contributed by Elizabeth Lawrence and Nicholas Turner, deals with similar issues to the chapter by Cinnamon Bennett. However, they have a broader approach, considering several dimensions of equal opportunities – sex, 'race', sexuality and disability – in a range of state organisations. They are concerned to analyse the role of social movements in relation to the equal opportunities agenda that the movements themselves produced and sustained. One interesting way in which the authors have done this is to examine how individuals have moved from being social movement activists to becoming equal opportunities officers. This detailed documentation of the 'professionalisation' of social movement activists is particularly significant and valuable. In relation to feminism in particular they suggest that the movement has undergone some degree of transformation, with some of those they interviewed feeling the lack of a wider publicly active women's movement. Whilst this implies the decline of feminist activism, Lawrence and Turner suggest that equal opportunities institutions within the state are perhaps acting as 'abeyance structures' at a time of relatively low mobilisation for feminism. However, since the waning of the wave of mobilisation of 'new' social movements initiated in the late 1960s, they suggest that the continuity and further development of equal opportunities policies may be at risk.

Ian Law takes up similar themes of state responses to the demands of social movements, and his focus is upon the attempts to develop equal opportunities practices in relation to 'race' and ethnicity in the Benefits Agency (for the delivery of social security benefits) and the National Health Service. Through an analysis of contemporary debates around the ambiguous and contradictory character of modernity and Enlightenment thinking, he identifies parallel tensions within equal opportunities practices and discourses. He specifies these ambiguities in terms of 'ethnic managerialism'. Using this concept Law's analysis is especially valuable in going beyond the purely theoretical speculations about the relationship between modernity, racism and anti-racism to explore these issues as they work out in particular state institutions and practices. In an argument similar to those put forward by Farrar, Bennett, and Lawrence and Turner earlier in this volume, he suggests that ethnic managerialism, as a bureaucratic and managerialist solution to problems of racialisation, has displaced relationships with Black-led social movements in the pursuit of equal opportunities. Linked with the wave of managerialist reform of the British public sector during the 1980s and 1990s, and riven with the ambiguities of modernist liberal egalitarianism, such as the faith in bureaucratic monitoring and a failure to recognise the dynamic character of ethnicity, ethnic managerialism is unlikely to deliver successful anti-racist policies.

The concluding part of the book examines the relationship between political transformations and intellectual debates. Valerie Hey's chapter develops a feminist critique of some contemporary conceptualisations of community and civil society. She argues that both the theory and practice of 'New Labour' has accepted much of the discourse and institutional reform of the last 20 years of radical right politics. This is often more evident in the ways in which the radical right's reform of institutions in a more disciplinary direction are often coded in a gendered manner. Institutional requirements and political demands for 'parental responsibility' really reflect concerns about 'inadequate mothering'. Extending this critique to related intellectual debates, she argues that some such as Bauman and Mulgan largely ignore relations of power in general and gender relations in particular, in their consideration of community and civil society. Such debates now occupy the intellectual spaces previously occupied by feminism in Britain, due to the partial demobilisation of the feminist movement (as addressed by Bennett and by Lawrence and Turner).

Ruth Levitas pursues issues closely related to the concerns of Valerie Hey's contribution. Levitas is struck by how contemporary political discourse, with its constant references to social cohesion, social integration, and so on, is so Durkheimian in tone to a sociologist's ears. She goes on to examine the Durkheimian presuppositions of one of the most popular political texts published in Britain in recent years – Will Hutton's *The State We're*

In. She argues that Hutton's work – often seen as a radical 'left' critique of British capitalism – is part of what she describes as the Durkheimian hegemony of political debate in Britain. This hegemony blocks out the consideration of certain kinds of political solutions to the problems it identifies.

The intellectual justification for direct action politics is the main focus of Paul Reynolds' chapter, in which he examines the debates around the strategy of the gay protest group OutRage; their strategy of 'Outing' gays who work in and apparently support homophobic institutions. OutRage is distinctive in its preference for direct action in contrast to lobbying for legislative change for 'gay rights'. The intellectual justification for this kind of direct action points to its use as a strategic means of raising public consciousness about heterosexism and homophobia. In doing so it also strikes at the heart of key homophobic institutions such as the church and the media.

The book concludes with a contribution from John Holmwood, who argues that the very enterprise of a radical sociology is inherently self-defeating. Considering a wide range of sociological theorising from Gouldner through to contemporary forms of postmodern sociology, he suggests that by making power the central concept of their analysis, and seemingly finding power to be all-pervasive in social life, self-styled radical sociologists have failed to face up to the implications of how power may operate in alternative social arrangements. Such supposedly radical sociology, by seeing power in operation everywhere, is unable to use the concept critically to distinguish between 'good' and 'bad' social relations.

Together, these chapters present a broad picture of the contemporary concerns of political sociology and the sociology of politics, especially as represented in the UK. They highlight both processes of transformation in contemporary politics and those features of political life that persist despite the appearance of transformation. They also provide a wealth of local detailed material to add complexity to the ongoing theoretical debates on power, resistance and their interrelations. Finally, the chapters make significant connections with and contributions to other sociological debates around not only social movements, identity, the state and social theory, but also environmentalism, social divisions, modernism and postmodernism.

Part I

Empowerment, Identity and Resistance

2 Empowerment and Resistance: 'Collective Effervescence' and other Accounts
Colin Barker

INTRODUCTION

In December 1946 there occurred a two-day general strike in Oakland, California. Chris Rhomberg (1995) writes that:

> The scene on the streets was described as a 'carnival-like atmosphere': men and women sang and danced to music from loudspeakers set up on the streets, a few pickets turned up on roller skates, and one journalist complained of 'young high school girls with their jeans rolled up above their bobby socks and their white shirt tails fluttering in the breeze'. Minor incidents of violence occurred, but union picket captains kept order and exhorted people to remain non-violent. One eye-witness recalled, 'The participants were making history, knew it, and were having fun. ... Never before or since had Oakland been so alive or happy for the population. It was a town of law and order. In that city of over a quarter million, strangers passed each other on the street and did not have fear, but the opposite.
>
> (p. 582)

Rhomberg describes an episode of collective action, during which we see people altering their forms of activity, their demeanour and social relations, and expressing views which most of the time were not publicly articulated. What interests me here is this rapid transformation.

Recorded elements of the phenomenon of 'people changing' in collective action include a sense of changed personal and collective identity, feelings of joy and well-being, altered forms of public speech and ideas, a sense of self-empowerment, the de-legitimation of existing authority, and the creation of new informal and formal institutions and networks.

11

One might expect such complexes of inter-related processes of social and personal transformation to be a central issue in social thought, and especially in theories of social change. However, these matters have attracted surprisingly little theoretical attention. 'Self-transformation in struggle' is hardly a major topic in sociological and social psychological theory – not even within the burgeoning field of 'social movement' studies.

This paper attempts to begin an exploration of this question. I briefly review several writers who have had something to say about the phenomenon of transformation in struggle. I then suggest that the recent shift towards re-attention to the 'temporal', i.e. to 'events' and 'social dramas' as specific objects of study within the social sciences, may provide a better framework for considering the question. I outline a phenomenological account of some ways in which 'episodes of collective action' may produce these kinds of transformation, and conclude with a few reflections on the implications of the suggested approach, with particular attention to questions of research strategies.

THREE THEORISTS

Emile Durkheim

There is an interesting germ of an idea in some of Durkheim's later writings, notably *Sociology and Philosophy* and *The Elementary Forms of the Religious Life*. This is the notion of 'collective effervescence', a process which Durkheim sees occurring at moments when social life takes on an especial intensity, marked by larger numbers of 'assemblies' of society's members.

> There are periods in history when, under the influence of some great collective shock, social interactions have become much more frequent and active. Men look for each other and assemble together more than ever. That general effervescence results which is characteristic of revolutionary or creative periods. Now this greater activity results in a general stimulation of individual forces. Men see more and differently now than in normal times. Changes are not merely of shades and degrees; men become different.
>
> (1961: 241)

> Society is the field of an intense intellectual and moral life with a wide range of influence. From the actions and reactions between its individuals arises an entirely new mental life of which we could not have the faintest idea had we lived in isolation. This we observe best at those signal epochs of crisis when some great collective movement seizes us, lifts us above ourselves, and transfigures us.
>
> (1965: 59)

Durkheim's account has two notable strengths. First, his account of 'collective effervescence' makes it clear that this is an 'interactional accomplishment', a product of the 'assembly' of individuals in ways outside their normal everyday experience. Second, his sociology is marked – here as much as anywhere – by a recognition of the significance of what David Lockwood (1992) terms the 'non-utilitarian' aspects of social life and organisation. However, Durkheim's idea of 'collective effervescence' remains under-developed in his own writings, and the possibilities of its further development are limited by some core assumptions of his sociology.

The most obvious limitation is what Lynn Hunt (1988) identifies as Durkheim's 'all-consuming emphasis on social consensus'. One would hardly gather from his account that the 'creative moments' in history which he sees as characterised by 'collective effervescence' are periods of intense social and political struggle. They are marked not simply by a process of 'regenerating' society's sacred symbols, but by their open contestation. As a result, not only are some individuals 'strengthened' as an outcome of these effervescent moments, but others are significantly 'weakened'.

This observation must be linked with another. Durkheim lacks any critical theory of 'ideology'. He refers to 'a general morality common to all members of a collectivity' (1965: 40), but without specifying the nature of the specific collectivity, or its relations with other collectivities. That the content and meaning of 'morality' might be itself subject to social conflict is seemingly beyond his sociological ken. The only such conflict he recognises is that between decaying ideals appropriate to the past and those relevant to the future. What Lockwood notes as Durkheim's lack of a theory of the 'utilitarian' sphere and its conflicts has significant consequences for his theory of consciousness.

Durkheim pays little attention to what Randall Collins (1988) terms the distribution of 'the means of ritual production'. Yet the question, who has the power to mobilise 'assemblies' and organise 'rituals', is relevant to determining their form and content. Such matters are often central in political contention: in contemporary Britain, for example, they concern rights in relation to such significant 'assemblies' as picket lines, gathering on premises and land, or organising and attending 'raves'. Nor does Durkheim distinguish between forms of 'assembly', except in quantitative terms. However, there is an important distinction, noted by Christopher Hill (1988) in seventeenth-century rulers' discourse, between 'assembly under authority' and 'self-assembly'. The former was held to be a worthy enterprise, the latter to be highly dangerous to order. We might translate this distinction into one between 'assembly from above' and 'assembly from below'.[1]

If Durkheim's notion of 'creative periods' were transmuted into a rather different register, identifying these as akin to the 'cycles of protest' that Sidney Tarrow (1989) and others have discussed, then possibly his insight might reveal more concrete possibilities for further theoretical and empirical exploration and development. As it stands, however, Durkheim's notion of 'collective effervescence' remains an interesting insight, by itself lacking much potential value for development.

Aristide Zolberg

In 1972, influenced by the events of May 1968 in Paris, Aristide Zolberg published an article on 'Moments of Madness'. Such moments of popular insurgency, he suggests, occur every so often, producing situations where, briefly, 'everything seems possible'. Zolberg draws on previous such 'moments' in Paris – the February 1848 Revolution, the 1871 Commune, the 1936 strike-wave of the Popular Front, the 1944 Liberation of Paris. At a descriptive level he brilliantly identifies the processes of social and personal transformation people experienced during these moments, especially so far as 'feeling' is concerned. He stresses the 'festive joy', the 'outpouring of speech' associated with the eruption of normally quiescent people into active political life.

In his conclusions, Zolberg suggests these 'moments of madness' possess several significant features. First, the 'torrent of words' characterising these moments releases into widespread public discourse novel and radical ideas which were, previously, the property only of small 'sects and coteries'. Second, these words and ideas anchor themselves in the new networks of social relationships which spring up at such times; thus a term like 'brotherhood' acquires a real, if temporary, power, because it appears to represent the birth of actual new relations. Third, during such moments new popular aspirations are voiced which, often, achieve some form of practical realisation either then or relatively soon afterwards: he mentions the expansion of the suffrage, universal state education, and the right to paid holidays. Thus tides of popular insurgency, though themselves temporary, may leave behind significant institutional sediments.

Zolberg's whole article is full of life and interest, and is valuable for his suggestion that social science pay more attention to such moments' historical significance. But there are also significant weaknesses.

Zolberg's descriptive materials focus on the transformation of 'feeling', but pay little attention to such processes within 'moments of madness' as the development of new organisational forms or shifts in what Charles Tilly (1993/1995) terms the 'repertoires of contention' deployed by people during popular struggles. His whole stress falls on broad elements of similarity in collective sentiments, and not on the factors which might enable a more concrete and differentiated appreciation of these varied occasions.

His explanations of the emergence of these situations are also very general. They arise, he suggests, in response to 'boredom'. There is hardly more specificity in his suggestion that 'moments of madness' arise from the tension between 'growing instrumentalism of everyday politics' and a 'yearning ... for a more dramatic political process in which fulfilment could be achieved through the act of participation itself'. There is no sense of more immediate, concrete issues and opportunities which may drive and enable these moments.

And Zolberg exaggerates. These moments, he proposes, are ones when 'everything seems possible'. The term catches the element of poetic enthusiasm and popular unity which often marks specific phases of revolutionary and near-revolutionary situations, but it also diverts attention away from the specific expectations and demands marking different groups and classes within insurgent populations, from the variations in content of such aspirations and their voicing within distinct moments, and from the problem of their relation to determinate conflicts and contradictions within the societies from which they erupt. To put the matter baldly, in an account of, say, the 1917 Russian Revolution, 'everything' lacks the evocative concreteness of 'Peace, Bread and Land'.

Finally, he notes that the public sentiments aroused in 'moments of madness' soon subside, leaving behind mixed feelings of cynicism and sadness. 'Post coitum omnia animal triste', he remarks. He does not offer a starting point for exploring the question, whether these events might have turned out differently. Sexual congress leaves some animals quite cheerful.

James C. Scott

James Scott has written two fascinating books, *Weapons of the Weak: Everyday Forms of Peasant Resistance* (1985) and *Domination and the Arts of Resistance: Hidden Transcripts* (1990), both of which bear strongly on the question of transformation in struggle. The first offers an ethnography of poor peasant struggles in a Malaysian village, but broadens its scope, in a seminal theoretical chapter, to a wide-ranging critique of current theorising about ideology. The second develops that theoretical argument further, drawing on a wide-ranging set of historical and sociological studies of popular resistance.

Scott's work emphasises the oppositional ideas and practices of the world's poor. He details the constant struggle against exploitation, in a class-divided world where the powerful seek means to maintain and extend both the material and the symbolic reach of their power, and where subordinate classes devise a variety of strategies of resistance. That resistance is offered against not only the material aspects of exploitation but equally the daily humiliations and indignities visited upon the oppressed. However, he stresses, the resistance of the poor is mostly constrained by their awareness of the brute facts of unequal power.

Scott organises his discussion around a key distinction, between a 'public transcript' and a 'hidden transcript'. The former represents the open ideology of the rulers, providing an account of the world as they would like it to appear. To this public transcript the oppressed are commonly required to, and do indeed, offer public deference. However, such deference is commonly only a tactical 'pose of the powerless'. For members of subordinate groups also develop quite different, and opposed, sets of ideas and practices, constituting a 'hidden transcript' with a content quite distinct from the 'dominant ideology'. Behind the backs of the powerful, to whom they offer public obeisance, the oppressed develop all manner of ways of acting which seek to limit the effects of exploitative relations on themselves, and they create and share a range of critical oppositional ideas which they keep largely concealed from their masters' ears and eyes. This hidden transcript is developed in its own 'sites', away from the gaze of the power-holders, in the slave quarters of the plantations, within informal village networks, in the cafés, pubs and meeting places where workers gather. These sites of the hidden transcript are partially autonomous places of self-assembly, where more or less covert alternative visions and critiques of the existing system are developed in relations of relative equality.

Such hidden transcripts – often concealed from the eyes of historians who rely on official documents to develop their accounts of the past – underlie the occasional 'eruptions' of popular protest in collective movements. These often reveal a sense of release, of choked-up feelings being expressed openly, in a festive, carnivalesque atmosphere. Such movements of collective struggle, on small and large scale alike, often generate just those phenomena of 'transformation' in which we are interested. What was previously concealed can now be spoken; those who before touched their forelocks to their 'betters' now speak more boldly, uttering what could not be said and acting in line with the visions developed in their concealed ideological underworld. Too many social theorists have ignored or played down the existence and significance of the hidden transcripts of the oppressed. They have developed one-sided and inadequate theories which assume that the effects of ruling-class power extend into the production of popular acceptance of existing systems of exploitation. Scott criticises a whole range of such theories of 'ruling-class hegemony', especially where they focus on the supposed ideological acceptance by subordinates of rulers' legitimacy claims.

Scott's work is enormously attractive. By comparison with Durkheim or Zolberg it represents a great advance. Many readers, on first encounter, are bowled over by his boldness and originality of argument. In drawing attention to the significance of a mass of evidence of everyday resistance practices among those whose struggles have too often been 'hidden from history', Scott, like Edward Thompson (for whose work he evinces great respect), also roots these half-concealed activities and ideas in the antagonistic relations of class appropriation. But this impressive work also contains some significant difficulties.

First, Scott focuses mainly on relations between the powerful and the powerless, but pays less attention to social interactions among the powerless, within this context of unequal power. He notes, almost in passing, that the sites of the hidden transcript are themselves arenas where power is exercised among relative equals. The concealed spaces within the social fabric, where oppositional ideas and practices are developed and shared, must themselves be counter-policed against spies, scabs and traitors. Through a whole variety of informal mechanisms, members of subordinate groups exercise social control over each other, over their workmates, neighbours, fellow slaves and peasants. The fact that this remains a necessity suggests a need to pay attention to the discourses and arguments going on among the oppressed. Scott, in bending the theoretical stick against theories of the 'dominant ideology', risks treating the world of the hidden transcript as marked by simple unity and harmonious amity among the oppressed.[2]

Second, this risk connects with another. We should not replace inadequate theories of ruling-class ideological hegemony with their simple opposite. Yet Scott's work tends at least to imply that within the hidden transcript lies a full-blown critique of existing systems of exploitation and subordination, only prevented from open expression by fear and caution in the face of overweening ruling-class power.

Third, in Scott's account it appears predominantly that what occurs in moments of collective action is that already-existing ideas and feeling are simply 'released' in a burst of enthusiastic open revelation of what was previously concealed. It is as if the cork of caution is simply loosened, and popular visions bubble forth. It may be that such mechanisms may be usefully invoked to account for some aspects of the 'transformations' wrought by popular collective action – indeed, participants themselves may report that their feelings take just this form. But not everything is explicable in these terms. Popular movements commonly reveal elements of practical innovation, theoretical creativity and internal argument in the face of novel circumstances, and such innovation and argument cannot be explained by simple notions of 'release'. Even if the 'capacity to innovate' may be released, the content of creativity and argument itself requires further exploration.

Fourth, except in his ethnography of the Malaysian village, Scott's account of ideas and their transformation focuses on 'general ideas' about society and its organisation. Thus, the public transcript accounts for the workings of society as the powerful would like to imagine it, while the hidden transcript develops a vision of an alternative form of society. The contest between the two transcripts is between general theories of social justice and social order. There is a difficulty here, which is by no means peculiar to Scott's work. It is the tendency – also apparent in Durkheim, in Zolberg, and in a mass of other work on consciousness, ideology and culture – to treat the world of the ideological as itself essentially – and solely – generalising and theoretical. What such conceptions lack is a sense of social life as a stream of incidents and events, large and small, which require immediate practical and linguistic responses; while these may themselves be patterned by general ideas, they cannot be reduced to them.

Finally, Scott's approach diverts attention from a complex of problems concerning both arguments within subordinate groups about how to respond to specific situations, and also related matters to do with leadership, strategy and tactics in collective action.

Summary

All three authors offer accounts in which forms of collective action promote changes in people's ideas and identities. Shifts in forms of action form an intrinsic aspect of such transformations, along with changes in language and practical social relations. In particular, such changes are highlighted during crises of sociopolitical action, periods and situations of more intense conflict. And Zolberg at least poses the question: What remains afterwards? Is there a sense in which new social relations and identities can be socially consolidated in new structures?

All three, although in distinct ways, pay insufficient attention to different-iation among actors, whether at the level of structure, historical setting or in everyday action itself. All three, despite their attention to change, focus more on the general than the specific, on structure more than practical action. All three also tend to assume an account of 'consciousness' rather dissociated from action, paying little attention to what people actually say and do during specific events.

EVENTS AND ACTION

One writer who begins to address the issue of the relationship between con-sciousness and action is Gordon Marshall (1983). Sociology, he suggests, tends to treat consciousness as 'a discrete component of social reality carried around inside people's heads and dipped into at pertinent moments'; thus it lacks a sense of 'reflective social actors engaging social structures in ways that might change their awareness and evaluation of the social world'. In order to grasp such matters, he argues for a shift towards a 'narrative mode' of analysis of ideas. That in turn suggests a focus on 'events' or 'social dramas', a topic attracting growing interest in sociology and anthropology as well as history.

At issue are the methods and theoretical assumptions required to study specific sequences of action and interaction, including, of course, episodes of collective struggle. Those involved in the contemporary discussion of 'eventful sociology' all write with an eye to the question, how such sequences contribute to the reproduction and/or alteration of social structures, including power relations, cultural meanings, and individual and social identities. That is, they are concerned with the very issues which lie at the heart of the problem of 'transformations'. All deal with the conceptual difficulties of handling 'moments', not necessarily of 'madness', but when real 'alternativity' (Shanin, 1986) becomes apparent. How may we account for phases of social interaction marked by open-endedness of outcome, uncertainty, choice, mobilisation, decision? These are moments when social life takes unforeseen direction, when history is reshaped on a larger or smaller scale, when 'forks' in development occur and when a single decision, incident or feature of a situation can 'make a difference'. Such 'events' offer a possibility for estimating the 'transformations' which are my main focus of interest here.

Rather than attempt an overall estimate of the many strategic research proposals offered by a variety of authors, I shall here follow through a few implications of one early approach, that outlined in Victor Turner's (1974, 1982) discussion of 'social dramas'. Social dramas, he proposes, follow analytically similar sequences, beginning with 'breaches', passing through phases of 'crisis' and 'redressive action' to a final process and outcome of 'reintegration' or 'fission'.[3]

In Turner's sequential schema, a drama is initiated by some kind of 'breach', an incident which in some sense upsets the social applecart. Some particular act threatens existing expectations, breaks a moral rule, threatens an existing way of proceeding. William Sewell (1996) suggests that, while such ruptures in social relations occur all the time, most are 'neutralized and absorbed into the preexisting structures' by one means or another – for example by direct repression, by rapid 'cooling down' interventions by others, by apology, by practical ignoring, and so forth. Other breaches or ruptures set off a chain of proliferating social processes which draw in other people and impact more widely on social life. Among such chains we can identify many processes of collective mobilisation and action. It is within such events or dramas that we are most likely to find the kinds of 'transformations' indexed at the start of this paper, for here there occurs that practical intersection between biography and history, between ideas, identities, actions and structures which apparently underlies changes in personal and social relations.

'INVESTMENT IN COLLECTIVE ACTION'

If the exploration of 'events' is a possible starting place for understanding 'transformations', we must still need some account of how such processes might occur. What phenomenological processes underlie the changes in forms of action and identity which are regularly reported as features of sequences of collective struggle?

'Transformation' implies some notion of a 'starting point' against which we can measure it. Paul Bagguley (1996), discussing the relation between working-class political consciousness and protest, draws on the notion of 'informed fatalism'. This, he suggests, involves a 'bounded rationality'. Here, people are both aware of their material circumstances and 'not entirely satisfied with them', but are held in check by their knowledge of the apparent impossibility of changing them. The study of protest, Bagguley suggests, should thus focus on those situations and contexts which 'unbind' that rationality. This approach has the advantage of pointing to the 'intricate inter-relations of agency, power and the structures of domination in a way that stresses their contingency, the essential uncertainty with respect to their permanence'. And, he comments, 'One never knows when some subtle shift of circumstance, some re-alignment of the institutional matrix will crack open the opportunities for collective action that multiplies its effectivity beyond the wildest dreams of the participants' (Bagguley, 1996: 21–2).

There is much to commend in this, especially the emphasis on the provisionality of 'binding'. But there is a risk that we think of 'informed fatalism' as a condition in which people concentrate their practical energy and attention on the 'impossibilities', almost straining at the leash. Such an image might draw us back to some 'uncorking' or 'release' account of collective action. More probably, most of the time, people in a condition of informed fatalism follow the famous advice, 'Be philosophical: Don't think about it.' That is, they focus their practical concerns not on their own incapacity to challenge existing structures, but on more immediate questions which absorb them: matters of everyday life, family, love and grief, work-task problems, lifestyle, cultural pursuits, hobbies and enthusiasms. Thus apparent 'political passivity' is really active engagement with a host of distinct matters.

The point is significant, for otherwise we shall envisage 'activation' as a sudden stimulation to artificial life of a previously static object, like dead muscle jerking under external electrical stimulus. Rather, we insist, the 'activated' are 'self-activated'. They don't 'become active', but alter their own mode of activity.

Of course, collective action does not come out of nothing. Among these diffused commitments we should look for continuing practical and ideal attachments to organisations and/or informal networks which in some sense embody a past history or future possibility of collective action. These remain part of the evolving cultural matrix. There are 'old' and 'new' organisations and networks of this kind – though they do not necessarily correspond to current paradigms of 'old' and 'new' social movements.

'Old' movements have periods of 'abeyance', in which they 'tick over' in relatively routine ways. Verta Taylor (1989) explores such periods of 'abeyance' in the women's movement in the USA; a similar notion could well be applied to formal and informal aspects of contemporary labour movements in Europe and elsewhere (e.g. Heaton and Linn, 1989). Alongside these, new 'submerged networks' (Melucci, 1989) may be constructed, within which new lifestyles are experimented with, new cultural critiques developed, new collective identities explored. Such new networks may be constructed not only among the disaffected urban young but also, for example, within 'new' workplaces, as previously unorganised groups of workers mutually explore their working conditions, patterns of subordination and exploitation, and develop partial critiques.[4] Such 'submerged networks' developed within the Black churches in the USA during the 1940s and early 1950s, before the launching of the Civil Rights Movement (Morris, 1984). In Poland the 'explosions' of 1956, of 1970–1, of 1976 and of 1980 were all presaged by the development of informal worker networks within plants and local neighbourhoods (Kolankiewicz, 1973; Barker, 1986; Laba, 1991; Goodwyn, 1991).

The degree of 'emotional investment' in such 'proto-organisations' and 'submerged networks' varies. Core individuals and groups provide their centres, drawing around them peripheries of contacts and connections, affiliates and sympathisers. They may form relatively closed subcultures and subcommunities, achieving sometimes via informal activities of everyday resistance a 'partial penetration' of authority's claims (Willis, 1977).

Such settings provide 'sites' where existing critical discourses are maintained, disseminated to new entrants, and reshaped, and where new kinds of critical discourse are also assembled and refined. However, what marks them – so long as they remain 'in abeyance' or 'submerged' – is that the transformations they achieve remain focused on the 'descriptive' categorisation of the social world and the self. They are, in a certain sense, 'discursive' rather than 'active' in their implications, oriented possibly towards the 'idea' of change but not yet imperative in their demands. Their inner life remains marked by the contours of 'informed fatalism'.

Within 'old' movements, such attachments are mostly low in intensity, and the formal and informal organisational matrices within which they are embodied remain in relative 'quiescence'. Ongoing 'investments' in such attachments may have weak practical salience, being overlain with a host of other more immediate commitments of interest and concern. Newer movements already require some 'emotional investment' in the development of new 'cultural critique', 'consciousness-raising' and the development of new 'collective identities'. But, as Carol Mueller (1994) suggests, even if their networks are oriented towards collective action there is still a distinction between possessing that 'orientation' and actually stepping forth into the public realm and declaring themselves with some public and irrevocable act. They are still marked by the diversity and tentativeness that Alberto Melucci reports in his accounts of the submerged networks of 'new' movements in

Italy. The possibility of collective action is 'latent' within such networks, but has yet to be activated. Within such settings, that is, we may find 'transformations' occurring, but not the relatively temporally concentrated and 'dramatic' ones that especially interest us here. Combustible materials may be assembled in submerged or abeyant networks, but the spark to fire them is still missing.

It is within 'events' or 'social dramas' that we may find the relevant sparks which set off more rapid sequences of social and personal transformation. To follow Turner for the present, we should look out for a specific 'incident' which constitutes a 'breach'. At least two sources of breach seem noteworthy as they involve social movements in collective action.

In the first, significant outsiders (for example, an employer, or a state agency) may initiate an 'incident' which others read as a 'breach' in existing patterns of interaction, to which participants within a 'proto-organisation' or 'organisation in abeyance' feel compelled to attempt a collective response. In the second, a proposal may arise from within a movement network or organisation for collective action which itself initiates a 'breach'.

What counts as a 'breach' is situationally determined. So is any collective response. The December 1955 arrest in Montgomery, Alabama, of Mrs Rosa Parks for refusing to give her bus seat to a white person was a 'signal' to local activists to attempt a collective boycott of the city's buses, but hers was not the first such arrest. A police raid on a café in the St Paul's district of Bristol in 1980 provoked a 'riot', but other such police raids have passed off without significant protest. Not every breach becomes a 'flashpoint' (Waddington *et al.*, 1989). In all such cases some group within the already-developed networks of those offended or threatened by the incident must both 'propose' a collective response, and succeed in mobilising others into common participation. They do not always succeed.[5] Similarly, if the decision of four students, from North Carolina A&T College, to 'sit in' at the lunch counter at the Greensboro Woolworth's provided a new 'spark' for the Civil Rights Movement, other demonstrations arising out of networks do not have this energising and proliferating effect. Some protests are 'routine' affairs, open to being contained by existing procedures and understandings. They signal neither urgency nor new opportunities to others.

Where it occurs, the switch to collective action involves a significant transition. Participants are called on to shift from 'talking' about a situation, to 'doing something' about it. They are summoned to make practical decisions and to enact them. The network or organisation is placed on a different, crisis, footing, with various consequences for its members, their identities and their social relations. From the decisional moment, a Turnerian 'limen' is crossed, a threshold between more stable social processes. Such a moment requires a kind of 'investment', a form of 'effervescence', distinct from those which Durkheim mostly has in mind in his discussions of ritual. Here there is no replication of one-ness with society, but the opening of overt conflict. Collective action has an element of the disturbance of ritual, the dishonouring of power and challenging of existing structure. A decision for collective action sets going a chain of incidents, decisions, counter-responses and mobilisations which together provide the inner temporal narrative of an 'event' as it moves from 'breach' to 'crisis' to eventual outcome. Commonly such 'events', of course, are relatively short-lived and limited in their overall effects on social structure and the self. Containment mechanisms come into play to 'cool' the issue, via compromise, repression or some other means. But when events begin, participants cannot know how they will turn out.

The taking of collective action, and the determination of at least its initial form, must be agreed among the participants. The decision must involve something of what Naomi Rosenthal and Michael Schwartz (1989) term a 'willingness to make and abide by collective decisions', however this is assessed and achieved. Some such willingness is the basic ingredient in what Rick Fantasia (1988) has termed emergent 'cultures of solidarity' among strikers. Entry into collective action implies a different kind of 'commitment' from that involved in 'submerged networks' in more peaceful periods. Here the bonds linking members of organisations and networks are tested in practice. Here those who disagree with the collective decision either cease to participate actively or indeed act against it. Others, in turn, who have previously stood apart from an organisation or network, may now enter: open collective action has a gathering as well as a dispersing character. Collective action decisions are thus likely to alter the actual membership and the functioning internal relationships of networks. The decision for collective action alters 'identities', as participants deliberate together about how to accomplish their plan of action.

The decision for collective action produces a 'collective actor' about whom it is then possible to make meaningful statements. Individuals *become* a 'crowd', a 'movement', a 'union', even a 'class' or a 'people', by acting together as such. Such a formation may be very temporary, and its inner configuration and its relationships with others may well alter considerably over time. However, a collective identity is formed, which is qualitatively different from the kind formed within the submerged networks analysed by Melucci and others. Melucci doubts that one may speak of real 'historic actors' when discussing social movements, as does Tilly (1993–4). But – as Mueller argues – the moment of stepping forth in collective action itself alters the social landscape, compels new responses from others, and permits the use of such collective terms. Collective identity here becomes something more definite, becoming a question of nameable actors, who do this and do not do that, in the public arena. Here history and biography intersect as people set out to 'make history' on some small or large social stage. They 'declare themselves' in action.

All of this compels a re-focusing of energy and attention on the immediate question. Diffuse and multiple commitments must be relatively concentrated and singularised. Individuals may respond with pleasure or grudgingly to a new call on their time and commitments, but there is an inescapable quality to such re-focusing. For once initiated, an 'event' will have reverberating consequences for participants, both individually and collectively, however it may turn out. Those consequences will be felt both internally and with regard to their relations with others. We should not, writes Rhomberg, 'underestimate the degree of risk and uncertainty inherent in moments of collective action' (1995: 582). That element of inherent risk and uncertainty necessarily sharpens people's attention, draws it ineluctably towards the specific arena in which it is fought out.

Collective action is threatening. It is an exercise of practical power. It blocks access to facilities or transforms their usage, it impedes or halts a pro-duction process, it offers a symbolic challenge to existing authorities and their capacity to issue practical commands. Collective action thus impels responses from others. However, the form of those responses is unpre-dictable. There are theorists who seek to reduce the analysis of events to 'games', but the analogy is poor. An episode of collective action is a contest whose players will not necessarily obey existing rules, or make the next moves according to the rules apparently governing their last. In Alasdair MacIntyre's nice expression, 'the problem about real life is that moving one's knight to QB3 may always be replied to with a lob across the net.' (MacIntyre, 1981: 94), Collective actors may set out to present themselves in one guise, but be understood and responded to in another, with unforeseen consequences.[6]

Collective action, in compelling others into responses, draws others into focusing on the issue, and into reshaping their own identities and commit-ments. Besides those who initiate the event through collective action, we may identify several other groups of significant actors. Bert Klandermans (1991, 1997) suggests that movements operate within a 'multi-organisation field', itself made up of 'conflict and alliance systems'. Collective action 'activates' various parts of that field and those systems, drawing them in and compelling them also to play various parts in an uncertain drama. In addition, it also draws attention to itself from a less directly involved but potentially significant 'audience interpretation system' in which, for instance, the media often play a dominant role. Collective action turns those who undertake it into public figures, focusing attention on their words and actions.

Those comprising a movement's 'conflict system' will seek to mobilise their own forces and resources, themselves entering onto a path marked by uncer-tainty and risk. They too must explore their own strengths and weaknesses anew, and focus their attention and energies on the struggle. The configuration of their forces and networks too may alter.[7] The sequence of interactions between the two sides is thus likely to change them both, in unpredictable fashion. The whole course of an 'event' is marked by unexpected incidents and situations, for which only the most partial preparation can be made. Participants must 'think on their feet', construct rapid responses to surprise sallies, advances, retreats, manoeuvres by opponents which shift the ground of the conflict.

Movements embarking on collective action normally seek to mobilise others. Beyond their own immediate forces, most of the 'resources' they can bring into action belong to potential allies. These are themselves located within their own, distinct or overlapping, organisation networks. Responses from potential allies may take a whole variety of forms. At one end of a continuum, additional groups and individuals may directly involve themselves in the processes of collective action initiated by the originators, or may initiate parallel and sometimes emulative forms of collective action. They may provide less directly 'active' support such as financial assistance, technical advice or that rather tenuous entity, 'moral support'. Or they may respond negatively. Patterns of response from potential allies will be shaped by a variety of considerations: what they are directly asked for, and how; the ways in which requests for support impact on their own readings of the situation and its possibilities; their own orientations and internal decision-making patterns, etc. Some responses will have little 'transformative' effects upon allies' own functioning, others may have extensive implications for their own futures.

Where collective action proliferates to involve others, new problems as well as opportunities are created. The entry of others into a conflict expands the range of centres of decision-making, posing new problems of coordination and organisation.[8] Those who are themselves 'activated' bring their own, sometimes new, commitments and understandings to the evolving drama, adding new voices with new proposals. The whole character of the initial protest may be altered by escalation.[9]

Thus it is not only the responses of opponents which may shift the field of collective action, but also those of allies – and public commentators too. The 'event' becomes a series of incidents, of particular conjunctures when further decisions have to be taken and enacted, each time with further uncertainty and risk. The decisional processes and commitments involved at the beginning of an event-sequence must be replayed any number of times, each time in a reconfigured situation, and with further consequences for the self, for social relations, for ideas, for the configuration of the group.

A crisis of the kind produced by many forms of collective action speeds up transformational tempos. Participants must make faster decisions, change tack, deal with the unexpected. They must make sense of and respond to momentary reverses and successful initiatives, often diverse and contradictory in their implications. Innovatory and impromptu decisions are commonly required, with a quickening of tactical and strategic intelligence. To be involved, even on a small scale, in 'making history' – for good or ill – has effects upon self-identities and collective identities. Commonly participants must undertake unfamiliar tasks, act differently, assume new personae, take initiatives and assume responsibilities. Existing divisions of labour and authority are liable to shift.

In all the theoretical attention devoted within social movement theory to questions of 'mobilisation', whether macro, meso or micro', there is a danger of forgetting a fundamental point. A process of 'mobilising' people into collective activity is also, for each participant, a process of 'self-mobilisation'. Those who respond to calls to devote attention, energy and commitment to some collective enterprise must reorganise their own lives in ways significant to themselves. They must, to a degree, 'singularise' their investments of concern, of time and cognitive direction, onto a new point of focus. They must simplify or reshape any previous diffusesness of commitments. People assuming new task and patterns of activity make new demands on their own personal resources.

Such self-mobilisation occurs, within collective action, as a social and not simply an individual process. Identities are inherently relational. This is the case both at an individual level, but also in respect of our collective identities. Who we think we are is a function of the groups with which are situationally affiliated and with whom others treats us as affiliated. Internal relations within such groups, their collective stance towards others, and those others' responses to these groups, are vital elements of our sense of self, of our powers, capacities, rights, our very aesthetic significance. Collective action embodies practical challenges to and transformations of these qualitative assessments. Sometimes they are directly registered as general cultural challenges: the marvellous slogan, 'Black is Beautiful', could not have emerged out of the 1960s without the battles fought by the Civil Rights and Black Liberation movements.

Participants in collective action regularly report that they 'discover' aspects of their selves, and their capacities, which they had not previously tested: speaking publicly, organising, taking initiatives which, before the event, they would not have imagined themselves doing. As a result they felt 'more alive'. These experiences, which might be termed 'empowerment', result from the necessity, imposed by the exigencies of collective action, of taking responsibility for new demands of speech and action which were, in their former pattern of existence, outside their everyday scope. What facilitates such experiences is the focusing of energy and attention on a new collective project, the concentrated 'investment' of cognitive and emotional resources in pursuing a collective decision. Gramsci remarked that 'strong passions are necessary to sharpen the intellect and help make intuition more penetrating. ... Only the man who wills something strongly can identify the elements which are necessary to the realisation of his will' (1971: 171). Drop the masculine reference, and the women of the Yorkshire pit villages or Liverpool's Women of the Waterfront can agree. Collective action, which focuses wills and strengthens passions, also sharpens intellects. Lenin's remark, that the masses learn faster in revolutions, also applies, if on a smaller scale, to less grand crises.

Collective action, undertaken in conditions of necessary uncertainty, is also a process of practical sociological investigation, an exploration of the social structure and the self which involves re-categorisation, a social re-theorising under pressure. Ron Eyerman and Andrew Jamison (1991) propose that movements are conceptually creative entities, which engage in 'meaning work', changing social evaluations; they are right, but we need to stress more that much of this 'meaning work' is undertaken within collective action itself.

New discoveries and new forms of action create the possibility of new forms of speech, new kinds of social relations, new audiences for minority ideas. Situations of collective action, in which actors are compelled through their practical engagement with the unfamiliar into making innovatory, spontaneous and impromptu responses, create circumstances in which new arguments gain plausibility. One weakness of 'resource mobilisation' theory is, as Alan Scott (1990) notes, that it treats grievances, preferences and values as relatively fixed. What movements often achieve – especially via collective action – is a process of alteration and not simply of expression of preferences and values, a re-focusing and re-articulation of grievances and demands.

New conjunctures, incidents and discoveries are liable to alter the appeal or resonance of various 'frames' and 'ideologies'. New possibilities and opportunities may disclose themselves, along with new measures of salience of commitments and social relations. Former patterns of obligation, loyalty and antagonism, may be recast. Previous cognitive, ethical and pragmatic assessments may be re-apprehended. The sequence of new incidents, actions and experiences provides actors with new materials against which to measure existing understandings, with which to confirm or refute arguments, and to assess competing arguments.[10] Collective action, in its short-term and long-term results, provides 'live' materials for altering the social and cultural context of meanings, for remodelling the comprehension of structures and totalities. What was formerly desirable may now seem irrelevant or insufficient, what was previously impossible now becomes an issue to be actively pursued. Existing patterns of influence and authority, of 'routine' action and speech, within movements as well as between themselves and their opponents, are open to alteration.

Such processes have effects on those who participate in them. Not uncommonly they entail considerable affective aspects. All action has both cognitive and affective sides, but 'extraordinary' action is liable to have 'extraordinary' affective qualities. Collective action, 'successful' or not, alters the balance of self-confidence within society.

CONCLUSIONS

The above sketch leaves far more questions unexplored than explored. One obvious issue concerns the possibility of 'consolidating' new identities and social relations formed during episodes of collective action. Is there, as Michels (1959) argued, simply a 'cruel game' which will continue without end, in which people struggle for democracy and self-empowerment only to recreate anew the conditions of oligarchy and domination? Or can and do collective struggles achieve smaller and larger institutional and personal transformations with a capacity to persist?

The issues broached above represent more a research programme than a set of definitive answers. The interesting question is not whether people change, and manage to 'fix' or consolidate some aspect of those changes, but under what conditions, and to what degree. In sum, what processes of 'restructuring' of society survive the phase of 'reintegration' with which a particular event-sequence concludes?

The exploration of such questions has, I think, implications for social movement theory, which I can do no more than indicate here. First, the relationship between 'social movements' and 'collective action', rather than having a taken-for-granted status, requires further investigation. Second, the matter of 'transformation' cannot be divorced from the study of 'strategy and tactics' in social movements, yet this is a field whose exploration has hardly begun. This issue is itself closely inter-woven with matters involving 'contention about contention' within movements, and thus questions about 'leadership' and 'hegemony'. Third, the issue necessarily implicates theorising about 'ideas', 'ideology', 'consciousness' and 'language', but in ways that most sociological theorising can barely touch. For these matters have been considered too often at far too general a level, without sufficient attention to concrete situations and speech-acts, and the relation between 'general' and 'situational' cognition and utterance. Fourth, the focus on 'events' and 'collective action' as a key locus of transformations suggests the need for research designs which permit the investigation of concrete sequences of practical and ideal action, and a consideration of 'narrative' modes of both study and explanation.

NOTES

1.   Such a distinction permits exploration of occasions like that in December 1989 in Bucharest, when participants in an 'assembly from above' converted it into a very different 'assembly from below', with death-dealing consequences for Nicolae and Elena Ceascescu.

2. For a parallel critique, suggesting that the related idea of 'free spaces' is a theoretical 'black box', see Polletta (1997).
3. Other writers use different terminologies. Sewell (1996) refers to 'ruptures' and 'moments of decision'. Sahlins suggests there are three moments within 'the structure of the conjuncture': 'instantiation', when social or cultural categories come to be embodied and represented in particular persons, objects and acts; 'denouement', when actual 'incidents' of practical interaction occur; and 'totalisation', when the consequences of an event are incorporated into a revised set of cultural categories and social relations.
4. Such 'submerged networks' have an obvious theoretical kinship with Scott's 'sites of the hidden transcript'. Evans and Boyte (1986) theorise these as 'free spaces'; Hetherington (1990) has suggested linking similar modern phenomena to the notion of the 'Bund' ('communion'), a form of sociation identified in the 1920s by Schmalenbach; cf. also Duka *et al.* (1995), on 'kitchen-cultures' in former Leningrad, or Mooney and Hunt (1996: 190–1) on 'halfway houses' in American agrarian movements.
5. There are interesting reconstructions of such moments in Waddington *et al.* (1989), in Rick Fantasia's (1988) account of the genesis of a wildcat strike, or in Lawrence Goodwyn's (1991) accounts of the events in Lublin in June 1956 and in Gdansk in August 1980.
6. For an excellent analysis of such a transformation, cf. Reicher (1996). See also Stott and Drury's analysis of the poll-tax riot in this volume.
7. How they act is itself conditioned by their own resources, their existing forms of organisation and understanding, their leaderships, and so forth. Kimeldorf (1988: chap. 3) offers a good analysis of the 'varying class capacities' of two groups of employers, those operating in American ports on the West and East Coasts respectively.
8. For a situation where weak coordination between an initiating group and a layer of enthusiastic supporters produced unforeseen results, see Goodwyn's (1991) fascinating reconstruction of the events in Lublin in 1956.
9. See, for example, Gareth Dale's account (1996) of the expansion of popular protest in East Germany during the revolution in 1989: the newly mobilised crowds pressed for changes more radical than envisaged by the 'early risers' from the intelligentsia-based 'civic movements', who rapidly lost their capacity to determine the pattern of events.
10. For a study which explores this, albeit rather holistically, see Ellingson (1995).

REFERENCES

Bagguley, Paul (1996), 'The Moral Economy of Anti-Poll Tax Protest', in Colin Barker and Paul Kennedy (eds), *To Make Another World: Studies in Protest and Collective Action* (Aldershot: Avebury), pp. 7–24.

Barker, Colin (1986), *Festival of the Oppressed: Solidarity, Reform and Revolution in Poland, 1980–81* (London: Bookmarks).

Blumer, Herbert (1969), 'Collective Behaviour', in Alfred McClung Lee (ed.), *Principles of Sociology*, 3rd edn (New York: Barnes & Noble), pp. 67–123.

Collins, Randall (1988), 'The Durkheimian Tradition in Conflict Sociology', in Jeffrey C. Alexander (ed.), *Durkheimian Sociology: Cultural Studies* (Cambridge: Cambridge University Press), pp. 107–28.

Dale, Gareth (1996), 'The East German Revolution of 1989', in Colin Barker and Paul Kennedy (eds), *To Make Another World: Studies and Protest and Collective Action* (Aldershot: Avebury), pp. 91–111.

Duka, A. N., Kornev, N., Voronkov, V. and Zdravomyslova, E. (1995), 'The Protest-cycle of Perestroika: the Case of Leningrad', *International Sociology*, 19, 83–99.

Durkheim, Emile (1961), *The Elementary Forms of the Religious Life*, translated by Joseph Ward Swain (New York: Collier Books).

Durkheim, Emile (1965), *Sociology and Philosophy*, translated by D. F. Pocock with an introduction by J. G. Peristiany (London: Cohen & West).

Ellingson, Stephen (1995), 'Understanding the Dialectic of Discourse and Collective Action: Public Debate and Rioting in Antebellum Cincinnati', *American Journal of Sociology*, 101 (1), July, 100–44.

Evans, Sara M. and Boyte, Harry C. (1986), *Free Spaces* (New York: Harper & Row).

Eyerman, Ron and Jamison, Andrew (1991), *Social Movements: A Cognitive Approach* (Cambridge: Polity).

Fantasia, Rick (1988), *Cultures of Solidarity: Consciousness, Action and Contemporary American Workers* (Berkeleys, CA: University of California Press).

Goodwyn, Lawrence (1991), *Breaking the Barrier: The Rise of Solidarity in Poland* (New York: Oxford University Press).

Gramsci, Antonio (1971), *Selections from the Prison Notebooks* (London: Lawrence & Wishart).

Heaton, Norma and Linn, Ian (1989), *Fighting Back: A Report on the Shop Steward Response to New Management Techniques in TGWU Region 10* (Barnsley: Northern College and TGWU Region 10).

Hetherington, Kevin (1990), *On the Home-Coming of the Stranger: New Social Movements or New Sociations?*, Lancaster Regionalism Group, University of Lancaster, Working Paper 39.

Hill, Christopher (1988), 'The Poor and the People in Seventeenth Century England', in Frederick Krantz (ed.), *History from Below: Studies in Popular Protest and Popular Ideology* (Oxford: Basil Blackwell), pp. 29–52.

Hunt, Lynn (1988), 'The Sacred and the French Revolution', in Jeffery C. Alexander (ed.), *Durkheimian Sociology: Cultural Studies* (Cambridge: Cambridge University Press), pp. 25–43.

Kimeldorf, Howard (1988), *Reds or Rackets? The Making of Radical and Conservative Unions on the Waterfront* (Berkeley, CA: University of California Press).

Klandermans, Bert (1991), 'New Social Movements and Resource Mobilisation: the European and American Approach Revisited', in Dieter Rucht (ed.), *Research on Social Movements: The State of the Art in Western Europe and the USA* (Boulder, CO: Westview Press), pp. 17–44.

Klandermans, Bert (1997), *The Social Psychology of Protest* (Oxford: Blackwell).

Kolankiewicz, George (1973), 'The Working Class', in David Lane and George Kolankiewicz (eds), *Social Groups in Polish Society* (London: Macmillan), pp. 88–151.

Laba, Roman (1991), *The Roots of Solidarity: A Political Sociology of Poland's Working-Class Democratisation* (Princeton, NJ: Princeton University Press).

Lockwood, David (1992), *Solidarity and Schism: 'The Problem of Disorder' in Durkheimian and Marxist Sociology* (Oxford: Clarendon Press).

Marshall, Gordon (1983), 'Some Remarks on the Study of Working-class Consciousness', *Politics and Society*, 12 (3), 263–301.

MacIntyre, Alasdair (1981), *After Virtue: A Study in Moral Theory* (London: Duckworth).

Melucci, Alberto (1989), *Nomads of the Present: Social Movements and Individual Needs in Contemporary Society* (London: Hutchinson Radius).

Michels, R. (1959), *Political Parties: A Sociological Study of the Oligarchical Tendencies of Modern Democracy* (London: Constable).

Mooney, Patrick H. and Hunt, Scott A. (1996), 'A Repertoire of Interpretations: Master Frames and Ideological Continuity in US Agrarian Mobilization', *Sociological Quarterly*, 37 (1), 177–97.

Morris, Aldon D. (1984), *The Origins of the Civil Rights Movement* (New York: Free Press).

Mueller, Carol (1994), 'Conflict Networks and the Origins of Women's Liberation', in Enrique Laraña, Hank Johnston and Joseph R. Gusfield (eds), *New Social Movements: From Ideology to Identity* (Philadelphia, PA: Temple University Press), pp. 234–63.

Polletta, Francesca (1997), 'Culture and its Discontents: Recent Theorizing on the Cultural Dimensions of Protest', *Sociological Inquiry*, 67 (4), 431–50.

Reicher, Stephen (1996) 'The Battle of Westminster: Developing the Social Identity Model of Crowd Behaviour in Order to Deal with Initiation and Development of Collective Conflict', *European Journal of Social Psychology*, 26, 115–34.

Rhomberg, Chris (1995), 'Collective Action and Urban Regimes: Class Formation and the 1946 Oakland General Strike', *Theory and Society*, 24, 567–94.

Rosenthal, Naomi and Schwartz, Michael (1989), 'Spontaneity and Democracy in Social Movements', in Bert Klandermans (ed.), *International Social Movement Research*, vol. 2 (Greenwich, CT: Jai Press), pp. 33–59.

Scott, Alan (1990), *Ideology and the New Social Movements* (London: Unwin Hyman).

Scott, James C. (1985), *Weapons of the Weak: Everyday Forms of Peasant Resistance* (New Haven, CT: Yale University Press).

Scott, James C. (1990), *Domination and the Arts of Resistance: Hidden Transcripts* (New Haven, CT: Yale University Press).

Sewell, William H. Jr (1996), 'Historical Events as Transformations of Structures: Inventing Revolution at the Bastille', *Theory and Society*, 25, 841–81.

Shanin, Teodor (1986), *Revolution as a Moment of Truth* (London: Macmillan).

Tarrow, Sidney (1989), *Struggle, Politics, and Reform: Collective Action, Social Movements, and Cycles of Protest* (Ithaca, NY: Cornell Studies in International Affairs/Western Societies Papers).

Taylor, Verta (1989), 'Social Movement Continuity: The Women's Movement in Abeyance', *American Sociological Review*, 54, 761–75.

Tilly, Charles (1993 and 1995), 'Contentious Repertoires in Great Britain, 1758–1834', *Social Science History*, 17 (2), summer 1993, 253–80; reprinted in Mark Traugott (ed.), *Repertoires and Cycles of Collective Action* (Durham, NC: Duke University Press, 1995), pp. 15–42.

Tilly, Charles (1993–4), 'Social Movements as Historically Specific Clusters of Political Performance', *Berkeley Journal of Sociology*, 38, 1–30.

Turner, Victor (1974), *Dramas, Fields and Metaphors: Symbolic Action in Human Society* (Ithaca, NY: Cornell University Press).

Turner, Victor (1982), *From Ritual to Theatre: The Human Seriousness of Play* (New York: Performing Arts Journal Publications).

Waddington, David, Jones, Karen and Critcher, Chas (1989), *Flashpoints: Studies in Public Disorder* (London: Routledge).

Willis, Paul (1977), *Learning to Labour: How Working-Class Kids get Working-Class Jobs* (Farnborough: Gower).

Zolberg, Aristide R. (1972), 'Moments of Madness', *Politics and Society*, 2, 183–207.

3 The Inter-Group Dynamics of Empowerment: a Social Identity Model

Clifford Stott and John Drury

THEORIES OF THE CROWD

In recent years, traditional psychological models of crowd action (Le Bon, 1895; Allport, 1924; Diener, 1980; Prentice-Dunn and Rogers, 1989) have been undermined by some very powerful critiques (Nye, 1975; Graumann and Moscovici, 1986; Turner and Killian, 1987; McPhail, 1991). These critiques have focused upon the extent to which this 'classic' account tends to reify crowd action, treating it as an inherently irrational atavistic intrusion rather than as an *outcome* of complex social processes. Moreover, historical studies of crowd events have demonstrated the normative structure of crowd behaviour, even in fast-moving and changing situations (Thompson, 1971; Reddy, 1977) further undermining the 'classic' accounts view of such action as a randomly destructive outburst.

However, most of the critiques of classic crowd theory have been limited by their inability to provide an adequate theoretical account of the normative structure of crowd events while at the same time accounting for its *dynamic* nature (cf. Barker, this volume). The social identity model of crowd behaviour (Reicher, 1982, 1984, 1987, 1996; Stott, 1996; Stott and Reicher, 1998a, 1998b) has gone a long way towards providing a theoretical model that can account for this apparent paradox. The social identity model derives from self-categorization theory (Turner *et al.*, 1987). It argues that people have available a wide range of self-categorizations corresponding to the social groups with which they identify. When a particular social category becomes salient in the perceptual system, people are able to act collectively in terms of the stereotypical dimensions of that social group.[1] Hence collective behaviour becomes possible when, and only to the extent that, people adopt and act in terms of the same social identity.

The explanatory power of the social identity model was illustrated through an analysis of the 'St Paul's riot' of April 1980. Reicher (1984, 1987) showed the close relationship between crowd participants' collective definitions of self and the normative structure of their collective action. By focusing on collective conflict in this way he was able to show that only action consistent with a specific identity became normative. For example, during the early stages of the event it was the police that were subject to collective 'violence' while other agencies such as the fire brigade were left untouched. Although, at a later stage, there were attacks on property, only attacks on shops and businesses owned by those outside the 'community' were engaged in *collectively* by participants in the crowd. This normative pattern to collective action reflected the nature of the social identity of the rioters, which they defined in terms of the antagonism between themselves as residents of St Paul's, and the power of outside agencies (such as the police and outside businesses) to have control over their lives.

The weaknesses of the St Paul's study, and hence this early version of the social identity model, are two-fold. Firstly, it focused on collective conflict only after it had already been initiated. The study and therefore the model were unable to account for changes in the normative structure of the event and consequently the *development* of conflict in the crowd event (Reicher, 1996). Crucially, the model's emphasis on normative structure at the expense of change is linked to questions of power. The study was unable to resolve whether the violence by the crowd was an inherent part of the collective identity, or whether it became legitimised in the crowd event itself. Moreover, it was unable to address how crowd members came to feel powerful enough to act out their identity as they did. Thus, in the early version of the social identity model, an emphasis on normative structure meant that dynamism, and hence power, were neglected.

Secondly, many studies of crowds have shown that collective violence characteristically originates with the intervention of outside agencies such as the police or army (Feagin and Hahn, 1973; Tilly *et al*. 1975; Stephenson, 1979; Smith, 1980; Fine and Millar, 1985). Nonetheless, the empirical focus of the original model was upon the crowd alone 'as if' in isolation. Subsequently, the theoretical model has remained ignorant of the role of out-groups in the development of collective conflict and has subsequently been unable to account for the inter-group dynamics of identity change (Stott and Reicher, 1998a).

MODELS OF COLLECTIVE POWER

The question of power in relation to crowd events and collective action more generally is raised by the large number of theorists in both sociology and social psychology. Subjective power in collectivities has commonly been theorised in terms of the concept of *'efficacy'*, which Chase (1992) defines as the (perceived) ability of the individual to bring about a desired state of the world or to avert an undesired state of the world. Klandermans (1992) points to the widespread agreement among recent social movement theorists that collective protest takes place in the belief among participants that the experienced grievances can be eliminated by the challengers' collective action – that the challengers have efficacy.

A number of studies concur with this argument. In a longitudinal questionnaire study, Breakwell (1992) found that self-efficacy (as measured by general efficacy and political efficacy scales) correlated significantly with involvement in political action such as marching on demonstrations. In a questionnaire study, Cocking (1995) found that environmental direct action activists had higher feelings of self-efficacy than non-activists for behaviours requiring relatively high levels of commitment (i.e. direct actions), but lower levels of self-efficacy for behaviours requiring relatively low levels of commitment (such as writing to MPs). In a study of women's participation in collective action, Kelly and Breinlinger (1995) found that feelings of individual efficacy were a powerful correlate of involvement in formal political organisation such as women's groups: '[i]t is the belief that getting involved does make a difference that distinguishes more active from less active individuals' (p. 53).

Following years of neglect within social psychology of issues of power (Cartwright, 1959; Tedeschi, 1974; Ng, 1980; Dépret and Fiske, 1993), the recent turn to issues of empowerment in collective action and intergroup relations has to be welcomed. Yet it is arguable that, as an account of empowerment, the concept of 'efficacy' is somewhat static.

Documentary studies of social movements and crowd events commonly point to the occurrence of empowerment not just as a precondition, but also as a process or consequence of involvement in collective action. For example, the US ghetto rioters of the 1960s who felt their action achieved something against a normally powerful out-group subsequently felt satisfaction, pride and confidence in their identity as participants – personally as well as collectively (Boesel *et al.* 1971). Similarly, commentators on the events of May 1968 in France describe how occupying students displayed increased confidence in their own abilities and capacities: 'The occupants of Censier suddenly cease to be unconscious, passive *objects* shaped by particular combinations of social forces; they become conscious, active *subjects* who begin to shape their own social activity' (Gregoire and Perlman, 1969, p. 37; emphasis in original).

While an account of the preconditions of empowered collective action is necessary, this must not preclude an understanding of the emergence of empowerment in the collective. Indeed, ideally what needs to be shown is the possible relationship between these two aspects of power in collective action. What is necessary, in other words, is an account of the *dynamics* of empowerment processes within crowd events.

It is within this framework that we shall now address the following issues. First, and more generally, we shall examine whether, and the extent to which, empowerment can arise from collective action. Second, and more specifically, we aim to investigate the impact of intergroup actions in altering social identities and hence power relations.

Our analysis takes as its premise the work already carried out by Reicher (1984, 1987, 1996) on the social identity model. This suggests a particular methodological approach – that is, to examine participants' identities, and to determine the actions that were generalised in the crowd. Going beyond Reicher's snapshot approach, however, we shall examine crowd participants' perceptions and identities not just once, but over the duration of the crowd event, and compare these with the perceptions of those acting in relation to the crowd – the police. In this way we aim to tackle the apparent paradox of social identity-based norms coinciding with dramatic change in crowd actions.

After a brief description of the particular crowd event we studied, we present an analysis of participants' accounts. The analysis details the changing perceptions and feelings of crowd members over the duration of the crowd event and points up significant contrasts between these and those of the police. We shall attempt to show the crucial relation between these various perceptions and the changes in power relations between crowd members and police.

THE TRAFALGAR SQUARE 'POLL TAX RIOT' OF MARCH 1990

The crowd event we examined was the anti-poll tax demonstration of 31 March 1990, in central London (Waddington, 1994). The poll tax was a new flat-rate tax imposed by the Conservative government (Burns, 1992; Bagguley, 1995) and the demonstration took place the weekend before the new tax was introduced. The march began in Kennington Park and was intended by the organisers to finish with a rally in Trafalgar Square. Estimates place the numbers in attendance at as high as 250,000 people. While congregating in the park, demonstrators took the opportunity to collectively express their commitment to a non-violent protest with a show of hands in response to a call from organisers. However, as the demonstration passed up Whitehall people stopped and a subsequent sit-down protest opposite Downing Street halted demonstrators' progress into Trafalgar Square. After repeated requests by stewards for those sitting down to move, the police intervened by firstly re-routing the demonstration and then by driving officers through the stationary crowd opposite Downing Street, pushing it as a whole north towards Trafalgar Square.

Subsequent to this intervention, generalised conflict between demonstrators and the police occurred for the first time. Large numbers of participants resisted police actions and attempted to drive the police back. This in turn led to the adoption of riot tactics by the police who used officers in protective clothing and on horseback to drive the crowd from Whitehall and Trafalgar Square. The consequent conflict involved as many as 5000 people in running battles with the police over a period of several hours, and also involved attacks on property in the West End and around Trafalgar Square.

ANALYSIS

The data we discuss comes from a wide variety of sources, including interviews, accounts, videos, newspapers and letters. Altogether, data were collected from around 40 demonstrators, as well as police and other commentators.

CROWD MEMBERS' INITIAL PERCEPTIONS

Initially all the participants interviewed consistently defined their identity at the beginning of the demonstration, and hence their rationale for collective action, in terms of a common non-violent opposition to an unjust tax. Consequently they understood the demonstration as a legitimate means for a variety of diverse groupings to collectively express their opposition to it:

> What united all these different people?
> Thinking the poll tax was really unfair. There was a feeling of, you know, you were quite justified to be there, which you don't always get on a lot of demonstrations. You know, this is going to be a good day out. I think the combination of the single issue and this feeling that you were doing the right thing.
>
> (Interview, R)

All of the participants that were interviewed drew a distinction between extremist factions who were associated with conflictual action and the majority who wished to act non-conflictually. Indeed, participants were explicit about the extent to which the demonstration shared a norm of non-violence.

> The mood was confident but not aggressive. A vote was taken as a statement of intent that demonstrators wanted a peaceful march. It looked as though every hand in the park was raised.
>
> [Participant account, D]

CROWD MEMBERS' PERCEPTIONS OF THE SITUATION IN
WHITEHALL

As participants arrived in the Whitehall area, they experienced the congestion and the sit-down protest as a product of the large numbers on the
demonstration filling the route beyond capacity. In line with their initial
identity, participants stressed that their presence in the area was not
conflictual or a threat to public order, rather they were congregating in the
area because they were unable to continue due to the sheer density of
people. This perception is illustrated in the following extract taken from a
conversation with a participant recorded in the crowd at the time.

> Why aren't you walking up to Trafalgar Square?
> Well as far as I understand it because Trafalgar Square is full.
>
> [Field notes]

As the congestion intensified there were some isolated incidents of conflict
towards the police and the sit-down protest took place. Participants in the
area again stressed the legitimate non-violent nature of protesters' behaviour, either by continuing to differentiate themselves from the small numbers
engaged in conflict or by emphasising the trivial nature of the conflictual
activity.

> The only slight confrontation was when I got to Downing Street where
> people have just started doing a sit-down protest. Once every ten minutes,
> like, an empty beer can would like clatter and, in fact, reach the pavement
> sort of ten feet in front of the police. There was no real threat to public
> order or anything like that.
>
> [Participant account, A]

POLICE PERCEPTIONS OF THE SITUATION IN WHITEHALL

However, in stark contrast, there is evidence to suggest that the police saw
the behaviour of the crowd as a whole as an illegitimate threat to public
order (Waddington, 1992). Interviews with riot-trained police officers more
generally suggested that, while the police accept that most crowd members
are ordinary law-abiding citizens, and that violence is the product of a dis-
ruptive minority, they also argue that ordinary people easily change in crowd
situations. They argue that even law-abiding citizens are liable to become
irrational, violent, and open to manipulation by extremist factions in situations where conflict is present. Consequently, they believe that the crowd as
a whole poses a threat to public order when only a minority is actually
engaged in initiating conflictual activity (Stott and Reicher, 1998b).

The spontaneous nature of the sit-down protest, the initial refusal of those sitting down to move on, and some minor incidents of conflict thus led the police to understand the situation as conflictual. Therefore, they regarded the crowd as a whole in that area to be posing a threat to public order. The following extract was taken from an interview with the commanding officer in Whitehall during the demonstration.

> Did you think that there was something in the nature of the crowd that made people more susceptible to this minority trying to influence people?
>
> I don't know, it's always hard. I think there were two thousand people causing us problems. Some of those, I am sure, the vast majority were good law-abiding people under normal circumstances. But when you are in a group like that, I am sure that, the fever of the cause, the fever of the day, the throwing and everything else, they get locked together and think 'oh we are part of this'. Something disengages in their brain. I am not a medical man or an expert in crowd behaviour, but something goes and they become part of the crowd.

[Participant police, Interview]

In addition to a perception of crowds as dangerous, the police emphasize the extent to which crowds are volatile. Consequently, the police are often concerned to remain in control of crowds at all times and to limit crowd action to that which has been agreed beforehand. Any deviation is seen as incipient disorder, warranting immediate intervention lest such crowd disorder should manifest its natural tendency to escalate. Thus having defined the situation as conflictual, the police would be predisposed to intervention.

Hence the police decided to intervene and forcefully pushed the crowd as a whole north towards Trafalgar Square. In terms of tactics, therefore, the police treated the crowd as a single unit regardless of any individual's prior activities or intentions. Thus, those demonstrators actively engaged in conflict and those who distanced themselves from it were equally likely to be subjected to aggressive policing activity.

The crucial point here is that it is not merely that the police *perceived* the crowd as a uniform danger, but that they had at their disposal a great deal of legislation, weaponry and manpower. As such they had the ability to *impose* their perceptions of uniformity upon crowd members through the use of indiscriminate coercive force.

CROWD MEMBERS' PERCEPTIONS OF THE POLICE INTERVENTION

Since crowd participants saw themselves as acting legitimately, they could see no legitimate reason for the police intervention. In addition, participants stressed the indiscriminate and violent behaviour of the police once they had entered the crowd:

> They were just hitting everybody and just being so violent towards everybody. I think the thing that struck me most was that there were people who weren't there for trouble, who were just there for the cause, getting beaten.
>
> [Participant account, V]

From the point of view of crowd participants, the use of such force in a crowded area posed a threat to all demonstrators' safety:

> Everyone started chanting 'Hillsborough' and that is when it really struck me, the full implication of what could happen to me and the people around me.
>
> [Participant account, N]

CHANGES IN CROWD MEMBERS' CONCEPTIONS OF LEGITIMACY

Given the perceived illegitimate and dangerous nature of the police intervention, participants subsequently *changed* the way in which they perceived conflict and those engaged in it. Recall that *prior* to police intervention participants described conflict as anti-normative and differentiated themselves from conflictual factions. *Subsequent* to police intervention, conflict came to be seen as an acceptable way of preventing further illegitimate police action:

> What did you think of those demonstrators?
> I think they were very courageous taking the police on. They were angry. I mean the poll tax [demonstration] changed my mind about what I think about violence against the police. I felt like the police were being complete bastards.
> Did you think the violence was justified?
> Oh yes.
>
> [Interview, L]

Thus, subsequent to the police intervention, crowd participants emphasised the legitimacy of their own response to the police by describing it not as violence, but as a means to *defend the crowd as a whole* from unjustified and indiscriminately violent police actions. Even demonstrators who were not directly involved in the conflict were understood to be condoning it:

> There were loads of people standing around that weren't involved in defending themselves. Every time something happened this enormous roar would go up from the crowd. So you had a group of people that were

actively involved and then you had this mass of people who were not involved but were clearly supporting what was going on.

[Participant account, P]

The use of coercive force by the police created a uniform social context for crowd participants which served to change both the content of the identity and the extent to which it was shared. In a context where crowd participants saw their own behaviour as acceptable, indiscriminate police action was defined as unwarranted and illegitimate. Consequently, where crowd participants previously saw conflict with the police as unacceptable, they subsequently saw it as both necessary and legitimate. Moreover, crowd participants who previously saw themselves as differentiated from those engaged in conflict subsequently came to see themselves as the same as these conflictual groups and individuals.

How could you tell that the crowd were united?
When we were faced by the police all the way through people were shouting 'you bastards'. The whole crowd was with each other. Everyone was outraged and were together in a certain feeling and together in what they did. The whole crowd seemed to have the same general feeling.

[Interview, K]

CHANGES IN POWER RELATIONS BETWEEN POLICE AND CROWD

Importantly, then, by using indiscriminate coercive force, police action changed the situation from one in which isolated individuals, or relatively small groups, were hostile towards them into one in which a much larger group of people were antagonistic. This altered the power relationship between those in the crowd and the police, in that unity and hence expectations of social support within the crowd were greatly enhanced. Hence demonstrators became able to collectively resist the police's use of coercive force. Thus the new identity was bound up with a change in the power relationships between crowd participants and the police; collective resistance of police action became not only acceptable but also possible:

There was a feeling of strength and of back up.

[Participant account, Pr]

Do you think being in a large crowd affects people?
Certainly affected me. It made me feel safer about being angry.

[Interview, P]

A number of crowd participants were explicit about the sense of empowerment they felt in being in a huge crowd united against the illegitimate actions of the police; they felt enabled to act in ways which they felt were right:

> The crowd went forward, because there was so many people and there was quite a strong feeling of power being in such a big group and like I said I felt I had the right to be there.
>
> [Participant account, T]

Moreover, being powerful and in a position – unusually, perhaps – to do what they felt was right opened up further possibilities to many crowd participants. They were able to go beyond merely defending themselves against the police to actually taking the initiative:

> So would you characterise this violence as defensive?
> It is being defensive by taking the offensive. The confrontation comes from there being the confidence of being a lot of you.
>
> [Interview, D]

However, collective actions by crowd members to resist the police would have confirmed initial police fears of a uniformly hostile crowd. Hence the dynamic of escalation where the police reasserted their dominant position by adopting riot tactics, so increasing the scale and intensity of their intervention. As a consequence the crowd was dispersed into the West End where widespread looting took place.

Crowd participants' experiences in the West End echo those when the police were initially forced back in Whitehall. Again the normal power relations had been reversed – temporarily, at least. This shift enabled many crowd participants to do things they had always wanted to do – to attack the world of wealth and privilege, themes which linked in with those motivating the poll tax demonstration itself. Crowd participants therefore had a rare opportunity to experience otherwise reified and congealed social relations as fluid and vulnerable, as the following interview excerpt illustrates:

> I've lived in London all my life and I've hated the West End. Just to see it as another world was really entertaining.
> Why were these kinds of places chosen? What was it about them?
> Well, symbols of wealth.
>
> [Interview, Z]

One is reminded of the conclusion of Reddy's (1977) study of riots over a 100-year period in Rouen. As he puts it, 'the targets of these crowds thus glitter in the eye of history as signs of the labourer's conception of the nature of society' (p. 84).

THEORETICAL IMPLICATIONS

This analysis of the behaviours and perceptions of demonstrations at the anti-poll tax riot has suggested a far more dynamic account than both the original social identity model and the efficacy accounts of power in collective action. Power was not a given feature of participants' identities which simply expressed itself unproblematically. Nor was the production of power in the crowd explicable outside of the changing relationship of crowd members to the police.

A dynamic social identity model of conflictual crowd action and hence empowerment within such action can be offered as follows.

1. The premise of behavioural conflict is a conflict of interpretations between crowd members and police, particularly as to what counts as legitimate behaviour.

Crowd participants perceive that the activity in which they and the majority of other crowd members are engaged is legitimate, and poses no threat to law and order. But police either hold a perception of crowd participants as uniformly dangerous from the outset or, despite initial perceptions of heterogeneity, see everybody in the crowd as equally potentially dangerous once conflict or 'disorder' has developed. Moreover, once conflict or 'disorder' has developed, police tactics dictate that it is both necessary and legitimate to treat the crowd uniformly, making all crowd members equally liable to repressive police action.

2. It is not enough that there is disagreement between groups; for such disagreement to develop into overt conflict, one group must have the power to impose its conception of proper practice on the other.

Thus the police, for example, may have the organisational and material resources – structures of command, technologies of communication, tactics and weaponry – to posit their own definition of 'public order' over that of the crowd.

3. Since identities are based on the actualities of social relations, the use of coercive force by the police creates a uniform social context for crowd participants within which the latter come to define themselves.

Assertive action by a powerful out-group may serve to change the nature of the intergroup relationship. For the poll tax demonstrators the intervention of the police meant that the issue became one not just of the poll tax but of illegitimate violence against them by the police. It therefore meant that self-defensive action was legitimate. Moreover, since the attack was on the crowd as a whole, then crowd participants who previously saw themselves as differentiated, came to see themselves as the same.

4. Finally, a common categorisation among in-group members in relation to an out-group leads to a change in the power relationship between crowd participants and the police, making collective resistance of police action possible.

Shared in-group membership means enhanced consensus and hence expectations of support. Where the crowd members are more numerous than the police – as in the poll tax riot – the power relationship has turned full circle. Hence the crowd was able to assert itself against the police, and even went beyond self-defence into more offensive action.

The account we have offered raises questions about the extent to which such changes in intergroup power relations extend beyond the crowd event itself. Did those who participated come to see their relationship with the police and state differently *after* the event? To what extent were any new, more empowered identities able to be sustained outside of the crowd event and in the face of subsequent persecution by the authorities? Although some of those we interviewed did indeed speak of feeling more empowered in the months following the event, this was not an issue we examined systematically in this case study. This question of the endurance of empowerment occurring in crowd events is a topic we have pursued elsewhere (see Drury, 1996; Drury and Reicher, 1998).

NOTE

1. Dimensions that are fundamentally social in origin.

REFERENCES

Allport, F. H. (1924), *Social Psychology* (Boston, MA: Houghton Mifflin).

Bagguley, P. (1995), 'Protest, Poverty and Power', *Sociological Review*, 43, 693–719.

Barker, C. (1999), 'Empowerment and Resistance: "Collective Effervescence" and other accounts', in P. Bagguley and J. Hearn (eds), *Transforming Politics: Power and Resistance* (this volume).

Boesel, D., Goldberg, L. C. and Marx, G. T. (1971), 'Rebellion in Plainfield', in D. Boesel and P. H. Rossi (eds), *Cities under Siege: An Anatomy of the Ghetto Riots, 1964–1968* (New York: Basic Books).

Breakwell, G. M. (1992b), 'Processes of Self-evaluation: Efficacy and Estrangement', in G. M. Breakwell (ed.), *Social Psychology of Identity and the Self Concept* (London: Surrey University Press).

Burns, D. (1992), *The Poll Tax Revolt* (Stirling: AK Press).

Cartwright, D. (1959), 'Power: Neglected Variable in Social Psychology', in D. Cartwright (ed.), *Studies in Social Power* (Ann Arbor, MI: Institute for Social Research, University of Michigan).

Chase, J. (1992), 'The Self and Collective Action: Dilemmatic Identities', in G. M. Breakwell (ed.), *Social Psychology of Identity and Self Concept* (London: Surrey University Press).

Cocking, C. (1995), 'Comparing Attitudes Towards the Environment: Does Direct Action Make a Real Difference?', unpublished MSc dissertation, University of Surrey.

Dépret, E. and Fiske, S. T. (1993), 'Social Cognition and Power: Some Cognitive Consequences of Social Structure as a Source of Control Deprivation', in G. Weary, F. Gleicher and K. L. Marsh (eds), *Control Motivation and Social Cognition* (New York: Springer-Verlag).

Diener, E. (1980), 'Deindividuation: the Absence of Self-awareness and Self-regulation in Group Members', in P. B. Paulus (ed.), *Psychology of Group Influence* (Hillsdale, NJ: Lawrence Erlbaum).

Drury, J. (1996), 'Collective Action and Psychological Change', unpublished PhD thesis, University of Exeter.

Drury, J. and Reicher, S. D. (1998), 'Collective Action and Psychological Change: the Emergence of New Social Identities', *Group Processes and Intergroup Relations* (submitted).

Feagin, J. R. and Hahn, M. (1973), *Ghetto Revolts* (New York: Macmillan).

Fine, B. and Millar, R. (eds) (1985), *Policing the Miners Strike* (London: Lawrence Wishart).

Graumann, C. F. and Moscovici, S. (1986), *Changing Conceptions of Crowd Mind and Behaviour* (New York: Springer-Verlag).

Gregoire, R. and Perlman, F. (1969), *Worker-Student Action Committees: France, May '68* (Detroit, MI: Black and Red).

Kelly, C. and Breinlinger, S. (1995), 'Identity and Injustice: Exploring Women's Participation in Collective Action', *Journal of Community and Applied Social Psychology*, 5, 41–57.

Klandermans, B. (1992), 'The Social Construction of Protest and Multiorganizational Fields', in A. D. Morris and C. M. Mueller (eds), *Frontiers in Social Movement Theory* (New Haven, CT: Yale University Press).

Le Bon, G. (1947), *The Crowd: A Study of the Popular Mind* (London: Ernest Benn; originally published 1895).

McPhail, C. (1991), *The Myth of the Madding Crowd* (New York: Aldine de Gruyter).

Ng, S. H. (1980), *The Social Psychology of Power* (London: Academic Press).

Nye, R. (1975), *The Origins of Crowd Psychology* (Beverly Hills, CA: Sage).

Prentice-Dunn, S. and Rogers, R. W. (1989), 'Deindividuation and the Self-regulation of Behaviour', in P. B. Paulus (ed.), *Psychology of Group Influence*, 2nd edn (Hillsdale, NJ: Erlbaum).

Reddy, W. M. (1977), 'The Textile Trade and the Language of the Crowd at Rouen, 1752–1871', *Past and Present*, 74, 62–89.

Reicher, S. D. (1982), 'The Determination of Collective Behaviour', in H. Tajfel (ed.), *Social Identity and Intergroup Relations* (Cambridge: Cambridge University Press).

Reicher, S. D. (1984), 'The St Paul's Riot: an Explanation of the Limits of Crowd Action in Terms of a Social Identity Model', *European Journal of Social Psychology*, 14, 1–21.

Reicher, S. D. (1987), 'Crowd Behaviour as Social Action', in J. C. Turner, M. A. Hogg, P. J. Oakes, S. D. Reicher and M. S. Wetherell (eds), *Rediscovering the Social Group: A Self-Categorization Theory* (Oxford: Blackwell).

Reicher, S. (1996), '"The Battle of Westminster": Developing the Social Identity Model of Crowd Behaviour in Order to Explain the Initiation and Development of Collective Conflict', *European Journal of Social Psychology*, 26, 115–34.

Smith, D. (1980), 'Tonypandy 1910: Definitions of Community', *Past and Present*, 87, 158–84.

Stephenson, J. (1979), *Popular Disturbances in England 1700–1870* (London: Longman).

Stott, C. J. (1996), 'The Intergroup Dynamics of Crowd Behaviour', unpublished PhD thesis, University of Exeter.

Stott, C. J. and Reicher, S. D. (1998a), 'Crowd Action as Intergroup Process: Introducing the Police Perspective', *European Journal of Social Psychology*, 28, 509–29.

Stott, C. J. and Reicher, S. D. (1998b), 'How Conflict Escalates: The Inter-group Dynamics of Collective Football Crowd Violence', *Sociology*, 32, 353–77.

Tedeschi, J. T. (1974), 'Introduction and Overview', in J. T. Tedeschi (ed.), *Perspectives on Social Power* (Chicago, IL: Aldine).

Thompson, E. P. (1971) 'The Moral Economy of the English Crowd in the Eighteenth Century, *Past and Present*, 50, 76–136.

Tilly, C. Tilly, L. and Tilly, R. (1975), *The Rebellious Century, 1830–1930* (London: J. M. Dent).

Turner, J. C., Hogg, M. A., Oakes, P. J., Reicher, S. D. and Wetherell, M. S. (1987), *Rediscovering the Social Group: A Self-Categorization Theory* (Oxford: Blackwell).

Turner, R. H. and Killian, L. M. (1987), *Collective Behavior*, 3rd edn (Englewood Cliffs, NJ: Prentice-Hall).

Waddington, D. (1992), *Contemporary Issues in Public Disorder* (London: Routledge).

Waddington, P. J. (1994) *Liberty and Order* (London: University College, of London Press).

4 Power, Politics and Everyday Life: the Local Rationalities of Social Movement Milieux

Laurence Cox

INTRODUCTION: THE CULTURAL ROOTS OF POLITICAL CONFLICT

Everyday language readily identifies social movement activity – campaigning, protesting, holding meetings, issuing statements – as 'politics'; perhaps not in the sense of parties and parliaments, but politics none the less. Much academic literature shares this view of social movements as 'politics by other means', from resource mobilisation and political opportunity structure approaches to analyses of movements as expressions of economic interests. It is interesting, then, that precisely in continental Europe, where contemporary movements have arguably made the greatest impact on the party system and engaged in the sharpest confrontations with the state, theorists have increasingly stressed the *cultural* aspects of social movements.

One such theme sees movements as rooted in specific *sociocultural milieux*: large-scale, 'lifestyle' responses to structured experience of inequality, with differing issues and priorities (Vester *et al.*, 1993; Hradil, 1987), local 'movement milieux' within these, and shifts in class *habiti* between generations in these milieux (Müller, 1990). Another approach identifies a shared culture as a *structural element* of social movement activity: as an identity enabling the networks between organisations, groups and individuals that constitute a movement (Diani, 1992a,b), or as 'cognitive praxis' combining world-view, issue-specific knowledge and modes of organisation (Eyerman and Jamison, 1991). Thirdly, social movements can be analysed as *cultural challenges*: movements may struggle to control the cultural definition of 'historicity', societal self-production (Touraine, 1981, 1985), their structural form may itself be a symbolic message to the wider society (Melucci, 1985, 1989, 1992), or 'political' and 'cultural' movement strategies may be alternative possibilities (Raschke, 1985).

The 'social movements' problematic, then, can be restated with an emphasis on the *culture of movement milieux*: as the source of mobilisation, of the internal culture of movement activity, and of wider challenges to the social order. The difficulty then becomes locating particular forms of engagement with power and the political within particular sociocultural formations. One possible response is the critical theory analysis of movements as defending the communicative rationality of the lifeworld against colonisation by capitalist and state rationalities (Habermas, 1984, 1987). Yet although particular, 'decommodified' lifeworlds are pointed to (Offe, 1985), it is quite a leap from a universal communicative rationality to the *specific* cultural logics of contemporary lifeworlds. If instrumental rationalisation has specific roots in Calvinist soteriology, so the roots of communicative rationalisation need to be identified.

A potential remedy is Eder's (1985, 1993) analysis of contemporary movements as expressing the *habitus* of the petite bourgeoisie and its struggle to impose its cultural definitions; yet this *habitus* is ascribed rather than examined, read off from the structural position of the class – and unsurprisingly contradicted by the Hannover project's findings of significant *transformations* in class *habitus* within movement milieux (Müller, 1990; Vester *et al.*, 1993). Both critical theory and Eder's approach thus offer to relate movement activities to movement milieux but fail to take account of the cultural *specificity* of the latter. The question is then how to theorise, and research, such specificity.

THE CONCEPT OF LOCAL RATIONALITIES

What is needed is a heuristic concept that could make it possible to link the culture of movement milieux with the forms of activity and challenges raised by social movements; avoid an *a-priori* exclusion of the political or the cultural; and enable an empirical engagement with the cultural specificities of actual movement milieux. I want to suggest the concept of 'local rationalities' as a means of doing this.

The specific cultures of movement milieux are 'local', contingent in relation to an abstract theory of modernity if not in relation to actual societies. To stress contingency is to avoid the purely rationalist ascription of a particular culture to such milieux on the basis of abstract considerations, hence to encourage the realist attempt to relate theory to the phenomenal world (McLennan, 1981) or, less grandly, to keep the question open.

'Rationality' then indicates the ontological level on which this culture is being sought. By analogy with the typologies of rationalities developed by Weber (1984) and Habermas (1984), it implies a *formal characteristic* about the *way we make sense of and engage with the world* which is capable of being *generalised* and taking on *a life of its own*. Thus, for example, the formal principle of a rational calculation of which means are best suited to achieve given ends enables that particular rethinking of the world we call modernity. Starting from a specific problem in a specific cultural milieu, it could be generalised to encompass all aspects of action and be used to restructure any other milieu. Thus the local rationalities of specific movement milieux are formal elements in the way participants act, talk and make sense of the world which could be generalised to restructure many areas of activity, notably linking everyday life with movement action.

ELEMENTS OF LOCAL RATIONALITIES

The discussion which follows is drawn from research in progress in Dublin 'movement milieux'. I am researching in particular a network formed *inter alia* in London squats, Dublin crashpads, a student occupation and anti-nuclear and ecological organisations, which has in turn formed a context for a variety of alternative 'political' and 'cultural' projects and experiments, such as:

(a) political projects, such as anarchist and green groups, street theatre, student politics and direct action;
(b) experimentation with living forms, in particular shared houses, squats and 'crashpads';
(c) economic projects, such as cooperatives, alternative bookshops and local trading systems (LETS);
(d) experimentation with sexual relationships, including bisexual, open and multiple relationships;
(e) experimentation with drugs, in particular hash, acid and mushrooms;
(f) cultural experiments, such as alternative music, Rainbow Gatherings, pagan and occultist rituals and groups, and so on.

This chapter draws on five interviews of my series with members of this network: three men and two women, all in their mid to late twenties when interviewed. Four are Irish, one is a European immigrant; class backgrounds range from skilled working class to professional, and occupations at the time of interview included unskilled worker, residential care worker, research student and computer programmer. All names have been changed.

As both collection and analysis of data are still in progress, this chapter is naturally very provisional. It should, however, be sufficient to make visible the possibilities and limitations of the approach I am suggesting. The 'local rationalities' of this network, as they appear above all in interview material, stress specific forms of *autonomy* and *reflexivity*: autonomy as self-development and what could be called 'lifeworld reflexivity' as the suspension of the 'taken-for-granted' attitude, and the willingness to make changes, in all areas of activity.

AUTONOMY AS SELF-DEVELOPMENT

The principle of autonomy is of course not a new one within modernity (Wagner, 1994). Yet most modern formulations take the self for granted: thus instrumental rationality treats both the self and its goal as assumptions, and enquires merely after the most effective way of getting from A to B. Even in its most hedonistic forms, possessive individualism is simply a special case of this approach. Romanticism, commonly ascribed to movement milieux, assumes a natural, pre-given self, albeit obscured by conventions and civilisation, and places this natural self first. Yet the logic of autonomy presented within this lifeworld places the self in question, as an open-ended project, something to be constructed or transformed. Thus participants make comments along the following lines:

> Ciarán is ambitious within himself, it's himself that he wants to develop, not a career or any of that kind of stuff.

(Josh)

Another participant speaks of

> People who do all kinds of odd and extremely innovative things, an awful lot of people whose top priority is sorting their head out, or whose top priority is something along the lines of enlightenment.

(Ruth)

In this context the pursuit of autonomy and self-realisation is explicitly contrasted to the goal-rational pursuit of material interests:

> It comes back to this idea that the way in which people perceive ambition as not a material ambition, which again links back to the ideas about people's attitude to property and that. Whilst they have fuck all of it, I don't think that is entirely responsible for their attitude. The development is sort of personal development, it's not material development. So the idea of going away to make money isn't really, you're not going to impress anybody, really. 'Oh wow, he's earning fuckloads of money, good for him, so what?'

(Josh)

The main theme is that of moving away from instrumental approaches, for example, seeking the best available employment, towards an exploratory approach to one's own life. This exploratory sense is underlined by the weak articulation of the nature of the alternatives and how to get there: it is not simply choosing an alternative strategy to achieve pre-existing goals. Rather, goals are something to be revised along the way. Thus, instead of identifying with a fixed self (whether the given self of instrumentalism or the 'true' self of romanticism), the self is seen as something to develop. One takes a distance from 'the self' in order to change it or observe it changing.

THE POLITICS OF AUTONOMY

In keeping with this logic, the instrumentally rational pursuit of politics in a narrow sense is often rejected outright in the name of autonomy:

> LC: Groups are bad things?
> Yeah, kind of limiting. If you try and set up anything a lot of these people will just go 'I'm not interested.' You know, if they happened to be somewhere and something happened they'd go for it, but anything organised they're not interested in, anything that sounds remotely political they don't want to know.
> LC: Why is that?
> Don't believe in politics, a lot of people just find it boring, or completely pointless, or they live their life the way they want to and they live and let live, if other people want to get into politics. You know, it would kind of be 'If you're into politics that's your trip, whereas me, I just want to wander round and play guitar.'
>
> (Ruth)

If politics is 'your trip', it is simply one way among many of pursuing the project of self-development. Alternatively, it may be a means of defending the free space required for the pursuit of autonomy:

> Politics is the mechanism by which decisions that affect my life are made, therefore if I wish to have any control over my life I must have an interest in politics, but it is not the driving force of my life.
>
> (Josh)

Thus political activity takes it place as one lifeworld interest among others, to be handled with tolerance. Speaking of a couple of heavily committed activists, for example:

> People know what Seán and Muireann are up to, but they're not very strongly influenced, and that's an example of Seán and Muireann being part of that group, coming from that group, and finding their own space.... But Seán and Muireann didn't ram it down anybody's throat, and nobody tried to make them conform to what was going on.
>
> (Josh)

This tolerance appears as a condition of autonomy:

> There is a sort of laid-back attitude which allows people to do their own
> thing and is very very tolerant of people's individuality and people doing
> their own thing and coming and going as they please.
>
> (Josh)

Thus movement activity can form a small or large part of an individual's
project of self-development, and it takes its place within the local rationalities of the network on this basis. This logic of autonomy as self-development,
however, has immediate effects in relation to the forms of politics which can
take root in it and the attitudes taken to the political.

On the one hand, political forms conducive to this type of autonomy are
preferred. Thus the direct democracy of the squat or the occupation and
their articulate counterpart in anarchist organising, and the network of alternative projects and *its* articulate counterpart in green politics, offer two possibilities of 'doing' politics. The immediate, lifeworld-bound activity of
demonstrations, direct action, the local project or the once-off event are preferred to more hierarchical political forms, whether of large-scale organisation or of clientele-building, whose only possible meaning is instrumental
and whose operation runs directly counter to the logic of autonomy:

> I think the fact that these people have the laid-back attitude of allowing
> people to do their own thing is a mechanism which allows very strong per-
> sonalities and very strong individuals to be able to interact with each other
> without stomping on each other's toes, and the sorts of ambitions that
> those people have, and the way in which they allow that ambition to be
> fulfilled, doesn't involve getting a group of people to centre round you.
>
> (Josh)

On the other hand, as we have seen, the political is itself relativised, as *one*
means of pursuing or defending the project of self-development among
others. As Melucci has said, activists engage in movement activities on the
basis that it has meaning for them, not in terms of its instrumental value: 'if it
doesn't make sense to me, I am not participating; but what I do also benefits
others' (1989: 49). In a Habermasian or Foucauldian perspective, this attitude is itself a form of resistance to the instrumental logic of the political
system: participants see the defence of personal, psychological and group
free space and independence as primary, and participation in more organised 'political' ways of realising this goal is always provisional. Thus local
rationalities themselves position the political and allocate it a very specific
place in terms of the pursuit of autonomous self-development. As we shall
see, this is also true in relation to reflexivity.

LIFEWORLD, REFLEXIVITY AND MOVEMENT MILIEUX

Implementing this project of autonomous self-development necessarily implies a reflexive attitude to social relations, and more specifically an *active* reflexivity, in the sense of the creation of meanings and practices which not only defend the 'free space' necessary for the project but directly enable this self-development, and develop the projects of the self as they move from the theoretical to the practical.

Movement milieux, then, are reflexive milieux, and we can speak with Lash (1994a) of a *life-world* reflexivity along with self-reflexivity or institutional reflexivity, and attempt to locate movement activities within this logic. In particular, if 'self-development' is to have any social reality, it must mean a change of the social relations within which people experience themselves and are confirmed in their identity. This implies a questioning of given social relations and a distancing from them; a search for alternative possibilities; and an exploration or experimentation with projects, including movement activities, which might enable the realisation of new 'identities' or a longer-lasting project of self-development. This move away from unreflexive life-worlds is immediately political, in the sense of raising questions of power and control, but not necessarily in the sense of an engagement with the institutions of political intermediation (Melucci, 1992).

DISTANCING FROM UNREFLEXIVE LIFEWORLDS

A logical prerequisite for any developed form of reflexivity is a certain measure of distancing from the 'normal' and 'taken-for-granted' assumptions of unreflexive lifeworlds. At its most basic, this appears as a personal attempt to find another path:

> People [in the Dublin suburbs] seemed to be content with just kind of shambling along, and into secondary school and out the other side, into a job, and not losing touch with their friends, in the pub every night of the weekend, but that wasn't enough for me. I was looking for something other and massively more, something to quench a deeper thirst for life. Like zombies, those people.
>
> (Mark)

This distancing operates in relation to the normal assumptions of people's class backgrounds:

> Even before I went to college I went 'I want to do a sort of liberal arts thing that isn't going to qualify me for one thing, so I can't just be pushed into doing a HDip [teaching qualification]', and a lot of people said 'Oh, so you're going to be a teacher.' I said, 'No, I don't want to be

a teacher.' I just wanted to leave Dublin for a while, do a lot of travelling, I'm grand.

(Ruth)

Most participants failed in one way or another to take the instrumental attitude to education demanded by conventional Irish assumptions about its role in providing secure employment. Similarly, many avoided the 'obvious' strategy of taking the available opportunities in, e.g., computers, translation or the music business:

I could get a job now, if I decided to, that I want to translate.

(Tina)

While this distancing from class assumptions is very general, there is also an ethnic distancing for a number of participants:

There are things you know, but they still have to be right in front of you to be obvious, like I always knew that the entire world wasn't white, Irish, all the rest of it, you know that all these other cultures exist, but it's when you actually meet them that it's different, because they live their whole life in a totally different perspective to you, which is great.

(Ruth)

Lastly, there is a distancing (for women at least) in relation to dominant gender assumptions:

You know, sometimes I wish 'Why'm I not like my sister?', you know? Why do I make life so hard for myself? Why don't I just want a normal job, and a husband, and two kids, and a house, and two cars?
LC: Well, why?
I don't know why, I just don't. [laughs] I just find it immensely boring.

(Tina)

As this last comment indicates, these are real choices that have to be made, and continually remade, within individuals' lives ('Why do I make life so hard for myself?'); but they are also made in relation to an alternative *habitus* ('I just find it immensely boring.') Distancing is not an easy exercise; and it depends crucially on the availability of local rationalities within which it makes personal and emotional sense. This very often implies a physical move towards known movement milieux:

People go there from all over the world. Usually people looking for something, or people who are too weird for the small town that they live in. I mean, people come from .... places where they're just too freaky for where they live, or they can't handle how racist where they are is. A lot of people say they couldn't deal with how racist it is.

(Ruth)

This suggests something of the working of this conflict between lifeworlds: the pursuit of autonomy leads both to rejection by unreflexive lifeworlds ('too weird', 'too freaky') and to rejection of those same lifeworlds ('they can't handle how racist it is'), pushing people towards movement milieux. Along with the usual forms of Irish emigration, it is noticeable that this life-world also includes a number of people who have emigrated *to Ireland* from western Europe, as well as a number of Irish people who have returned from significant periods of time in the movement milieux of e.g. London, Paris o r Berlin. A similar clash between unreflexive and reflexive lifeworlds is evidenced in this returner's perspective:

> So after I got back from there, I ended up in college, which was like being right back in secondary school again, which was about as far removed from where I'd been as I could have got at the time. So I wasn't very well acculturated, I kind of disacculturated myself somehow from all that kind of thing, I didn't relate to it very well. I'd lost all fear of loss of social prestige or position, all the subtle motivations for the middle-class Dublin life, they're all based on social position, standing and material comfort. All those kind of values I kind of shed [abroad].
>
> (Mark)

The reflexive (re-)creation of self starts from deliberate acts of distancing from one's lifeworld background, but for its stabilisation requires an association with the alternative rationalities represented by movement milieux.

THE USES OF OTHER MOVEMENT MILIEUX

If this association cannot be face-to-face, mediated participation in other milieux, relativising the here-and-now by making present other cultural possibilities, can be an important building block for local reflexive milieux. Other milieux are rarely seen as something to be imitated verbatim; rather, they are used as a tool for opening up a sense of possibility with regard to one's own life – in other words, to enable reflexivity. Thus one participant stresses:

> … the fact that [those involved] are very well read and are involved in, interested in most things.
>
> (Josh)

These are not just individual attributes, but relate to a reflexive *habitus* of (literally) reading other ways of life as a means of gaining distance from one's own background and of creating new possibilities. So, for example, the American counter-culture of the 1960s is critically examined as a sort of map of the territory opened up by the reflexive perspective:

What I thought happened in the sixties was that people started thinking very differently, not for the first time ever, but that they had this wealthy class of people who should have been happy as flowers, ... and instead they went 'Well, sod this for a game of soldiers, I don't want to go to college, get a degree, get a good job and have a huge house, mortgage and 2.5 kids.' So then they'd started, you know, they started exploring alternatives, and as always happens with that a lot of people just spent a lot of time doing a lot of drugs, wandering round, getting fucked up, and trying to be enlightened. And of course a lot of them weren't enlightened, a lot of them ended up doing heroin, but a couple were, so it was well worth trying.

(Ruth)

Other ways of life, then, are not imitated but rather used as a means of setting provisional goals for the project of self-development, for its reflexive implementation and for the discovery of appropriate contexts for both. Such maps of the American 1960s serve as a reference point for finding a reflexive lifeworld:

I suppose I had this idea in my head of coming across a kind of Merry Prankster-ish bunch of people who were interested in bouncing off each other as much as they could, rather than going to the pub.

(Mark)

ATTITUDE TO MOVEMENT PROJECTS

Reflexivity, then, involves a certain distancing from customary expectations and a greater awareness of alternative possibilities. If it is taken to its logical conclusion, it naturally means making some use of these: rather than reproducing existing social relations (albeit with an 'ironic' awareness of their contingency), experimenting with alternatives, adopting a reflexive attitude not just in theory but also in practice.

I have already mentioned the variety of projects developed within this milieu (see also Cox, 1998). I am interested here in the cultural *habitus*, in the sense of a general orientation to the world, that enables this experimentation, that makes it possible to 'try out' the implications of reflexivity. The best way of summarising this is in terms of a general valuation of creativity and 'makeability', which as we have seen applies to the self as well as to the external world.

One way in which this habitus appears is in a fascination with form. This is of course a very visible feature of contemporary social movements, where the effort devoted to formulating and implementing an organisation form will often exceed the effort devoted to its ostensible purpose (Melucci, 1995).

It also appears, however, in the enjoyment of simply playing with form and ideas, in the elaboration of purely verbal projects, the enjoyment of formalistic 'mind games', and the 'techie trip' of elegant and baroque technical activity. It can, of course, become the case that form takes over completely from content, or means from ends; this is undoubtedly part of the reason for the inordinate focus on rules and procedures that paradoxically plagues many movement institutions. If I am right, however, this is a necessary price for reflexive rationality.

One corollary of this experimental and playful attitude can be a lack of commitment. The world appears as a series of not entirely binding personal or collective projects and attempts at 'getting things together', with a generalised expectation that different people will be 'into' different projects at different times. Hence commitment has its costs:

> Most people I know don't want to be committed to anything. Or anybody because they're so desperate to get their lives together, get whatever it is that they want to do together that that takes up an awful lot of time, so they don't want to compromise that by being stuck in one place or one job or with one person or in one country.
>
> (Ruth)

'Getting it together' – creative and reflexive activity in general – is potentially threatened by too great a degree of commitment to any specific project. The logical conclusion is that it is normal for participants to see the milieu as something that is ultimately provisional and external, in other words, to maintain the reflexive attitude towards the movement itself. As one participant comments:

> It's kind of paradoxical to want to be part of a group and at the same time not yet part of the group. To want to create a comfortable subset or define its boundary or something.
>
> (Mark)

The lifeworld, then, is legitimated by its contribution to reflexive projects, and if it moves towards becoming 'taken-for-granted' in its turn it needs to be ditched, and for the same reason it was initially entered. Thus it is always an open-ended exercise: too tight an articulation would defeat the purpose. The fascination with experimentation, and the double-edged tolerance and refusal of commitment, are ways of structuring interaction within this 'free space', the skills of living together in a particular way. This may be formalised at times in particular institutions, but exists primarily as a way of doing things, a common 'structure of feeling' geared towards reflexivity.

This has important implications for movement mobilisation. Not only is commitment only likely to projects that have strong personal value, but the lack of commitment to the milieu itself makes stable organisation difficult. Virtually all participants have spent considerable periods of time abroad, for example; the very mobility that facilitates reflexive creativity also makes sustained involvement a difficult achievement. The problem is exacerbated by the tendency of social relationships to lose their reflexive edge and become 'retraditionalised'. One participant says of his decision to emigrate:

> [The difference new people make is] new influences, new ideas. If I can be excused using a sort of Americanism cliché, personal development, in the sense that my interaction with these people, whilst it is completely wrong to suppose that I can't get anything more out of interacting with these people, I had got caught in a rut, where my relationship with them was such that something had to change before I could get more out of my interaction with these people. That something needed to be other people bringing new attitudes, new ideas, fresh outlook on old ideas, anything, into it, would have possibly changed that and sort of got me out of that rut.
>
> (Josh)

Thus if lifeworld reflexivity and self-reflexivity are blocked by routinisation, 'creativity' turns to 'stagnation', and the likely response is to move on. But I want to argue that 'creativity' and 'stagnation' are also linked in other ways.

THE COSTS OF REFLEXIVITY

The principle of lifeworld reflexivity implies that all activity, not only work processes or political organisation, requires clear reasons and articulate decisions. Giddens (1994) has recently explored the pathological effects of the impact of reflexivity 'from outside' on lifeworld contexts in the generation of compulsive and obsessive activity. Here, however, is a lifeworld where the demand for reflexivity comes very much 'from within'.

It is something of a sociological commonplace (e.g. Berger and Luckmann, 1967) that routine, convention, tradition and ritual are enabling mechanisms: they enable the regular production of action without much need for prior thought and discussion, they enable a sedimentation of 'how-to-do-it' knowledge and skill, and so on. For the same reason they privilege means rather than ends, exclude the operation of reason, reinforce local power structures, and prevent the exploration of new possibilities. Yet consider the implications.

If a reflexive orientation to the lifeworld demands a focus on ends and the elaboration and coordination of reasons for action, democratic agreement on the forms of activity, and the exploration of all the possibilities that can be imagined or read about, this makes activity of any kind an extremely demanding business.

The interest in other ways of life and other ways of thinking about the world, the fascination with form and technique, the interest in talking about impossible projects and so on then acquire another, immediately practical meaning, as ways of discovering problems in play and talk rather than in action and conflict. As one participant puts it:

> It does help you if you've got a slight idea about something but it's vague, and you're really not that sure, and then you'll be sitting in a room with somebody who'll be talking about it and you'll go 'Yeah, that's it, that's exactly what I was looking for. Where is that?' Or 'What book was that in?' And they can tell you… . If you find somebody who's already done what it is that you're about to do you can get a lot of advice from them. You can get some pitfalls, as well. It's like 'I did this for ten years, and it's not worth it. Try something else instead.'
>
> (Ruth)

The stakes are high when neither the nature of the self, nor its goals, can be taken for granted, and the risks include criminalisation, homelessness, emigration and so on. Where reflexivity widens the range of *actual* options to include all *possible* choices, with no fixed yardstick to evaluate these possibilities and their consequences, choice becomes difficult, if not impossible. Choosing itself becomes an almost impossibly high barrier:

> If you do have that amount of choice, if you sit down, like for instance, at the moment I'm in completely the ideal situation, because … I've got no ties whatsoever, I don't have to be back in Dublin for anything, I don't have to come back for a course, I don't have to come back for a job, I've got a job where I don't have a contract. I could leave tomorrow … my only limitations are money, that's the only thing. There's nothing else. Which is great. But it also means 'Oh no, what should I do next?' Cause if you can do anything at all, it's difficult to narrow it down.
>
> (Ruth)

Given the costs of reflexive action, then, it is hardly surprising that life in this milieu alternates between bursts of enthusiastic activity and new projects which do fit the bill of reflexive creativity, and lengthy stretches of 'null-space', of talk and play, of understructured inactivity. Thompson (1993) saw this alternation of intensive activity and relative inactivity as normal prior to the imposition of industrial labour discipline; its reflexive variant, however, carries with it an alternation between elation and depression that was presumably foreign to the annual agricultural cycle. The difference between this and the motivational structure of unreflexive contexts is striking:

At the moment he's still officially temporarily employed by [a removals firm], which he has said himself is doing him an absolute world of good in that there is a degree of externally imposed discipline which has a knock-on effect in that he's able to achieve whatever the hell he wants to do, he values his spare time, he uses it efficiently, he gets things done, whereas previously he had so much bloody time to do anything he achieved nothing.

(Josh)

The few activists who overcome the barriers of action on a *regular* basis without such external constraints do so at a very high cost: continually forcing themselves into action, and resolving the difficulties of choice and commitment by placing themselves under extreme moral pressure. The levels of burnout among such activists are then very high, since the amount that needs doing is effectively infinite once reflexivity is applied to one's political persona, and because of reflexive modes of organising are not just extremely labour-intensive but also extremely emotional, since they place one's own personal project continually in question and depend on self-exploitation and the mining of this very insecurity.

This is one reason why movement institutions commonly suffer from what Raschke (1993) identifies as a conflict between legitimacy and efficiency. The reflexive attitude is highly legitimate but not particularly efficient; goal-rational behaviour is illegitimate in terms of both reflexivity and autonomy. Activists who see the need for goal-rational behaviour commonly suffer from a lack of identification with the way in which they need to behave in order to achieve their aims: an acute form of the Weberian paradox.

LOCAL RATIONALITIES AND MOVEMENT MILIEUX

These local rationalities are initially formed in the specific contexts of movement milieux. Thus one participant comments of a student occupation that it set:

... a framework of the way in which the social interactions that that particular group of people have subsequently continued to use: a lot of music, people sitting round playing music, talking, often about trivia, but there have often been, you know, good serious discussions as well.

(Josh)

The resources for the development of autonomy and reflexivity, such as books or music (see Cox, 1997), are made available through the networks of these milieux:

There's a very laid back attitude to property. People are not particularly possessive or protective of what is their property, you know, people borrow things from, there's an awful lot of kipple that transfers and ends up in various flats. It's not uncommon to arrive in somebody's flat, 'Oh, can I have a look through your tapes?' – 'Yeah, sure, go for it.' – 'Oh fuck, that's mine, where'd you get that?' – 'I dunno, oh, take it back.' – 'Oh yeah, well haven't seen that in years.' You know, people don't get wound up about it, they just 'Ah shit, I haven't seen that, I was wondering where it went.'

(Josh)

The local rationalities we have examined are formed within milieux structured by very specific cultural assumptions, as another participant stresses:

The only philosophy I thought that was behind all that group of people was, you know this thing, 'What goes around comes around', you know, the idea of like, at a simple level, somebody bums a cigarette off you, you bum a cigarette off somebody else? This kind of thing, at a really low level, but it's true, what goes around comes around. You do things for people, the idea is, instead of, I was brought up with a favours system, you know, I do this for you therefore you have to do this for me. Somebody gives you a Christmas present, you're morally obliged to give them one, this kind of thing, whereas I just liked that, you know, that people would do things for other people for no apparent reason. It's like, I have something that I don't need. You need it, take it.

(Ruth)

The net effect of this cooperation with each other's projects of autonomy is a reflexive lifeworld built on strong personal links:

I think it was like a support group. It was one of the closest groups of people I ever came across. I hadn't come across groups of people who knew each other that well and were that close, which was really nice. Knew everything about each other, had been through lots together.

(Ruth)

Such socially organised practices enable an apparently individualistic mode of life to maintain its separate identity. There is naturally a close relationship in this milieu between individuals' continued participation in such practices and the networks that sustain them, and their continued development of personal and lifeworld reflexivity. At the same time, these practices support rationalities that are capable of abstraction and generalisation far beyond these contexts.

I have suggested that a concept of local rationality can bridge the gap between the sociocultural basis of contemporary movements, their characteristic modes of formation, and their impact on the wider society. The implication is that we could consider individualisation and the development of reflexivity (Giddens, 1990; Beck *et al.*, 1994) not as a structural feature of high modernity *reflected* in contemporary movements, but as a rationality formed *within* movement milieux. The suggestion that contemporary social movement milieux are a key source of cultural change (Lash and Urry, 1987; Lash, 1994a,b; Sulkunen, 1992) would then be directly analogous to Weber's (1985) arguments about the cultural roots of modernity. This leaves open the question of *how* such rationalities are generalised beyond their sources. Before dealing with this, I want to return to the ways in which we interpret social movements.

HIDDEN DISCOURSES

If social movements, and their milieux, operate under very specific cultural assumptions, researchers who do not take this explicitly into account will misread what they see in terms of their own taken-for-granted assumptions. Despite some honourable exceptions (Diani and Eyerman, 1992), movement research is often unreflexive in this specific sense of failing to thematise – and hence notice – differences in culture.

The problem is reinforced if the researcher's perspective corresponds to that of some participants. Much of the literature in practice offers an uncritical (because implicit) identification by researchers with movement organisers. The researcher's construction of movements as primarily political is likely to be shared by the most politically active and organised among their movement contacts, and both can collude in this analysis. There is of course a parallel between their situations: both are intellectuals, engaged not only in the theoretical construction of a 'movement' as an essentially political entity, but also in the practical organisation of social relations (of mobilisation, of research) which attempt to involve other participants on these terms. Participants who have held formal positions in political organisations are also more likely to have followed conventional career paths in other respects, and hence to inhabit a world more familiar to the researcher.

Yet committed activists (like researchers) are a rather small minority within the networks of those they (occasionally) mobilise, and only one element, albeit an important one, of movement milieux. A focus on the most politicised, organised and articulate elements of the lifeworld is in some ways a focus on its *least* characteristic elements, and on those which are in some important ways least different from the dominant lifeworld. By extension, activists' orientation towards mobilisation may even render the cultural logics of other participants partially opaque to them.

There might then be some value in examining how those other participants view mobilisation. This can be illustrated by the example of a student occupation. Reflecting on that, one participant says:

I think most people realistically were in the occupation because it was damn good fun. To me, from my perspective, politics is something that, and I think it's reasonably common within this group of people, politics is an interest, but not the driving force, and those for whom it is the driving force, such as Seán and Muireann, are now very much peripheral to the group.

(Josh)

Another agrees:

Obviously, the whole thing was politically motivated, but once you got in there you were, I spent quite a lot of time in there at the start of it, that you had a lot of time to fill, that, you know, you had your time when you were doing things and where you were just basically hanging round with the other people who were there all the time, and getting to know them intimately and getting introduced to things that you hadn't been introduced to before.

(Joe)

While these participants are aware of the other logics of full-time activists, they locate them in terms of their own perspective of a reflexive milieu made up of a series of projects, and in terms of their own rationality:

I remember sitting in the Coffee Inn, and Pat gave everybody a conker, for some weird reason, and we were sitting in the Coffee Inn with these weird plans for building this windmill in Dermot's back garden, and Harry had this kind of odd plan for world domination, trying to [laughter] bring the Sixties back to Dublin because they'd never really hit, which I remember I kind of went 'Well, OK, that's weird, but I've nothing better to do for the summer and [laughs] it might be fun.'

(Ruth)

Thus the hidden discourses of ordinary participants coincide with Melucci's analysis of movement action as simply one part of a broader way of life for the majority of those involved. These participants are fully capable of inserting political action into their own local rationalities, and of relating the two:

There were a lot of discussions going on about what was happening and what people were trying to do and stuff. I wasn't really all that involved in many of those. And I don't think I was at any of the big sort of decision meetings. If anything, I was sort of a hanger-on rather than seriously involved in it. ... I was in the party end of it, and one of the things that people there were trying to do was make sure that there was sort of a minimum number of people around, so as not to give security an opportunity to come in en masse and throw everybody out, and I certainly would have been there as cannon fodder in that sense, but really just another face more than anything else.

(Josh)

The point is not to argue that only the most inarticulate and disorganised of participants can speak for movements. It *is* to say that researchers who fail to notice this double hermeneutic, whereby movement cultures are both *other* than the dominant culture and *divided* between those engaged in their instrumental rationalisation (for political or indeed economic reasons) and those for whom local rationalities prevail, are very likely to systematically misunderstand what is going on in the cultural milieux from which movement mobilisations grow. A fully reflexive sociology of the broader movement, by thematising these issues, might make it possible to move beyond this self-confirming situation.

CONCLUSION: THEORISING MOVEMENT MILIEUX

Movement milieux, then, are reflexive lifeworlds where the local rationalities I have described are developed, explored, (partially) institutionalised and from which they may be generalised. This can be phrased in terms of Eyerman and Jamison's definition of a social movement as 'a cognitive territory' (1991: 55), of Wainwright's (1994) analysis of movements as engaging in a grassroots politics of knowledge, or in Gramsci's (1991) concepts of intellectual activity as at once 'theoretical' and 'directive' (organising) activity. The local rationalities of movement milieux then appear as the rethinking and *reorganisation* of everyday life from below. This naturally comes into constant conflict with the instrumental rationalities of capital and the state, within the lifeworld but also within the individual.

This everyday conflict is then a 'war of position', in Gramsci's metaphor – a struggle over power relations within the social relations of 'civil society' (and the 'soft' fringes of the welfare state), rather than the 'war of movement' represented by direct challenges to the coercive core of the state. The construction of hegemony, or the articulation of counter-hegemony, are precisely this practical extension or repulsion of these different rationalities within everyday lives, as agents attempt to structure lifeworld contexts in terms of one or the other. It is in this active way that a local rationality can be generalised beyond its original lifeworld context, and that social movements can be seen as cultural challenges.

Within contemporary capitalism, groups such as the unemployed and students are 'decommodified' (Offe, 1984): they are temporarily or permanently marginalised from the production process and its associated structures of domination. From Berger *et al.* (1974) to Bey (1991), this situation has been identified as an important site for the generation of cultural resources for challenges to the dominant forms of late modernity. In particular, autonomy and reflexivity seem 'locally rational' responses, exploiting this relative weakness of direct domination (Cox, 1998). Such lifeworlds, then, are neither simply passive victims of radical modernity nor locations of purely defensive struggles against colonisation by instrumental rationality: their own local rationalities are capable of 'communicative rationalisation' to a point where they can break the bounds of the lifeworld and spread to others. Whether they succeed in doing this is of course a question of the politics of culture.

In Western states since 1968, the challenge to previously 'taken-for-granted' modes of cultural domination has since been met with responses geared to enabling a resumption of 'business as usual'. If Touraine (1981) is right in identifying struggles over 'historicity' as definitive of social formations, then the shift from 'organised' to 'disorganised' capitalism is a shift from a 'struggle over closure' (between the dominant 'old right' and subordinate 'old left') to a 'struggle over openness', in which the conflict between the dominant forces of disorganised capitalism and subordinate 'new left' movements over *just how far* openness (reflexivity, autonomy) is to be taken, defines the new stakes at issue, and marginalises other forces.

Reflexivity tends to mean a situation where social relations are 'consumed' reflexivity, but 'produced' unreflexivity; in other words, a diversity of 'negotiated' readings, which represents a *precondition* for effective cultural hegemony – the ability of the dominated to find their own value in the cultural construction of their own domination (Gramsci, 1991: 12–14). Similarly, autonomy tends to mean a situation of atomisation, possessive individualism and goal-rational action. The local rationalities of movement milieux can radicalise both towards an active lifeworld reflexivity which applies to the actual production of social relations as much as to the attitudes adopted towards them, and towards a reflexive autonomy which does not restrict itself to the pursuit of given goals.

The conflict is then precisely over the practical meanings of reflexivity and autonomy: whether they can form part of a new hegemony to contain social conflict, geared around instrumental rationality, or whether they can be radicalised to the point of rupture within the kinds of local rationality I have been describing. In his important new book McKay (1996) asks why the British state has adopted such a brutal strategy against the free festival scene, the New Traveller lifestyle, rave culture and so on, and notes the paradox that these groups are among the most 'enterprising' representatives of 'personal initiative' and 'individual freedom'. Perhaps this chapter offers a pointer to the answer.

ACKNOWLEDGEMENTS

I want to thank the participants for the interviews this chapter is based on, and Hilary Tovey and Anna Mazzoldi for comments on earlier versions.

REFERENCES

Beck, U., Giddens, A. and Lash, S. (eds)(1994), *Reflexive Modernization* (Cambridge: Polity).

Berger, P. and Luckmann, T. (1967), *The Social Construction of Reality* (London: Allen Lane).

Berger, P., Berger, B. and Kellner, H. (1974), *The Homeless Mind* (Harmondsworth: Penguin).

Bey, H. (1991), *TAZ* (Brooklyn: Autonomedia).

Cox L. (1997), 'Reflexivity, Social Transformation and Counter Culture', in C. Barker and M. Tyldesley (eds), *Third International Conference on Alternative Futures and Popular Protest*, vol. 1 (Manchester: Manchester Metropolitan University).

Cox, L. (1998), 'Towards a Sociology of Counter Cultures?', in E. McKenna and R. O'Sullivan (eds), *Cultural Diversity in Modern Ireland* (Aldershot: Avebury) (forthcoming).

Diani, M. (1992a), 'The Concept of Social Movement', *Sociological Review*, 40 (1), 1–25.

Diani, M. (1992b), 'Analyzing Social Movement Networks', in M. Diani and R. Eyerman (eds), *Studying Collective Action* (London: Sage).

Diani, M. and Eyerman, R. (eds) (1992), *Studying Collective Action* (London: Sage).

Eder, K. (1985), 'The "New Social Movements"', *Social Research*, (52) 663–716.

Eder, K. (1993), *The New Politics of Class* (London: Sage).

Eyerman, R. and Jamison, A. (1991), *Social Movements* (Cambridge: Polity).

Giddens, A. (1990), *The Consequences of Modernity* (Cambridge: Polity).

Giddens, A. (1994), 'Living in a Post-traditional Society,' in U. Beck, A. Giddens and S. Lash (eds), *Reflexive Modernization* (Cambridge: Polity).

Gramsci, A. (1971), *Selections from Prison Notebooks* (London: Lawrence & Wishart).

Gramsci, A. (1991), *Il materialismo storico e la filosofia di Benedetto Croce* (Rome: Riuniti).

Habermas, J. (1984), *The Theory of Communicative Action,* vol. 1 (London: Heinemann).

Habermas, J. (1987), *The Theory of Communicative Action*, vol. 2 (Cambridge: Polity).

Hradil, S. (1987), *Sozialstrukturanalyse in einer fortgeschrittenen Gesellschaft* (Opladen: Leske & Budrich).

Lash, S. (1994a), 'Reflexivity and its doubles', in U. Beck, A. Giddens and S. Lash (eds), *Reflexive Modernization* (Cambridge: Polity).

Lash, S. (1994b), 'Expert-systems or Situated Interpretation?', in U. Beck, A. Giddens and S. Lash (eds), *Reflexive Modernization* (Cambridge: Polity).

Lash, S. and Urry, J. (1987), *The End of Organized Capitalism* (Cambridge: Polity).

McKay, G. (1996), *Senseless Acts of Beauty* (London: Verso).

McLennan, G. (1981), *Marxism and the Methodologies of History* (London: New Left Books).

Melucci, A. (1985), 'The Symbolic Challenge of Contemporary Movements', *Social Research*, 52, 789–816.

Melucci, A. (1989), *Nomads of the Present* (London: Hutchinson).

Melucci, A. (1992), *L'invenzione del presente*, 2nd edn (Bologna: Il Mulino).

Melucci, A. (1995), 'The New Social Movements Revisited', in L. Maheu (ed.), *Social Movements and Social Classes* (London: Sage).

Müller, D. (1990), 'Zur Rekonstruktion von Habitus – "Stammbäumen" und Habitus – "Metamorphosen" der neuen sozialen Milieus', *Forschungsjournal neue soziale Bewegungen*, 8 (3), 57–65.

Offe, C. (1984), *Contradictions of the Welfare State* (Cambridge, MA: MIT Press).

Offe, C. (1985), 'New Social Movements', *Social Research*, 52, 817–68.

Raschke, J. (1985), *Soziale Bewegungen* (Frankfurt: Campus).

Raschke, J. (1993), *Die Grünen* (Köln: Bund-Verlag).

Sulkunen, P. (1992), *The European New Middle Class* (Aldershot: Avebury).

Thompson, E. P. (1993), *Customs in Common* (Harmondsworth: Penguin).

Touraine, A. (1981), *The Voice and the Eye* (Cambridge: Cambridge University Press).

Touraine, A. (1985), 'An Introduction to the Study of Social Movements', *Social Research*, 52, 749–88.

Vester, M. V., von Oertzen, P., Geiling, H., Hermann, T., and Mueller, D., (1993), *Soziale Milieus im gesellschaftlichen Strukturwandel* (Cologne: Bund).

Wagner, P. (1994), *A Sociology of Modernity* (London: Routledge).

Wainwright, H. (1994), *Arguments for a New Left* (Oxford: Blackwell).

Weber, M. (1984), *Soziologische Grundbegriffe* (Tübingen: Mohr).

Weber, M. (1985), *The Protestant Ethic and the Spirit of Capitalism* (New York: Scribner's).

5 Resisting Colonisation: The Politics of Anti-Roads Protesting
Wallace McNeish

INTRODUCTION

Habermas (1976, 1987) argued that the incremental extension of state authority coupled with economic restructuring in advanced capitalism has generated an ongoing crisis of legitimation. A primary manifestation of this crisis is the growth of new movements of protest and resistance which are a reaction against the dominant paradigm of unmitigated capitalist growth and the concomitant expansion of a technical logic and instrumental rationality which impoverishes culture, democracy and the environment. Using quantitative data from a postal survey of the social and political attitudes of protesters affiliated to the national anti-roads coalition Alarm UK, and qualitative data from in-depth interviews with individual activists and protesters,[1] I shall argue that the highly innovative and oppositional anti-roads protests which have taken place in recent years in the UK are a prime example of what Habermas describes as 'resistance to the colonisation of the lifeworld'.

Habermas's stance towards such resistance can best be described as one of critical support; he is critical because of the tendency of new social movements towards a narrow defensive particularism, but is at the same time supportive because he recognises that the new movements contain a latent emancipatory potential which stems from their counter-state practices and their creation of dialogue and debate around new political issues within the public sphere. The paper will begin by tracing the origins of the direct action anti-roads movement of the 1990s, it will then move on to draw upon the above research in order to critically analyse the validity of Habermas's theoretical position while advancing some tentative conclusions as to the wider political significance of such protests. The paper concludes with a brief consideration of some of the key contradictions, possibilities and problems which exist within the anti-roads movement.

THE EVOLUTION OF ANTI-ROADS PROTESTING IN THE UK

Motorways were something that had been discussed at length by engineers, government and planners in Britain from the mid-1930s onwards, but it was not until 1958 that the first one in the form of the Preston Bypass was built (Starkie, 1982: 1). Britain in fact lagged far behind its European neighbours in this respect where, for example, Italy had built its first autostrade in the mid-1920s and Germany had laid the keystones of its autobahn system by 1904. Motorways were, however, very much part of the modern 'zeitgeist' and it is therefore hardly surprising that successive post-war governments, when faced with the task of reconstruction, steadily growing levels of car ownership and the need to re-create a competitive economy, embraced them whole-heartedly. In 1946 the Labour government's Ministry of Transport announced plans for an ambitious programme to construct 1000 miles of new trunk roads and motorways to link all major industrial conurbations and centres of commerce. Due though to financial constraints, construction work did not begin until the mid-1950s, although it was not until the 1960s that work began in earnest. Subsequently, the government began a process of revising its programme, so that by 1971 a total of 3500 miles of new and upgraded trunk roads and 2000 miles of motorway were projected (Painter, 1981: 210–11).

Painter (1981), identifies three distinct phases in the growth of opposition to road and motorway schemes in the UK up until 1979. In the first phase during the 1950s, opposition to road schemes was confined to individual property owners who objected on the grounds of loss of value to their properties, and farmers who objected on the grounds of a threat to their livelihood. This type of objection was, however, managed successfully by local authorities and the Ministry of Transport through a process of negotiation and compensation. The second phase involved local and national amenity societies during the 1960s but in general the objections were safely channelled into areas of aesthetics, design and questions of routes 'fitting the landscape' which posed no real threat to the overall shape of the roads programme.[2] In the 1970s, however, anti-roads opposition entered a third and more militant phase with local protesters not only questioning the need for new roads in their localities but expressing scepticism and disapproval about the rationale for the roads programme as a whole (*ibid.*: 214). Despite the Skeffington Report's (1969) recommendations concerning participation and openness in the planning process, little of this agenda was being implemented,[3] and local objectors during this period began to disrupt what were widely perceived to be 'loaded' and undemocratic public inquiries, while a newly radicalised environmental movement involving new pressure groups such as Friends of the Earth (FoE) began a concerted propaganda offensive against cars and motorways.[4] This was also the period when numerous tenants associations and grassroots citizens action groups began to spring up in inner-city areas to fight for fair rents and improved housing conditions, and to oppose urban redevelopment and motorway schemes that would break-up long-standing communities, such as the 'Westway' in London (Clark, 1972).

The grandiose road plans of the 1960s and early 1970s were, though, never to be fully realised because by 1974/5 the deep economic crisis, coupled with an increasingly vociferous anti-roads and environmental lobby, made a reduction in construction expenditure politically prudent. With the inter-urban network, virtually complete, the financing of new road and motorway projects tailed off from the mid-1970s as the government switched its policy emphasis towards the improvement of public transport (McKay and Cox, 1979: 185–8). Much to the chagrin of the BRF (British Roads Federation) a spending ceiling for new highway construction of £300 million per year was fixed by the Labour government's 1977 Transport White Paper – a figure that was to last into the early 1980s (Painter, 1981: 215). Under the Thatcher government, however, the creation of out-of-town retail, leisure and business parks was actively encouraged and naturally with these developments came the need for more roads. Thatcher talked positively of what she called the 'great car economy', and the BRF finally got the breakthrough it had been waiting for in 1989 with the government's announcement of its £23 billion 'Roads to Prosperity' road-building programme. It is this programme which has been the catalyst for the fourth and most militant phase of opposition to road building in Britain – something which has manifest itself in the growth of the mass direct action anti-roads movement of the 1990s whose widespread impact has played such an important role in making the government pay particular attention to road building when under fiscal pressure to cut public spending.

ANTI-ROADS PROTEST IN THE 1990s: THE ROLE OF ALARM UK

Although the highly publicised protests which took place at Twyford Down in 1992 have correctly been identified as the most significant catalyst for the birth of the national direct action anti-roads movement of the 1990s (Rowell, 1996: 320–55), this 'fourth phase' in the evolution of opposition to road building in fact has its precursor in the earlier mass opposition to the '*London Road Assessment Studies*' that erupted when the official reports were released in 1988. The Department of Transport planned to spend between £12 and £20 billion on road widening, new bypasses and the construction of an inner-M25 in order to ease the capital's traffic congestion problems. In opposition to these proposals, a London-wide alliance against road-building was formed in the shape of Alarm, which by the end of 1989 was composed of over 150 local groups including the public transport pressure group Transport 2000, local FoE and local residents' action groups.

Alarm adopted a highly decentralised structure with each local group retaining autonomy of action and with only one simple rule binding them together, i.e. that 'each group had to oppose all roads in the Assessment, not just those in their backyard' (Stewart *et al.*, 1997: 9). After a campaign involving innovative publicity stunts, mass letter writing and the circulation of well-researched counter-information to local action groups and the media, Cecil Parkinson announced in 1990 that every single one of the road proposals included in assessment studies would be withdrawn. This victory was significant in that it was a victory for a new style of anti-roads campaigning that aimed to win before public inquiries took place, and before even the statutory public consultation period. Alarm had achieved what it set out to do, i.e. 'to create its own framework for protest, dismissing the DoT's structures as merely techniques designed to get its plans through with the minimum of fuss. Alarm's approach deliberately set out to liberate people from meek adherence to the DoT, to empower them, to enable them to set their own agenda and to put the Department and its officials on the defensive. It set out to create such a mass protest movement that the Road Assessment studies would become politically untenable' (Stewart *et al.*, 1995: 13). Perhaps though, even more importantly, the campaign in London laid the foundations for a network of grassroots activists who, in contrast to many of the established environmental groups, preferred to work outside of the official environmental lobby system and had no faith in the official inquiry and legal consultation processes. It was these activists who in the 1990s would play a central role in coordinating and sustaining the national movement against the DoT's 1989 plans.

In 1990 Alarm UK was launched with the aim of reproducing the success of the London campaign on a nationwide basis, and within two years another 100 local anti-roads groups from around the country had affiliated. There were early successes at Birmingham, Preston, Yorkshire, Woodstock and Exeter, and when the protest at Twyford Down began to 'heat up' in late 1992, Alarm UK supported the protesters' new direct action tactics. When interviewed about Alarm's position *vis-à-vis* direct action, one of the leading organisers said:

I think that most of our people when they join don't think they are going to take direct action and most don't need to go that far – we obviously try to stop the road at the earliest possible stage – yet if it comes to it they are usually prepared to take direct action although we didn't start out as a direct action movement we have always taken the view – and this is where we differ with other organisations like FoE in the early days – that we support direct action and we've never had a problem with breaking the law.

Unlike FoE, which officially pulled out of the protests at Twyford due to legal intimidation from the government (Rowell, 1996: 334), Alarm UK lent its active support to the local groups and, despite some philosophical differences, it also lent its support to the actions of the young protesters involved with the 'Dongas Tribe' and the newly formed radical environmental organisations Earth First! and Reclaim the Streets. It was also at Twyford that Road Alert! was born as a sister organisation to Alarm UK, with a specific remit to concentrate on educating protesters in direct action skills. However, this organisation has since folded due to the pressures on resources brought about by the Newbury campaign in 1995. Although the motorway extension at Twyford was eventually built, the positive experience of the local groups, the national umbrella organisation and the radical environmental groups working together cemented a partnership which, although at times it has been tense, has nevertheless been sustained throughout the keynote protests of subsequent years.[5]

In 1997, with the government's 1989 plans in tatters, the Newbury Bypass campaign largely over, and the eviction of the Fairmile camp in Devon complete, many of the young 'hardcore' deep green protesters are now turning their attention away from roads to oppose other forms of development, for example open-cast mining, the building of shopping centres on greenbelt land, and the creation of new airport runways as at Manchester. Reclaim the Streets has, however, taken a different direction as, alongside its provocative 'street parties', it has staged actions in support of the sacked Merseyside dockers and striking tube workers in London. Alarm UK continues to operate and is currently campaigning against the 114 publicly funded road schemes and the 33 privately funded DFBO (Design, Finance, Build and Operate) schemes that remain out of the overall total of 600 in the original 1989 plan (*Alarm Bells*, 1997, No. 19: 1). It has also signed up to the 'Real World' Coalition[6] and is working with Transport 2000 on developing an alternative sustainable transport strategy – it may in the future merge with (and perhaps radicalise) the latter organisation. Anti-roads protests based upon the direct action British model are now starting to spread across Europe, most notably in Germany and Luxemburg where road building is threatening the future of ancient forests. In the UK, however, the alliances of the past few years are set to come under increasing strain in the face of competing social, political and class interests, and it is an open question whether or not the alliance of the past few years will continue to hold or perhaps develop new alignments which will go further in challenging the social, political and environmental *status quo*.

THE ANTI-ROADS MOVEMENT AND THE CRISIS OF LEGITIMATION

Since the early 1970s a large body of social research and political theory has grown up on the contemporary significance of the 'new social movements', a generic term which has come to encompass the vast array of oppositional currents and organisations that grew out of the flowering of New left radicalism, student rebellion and 'counter-culture' in the late 1960s. Although the ardour of the 1960s militancy was short-lived, its impact in the advanced liberal democracies has been immense in that it both signified and contributed to the wider societal development of new 'participatory' ideologies, non-institutionalised modes of political action and the politicising of cultural, environment and moral issues that were hitherto generally considered apolitical. Offe (1987) points to the contemporary significance of this politicisation process when he argues that 'not only are the institutional channels of communication between the citizenry and the state used more often and more intensely by a greater number of citizens and for a wider range of issues; in addition, their adequacy as a framework for political communication is being challenged' (p. 63). The anti-roads movement is the latest expression of this 'new politics' which in Britain has a long tradition in movements such as CND, the wider peace, anti-nuclear and environmental movements, the women's movement and movements for minority rights, as well as more specifically urban social movements which have campaigned around issues of collective consumption.

Within recent theories of the new social movements, as indeed within all areas of social and political theory, postmodernism has become the salient trend (Laclau and Mouffe, 1985; Boggs, 1986; Melucci, 1988; Dalton and Kuechler, 1990; Aronowitz, 1992; Crook *et al.*, 1992). Influenced by the anti-foundationalist epistemology espoused by poststructuralist philosophers such as Derrida, Foucault and Baudrillard, postmodern social theorists argue that referent categories such as class, income, status or occupational group no longer have any meaning in an increasingly postmodern world that is heterogeneous, rhizomic and devoid of any discernible structure. Dalton and Kuechler (1990), express this view in relation to the 'new politics' when they propose that the:

> ... new social movements signify a shift from group based political cleavages to value and issue based cleavages that identify only communities of like minded people. The lack of a firm and well defined social base also means that membership tends to be very fluid, with participants joining in and then disengaging as the political context and their personal circumstances change.
>
> (Dalton and Kuechler, 1990: 12)

Leading the opposition to this interpretation are the critical theorists Jurgen Habermas (1976, 1987) and Claus Offe (1984, 1987), who, rather than viewing the new movement politics as indicative of a shift towards post-modernity, have instead reworked the Marxian theory of crisis in order to explain the new struggles that characterise the present historical juncture. Moreover, Habermas has been one of the most outspoken critics of post-modernism, arguing forcefully that its relativism is simply conservatism in a radical guise. For Habermas, postmodernism's inherent perspectivism must ultimately lead to political impotence because in abandoning the normative evaluative criteria of modernity the ground is cut away from any universal standard that social and political phenomena can be measured against (Habermas, 1992).

Habermas's and Offe's crisis theories are premised upon the inbuilt contradictions that exist between the economic, administrative-political and sociocultural subsystems of modern society. In the contemporary era the growing disparity between public expectations of these subsystems and the state's ability to satisfy both these expectations and the acute demands of economic restructuring, has created a crisis of legitimation which defines the new political paradigm of late as opposed to liberal capitalism (Habermas, 1976; Offe, 1984). The political and economic system requires a mass input of loyalty in order to sustain it, but because of its inability to deliver ever-multiplying demands, individual motivations for participation are increasingly coming to be questioned. Habermas and Offe posit that in order to offset this crisis the state has attempted to extend its authority through the incremental extension of public policy into previously autonomous subsystems of action. This strategy has, however, had something of a paradoxical effect, for although the state's functions have increased, and thus its formal authority has been extended, at a deeper and more substantive level that authority has been subverted through its own striving for inclusiveness. As the scope of political authority grows it politicises its own non-political underpinnings and in doing so negates the very source of its original legitimation. In essence, then, the intervention of the state into spheres that were previously autonomous and associated with the private concerns of morality, the family and the community has turned them into public and hence political issues. Work is no longer the sole source of oppression in late capitalist society, rather the growth of state authority has created new multiple forms of deprivation in the social and cultural spheres to which the new social movements are a defensive response.[7]

Del, an activist from Reclaim the Streets, very much captures the practical essence of Habermas and Offe's argument in the following lines:

I think that the state is becoming more and more paranoid because it is starting to realise that people have less and less faith in it and don't believe in it or recognise its worth – and therefore they need to bolster themselves up at every opportunity and they'll do that by new legislation and clamping down on those they consider to be a threat – and we are a threat to them ... we are saying that we want to get rid of you, you are exploiting, oppressing, dominating and fucking over the planet and its people – but it's difficult for them because of the way we organise – their main tactic will be to make us as paranoid as hell and to try to make us work secretly – we have to oppose that by trying to build a mass movement.

A good contemporary example of this politicisation/delegitimation process taking place is the introduction of the *Criminal Justice Act* in the UK in 1994. This was an Act of Parliament which was designed to effectively criminalise and thereby regulate various forms of behaviour and protest which had hitherto been considered legal, for example trespassing on private property was made a criminal as opposed to civil offence. This Act also gave the police sweeping powers to deny permission for protest marches and demonstrations, to clamp down on 'illegal' parties and raves, and to make traveller convoys illegal. Now while in one sense the formal regulatory authority of the state has been extended, what the Act has effectively done is to politicise a whole new layer of people, and particularly the young, who resent this interference with their chosen lifestyles, i.e. going to illegal raves has taken on a certain, more explicit, political significance as has 'going on the road' with the 'travellers'. Moreover people have joined anti-roads protests just to defy what they view as an anti-democratic and draconian Act while the roads protests, in bringing protesters into conflict with the forces of the state, have themselves had a radicalising effect upon many of those who have taken part.

Rosie, a Glasgow activist, described her experience of the 1995 anti-M77 protests in the following terms:

When you come to the M77 and there are four hundred police they are like an army ... when they became that I no longer had any respect. I no longer saw individual police at that point and I surprised myself as I had been brought up to show them that respect. At Pollok I pushed against them physically and I had no problem with that – in another circumstance I would never have done that ... the CJA? I don't even see it as a just or proper law ... any intrusion into my space I have a right to resist it and I know that I am not alone in that.

The other important effect that the CJA has had politically is in provoking the setting up of networks and alliances across the country against it, thus drawing together and creating a cross-fertilising communicative dialogue between individuals campaigning on a wide array of diverse issues.[8]

Following the research carried out by Inglehart (1977, 1990) on the growth of postmaterialist values, Habermas (1987) argues that adherents to the new social movements are young, well educated and primarily rooted in the new middle class.[9] This is a class which is not involved in the 'productivist core of performance' in late capitalist societies and is also by nature of its location in the welfare and education systems most sensitised to the self-destructive tendencies of unmitigated industrial growth and the risks associated with increasing complexity (Habermas, 1987: 392). Habermas's thesis about the important role of the new middle class is broadly confirmed by survey data from Alarm UK which reveal the ideal type of member or supporter for this organisation to be a white (98 per cent), middle-aged (the median age group is 40–44), male (69 per cent), home-owner (71 per cent) who is highly educated (69 per cent have a university degree or above) and does white-collar work (22 per cent 'higher' professionals, 22 per cent lower professionals, 10 per cent in creative/technical/consultancy services, 9 per cent self-employed).[10] The sample also confirmed Inglehart's thesis about the relationship of postmaterialism to the new social movements because, in a modified version of his test, respondents consistently chose priority options that pertained to the quality of life as opposed to those associated with old-style materialism.[11]

The age breakdown of the respondents, however, did differ significantly from Habermas's assertion that new social movement activists are primarily young – perhaps one reason for this is because in Britain, unlike in Germany, material security is not really achieved at an early stage in individual middle-class career development and therefore postmaterialist values take longer to develop. Another reason that is pertinent here is that many of the original new social movement activists who continue to be active have now aged significantly; for example the age profile for CND and FoE members who were also involved with Alarm UK was predominantly over 40. Here, though, it is important to note that the anti-roads movement is characterised by an alliance between two wings, i.e. the local protest groups and the younger 'hardcore' eco-activists. Alarm UK is much more representative of the former wing and is much less so of the latter, who tend to be affiliated to organisation such as Earth First! and Reclaim the Streets if they claim any group affiliation at all. The 20 per cent of Alarm UK respondents who are also members of Earth First! indeed do have an age profile which is concentrated in the late 20s and early 30s and is thus significantly younger than activists affiliated to the older environmental organisations. Aside from being younger those from the eco-activist wing of the movement tend to come from all social class backgrounds including the traditional working class, tend to be less well formally educated and tend to be either unemployed or underemployed.

COMMUNICATIVE ACTION AND THE ANTI-ROADS MOVEMENT

According to Habermas, the new conflicts articulated by the new social movements 'are manifest in sub-institutional, or at least extra-parliamentary forms of protest, ignited by questions having to do with the grammar of forms of life' (Habermas, 1987: 392). The new movements thus for Habermas represent a shift away from the institutionalised parties and representative democracy that characterised the 'old politics', and are motivated instead by problems centring on the quality of life, individual self-realisation, norms, values and human rights. Giddens (1987) describes this kind of political action as 'life politics' and it is in many ways an apposite description of the type of activity that the roads protest movement is engaged in.[12] There is nevertheless a counterbalancing tendency at work within the protest movement which sits rather uneasily with this general orientation. Rather than rejecting one type of politics for another the Alarm UK survey respondents tended to combine an identification with both 'old' and 'new' politics. Whilst on the one hand they stressed 'quality of life' and an unresponsive, undemocratic political system as a reason for protesting, on the other hand they were overwhelmingly planning to vote at the next election. They also largely defined themselves in 'traditional political terms; 60 per cent defined themselves as being on the centre left or far left politically, (including 27 per cent socialist or green socialist), and 32 per cent were members of political parties (another 20 per cent had been active in political parties in the past).

Age, though, plays an important role in differentiating the anti-roads protesters in political terms. In general the younger the respondents the less interest they have in traditional political processes and for the eco-activist wing of the movement the political system is simply anathema. When asked if voting at the next election the following responses from young activists were typical:

There's no point – I mean they talk about us doing single issue politics when it's them – their single issue is to get intae parliament and then sit on their arses for five years.

> Rab: RAM 74 (Residents Against the M74, Glasgow)

I don't vote, and I've never voted and I never will vote either because it doesny matter who gets intae power they're still oot fur themselves … .every time I protest that's my vote – I vote through protesting … .and I get more votes than anybody else cos my vote's a protest.

> (Alec: Pollok Free State, Glasgow)

Well to me I can't say yes to something I don't believe in – I don't believe in going for the lesser of two evils.

> (Laura: Newbury protester)

These responses are, however, not only typical of young anti-roads protesters but according to the 1995 *'The Kids are Alright?'* survey of young people's political attitudes they are also indicative of young people's attitude to mainstream politics in general (Garner, 1997). If looked at in tandem with the growth of protest movements like those over roads, animal rights and the

CJA, this survey supports the views that young people in particular have become alienated from the traditional parties and decision-making processes of British representative democracy, but that nevertheless they are far from being apolitical.[13]

Habermas contends that the new social movements represent modes of resistance to the 'System's colonisation of the lifeworld' (Habermas, 1987: 394). Thus the new movements respond to highly specific problem situations which arise when the foundations of the lifeworld are under attack and the quality of life is threatened. These conflict situations emanate from a variety of sources. Firstly 'green problems' – for example, urban and environmental destruction, pollution, health hazards, etc. Secondly, problems of excessive complexity – for example, risk and the fear of military potentials for destruction, nuclear waste and nuclear power, etc. Thirdly, an overburdening of the communicative infrastructure which results in a cultural impoverishment that in turn engenders the growth of particularistic communities based upon gender, age, skin colour, neighbourhood, locality or religious affiliation (Habermas, 1987: 394–5). What unites most of these diverse groups which have arisen in response to these specific issues is that they all are critical in one way or another of unmitigated economic expansion and development.

For Habermas, economic development within late capitalism is controlled by a technocratic elite of experts which looks at problems of growth in strictly instrumental economic terms. A good example here is the planning process for new roads where routes are planned to go from A to B in the least possible time and at the least possible cost. Public consultation over new routes is negligible, and when there is a public inquiry the results almost invariably go the planners' way due to the 'experts' evidence, and if a choice is offered it is always either A or B, as opposed to no road at all or one that has not yet been suggested by the experts.[14] Statistics bear this argument out, for out of 146 public inquiries into English trunk road schemes in a five-year period only five were rejected by the inspectors (Rowell, 1996: 332). In Habermasian terminology this example of road planning residing in the hands of experts who are not democratically accountable and to which there is little or no public consultation is but one aspect of the progressive 'scientization of politics and public opinion' (Habermas, 1971: 62–80). Decisions are thus made in purely instrumental terms, leading to both a further erosion of the lifeworld's autonomy and a further suppression of communicative reason.

Habermas argues that the conflicts which the new social movements engage in and articulate 'arise at the seam between System and lifeworld', by which he would seem to imply that there are islands of communicative action and reason that have not yet been completely overrun by the instrumental purposive rationality propagated by the System. By this count he is much more optimistic than postmodern thinkers like Foucault, for whom power permeates all aspects of social life. Habermas nevertheless adopts a somewhat ambiguous stance towards the new social movements and his position is best described as one of critical support. He is critical because there is often a tendency within the new movements towards particularism – something which is ever open to the poss-ibility of irrationalism and indeed such tendencies can be counterproductive to the release of communicative rationality because insularity prevents discussion and consensus formation in wider society. Within the anti-roads movement, however, only a minority of 'deep Greens' take a consciously particularist and isolationist perspective. Although NIMBYism is often a key factor in the initial mobilisation of local action groups, over time, as the Alarm survey indicates, many individual activists come to link anti-road protesting to wider issues of the relationship of the environment to democracy, social justice, transport policy and economic sustainability. Particularism is regressive politically for Habermas because unless individual interests are universalised from a norma-tive point of view then the grounds for a recovery of communicative rationality *vis-à-vis* the System cannot be revived.

While critical of the dangers of particularism, Habermas takes a positive view of the latent emancipatory political potential of the new social move-ments stemming from their disposition to create alternative institutions and practices that run counter to those organised according to the dictates of the state and capital. Moreover the new movements encourage experimental forms of participatory democracy which are vital for the revival of commu-nicative reason in society while their alternative institutions and counter-practices defend the lifeworld from System intrusion. On the eco-activist direct action wing of the anti-roads movement this is something that is clearly understood, and especially from those who take a more social as opposed to strictly environmental perspective:

> I suppose the idea is to build up these networks in opposition to state insti-tutions and you build them up to make more and more people realise that they have control over their own lives and that they have that by taking it and doing it – then eventually they will come up against the opposition of the state and no doubt there will be a bit of a brawl about that stage... these are I suppose new terms for old ideas no doubt – so it's the growth of that kind of counter-culture and counter-institutions which is the way forward.
>
> (Del: Reclaim the Streets)

Finally, for Habermas the new social movements in carrying out these func-tions provide examples and prototype models for the possible birth of a new society that is predicated on equality, universal rights and radical democracy. The anti-roads movement in many respects fulfils each of these positive crite-ria, e.g. in its base community like protest camps and free states, in its law-breaking non-violent direct action, in its grassroots participatory orientation and in its refusal to abide by the state's repressive laws or planning decisions. In fulfilling these criteria the anti-roads movement and other social movements like it not only bring to light those policy decisions which run counter to universal interests but, more importantly, they open them, and indeed other wider related issues, up to debate in the public arena. As Hewitt argues in his commentary on Habermas, 'a defence of specific identities and needs provides the grounds for raising more universalistic concerns' (Hewitt, 1993: 63). Thus in Habermas's theory, and unlike the theories of the new social movements which rely on postmodern premises, there is an attempt to align their diverse interests and activities within a single unitary project of human emancipation. In this sense Habermas's theory can be seen as a supplement to historical materialism that has borrowed from and radicalised Weber's theory of rationalisation to give it a deeper power of explanation and critique.

ALLIANCE CONTRADICTIONS WITHIN THE ANTI-ROADS MOVEMENT

In terms of activism, support and membership the anti-roads movement crosses traditional class boundaries and unites the members of different classes depending upon the locality of the protest, i.e. city, town, village, countryside. Thus in Glasgow the protests against the M77 extension had large numbers of working-class people from the local community participating, whereas at Newbury the protests tended to be largely middle-class n composition. The government's 1989 road-building programme was, however, largely centred upon the shires of 'middle England', and this accounts for the dominance of the latter classes in the umbrella organisation Alarm UK. The different factions of the middle class have united in local action groups, sometimes even with members of the landed class, to counteract a threat to their 'quality of life' and to their property. What, though, is striking about this alliance is that members of these classes have done so in conjunction with young 'hardcore' eco-activists who are mostly unemployed or students, often hold much more radically critical sociopolitical views (green variations of anarchism are a key trend), and have very different reasons for protesting. Moreover members of the local action groups have supported the young eco-activists materially, financially and also physically – a third (34 per cent) of respondents to the Alarm UK survey had taken part in various forms of non-violent direct action, and three-quarters (74 per cent) agreed with breaking the law if it was necessary to do so.

One possible point of contact that joins these social groupings in a common opposition to road development is an anti-modernist tendency that is manifest in a nostalgia for rural life and an idealised picture of the past. The landed class have, since the onset of industrialisation in the late 18th/early 19th century, harked back to an idealised pre-industrial Britain – a vision that goes back to the revolt of the romantics. The middle classes are also caught up with the culture of nostalgia but in a different way, i.e. in their consumption of romantic kitsch, e.g. mock Tudor houses, Laura Ashley, William Morris designs, antique fairs, etc. This class have also viewed themselves as escaping the worst aspects of urbanisation and industrialism by living either in the suburbs of cities or in the commuter towns and villages of the countryside. Finally the young eco-activists, many of whom have been brought up in urban settings, also tend to illustrate an idealised vision of the past in their treehouses and 'medieval' encampments, their revival and re-invention of folk songs, stories, and pre-industrial mythologies, and in their attempt to revive the arts and crafts tradition in decentralised self-sufficient ecological communities. Although this romanticisation of the past provides a meeting point for each of these social groupings it is also a source of potential conflict because each social grouping has a very different vision of an ideal way of living and therefore the alliance that exists between them against road building and other forms of development is very tenuous one.

The tensions which exist in terms of varients of romanticism are further compounded by conflicts over the status of science and technology. For some in the anti-roads movement, particularly elements of the new middle class, technology and 'positive' science have the potential to make possible the creation of a 'post-industrial utopia' whereby the 20th-century decentralising shift from urban to suburban living and working is further extended outwards so that in the future cities will become redundant for the majority of the population. Equally e-mail and the internet have made new modes of posting and retrieving anti-road campaign information possible for those with access to the requisite technology.[15] In contrast to this positive perspective, however, lies the perception prevalent on the movement's deep Green wing that science and technology are in the process of creating a Gibsonesque dystopia which both represents and flows from humankind's Promethean and alienated relationship with inner and outer nature. It is only, though, in rare cases that these positions are clear-cut, and it is much more usual for activists to adopt a pragmatic attitude to science and technology, using it where and when it is advantageous to do so and criticising the lack of accountability and democratic control over its use by government, the scientific establishment and large corporations. It should also be noted here that there are distinctive elements within the anti-roads movement who neither romanticise the past nor pursue defensive sectional interests, but are rather offensively orientated towards the creation of a future-looking ecologically sustainable and socially just society.

The splits that are manifest in the anti-road protest movement in terms of progressive and regressive visions also very much mirror the ideological divisions that exist within the wider Green movement. Here Scott's (1990) typology is useful for the purposes of clarification and for the illumination of the types of internal conflict which are likely to occur. According to Scott there are four main ideological positions within the Green movement: the 'fundamental-ists' who are uncompromisingly anti-capitalist and are more orientated towards 'movement' politics than institutional politics; the eco-socialists who oppose the capitalist state and link social and ecological issues; the conserva-tives who take a romantic anti-capitalist stance; and the 'realists' who view progress as ultimately coming through 'feasible' reform of capitalist economic and social structures, and thus advocate alliances with political parties and the lobbying of government (Scott, 1990: 81–7). Thus there is the distinct possibil-ity of ideological conflict between, for example, the 'realists' and the 'funda-mentalists', or between the eco-socialists and the conservatives, etc.

Intrinsically linked to these ideological divisions is, of course, the issue of class division which, as Keating (1991) argues, is the inherent weakness of 'rainbow coalitions' which lack a cohesive and cogent over-arching ideology. Keating points to the fact that 'the economic class interests of individuals are likely to take precedence over shared neighbourhood or other values in the long term'. He also notes that by making 'staged and modest concessions' those in authority can split off sections of social movements and effectively achieve 'a progressive demobilisation' (Keating, 1991: 88). The contradictions in terms of ideology and class that Scott and Keating respectively emphasise reinforce the argument that the alliance against road-building is a tenuous one. These ten-sions have, though, been present in the anti-roads movement since its incep-tion, and yet it has shown a remarkable cohesiveness, drive and determination in pursuing its goal. Now, however, that the goal of stopping the government's road-building programme has largely been achieved, the inbuilt contradictions which had hitherto been suppressed by the concentration on a 'single issue' are likely to increasingly come to the fore as the movement fragments and the dif-ferent ideological strands being to pursue other, often broader, issues and inter-ests. One fundamental question that remains, though, is a political one; i.e. whether or not the anti-road protest movement and others like it can provide inspiration and perhaps form the catalyst for the development of a wider 'offen-sive' social movement that, in terms of both theory and practice, will funda-mentally challenge the social and environmental status quo?

NOTES

1. This research has been conducted as part of an ongoing ESRC-funded PhD project. With the generous aid of Alarm UK, 500 postal questionnaires were sent out in September 1996, to which there has been a 47 per cent response rate. Semi-structured interviews with individual activists and protesters from Alarm UK, Earth First!, Reclaim the Streets, local action groups and the Pollock Free State protest camp in Glasgow were conducted between June and December 1996.

2.   For an excellent sociological analysis of amenity societies opposing a road development see Keating (1978).

3.   This government report made the modest recommendation that 'authorities preparing plans voluntarily accept an obligation to give full publicity to their proposals as they are being drawn up and to give the public an opportunity to participate in the plan-making process' (Skeffington, 1969: 41). The main problem was, of course, the 'voluntary clause' but there was also a lack of concrete detail as to how to actually involve the public in planning.

4.   For an activist's critique of the public inquiry system as it relates to motorway planning during this period see Tyme (1978). Tyme was a leading figure in the National Motorways Action Committee which was set up in 1974.

5.   The most high-profile of these protests occurred at Oxleas Wood in southeast London (1993), the Wanstead and Leyton areas of London (M11, 1994), Bath (1994), Glasgow (M77, 1994–5), Newbury (1995–7) and Fairmile (1995–7).

6.   See Jacobs (1996). The 'Real World' Coalition is an alliance of 30 non-governmental organisations, voluntary organisations, campaigning and pressure groups which aims to force the issues of environmental sustainability and social justice onto the party political agenda. Alarm UK's acceptance by the 'Real World' is perhaps a sign of its increasing respectability.

7.   There is a notable similarity here to the early work of Manuel Castells on urban social movements. Castells (1977) viewed the growth of state authority in managing the means of collective consumption as being a source of politicisation and inevitable conflict over the allocation of resources.

8.   The survey of Alarm UK revealed that 24 per cent of members and supporters have been involved in campaigns against the CJA, of whom the vast majority were aged under 30. It also reveals the way in which activists tend not to confine themselves to one campaign, but are often involved with several at one time. In Glasgow the RAM74 (Residents Against the M74) protest group, which is leading the campaign against an extension to the M74, grew out of a group called Soosiders Against the Criminal Justice Act.

9.   For debates about the political nature of the new middle class, see Bagguley (1995).

10. An earlier survey at the Alarm UK conference in March 1996 revealed a rough 50/50 gender split amongst 80 or so core activists.

11. See Inglehart (1990: 74–5). Respondents were asked to prioritise the following categories in order of importance to them politically: fighting crime, protecting the environment, fighting inflation, creating a less impersonal society, maintaining order within the nation, the protection of civil liberties, creating more beautiful cities, maintaining economic growth, giving people more control over their own lives, and maintaining strong defence forces.

12. Giddens (1987) characterises the new movement's orientation towards 'life politics' as a revival of the classical distinction in political philosophy between 'freedom from' and 'freedom to'. The 'old' movements, i.e. the labour, free speech and democratic movements, he argues, work within the paradigm of emancipatory politics and struggle to attain freedom from inequality and oppression, whereas the newer movements, e.g. ecological, peace, etc., are in general orientated towards 'self-actualisation', i.e. the freedom to have a fulfilling and satisfying life for all.

13. This survey, conducted in 1995 by London Youth Matters, found that only 40 per cent of the 18–24 age band intended to vote at the next general election. On specific issues, though, young people felt strongly, e.g. extra funding for the

National Health Service (66 per cent), helping the homeless (73 per cent), supporting single parents (56 per cent). What the survey also found was that young people overwhelmingly defined politics as 'a thing that directly affects my life' (54 per cent), as opposed to 'what goes on in parliament' (24 per cent).

14.   For a Habermasian critique of the 'techno-decisionistic' logic of the Public Inquiry System, see Rodger (1978).

15.   Results from the Alarm UK survey revealed that only 20 per cent of respondents 'do not use a computer regularly' and that 21 per cent used the internet frequently as a source of information and communication. A quick search on the net reveals just how important an information medium it has become in relation to anti-roads protests and other 'alternative' campaigns and politics. For anti-roads campaigns one of the best sites is the RTS links page at: http://www.hrc.wmin.ac.uk/campaigns/RTS/links.html; see also the *Red Pepper* links page at: http://www.netlink.co.uk/users/editoria/dir/index.html

REFERENCES

Aronowitz, S. (1992), *The Politics of Identity: Class, Culture, Social Movements* (London: Routledge).

Bagguley, P. (1995), 'Middle Class Radicalism Revisited', in T. Butler and M. Savage (eds), *Social Change and the Middle Classes* (London: UCL Press).

Barker, C. and Tyldesley, M. (eds) (1996), *Alternative Futures and Popular Protest Conference Papers*, vol. 2 (Manchester: MMU Press).

Blowers, A. Brook, C., Dunleary, P. and McDowell, L. (eds) (1981), *Urban Change and Conflict* (London: Harper & Row).

Boggs, C. (1986), *Social Movements and Political Power* (Philadelphia: Temple University Press).

Bray, J., Must, E. and Stewart, J. (1995), *Roadblock* (London: Jugatsu).

Castells, M. (1977), *The Urban Question – a Marxist Approach* (London: E. Arnold).

Clark, G. (1972), 'The Lesson of Acklam Road', in E. Butterworth and D. Weir (eds), *Social Problems of Modern Britain* (London: Fontana/Collins).

Crook, S., Pakulski, J. and Water, M. (1992) *Postmodernization: Change in Contemporary Society* (London: Sage).

Dalton, R. J. and Kuechler, M. (eds) (1990), *Challenging the Political Order* (Cambridge: Polity).

Garner, C, (1997), 'The Gospel According to Swampy', *The Independent*, 6 February.

Giddens, A. (1987), *The Consequences of Modernity* (Cambridge: Polity).

Habermas, J. (1971), *Toward a Rational Society* (London: Heinemann).

Habermas, J. (1976), *Legitimation Crisis* (London: Heinemann).

Habermas, J. (1984), *The Theory of Communicative Action*, vol. 1 (London: Heinemann)

Habermas, J. (1987), *The Theory of Communicative Action*, vol. 2 (Cambridge: Polity).

Habermas, J. (1992), *The Philosophical Discourse of Modernity* (Cambridge: Polity).

Hewitt, M. (1993), 'Social Movements and Social Need: Problems with Postmodern Political Theory', *Critical Social Policy*, 37, 52–74.

Inglehart, R. (1977) *The Silent Revolution* (Princeton, NJ: Princeton University Press).

Inglehart, R. (1990), *Culture Shift in Advanced Society* (Princeton, NJ: Princeton University Press).

Jacobs, M. (ed.) (1996), *The Politics of the Real World* (London: Earthscan).

Keating, M. (1978), *The Battle of the Western Approaches – A Study in Local Pressure Politics and Amenity in Glasgow* (Glasgow: Glasgow College of Technology Policy Analysis Research Unit).

Keating M. (1991), *Comparative Urban Politics* (Aldershot: Edward Elgar).

Laclau, E. and Mouffe, C. (1985), *Hegemony and Socialist Strategy* (London: Verso).

McKay, D. H. and Cox, A. W. (1979), *Politics of Urban Change* (London: Croom Helm).

Melucci, A. (1988), *Nomads of the Present* (London: Radius).

Offe, C. (1984), *Contradictions of the Welfare State* (London: Hutchinson).

Offe, C. (1987), 'Challenging the Boundaries of Institutional Politics: Social Movements since the 1960s', in C. S. Maier (ed.), *Changing Boundaries of the Political* (Cambridge: Cambridge University Press).

Painter, M. (1981) 'Policy-making on Inter-Urban Highways in Britain, 1945–79', in Blowers, A., Brook, C., Dunleary, S. and McDowell, L. (eds), *Urban Change and Conflict* (London: Harper and Rowe).

Rodger, J. J. (1978), 'Inauthentic Politics and the Public Inquiry System: a Discussion Based on the Moss Moran Controversy', *Scottish Journal of Sociology*, 3(1).

Rowell, A. (1996), *Green Backlash* (London: Routledge).

Scott, A. (1990), *Ideology and the New Social Movements* (London: Unwin Hyman).

Skeffington, A. M. (1969), *Report of the Committee on Public Participation in Planning* (London: HMSO).

Starkie, D. (1982), *The Motorway Age* (Oxford: Pergamon).

Stewart, J. (ed.) (1997), *Alarm Bells* (London: Alarm UK).

Tyme, J. (1978), *Motorways Against Democracy* (London: Macmillan).

Part II

Resistance and Change in Social Movements

6 Social Movements in a Multi-Ethnic Inner City: Explaining their Rise and Fall over 25 Years
Max Farrar

INTRODUCTION

Chapeltown is a district just north of the centre of the city of Leeds. This chapter provides brief details of a number of social and political mobilisations around issues of racism and ethnicity in the area between 1972 and 1997. Setting these campaigns in the context of rising unemployment and improved environmental conditions, the chapter argues that the 1970s saw the emergence of effective urban social movements, and seeks to explain the decline of these movements into smaller campaigns in the 1980s and partial struggles in the 1990s.

Over the past 25 years Chapeltown has been persistently represented in the national and local newspapers as a black ghetto seething with crime and violence (Farrar, 1995, 1996, 1997a). Less often do the media point to its persistent levels of high unemployment: 12.6 per cent in 1974, four times the national rate (Leeds City Council, 1974), and 32 per cent in 1991, almost three times the rate for Leeds in that year (Farrar, 1999). Nor does the media refer to the variety of ethnic groups who reside in this area (of its 14 000 residents in 1991, 39 per cent were classified as white, 28 per cent as South Asian and a further 28 per cent as African, Caribbean or Black Other).[1]

Compared to areas of Leeds in which middle and upper income families reside, Chapeltown is significantly disadvantaged (see Table 6.1). Poverty may not open itself to the easy certainty of 'fact', but the life experience that is associated with long-term extreme rates of unemployment is an over-riding reality for significant numbers of people in the area. Just as the statistics show that unemployment has increased by 250 per cent in the past 20 years or so, in several respects the material life of people in the area has declined catastrophically. If a third of the nation's under-16s live in poverty, risking four times the chances of dying by the age of 20 compared to the affluent, at least a third of

Table 6.1   *Comparing Households in Chapeltown and Leeds: Lifestyle Indicators*

Percentage of households	Chapeltown	Leeds
Owner occupiers	44	61
Privately rented	14	7
Council rented	26	27
Exclusive use of bath and toilet	97	99
As above, plus central heating in all or some rooms	47	65
Room occupation of over 1.5 persons per room	2	0.3
Household does not own a car	67	41

Source: Tables 20a, 21, 23 and 58, *1991 Census of Population: Small Area Statistics* (OPCS).

Chapeltown's children will be in this category (Dennehy *et al.*, 1997; *Observer*, 23 April 1997). While a 1991 'single parenthood statistic' of 47 per cent of all households in Chapeltown must be read in the light of local arrangements of familial responsibility, the real difficulties imposed when many parents are alone and unsupported with their children cannot be ignored. But, to some extent, material progress has been made in Chapeltown over the past 25 years. Housing conditions have improved, and the provision of a variety of local facilities has also been extended (Farrar, 1996). To lose sight of these 'facts' is to fail to see the material context in which political struggle has taken place in the area. The politics of Chapeltown are the politics of people who, overall, are not immiserated, and should not be thought of as mere victims. Real material gains have been made over the past quarter-century, largely as a result of the struggles of confident, experienced and effective organisations representing, at their height, large sections of the local population. Nevertheless, exclusion from work, the removal of welfare benefits for 16-year-olds and the existential terror of life in the most uncertain and oppressed margins of society are persistent realities for a significant proportion of Chapeltown's population. The increased use of hard drugs in the late 1980s and early 1990s, the sharp rise in street robbery and burglary in Chapeltown between 1987 and 1995[2], are evidence of the detrimental effects of this social exclusion of a small but significant proportion of the local population.

SOCIAL AND POLITICAL CAMPAIGNS IN CHAPELTOWN FROM THE 1970s

Table 6.2 gives brief details of the social and political campaigns in Chapeltown between 1970 and 1995. Although there is no space here to give

Table 6.2   *Social and Political Campaigns in Chapeltown, 1970–95*

Date	Campaign name	Issue
Oct. 1972	Chapeltown Parents and Friends Association	Local control of Play Centre
July 1973	Chapeltown Parents Action Group	Elimination of racism at Earl Cowper Middle School
May 1973	Scott Hall Action Group	Provision of pelican crossing on dual carriageway
Aug. 1973	Chapeltown Community Association *Ad-Hoc* Group	Street cleaning in Chapeltown
July 1974	Ditto	Ditto in Sholebrokes area
July–Nov. 1974	(Sikh Temple, CRC, IWA)	The right for Sikhs to wear turbans on Leeds buses
Nov. 1975– July 1976	(Bonfire Night 12)	Defence of black youths arrested at 'riot'
July 1981	(Leeds Uprising)	'Riot' in Chapeltown/ Harehills
Nov. 1986	(Rutland Lodge)	Racism at a council training centre
Nov. 1987– Mar 1988	Root Out Racism in Education	Non-appointment of qualified black worker to senior post in Education Department
Aug. 1987	Ellis Must Go!	Removal of senior police officer after racist remarks
Dec. 1990	Chapeltown Defence Campaign	Against police harassment
Dec. 1994	Black Direct Action for Equal Rights and Justice	Defence of youths arrested at mini 'riot'
Jan. 1990	Anti Hard Drugs Campaign	Campaign and education against crack cocaine, etc.

Note: Where the 'campaign name' is given in parenthesis this indicates that no formal, single organisation was created to deal with the issue.

full details of each of the campaigns that have taken place in this small area of Leeds over the past 25 years, I have analysed some of them elsewhere (Farrar, 1981, 1988, 1992). I will provide specific information where it is relevant to the primary purpose of this chapter – a sociological explanation of the changing forms of protest.

From Table 6.2 it appears that there is a rhythm of protest – short bursts followed by long pauses. One of my aims here is to show that there is nothing natural about these waves of activity; they are explicable by demonstrating the connection between social, economic and political processes outside Chapeltown and the emergence of specific life orientations within Chapeltown.

IDENTIFYING URBAN SOCIAL MOVEMENTS

Manuel Castells' (1983) analysis of urban social movements has been roundly criticised (see Saunders, 1986; Lowe, 1986; Zukin, 1987). By 1988 Peter Jackson could write: 'the last six years [have] witnessed the rise (and fall?) of urban social movements as a theoretical framework' (Jackson, 1988: 263–4). Social movements in general, however, have continued to be the focus of theoretical and empirical discussion (e.g. Maheu, 1995). Paul Gilroy (1987) is one of the few British theorists positively to employ Castells' concept of urban social movements. Fourteen years later, Castells (1997: 60–4) revisited his earlier work on urban social movements, but failed to identify contemporary European and North American examples commensurate with the utopian and proto-revolutionary movements he found in those continents in the 1970s. Analysing movements organised by the Zapatistas in Mexico, the American Patriots and Japan's 'Aum Shinryko', Castells (1997: Ch. 2), adapted Touraine's typology proposing that 'identity', adversary' and 'societal goal' are the concepts with which social movements should be analysed (1997: 71). Significantly, only the Japanese organisation was based in the city, but its predominantly mystical orientation divorces it from the usual concerns of urban movements. This approach highlights the problem that became evident in Lowe's (1986) discussion of tenants' and ratepayers' associations: Castells presents not so much a theory of urban social movements as a set of criteria by which one kind of protest group (such as a pressure group) might be distinguished from another (such as a social movement).

To reduce the argument to whether or not a city-based protest group can be categorised as an urban social movement, and to reduce the discussion of social movements to a descriptive typology, is to miss the most useful point of the analysis of social movements, urban or otherwise. Castells (1983, 1997) continually focuses on the prospects for resistance to, even revolution against, capitalist society. This question – in what social formations can racism, sexism and class exploitation be confronted in the last decades of the 20th century? – should be a central problem for sociology. Castells' typology (1983) for the analysis of urban social movements obliges us to examine organisations and actions such as those Chapeltown has witnessed over the past 25 years in some detail. It does not explain why movements emerge, but it does provide the means by which we may evaluate the extent of the challenge posed to the local and central state by these campaigns and *ad-hoc* groupings. For Castells the most far-reaching threat (outside the workplace) to the established order emanates from urban social movements.

Castells' theory has been so frequently summarised briefly, and then criticised unfairly, that it is worth setting out his views in some detail. To deserve the label of urban social movement, Castells argued, it must meet the following criteria:

1. To accomplish the transformation of urban meaning in the full extent of its political and cultural implications, an urban movement must articulate in its practice the three goals of collective consumption demands, community culture, and political self-management.
2. It must be conscious of itself as an urban social movement.
3. It must be connected to society through a series of political operators, three in particular: the media, the professionals, and the political parties.
4. While urban movements must be connected to the political system to at least partially achieve their goals, they must be organisationally and ideologically autonomous of any political party.

(Castells, 1983: 322)

Since he stresses that point 1 above 'must command all others' (*ibid*.: 323) it is important to be clear what he means by the 'three goals':

'Collective consumption demands' are those which seek to de-commodify the services provided by the city, to transform them from exchange values into use values. He calls movements which pursue these demands 'collective consumption trade unionism'.

(*Ibid*.: 321)

'Community culture' is a shorthand for 'the search for cultural identity, for the maintenance or creation of autonomous local cultures, ethnically-based or historically originated'; the effort to defend people's face-to-face communication, their 'autonomously defined social meaning' against the invasion from above of media messages and its standardised culture. 'Community movements' pursue these aims.

(*Ibid*.: 319)

The third goal is for neighbourhood self-management, local participation and autonomy, against centralised power structures, and is characteristic of what Castells calls a 'citizen movement'.

(*Ibid*.: 320 and 321)

Castells' overall theory was principally concerned with the processes by which the meaning of urban life is spatialised (*ibid*.: 14), and thus the theorising of urban change. Since Castells defines urban meaning in somewhat technical language which seeks to associate meaning with economic processes and class conflict (*ibid*.: 303), I should indicate that, complementary with Castells, I use the term to grasp the subjective processes of 'making sense' of the city. While the presentation above is an attempt to offer a classification of urban movements according to their particular goals and organisational forms, Castells' broader theoretical concerns are raised in the concept 'the transformation of urban meaning'. While this phrase might be thought vague, Castells' approach remains productive, at least so far as the politics of Chapeltown are concerned.

THE EARLY 1970s IN CHAPELTOWN

Three rather different organisations in Chapeltown were engaged in the process of attempting fundamentally to alter the meaning of living in an inner-city area during the early 1970s.[3] One, the Chapeltown Parents Action Group (CPAG), had an exclusively African–Caribbean membership; the second involved the local Sikh temple; and the third, the Chapeltown Community Association (CCA), was composed of whites (English, Irish and Eastern European), African–Caribbeans and Indians.

The CPAG organised the parents of children at a school in the heart of Chapeltown, Earl Cowper Middle School, to withdraw their children for two days in pursuit of their demands. These included: that the headteacher be sacked for his racist descriptions of black children, that facilities at the school be improved and that black people become more involved in the management and education at the school (Farrar, 1992). This action, which, unprecedentedly, succeeded in having the headteacher removed and in improving staffing and conditions at the school, satisfied several of Castells' criteria. It achieved advances in the area of collective consumption by expanding educational resources for local children. It did much to enhance the cultural identity of African-Caribbeans. A highly politically educated group at the core of the CPAG (the West Indian Afro Brotherhood) ensured that the campaign was led by parents of children at the school. The confidence of those parents in articulating their sense of injustice at the racist denial of the value of their culture was visibly increased as white officials in suits were subjected to rigorous cross-examination in public meetings. This was a campaign which fulfils Castells' notion of a 'community movement' in that it effectively enhanced 'face-to-face' communication and resisted media stereotypes of black people. In addition, the movement initiated by this grouping was in pursuit not simply of material improvements, but of the dimensions of postulated community which could be called metaphorical – the dream/desire for equality, justice and meaningful social existence.

Although the CPAG did not immediately achieve its aim of obtaining more local control of the school (via the appointment of black governors, as it had demanded) it is clear from subsequent developments that the Education Department recognised that the balance of power between itself and Chapeltown's African–Caribbean population had decisively shifted – in favour of the local people. Similarly, at the level of organisation, this campaign fulfilled Castells' strictures. It was completely autonomous of all political groups, either of the orthodox parties or the Marxist organisations which, at that time, were desperate to influence black politics. But it placed its demands squarely within the political arena, and ensured that the media, professional educationalists and city councillors were forced to respond. Most crucially, perhaps, it transformed urban meaning in this sense: no longer could the (white) city treat its black population as an alien Other, to be merely vilified or ignored. The CPAG was a manifestation of an emerging consciousness of the relationship between black migrants and the white metropole. Just as the meaning of being black was fundamentally changed by this confident, conscious movement, so too was the meaning of being white – at least for those who ran the city, and for those of us who lived or worked in Chapeltown.

A second example is the mobilisation of Leeds' Indians of the Sikh faith, most of whom lived in Chapeltown, during 1974. This activity was sparked by the suspension by the bus company of two Sikhs who clocked in for work on 3 July 1974 wearing, for the first time at work, their turbans. Initial activity involved behind-the-scenes negotiations by the Community Relations Council and leading members of the Sikh Temple. With increasing hostility towards the Sikhs from the bus-workers' union, the TGWU, and in the absence of progress in the negotiations, the Indian Workers Association organised a demonstration by Sikh men and women outside the union offices in September. The United Caribbean Association issued a public statement of its support for the Sikhs (*Chapeltown News*, No. 21, 1974).[4] By the time a second demonstration was planned in November, this time with the full backing of the Temple, the management and the union conceded the right to wear turbans on the buses. Here again we see some characteristics of an urban social movement – in particular the ability of the Sikhs to assert their organised presence in the public places of the city. In defying the white stereotype, particularly strongly articulated around that time, that all 'Asians' (and particularly 'Asian women') are docile (but deceitful) (see Southgate, 1982), and in defying the assumption that Asians and African–Caribbeans do not seek common cause, this action, like that of the CPAG, intervened in the black–white power relations in the city, and thereby altered the meaning of urban life.

An analysis of some of the activities of the third case, the Chapeltown Community Association strengthens the applicability of Castells' thesis. While the CPAG would dissolve itself, and leave the ongoing process of political and cultural activity to local organisations such as the Brotherhood, the United Caribbean Association, the Jamaica Society and the Barbados Overseas Association, the CCA established itself as a formal organisation with an Annual General Meeting and a committee structure. It maintained a high profile of activity from 1971 to 1974, finally dissolving in 1975. Its sub-committees reflected its aims: to improve housing conditions, road safety, play facilities for young children and youth, and street cleaning. In its first two years it pursued these goals by entirely orthodox means. It produced plausible plans (its first Secretary was a Town Planner), wrote letters and held meetings with council officials. The gains actually made by the CCA in improving the provision of items of collective consumption were minimal. On the other hand, the CCA's proposals – for a community centre, redesign of the road layouts and so on, were far-sighted and, in many cases, delivered some years later. In 1973 and 1974, however, under the influence of those (including myself) in the CCA whose politics had been shaped by the contemporary radical and international movements of students, women, gays and black people, an approach was adopted which more closely conformed to Castells' criteria. It began to define itself explicitly around demands for wholesale change in the infrastructure of the neighbourhood, such as: 'an immediate £2 million programme to set up teams of builders and trades-people to work on every house in need of improvement or repair, work to start immediately on the proposed new houses, health clinic, school, community centre and play park' (CCA leaflet, September 1974). It adopted direct action tactics such as blocking Chapeltown Road with rubbish and an abandoned car in August 1973, and dumping rotten fish in the council's Cleansing Department office in July 1974 (see *Chapeltown News*, No. 11, 1973 and No. 19, 1974). Like the CPAG, the CCA was organisationally autonomous, but it attempted to use the media, professionals and powerful politicians in pursuit of its aims. It was persistently hostile to local Labour councillors and the Labour Chair of the Housing Committee (despite its demand that they improve facilities) and made life very uncomfortable for its one member who was a Conservative Party member. Implicitly, it demanded greater local self-management but, unlike the CPAG, it never articulated this as a clear demand.

In two respects, however, the CCA could not be called an urban social movement. Firstly, in transforming itself from its origins as a public, open pressure group into a small activist grouping with radical demands, it was unable to mobilise the popular support which would earn the label of 'movement'. Second, its cultural amorphousness meant that it could never make a clear intervention into the structures of meaning within the city, or the locality. 'Transformation of urban meaning' requires a real shift in the way that a city thinks about itself, if such a reification may be allowed for a moment. Major changes at this level are only likely when relationships of power are disrupted by the emergence of new social actors, who are able to impose new urban meanings on the city. The CCA – remarkable in one sense for its multi-culturalism, its coalition across ages, genders and class – was never able to generate a particular set of meanings which were capable of wider replication within the neighbourhood. The content of one possible mobiliser of common meanings, 'community', was never specified, probably because its members would never agree on what they meant by the term, still less about how it should be achieved. Castells' invocation of the phenomenological concept of meaning seems to me to be a major contribution to the analysis of social movements, urban or otherwise. Although it is rarely explicitly invoked, it is the search for new 'modes of Being', the new sense of meaningfulness that can arise when the dominant power is disrupted or overturned, which is required in the analysis of the anti-road protests and the alternative, ecological lifestyles we have seen in Britain in the 1990s (Maffesoli, 1996; McKay, 1996). It is perhaps ironic that the CCA utilised the term 'community', which still connotes the utopian aim of creating places in which relationships of warmth, solidarity and (in its radical formulations) equality might prevail, but was never able to spell out such yearnings. Unlike the CPAG and the action by the Sikhs, it could not appeal to the common experiences of its members: it had no way of knowing what experiences they had in common.

'RIOT' AND URBAN SOCIAL MOVEMENTS

Chapeltown has been the site of two major events which the media refer to as riots, in November 1975 and in July 1981. These events challenged both the practice of local politics and the theory of urban movements. In 1975, on the evening of 5 November – celebrated throughout Britain as the night of an unsuccessful attempt to blow up Parliament in the 17th century – the first effort by black British youth to physically defeat the police force took place. In a planned retaliation against the police and fire brigade's dowsing of their bonfire the year before, young African-Caribbean men hurled bricks at police cars as they patrolled Spencer Place, one of the main thoroughfares of Chapeltown, where this grouping traditionally held their bonfire. Two police officers were seriously injured and several cars were wrecked. Over the next few days 11 black youths and myself were arrested. We appeared in court in June 1976, some of us facing affray charges, others accused of grievous bodily harm and possession of an offensive weapon. On most charges we were acquitted, but three received short spells of detention.

The events of 12 and 13 July 1981 caused much more serious damage to property, including the looting of shops and the burning-down of buildings. The damage was estimated at £2 million. Perhaps 200 to 300 youths were involved, many of them white, from other lower-income areas of Leeds.

Twenty-four people were arrested and almost all were convicted. In my initial analysis of the 1981 events, which I linked to both the Bonfire Night events and the campaigns by the CPAG and the CCA of the previous decade, I attempted to show that these were proto-revolutionary 'uprisings', not 'riots' (Farrar, 1981). In analysing similar events of even greater physical violence in other British cities (Birmingham and London) during 1985, Paul Gilroy also argues that what is conventionally dubbed 'riot' is actually infused with potent political meaning. To support his argument he uses the work of Alain Touraine and Alberto Melucci on social movements. Touraine argued that the social movements universalised the issue of emancipation and the control of historicity; no longer was it the prerogative of the industrial workers (Touraine, 1981). Gilroy outlined Melucci's characteristic features of a social movement as: the non-negotiable nature of their demands; their aim for complete autonomy from the system, rather than for political power within the system; the immediate satisfaction of collective desires; the central place they give to the body as a medium for understanding that human beings are part of the natural world; a religious or spiritual component (Gilroy, 1987: 224–7, and Melucci, 1996). According to Gilroy, 'Britain's social movement around "race" exhibits all the characteristics suggested by Touraine and Melucci' (Gilroy, 1987: 227). It might be stretching the point a bit too far to claim that young black men engage in physical confrontation with the police in order to take control over the course of history. On the other hand, those who in this period were influenced by Bob Marley's militant Rastafarianism would, perhaps, have argued that they were struggling against the Babylon system as a whole, and aiming for a new, spiritually informed social justice, as outlined in Haile Selassie's famous speech to the United Nations on 'war' (and set to music by Marley in the song of that name). Rastafarianism is explicit in its longing for a new spiritual community where racism and oppression is extinguished (McKnight and Tobler, 1977; Plummer *et al.*, 1978; Owens, 1979; CCRJ, 1982).

Melucci's criteria fit the characteristics of some aspects of the 1975 'riot', and the 1981 events, but Melucci (and Gilroy) are excessively optimistic if they claim that these capture the motives of all, or even a majority, of those who burned and looted in Chapeltown in July 1981. Significantly, Castells' criteria are not mentioned by Gilroy at this point in his argument. Only in one respect do the conflagrations of 1975 and 1981 meet with Castells' criteria. They did have an impact on collective consumption patterns in the neighbourhood. The 1975 events galvanised the Education Department into further provision of adult education and community centre facilities (Farrar, 1988). The 1981 events led to wholesale restructuring of housing, leisure and youth facilities. They also had a significant impact on the power relations between the locality and the city council – an official body, the Harehills and Chapeltown Liaison Committee, was established by the leader of the city council as an immediate response to the 1981 'riot' (Farrar, 1988, 1996). But Castells stresses that – in an echo of Marx's dictum about class in itself as opposed to class for itself – if a mobilisation is to be called an urban social movement, it must be conscious of itself as such. Those who rose up in 1975 and 1981 were undoubtedly conscious of their power, but they were never able to specify wider social or political goals, and had no interest in formulating themselves as a movement. The re-allocation of welfare resources to Chapeltown was a consequence of their action which they did not foresee (although some in their ranks would later retrospectively justify their actions in terms of services thus delivered to the people of Chapeltown). When Gilroy does utilise Castells' work on urban social movements, he does not make the link with violent protests. He refers to the types of campaign Chapeltown saw in the early 1970s – what Castells would call 'collective consumption trade unionism' and 'community movements' – as fulfilling Castells' criteria (Gilroy, 1987: 230).

EXPLAINING THE DECLINE OF MASS POLITICS

One of the problems with Castells' analysis is its lack of focus on the reasons why urban social movements fail. Indeed, after 1981, the proto-urban social movements of the 1970s were unable to re-form with anything like their former vigour. To explain this, several concepts, outside the domain of Castells' 1983 work, are required. To understand the decline in salience of the social movements in Chapeltown, three processes require investigation: hegemonic incorporation, individualisation and processes of ethnic segregation. Each process rests on the elaboration during this period of specific discourses: of non-violent/corporatist politics, of equal opportunities and of ethnic particularism. In some respects the argument here parallels those of Ian Law and of Elizabeth Lawrence and Nicholas Turner in part III of this volume. The 'ethnic managerialism' identified by Law has prevailed within Leeds City Council, to the detriment of social movement formation, but where Law identifies Conservative government, scientific management theory and the New Right as the culprits, it is clear from my research that a Labour-controlled bureaucracy willingly took the same route (Farrar, 1988, 1999). Where Lawrence and Turner note the deference paid by equal opportunity officers to the social movements, my argument is that the wider discourse of equal opportunities has promoted an individualistic career-identification among a layer of people who, a few years earlier, would have pursued a 'community politics' identification. The end-result of each of these processes, in Chapeltown at least, has been the segmentation of ethnic groups, further undermining the prospects for movements which pursue the generalisation of use values and autonomous political organisations.

Given the political history of the area, the 1975 'riot' might have been expected to galvanise the local Caribbean activists into forming a movement around the youth arrested. No such movement emerged. A significant number of people paraded with placards on the steps of the Town Hall on the first day of the trial, and a formidable team of largely black barristers, organised largely by the women who had once been in the West Indian Afro Brotherhood, conducted a spirited (and successful) defence. (The sexism connoted by the Brotherhood's name was never fully reflected in the internal life of the group.) But the majority of local black people were under the sway of that most powerful aspect of the hegemonic culture of England: the view that violence has no legitimate part to play in politics. Raymond Williams' gloss on Gramsci's use of the term 'hegemony' is instructive. It refers to 'the central, effective and dominant system of meanings and values, which are not merely abstract but which are organised and lived' (Williams, 1980: 38). He saw this system as 'deeply saturating the consciousness of a society' (Williams, 1980: 37). Williams argued that, in order to achieve this deep saturation, 'incorporation' must take place. He stressed the role of the family, education, intellectual practices and the organisation of work in instilling dominant values and meanings, but it also takes place in the aftermath of organised protest. Campaigns, such as those which predominated in Chapeltown until 1975, were a challenge to the hegemonic notion that black people were a passive underclass to be exploited and oppressed at will. Engaging in organised activity, people 'lived out' and embodied their opposition to those institutions that had symbolised their oppression. As we have seen, more often than not the dominant institutions gave way to their demands. Their challenge was legitimated. As Williams pointed out, however:

> alternative meanings and values, the alternative opinions and attitudes, even some alternative senses of the world, can be accommodated and tolerated within a particular effective and dominant culture.
>
> (William, 1980: 39)

To the extent that these alternative meanings are institutionalised and significantly disrupt the hegemonic meaning system, the tag of urban social movement applies. But their very success may well usher in a process of incorporation, as aspects of their values and meanings are either taken on or blunted by those who run the dominant institutions in the local system. The young people who, in 1975 and 1981, engaged in physical violence were also living out, and embodying in an even more dramatic form, their challenge to that institution (the police force) which is itself most physical in its imposition of hegemonic meaning. Unlike their predecessors in protest, they experienced the full weight of the judicial apparatus. Nor was this form of challenge legitimated by black organisations. The older leaders of these organisations had, in the main, adopted long ago the discourse of political non-violence: they broadly accepted that element of the dominant meaning system which proscribes violence in pursuit of any goals, even those which 'rioters' might attempt to define as political. It is quite possible that their violent actions actually reinforced the commitment of some key figures in the black organisations to the hegemonic condemnation of such methods of protest. Only the Chapeltown News Collective, influenced as it was by the discourse established by Malcolm X and the Black Panthers, wholeheartedly supported the defendents from the night of the 'riot' through to their trial. It was only on acquittal that the 1975 defendants were briefly celebrated by those in the black organisations who had failed to support them during the trial. The absence of militant organising in Chapeltown over the next five years can be ascribed to the fundamental shock wave that the Bonfire Night events sent through the local organisations. 'Politics', if the *Chapeltown News* definition was to be allowed, now veered too close to a terrain which could no longer be justified within the boundaries of English political discourse. The response of some of the radicals, black and white, who had been involved in the defence of these youth was to set up a Law Centre – an organisation which, it was thought, could pursue progressive policies through legitimate channels. The CCA went out of existence and *Chapeltown News* soon ceased to publish. No other initiatives were taken by local organisations. By 1981 the only organisation willing to offer any support to those arrested after the burn-down of Chapeltown Road was a small, multi-racial group of politically minded people called the Come-Unity Collective. Its effort to explain the events in terms Martin Luther King's words – 'How long must we live under the Iron Boot of oppression?' (*Come-Unity News*, No. 3, 1981) – and its appeal for a Defence Campaign, fell on completely deaf ears (*Come-Unity News*, Nos. 5 and 6, 1981). After two years of organising political and cultural activities, the CUC dissolved in 1982.

The explanation for this down-turn in political activity in Chapeltown starts with Williams' notion of incorporation, which the Fainsteins (1996) re-phrase in terms of the acquisition of civil, political and social rights of citizens. It should be recalled that the events in July 1981 in Chapeltown were part of an enormous wave of violent protest throughout England, initiated in April in Brixton and which spread to all the major cities, and many smaller ones during July (Benyon and Solomos, 1987). The Leeds City Council responded rapidly to the events of July 1981. Under the control of a former full-time trade union official, George Mudie, now Labour MP for Leeds North East, the initiative taken was that which has served social democracy through the ages: set up a consultative body and consolidate the discourse of corporatist politics. The Harehills and Chapeltown Liaison Committee initially gathered all the leading figures in the African–Caribbean organisations, and within a short time attracted their equivalents in the Asian organisations. Skilfully steered by Mudie, then Leader of the Council, who insisted on the attendance at its regular meetings of all his Heads of Department, the Committee had great credibility with the local people who attended. The initiatives which were fed through the Committee delivered major material gains for the neighbourhood (Farrar, 1996). But, by drawing so much of the energy of the local organisations into the Committee and its subcommittees, the possibility of independent action, such as that of the social movements of the 1970s, was severely undermined. Even the few radicals at the Law Centre (by 1980, I was one of them) increasingly worried about cuts in their funding from the council found themselves somewhat incorporated into the Liaison Committee's structures.

There were, however, two more significant processes, only partially connected to incorporation, taking place during this period: the process of individualisation and ethnic segmentation. Durkheim's (1964) argument that modern society is characterised by the increasing public prominence, and self-confidence of a category called 'the individual', is rarely challenged. Clearly, however, the process of individualisation is not one which continues at an even pace. Maffesoli (1996), for instance, argues that it is now in decline, and it seems likely that, at times when a social democratic party is in power, there is less discursive support for, and perhaps less of the practice of, individualism, than at times when free-market entrepreneurialism is hegemonic. It would be equally wrong to expect the process to take the same form in all sectors of society. In Chapeltown there was little support for the brand of individualism which was promoted by the Conservative government during the 1980s. Strong collectivist traditions within the African–Caribbean and Asian populations of the area, combined with the remains of class hostility among much of the white population, opposed most aspects of Thatcherism.

However, there was an alternative discourse to that offered by Thatcherism which became available with the Labour council's effort to ameliorate the problems of Chapeltown. 'Equal opportunities' is a strange brew of conservative, liberal and social democratic political theory. The institution of an Equal Opportunity Unit within the city council in 1983 signalled the slow march of black people into the corridors of local government. In many cases jobs went to educated and politically aware black people from Chapeltown. As time went on, quasi-independent council and government-funded 'community' projects expanded and offered further job opportunities for local people. Their aim, in most cases, was significantly to improve the provision of services and the employment prospects of local people like themselves. Fuelled by an explicit commitment, if not to anti-racism, then at least to multi-culturalism, the 'equal opportunity' discourse was able to disguise its implicit individualism – for the root of 'equal opportunity' is just reward for individual effort – in the guise of 'serving the people'. In the hands of a social democratic council it is administered on the basis of improving collective provision, and many such improvements took place. Black people in council and voluntary sector jobs, and the many white colleagues who supported them, could justifiably pride themselves on these collective achievements. But the impact on the structures of value and meaning within Chapeltown was not to enhance collectivist aspirations. The message that was received locally was: there are now well-paid careers doing worthwhile work to be had for the appropriately qualified individuals. Socially useful, paid work is a primary value in any society; it is a bulwark of almost everyone's system of meaning. The emphasis on the social value of the work, its relevance to the collective needs of local people, must be fervently sustained in local and city-wide discourse if 'equal opportunities' is not to decay into a softer version of conservative individualism. No such fervour emanated from the council or from local organisations. Self-interested individualism was allowed to flourish.

Ethnic segmentation proceeded simultaneously with individualisation throughout the 1980s. After the initial delivery of collective provision, in terms of housing and environmental improvements, the Liaison Committee became a springboard for the pursuit of local facilities tailor-made to the professedly separate needs of each of Chapeltown's ethnic groups. While special pleading rarely took place in public, the Committee provided the mechanism for private lobbying. The West Indian Centre was built. The Jamaica Society and the Barbados Overseas Association acquired improved premises. By the end of the decade the Islamic Centre on Spencer Place had been considerably extended, the Bangladeshi Muslims acquired a Mosque on Markham Avenue (in the early 1990s they acquired a training and community centre on Roundhay Road), the Ramgahria Sikhs opened extensive premises at the south end of Chapeltown Road, the Namdari Sikhs obtained smaller premises on Louis Street and the main Sikh Temple on Chapeltown Road built a new hall opposite its Temple. Much of the funding for these buildings came from non-council sources, but the support of the city council was crucial in the provision of land, some funds and in supporting applications to other bodies. Each of these institutions was sorely needed. Their consequence however was to lessen the opportunity for inter-ethnic communication, since there was no commensurate pressure from any source to improve facilities at the one centre supposed to serve the whole 'community'. The Education Department's 'Chapeltown Community Centre', one of the major demands of the CCA, had never fulfilled the function its name implied. As each particular organisation acquired its own premises only an organisation advocating an inclusivist, inter-ethnic ideology would counter the process of segmentation that developed during the 1980s. No such calls were heard. Instead, the discourse of ethnic particularism (Gilroy, 1987, 1993) was further elaborated by local organisations, and reinforced by local councillors and their officers at every opportunity.

PARTIAL STRUGGLES IN THE 1980s

'Community struggle' did not disappear from the streets and meeting places of Chapeltown during the 1980s and 1990s (Table 6.2). Several campaigns provide evidence that the processes which gave rise to the urban social movements of the early 1970s have not departed. One very brief, successful, mobilisation in November 1986 against allegations of racism by white instructors towards black youths at an Education Department training centre (then called Rutland Lodge, later the Scott Hall Skills Centre) laid the basis for a prolonged campaign between November 1987 and March 1988 (Root Out Racism in Education, RORIE). Initiated by black employees of the Education Department in protest against one of their number being rejected for a senior post to which he had acted-up for several months, the campaign involved a hundred or so African–Caribbean, white and Asian people (many, but not all, were council employees). Twice occupying council committee rooms in direct action reminiscent of the urban social movements, RORIE was an organised, militant grouping which indicated that there were still layers of people in Chapeltown who were opposed to the processes of ethnic segmentation outlined above. Equally significantly, RORIE included people whose identities were supposed, by some, to be fixed in lesbian separatism. Since the person whose rejection stimulated the campaign eventually obtained the post he applied for, it might be counted as successful. In that it was organisationally autonomous, saw its wider goals as improving educational provision for all non-white people, and was conscious of itself as a political force, RORIE comes close to fulfilling Castells' criteria. But its focal concern – equal opportunity employment policies – opens it to the charge of promoting the very individualism which social movements disavow. Its instability as a coalition recalls the problems of inter-ethnic solidarity that emerge when the discourse of unity is being countered by that of particularity.

The successful campaign (August 1987 to May 1988) to remove a senior police officer, Superintendent John Ellis, whose racist remarks about 'West Indians' had been tape-recorded, was similarly large and almost as militant in its tactics. It brought into common cause working-class Asians, led by Omparkash Sharma, who had recorded Ellis' words, together with younger African–Caribbeans who were already critical of policing methods in Chapeltown. Although the UCA had supported the Sikhs in 1974, and some Asians were involved in RORIE, never before (or since) had there been a politically militant type of alliance between Asians and African–Caribbeans in Chapeltown. The challenge thereby posed to those who believe that cultures are hermetically sealed from each other would at first appear considerable. Close inspection of the transcript of the tape, however, reveals what was known privately at the time. Mr Sharma was in severe conflict with his

African–Caribbean neighbours and he, and his members, were threatening violence towards local African–Caribbean youths whom they regarded as criminal ('Ellis Must Go!' pamphlet, May 1988: 5). The alliance was purely tactical from both parties' points of view. This was a noisy demonstration of local power, but it was not an urban social movement. Two further demonstrations against the police were equally partial and tactical. The Chapeltown Defence campaign attracted about 80 people to march through freezing sleet to the city-centre police station in December 1990 in protest against the rough treatment of a woman whose son was being sought by the police, following a series of representations to the Chapeltown police about their inappropriate behaviour in making arrests. Black Direct Action for Equal Rights and Justice mobilised around 100 in a demonstration through the town centre in December 1994 following the arrest of young people in altercations outside a youth club held at the Chapeltown Community Centre. Although the latter organisation initially had a wider social base than the Defence campaign, in that it involved several of the parents of the young people arrested, it was unable to sustain itself, despite highly professional publicity and support from the National Black Caucus. While all these actions are testimony to the willingness of small groups of people to maintain the tradition of local organising which characterises the area, none of them either raised general demands (relating to use values or to autonomous local institutions), or transformed urban meaning.

CONCLUSION

This small 'inner-city' district of a major British city has witnessed a remarkable succession of political assaults on the local state over the past 25 years. Some of these have been launched by organisations which, it has been argued, conform closely to Castells' (1983) criteria of urban social movements. In struggling for use values, for communal and ethnic solidarity and for local political control, several organisations in Chapeltown in the 1970s provided evidence that local people, black and white, have organised themselves for the social control of historicity. To explain their inability in the 1980s and 1990s to mount campaigns which reached such high levels of political consciousness and organisation, this chapter has pointed to processes such as hegemonic incorporation, individualisation and ethnic segmentation, and to their associated discourses (non-violence/corporatism, equal opportunities and ethnic particularism).

Finally, it seems important to add that an adequate account of the rise and fall of social movements requires as much attention to the subjective processes at stake in political mobilisation, and de-mobilisation, as is given to the social and economic processes (Farrar, 1997b; Hall, 1997, 1998). Political creativity can flourish when sufficient numbers of people feel secure enough and when alienation is – perhaps temporarily – lessened. On the other hand, anxiety suffuses large numbers of people when exclusion is hardened and anti-social behaviour by the chronically ontologically insecure increases. These subjective dispositions have a distinct bearing on the possibilities for progressive transformation of the inner city.

NOTES

1.   All 1991 statistics have been derived from an Enumeration District analysis of the 1991 OPCS Census. The Enumeration District used were those for the area known to local knowledge as Chapeltown (Farrar, 1999).
2.   For detailed figures and analysis of crime in Chapeltown see Farrar (1999). Crime rates levelled out after 1995.
3.   The following analysis is based on my participant observation of the campaigns and groupings referred to. As will become clear, I never claimed any neutral, observational status during this work. On many occasions I actively took the side of the local organisations in their campaigns against the council and the police. My methodology is discussed in Farrar (1999).
4.   *Chapeltown News* was an entirely independent local 'community' newspaper written and published by a collective of which I was a member. Its successor, the similarly produced *Come-Unity News*, is referred to later in this chapter. Both are archived in the Local History Section of Leeds City Council's central library.

REFERENCES

Benyon, J. and Solomos, J. (1987), 'British Urban Unrest in the 1980s', in Benyon, J. and Solomos, J. (eds), *The Roots of Urban Unrest* (Oxford: Pergamon Press).
Castells, M. (1983), *The City and the Grassroots* (London: Edward Arnold).
Castells, M. (1997), *The Power of Identity* (Oxford: Blackwell).
CCRJ (1982), 'Catholic Commission for Racial Justice', *Notes and Reports*, No. 10: 'Rastafarians in Jamaica and Britain' (London).
Dennehy, A., Smith, L. and Harker, P. (1997), *Not To Be Ignored – Young People, Poverty and Health* (London: Child Poverty Action Group).
Durkheim, E. (1964), *The Division of Labour in Society* (New York: Free Press).
Fainstein, N. and Fainstein, S. (1996), 'Urban Regimes and Black Citizens: the Economic and Social Impacts of Black Political Incorporation in US Cities', *International Journal of Urban Regional Research*, 20(1), 23–37.
Farrar, M. (1981), a.k.a. Paul Holt, 'Riot and Revolution: the Politics of an Inner City', *Revolutionary Socialism: the journal of Big Flame*, Winter.
Farrar, M. (1988), 'The Politics of Black Youth Workers in Leeds', *Critical Social Policy*, 23, Autumn.
Farrar, M. (1992), 'Racism, Education and Black Self Organisation', *Critical Social Policy*, 35, Autumn.

Farrar, M. (1995), 'Re-presenting the Inner City', *Regenerating Cities* [now City], January.
Farrar, M. (1996), 'Black Communities and Processes of Exclusion', in G. Haughton and C. Williams (eds), *Corporate City? Partnership, Participation and Partition in Urban Development in Leeds* (Aldershot: Avebury).
Farrar, M. (1997a), 'Migrants and Settlers: Space and Time in an English Inner City', in S. Westwood and J. Williams (eds), *Imagining Cities – Scripts, Sign, Memories* (London: Routledge).
Farrar, M. (1997b), 'Urban Social Movements: Now You See Them, Now You Don't – Explaining the Politics of an English Inner City, 1970–1995'. Paper presented to the British Sociological Association, York, April.
Farrar, M. (1999), 'Constructing and De-constructing "Community": A Case Study of a Multi-Cultural Inner City Area – Chapeltown, Leeds, 1972–1997', PhD thesis, currently submitted for examination.
Gilroy, P. (1987), *There Ain't No Black in the Union Jack* (London: Hutchinson).
Gilroy, P. (1993), *Small Acts – Thoughts on the Politics of Black Cultures* (London: Serpents Tail).
Hall, S. (1992), 'The Question of Cultural Identity', in S. Hall, D. Held, and T. McGrew (eds), *Modernity and Its Future* (Cambridge: Polity).
Hall, S. (1997), 'Black Bodies', *New Times*, 1 February.
Hall, S. (1998), 'Aspiration and Attitude – Reflections on Black Britain in the Nineties', *New Formations*, 33.
Jackson, P. (1988), 'Social Geography: Social Struggles and Spatial Strategies', *Progress in Human Geography*, 12(2), 263–9.
Leeds City Council (1974), 'Chapeltown Residents Opinion Survey' (Leeds: Department of Finance, Department of Housing).
Lowe, S. (1986), *Urban Social Movements – the City after Castells* (Basingstoke: Macmillan).
Maffesoli, M. (1996), *The Time of the Tribes – The Decline of Individualism in Mass Society* (London: Sage).
Maheu, L. (ed.) (1995), *Social Movements and Social Classes: The Future of Collective Action* (London: Sage).
McKay, G. (1996), *Senseless Acts of Beauty – Cultures of Resistance since the Sixties* (London: Verso).
McKnight, C. and Tobler, J. (1977), *Bob Marley – The Roots of Reggae* (London: W. H. Allen; Star Books).
Melucci, A. (1996), *Challenging Codes – Collective Action in the Information Age* (Cambridge: Cambridge University Press).
Miles, R. (1989), *Racism* (London: Routledge).
Owens, J. (1979), *Dread – the Rastafarians of Jamaica* (London: Heinemann Educational).
Plummer, J., Bishton, D. and Homer, B. (1978), *Movement of Jah People – The Growth of the Rastafarians* (Birmingham: Press Gang).
Saunders, P. (1986), *Social Theory and the Urban Question* (London: Hutchinson).
Southgate, P. (1982), *Police Probationer Training in Race Relations, Research and Planning Unit Paper 8* (London: Home Office).
Touraine, A. (1981), *The Voice and the Eye* (Cambridge: Cambridge University Press).
Williams, R. (1988) 'Base and Superstructure in Marxist Cultural Theory', in R. Williams (ed.), *Problems in Materialism and Culture* (London: Verso).
Zukin, S. (1987), Review of Castells (1983) and Lowe (1986) in *American Journal of Sociology*, 93(2), 459–62.

7 'Very British Rebels': Politics and Discourse within Contemporary Ulster Unionism

James White McAuley

> 'When *I* use a word,' Humpty Dumpty said, in a rather scornful tone, 'it means just what I choose it to mean – neither more nor less.'
>
> The question is,' said Alice, 'whether you *can* make words mean so many different things.'
>
> 'The question is,' said Humpty Dumpty, 'which is to be master – that's all.'
>
> Lewis Carroll, *Through the Looking Glass*, pp. 229–30

> The idea of Irish unity by stealth is actually what you are talking about, and what you have is not a peace process but a 'piece-by-piece' process. That is a frustration, that is a fear ... perception here is the reality, and we have got to deal with that perception.
>
> Ian Paisley Jr, *The Observer*, 11 January 1998

INTRODUCTION

Ulster unionism has reacted to political events surrounding what has become known as the 'peace process',[1] with hostility, with clear expressions of suspicion and with loud outcries of treachery by the British government. Events throughout the contemporary period have, for many observers, simply reinforced their understanding of unionism as an ossified and phlegmatic social movement. This chapter, however, will seek to question this and to view unionism as a social movement constantly subject to processes of redefinition and renegotiation.

The emergence of Ulster unionism must from its outset be seen as an expression of resistance to the political desires of Irish nationalism. Ruane and Todd (1996: 88–9) correctly identify two main strands from the beginning: a defence of Protestant interests, and a strong argument that the union could be seen to bring benefits to the whole of Ireland, the British Isles and the empire. Since then, to support this, unionists have been engaged in the invention and reinvention of their histories and traditions (cf. Anderson, 1991; Hobsbawm and Ranger, 1983; Gellner, 1993; English and Walker, 1996; Walker, 1996). Like other social movements Ulster unionism has sought to identify and reproduce the symbols of its 'nation' and to reinforce its social and geographical boundaries by the social construction of its separateness from others on the island of Ireland.

UNIONIST POLITICAL IDEOLOGY AND CULTURE

Against this background this chapter seeks to outline the contemporary politics and ideology of unionism and analyse it as a contemporary social movement. It will consider the direct responses of unionism to political events and the attempt to find a negotiated settlement to the conflict in Northern Ireland. In trying to understand unionism as a social movement, it will importantly focus not only on the structures of formal political parties and pressure groups, within Northern Irish society, but also on what people believe about those structures, how they work, and how they are oriented.

These beliefs may take several key directions, including: the desirable goals of political and social life; the perceived aims of the roles of the state; or the values within the political system. Unionist political culture is, therefore, best understood as the product of a specific constructed history, expressed both in the public and private areas of life. Unionism developed as a response to the perceived threats from Home Rule throughout the whole of Ireland. It was in the northern Protestant-dominated counties, however, that it became a mass social movement. That does not mean that as a political culture unionism is homogeneous: far from it. Within unionism there exist segments of the population with distinct values, differences and subcultures. As a movement it was, and remains, cross-cut by tensions involving politics, culture, class, region, popular culture and religious denomination.

Indeed, the continued fragmentation of Northern Ireland's political culture remains one of its most enduring features. In other societies where a range of political subcultures exists, they are not incompatible with the development of a unified national political culture. It is, however, obvious that Northern Ireland does not share a political culture either with of the rest of the United Kingdom, or with the rest of the island. The political cultures that emerged, although often based on the same resources, both physical and social, and the same symbols, manifested in intensely different political values, highly antagonistic to each other. As O'Neil (1971: 493) once pointed out, the major values of the two political cultures in Northern Ireland surround the ability to inhibit the fundamental goals of the other, reducing politics to a 'sum-zero' game.

In Northern Ireland, political socialisation is restricted almost exclusively to one's respective community. Socialisation is still largely a process of a growing awareness of the parameters of the construction of social difference and a particular understanding of the reasons for political conflict. Much of Northern Irish political culture involves the construction and demonisation of the 'other'. This process often reinforces and is reinforced by social conflict and violence. It is within this context that the invention of traditions must be seen and the continued formation of the 'imagined communities' of unionism and nationalism is ensured. A key task for unionism as a social movement is to link the past and the present in an understandable way, through particular patterns of socialisation, which rely heavily on distinctive social histories and collective remembering (cf. Taylor, 1989; Gillespie *et al.*, 1992: 135–68; Robb, 1992; Jarman, 1997).

REALIGNMENTS WITHIN UNIONISM

Several recent works have, in total or in part, sought to analyse the nature of contemporary unionism and loyalism (cf. Coulter, 1994; McAuley, 1994a; Bew *et al.*, 1995; McGarry and O'Leary, 1995; Clayton, 1996; Porter, 1996; Ruane and Todd, 1996; Gilligan and Tonge, 1997; Shirlow and McGovern, 1997). This assessment will begin with the contemporary peace process and the cessation of violence by both loyalist and republican paramilitary organisations. The initial response of the wider unionist community to the IRA cease-fire was a mixture of relief and scepticism. Overall, it was the DUP (Democratic Unionist Party), who took the lead in overt opposition, dismissing the IRA cease-fire as a simple 'tactical manoeuvre' to extricate as many concessions as possible from the British government. The message from the DUP was clear, that the British government could not be trusted, and any grouping involved with them were also culpable of perfidy.

One other expression of this was the open hostility many DUP members expressed towards the Ulster Unionist Party (UUP), for their, albeit limited, support of peace process. These criticisms reflected both ideological and social differences, and rested on two core DUP beliefs, that the Ulster Unionists are ineffectual in their commitment to the defence of unionism, and that the Ulster Unionists remain distant from the 'ordinary' unionist people. In turn, the Ulster Unionists have consistently claimed that the political tactics of DUP have merely weakened the unionist cause. Such tensions were revealed in a speech by David Trimble, the UUP leader, in which he strongly criticised the leadership tactics of the DUP. In direct reference to the leadership of Bob McCartney, and particularly Ian Paisley, he said:

> Their actions and attitudes have been counter-productive. They have let nationalists off the hook: they have driven London into the arms of Dublin. We must warn against supporting them. ... Unfortunately the methods of those who denigrate us continue to do damage to the Union at home, in the rest of the United Kingdom and elsewhere. The reasonable case we present is being obscured by aggressive, loudmouth Unionists.
>
> (Ulster Unionist Council, Press Statement, 22 March 1997)

The DUP responded by claiming that it was only the DUP 'which stands effectively in the way of his betrayal policy'. Ian Paisley further claimed that Mr Trimble and the UUP were 'on a sell-out programme', looked upon as a soft touch by the British government, Dublin, the White House, the IRA, the Pan-Nationalist Front and all Ulster's enemies and Ulster's 'Achilles heel in this time of trial' (DUP, Press Release, 24 March 1997). Such positioning and arguments have long been typical of the DUP. During the early 1970s, in the face of radical and rapid social and political change, Northern Irish society split along communal lines. In part, the response of the DUP actively promoted themselves as the bearers of unionism's traditional values. Since then, their major political articulation has always been that the union is increasingly under threat, and that they are its true and most able defenders.

There have been other important fissures within unionist politics. Recent times have seen the loyalist paramilitaries also attempt to construct a more overtly politicised role, initially to the IRA's cease-fire, and later to the formal peace process. The increasing prominence of the UDP and the PUP has brought into sharp relief the relationship between the DUP and much of the Protestant working class. While the DUP have, in the past, succeeded in articulating and coordinating the concerns of working-class loyalism, certain key groups have looked elsewhere for outlets to their political expression. One example of this is the paramilitaries; another, those who had found political expression at the level of community politics. A clear message coming from such groups, for many years, has been discontent with the political representatives of unionism, including both the UUP and the DUP. Following the cessation of violence in 1994, it appeared that key sections of the Protestant working class were no longer content to recognise the DUP as their sole legitimate representatives. These tensions have been seen in a series of statements made by Ian Paisley, in which he was unequivocally hostile to the political leadership both of the PUP and UDP (cf. *Belfast Telegraph*, 14 and 18 October 1994).

The conflict between these sections of unionism was also clearly seen at the time of the Forum election in a statement issued by Gary McMichael, of the UDP when, in a clear reference to both the DUP and UUP, he claimed that one of the major objectives of the UDP was to represent those who had been without a voice for the past 25 years (*The Irish Times*, 18 May 1996). The ideological and pragmatic conflicts between those political groupings representing the paramilitaries, and the DUP, have continued throughout the period of the peace process. Ian Paisley, for example, has referred to both the PUP and UDP as 'marionettes' and 'puppets' of the Northern Ireland Office, themselves falling directly in step with Westminster's lead. As one leading figure in the DUP recently put it, they:

> have rolled over, stuck their legs in the air and their bellies up ... they are puppets, because they are getting their strings pulled.
>
> (*The Irish Times*, 1 December 1997)

In trying to dismiss these groups it is Paisley and the DUP who are still seeking to project themselves as the authoritative bulwark of the union. Indeed, this position was at the heart of the DUP's campaign for the 1996 Forum election, when they campaigned under the slogan 'the Unionist team you can trust'. Throughout the campaign they offered a 'covenant with the Ulster people' (*UDUP, Election Communication*, 1996), assuring voters that, in any talks, 'the DUP will negotiate only within the parameters of the UK' and 'will take only to constitutional politicians and parties' (*UDUP, Election Communication*, 1996).

In response the UDP and the PUP have been highly critical of the 'traditional' unionist political leadership. The PUP in particular have remained openly antagonistic to the leadership of Ian Paisley, whom they claimed was destroying any unified unionist response, and was increasingly disconnected from the response of 'ordinary people' to the peace process. There was also an overt articulation of the belief that the DUP were unrealistic in the way they have sought to direct unionist politics, and the DUP decision to exclude themselves from any meaningful input into the peace process. Both the PUP and the UDP have continued to claim that it is they that best reflect the views expressed by the broader loyalist community, and best seek to highlight working-class opinion and social conditions. Throughout the contemporary phase it is the PUP that has expressed this position in its most consistent, coherent and accessible form.

(RE)CONSTRUCTING UNIONIST IDENTITY AND POLITICS

So can these different trends within loyalism be seen in political terms? As a political ideology unionism as a social movement often manifests itself around an expression of the claim for a distinct British identity on the islands of Ireland. Unionism constructs this Britishness in ideological terms which are multi-discursive, mobilising across a wide range of social categories.

The unionist bloc through the Stormont government structured Northern Irish society in a particular social and economic direction. This process itself was underpinned by a specific alliance of class forces, by which certain political groupings dominated certain areas of political discourse. This response has again been seen in recent times, as in, for example, the unionist reactions to the Anglo-Irish Agreement, the Downing Street Declaration and the peace process. Unionists have constantly referred to such macro-political innovations as being the first step to a united Ireland, thus arousing many of the fears held by the different factions of unionism, from those who place greatest emphasis on the British link to those who regard the British with deep suspicion.

The extent of unionist fears and insecurities can be seen in editions of the *Orange Standard*, in which it is claimed that, during the past quarter of a century, Protestants had consistently been driven from large areas of Northern Ireland. Other recent issues (May 1996, June 1996, September 1996, December 1997, January 1998) have spoken of 'de-Protestantisation' and 'ethnic cleansing', of Irish Protestants both historically and in the contemporary period. For them the analysis of events is straightforward, ethnic cleansing is highly effective for republicans, in that 'it removed Protestants from large tracts of territory in the Province and enabled the IRA to operate even more effectively' (*Orange Standard*, December 1997/January 1998: 12). For many unionists the response should be equally direct; Ulster Protestants and unionists have made it clear that they will not be surrendering any more of their territory to the enemies of Ulster (*Orange Standard*, June 1996: 1). It is in the context of such ideas that the political response of loyalism must be understood. The restatement and reorganisation of traditional loyalism, manifest around the DUP, is central to the figure of Ian Paisley. In doing this, Paisley and the DUP are seeking to try to reassume their central hegemonic position within loyalism. Many unionists and loyalists hence perceive their Britishness, their core identity, as increasingly being threatened by contemporary events.

Given the prominence of this position within unionism, does it make sense to speak of a 'new loyalism'? Certainly some of the strongest arguments promoting a cultural pluralism and progressive citizens' rights have, in recent times, come from representatives of the UDP and PUP. Within the narrow confines of the formal politics of the contemporary peace process, both are agreed on the idea of a Northern Ireland Assembly. The PUP seek an administrative assembly, with power sharing, while the UDP endeavour to bring about a more powerful institution with 'proportionality' for elected representatives, while both are equally committed to a Bill of Rights. Clearly, there may be some room for political movement here. A more important question, however, is whether the UDP and PUP mark any ideological change in loyalism.

For many loyalists, however, their contemporary experiences also need to be seen in the context of dramatic deindustrialisation, economic decline, political disarticulation and ideological disintegration. The peace process has opened up some room for debate around such issues within loyalist working-class communities. As I have argued elsewhere, however (McAuley, 1991b, 1994a, 1996b, 1997a,b) that does not necessarily mean that groups such as the PUP or UDP have superseded sectarianism or replaced it. Rather their position should be seen in the context of negotiating the ideological terms within which contemporary unionism seeks to re-express and redefine ideas of a British identity. Certain political groupings within unionism still dom-inate, or at the very least seek to dominate, particular areas of political life and political discourse. This can be seen in the lexicon of the DUP's response and their belief that what is currently under way is a negotiation on the very future of Ulster (UDUP, n.d., c: 1). They also claimed full vindica-tion of their analysis of recent events, including, as they put it, the 'Downing Street Declaration sell-out', the 'treacherous Framework Document' and the 'bogus IRA cease-fire'. In fact the DUP largely campaigned on a mandate not to take part in any negotiations. They indicated that they would not sit down with Sinn Fein, even if the IRA cease-fire was restored. As part of the manifesto for the Forum election in 1996 stated, there would be no negotia-tion, 'on the basis of the Downing Street Declaration and the Framework Documents' (UDUP, *Election Communication*, 1996).

The DUP's manifesto further sought to ensure Northern Ireland's constitu-tional position within the UK be accepted without any ambiguity. Underpinning this was the clearly articulated belief that the union is not safe under the terms brought about by the closer workings of the British and Irish governments. Much recent DUP thinking has sought to challenge Dublin's 'illegal claim over Ulster', and strongly argued that there can be no role for Dublin in Ulster's affairs. Elsewhere the DUP have promoted the establish-ment of democratic and accountable structures of government for Ulster, and demanded that IRA/Sinn Fein be made to dismantle its terrorist machine. These terms are applied to a wide range of opponents, from the political leadership of the USA to members of loyalist paramilitary groupings; from the Irish government to the Ulster Unionist Party, and from the international media to the Social Democratic and Labour Party (SDLP). The strength of this position can be seen in the broader loyalist response to the peace process.

(RE)'FRAMING' UNIONISM

Useful in understanding unionism is the concept developed by several social movement theorists of 'framing' (Gamson, 1992; Snow and Benford, 1992;

McAdam and Rucht, 1993; Tarrow, 1994: 118–34; Johnston, 1995; Garner, 1996: 16–17, 56–61). This is used to explain the ways in which movements organise their discourses and align them with the central values and ideas that they believe to be prevalent in society. The major differences in representations are concentrated into a variety of symbols, icons and slogans. The discourses and symbolism that legitimise unionism as a defence of identity, and as security against external and internal threat, are understood and broadly accepted by many unionists, across all social and economic groupings. One response, in the contemporary period, has simply been to try to return unionism to rudiments. In particular this can be seen in the discourses of those who were extremely sceptical of the entire peace process in the first place, and who saw it, at best, as a dilution of the unionist position and, at worst, as another victory for republicanism.

There are several further discourses around which traditional unionism has restructured. Central are particular constructs of the concepts of 'democracy', the 'democratic process' and the refusal to capitulate to 'terrorism'. As Peter Robinson of the DUP put it:

> Government policy has one common and consistent purpose – to provide a smooth and gradual transition towards a united Ireland. The motivation is as conspicuous as the intention. IRA terrorism – and in particular IRA terrorism on the British mainland – has brought them to this point.
>
> (DUP, Press Release, 27 October 1997)

Such sentiments are reflected throughout other sections of unionism. Take, for example, this statement from Ken Maginnis following a meeting between John Hume with Gerry Adams and the IRA leadership:

> The reiteration of the 'IRA's commitments to its republican objectives', is not a simple restatement of aspirations but an ominous threat that violence will continue so long as it fails to achieve its objectives. With the support of only 4.8% of the total electorate the IRA is not going to achieve its objective of a United Ireland; it knows that and, with its ethos of violence, it is unlikely that it will act in the best interests of society in Northern Ireland.
>
> (UUP, News Release, 29 February 1996)

Further consequences for unionism have been increasing indications that the 'Unionist middle classes have begun to emerge from their political and ideological slumber' (Coulter, 1997: 138–9). One manifestation of this has been the electoral success of Robert McCartney as an independent United Kingdom Unionist. For Coulter this indicates that McCartney has, among others, harnessed 'the energies of that body of Unionist professionals dismayed at the substance and form of contemporary Unionism'.

At one level there is evidence to support Coulter's argument. McCartney has engaged in some important fault-finding exercises from within unionism. Since the formation of the Northern Irish state, for example, he argues that the Unionist Party has relied on two main factors: an inbuilt unionist majority and the manipulation of pro-union paranoia about Northern Ireland's place within the United Kingdom. This constitutional anxiety was compensated for by an extreme sectarian loyalism. It is this McCartney challenges, arguing that if the benefits of the union are to be made clear to all, and the union is to be preserved, then there must be dramatic changes in the formation of Northern Irish society. At another level, however, McCartney has readily aligned with the values of traditional unionism and the view that the peace process is part of a broad conspiracy against the union. From this perspective a central task of the British government has been to promote and persuade the pro-union majority that the IRA cease-fire is a fair exchange for the sacrifice of its British identity (*News Letter*, 23 February 1995). For McCartney the strategy for a political settlement proposed in the Framework Document long pre-dates the cease-fires. The suspension of violence was, however, necessary as a precondition for the 'selling' of it to the unionist population. The very best unionism can hope for, within the parameters of an agreed peace process, is some stay of execution for the union. McCartney too thinks that the traditional unionist leadership has failed, and that without the decisive leadership, which unionism has failed to give, the current constitutional arrangements will go by default.

Increasingly, the UKU have politically synthesised with the DUP, who have talked in terms of continued 'Unionist alienation'. The DUP have also argued that the British Government has 'psychologically abandoned Northern Ireland', and that they planned to 'physically disengage as soon as circumstances permit a total withdrawal' (*The New Protestant Telegraph*, June 1995). Hence, both the DUP and the UKU have projected the peace process as part of the final conflict in the battle for Ulster. They have responded politically by restating the most basic of unionist principles.

The importance for the future of unionism of an increasing equilibrium between the DUP and UKU positions should not be underestimated, particularly as they draw on dramatically different constituencies and social strata for their support. At the heart of McCartney's project remains the desire to project unionism as a rational political choice, in the interests of the majority of Northern Ireland's citizens. This form of unionism represents itself as standing against a perceived Irish irredentism with a resolute endorsement of the union's economic and social benefits. The UKU see sectarianism as an atavistic ideology, endorsing their conception of the union as something that should be based upon the values of pluralism, multi-culturalism and equal citizenship. In recent writings, McCartney (n.d., a, b) has outlined what he sees as the dynamic behind the peace process. The British and Irish governments, will with the assistance of the Irish-American lobby:

seek by a massive propaganda campaign to persuade the pro-Union people that the benefits of a terrorist controlled ceasefire are a fair price to pay for the sacrifice of the Union and their British identity.

(n.d., b: 2)

As such these views draw on, and overlap with, other areas of contemporary unionist discourse, such as that promoted by unionist intellectuals (cf. Aughey, 1994, 1995; Aughey *et al.*, 1995; Cardogan Group, 1992, 1994, 1995, 1996; Foster, 1995; Nesbitt, 1995; Porter, 1996; Roche and Birnie, n.d., 1996). The active defence and promotion of the link between Northern Ireland and Great Britain by such a grouping is a reasonably recent phenomenon. Central to their argument is the view that unionists themselves have been extremely poor ambassadors for their own cause. It is not the message, but the messengers, that are primarily to blame.

As key task for this grouping is to counter the main arguments forwarded by the Republican Movement (Foster, 1995). Their 'dogma', that the union of Northern Ireland with Great Britain is merely a negotiable political arrangement, has become an accepted wisdom and the driving force behind the peace process. For such unionists this reading of 'republican history' has become deeply rooted in the understandings and strategies of all the major British political parties, the administration of the United States of America and much of the world's public opinion. Such an analysis for them represents a clear fabrication. Rather the union is fundamental, resting as it does on the most desirable expression of the political, social and cultural realities of the Irish situation.

This approach can also be clearly seen in other works, such as those of Dennis Kennedy, Patrick Roche and Esmond Birnie. For example, Roche and Birnie have argued that the 'betrayal of Ulster' has largely come about because of the failure of unionists to 'undermine the intellectual creditability of Irish nationalism' (1996: 14). For Roche and Birnie (n.d., 1996) there are fundamental flaws in the Irish nationalist position. Irish nationalist ideology is 'the politics of the absurd', driven by the defective core belief that there is a single nation on the island of Ireland. A central task for these writers is to reveal the weakness of the Irish nationalist position. For Roche and Birnie there is no sustainable objective claim to support Irish nationalism. Indeed, for them, Irish nationalism has been reduced merely to some form of geographical determinism, whereby 'location of birth determines national identity'. Hence, they further conclude that Irish nationalism is 'entirely without validity' (1996: 15).

Such views would, no doubt, find favour with Dennis Kennedy, another member of the Cardogan Group, He has argued (*The Irish Times*, 14 November 1997) that the definition of Irish nationalism and identity that has developed in the 20th century has bonded together the nation and State. This makes talk of 'national allegiance' as meaning anything other than allegiance to a 32-county Irish Republic almost impossible. Central for Kennedy is the dominance of the idea of the unfinished political business of the unification of Ireland. This perspective he believes has been directly reflected in the closer workings of the British and Irish governments and in the subsequent publication of the Anglo-Irish Agreement, the Framework Documents and the Downing Street Declaration, especially by their references to the possibility of Irish unification and their undertakings to facilitate it in certain circumstances. At the heart of Kennedy's analysis, as with most unionist intellectuals, is the belief that those in the northeast of Ireland remain a distinct community, differing from the people of the rest of the island, in core matters such as religion; place of origin; cultural, social and national identity. What binds together such writers is an inherent belief of the superiority of the union as a political, social, economic, perhaps even moral, arrangement for those living in that part of Ireland.

UNIONISM AS A CONTEMPORARY SOCIAL MOVEMENT

If the reading of the peace process suggested above is correct, then the period beginning with the 1994 cease-fires has revealed several fractures within unionism. This, in part at least, reflects the experience of differing sections of loyalist society that have previously been excluded from the public arena and policy-making in Northern Ireland. One such grouping is women from a unionist background. Traditionally, the social and political conservatism of mainstream unionism has often made it difficult, if not impossible, for many women to engage in 'the political'. Whilst recognising that this grouping is a highly diverse set of individuals, a common experience is that they have been excluded from any visible participation in politics (McAuley, 1994a; NIWC, 1996; Democratic Dialogue, 1997; Sales, 1997).

There is recent evidence that women from loyalist backgrounds and communities have increasingly created the opportunity to discuss their own identity and social relations in a more meaningful way. This seemed particularly the case in the period following the initial paramilitary cease-fires. It would be wrong, however, to suggest that all women from these backgrounds desire peace on any terms, or are politically progressive in their outlook. Indeed, Morgan (1995) and Morgan and Fraser (1995) have effectively demonstrated that this is far from the case. In periods of absence of overt paramilitary violence, however, the increasing debate within the broad loyalist community has accommodated those who traditionally have been most excluded. The fear must remain, however, that if there is a return to political violence then such groupings will again be forced to the margins.

Indeed, throughout the contemporary period, the contest for the 'soul of loyalism' has intensified. Following the Forum elections, with the UDP and

PUP taking around 10 per cent of the unionist vote, the struggle for control of the political leadership of loyalism is apparent. The current strength and appeal of DUP discourse and their social construction of unionism should not, however, be underestimated. Many writers (cf. Anderson, 1991; Billig, 1995; Eriksen, 1993; Gilroy, 1987; S. Hall, 1985, 1993; Jackson and Penrose, 1993; Said, 1980, 1985, 1990, 1997; Sarup, 1996) have increasingly made manifest the importance of the social construction of 'nationhood' and the relationships between discourse and power in constructing such identities. All have provided ample evidence to suggest that language is never neutral, but rather expressions of broader power relations.

The contemporary period has seen a reinvestigation of the notion of British identity from within core sections of loyalism and particularly the Protestant working class. Much of the debate organised by community activists in loyalist districts has been well documented (cf. Belfast Community Economic Conference, 1995; M. Hall, 1994b, 1995, 1996, 1997; Shankill Think Tank, 1995). It involves the changing form of Protestant and unionist culture and politics, and the possible shape of a restructured union- ism in the next century. To a great extent it has been structured by ex- prisoners, local councillors and community activists, some of whom were members of the paramilitaries and/or the Ulster Democratic and Progressive Unionist Parties. What is also clear, however, is a level of engagement by those not involved in such organisations. Overall it indicated, certainly in the period after the initial cease-fires, a degree of self-criticism and internal reflection unusual for unionism.

This has been reflected in the political positioning of the UDP and the PUP in particular. In their Forum election material, for example, both the UDP and the PUP sought to put distance between themselves and the repre- sentatives of traditional unionism. The PUP claimed, for example, that 'because of political instability in Northern Ireland' the real issues had 'gone by the board'. Further, mainstream unionist politicians have consistently 'failed to consult and therefore misrepresented the views of the unionist people especially in working class areas' (PUP, *Election Communication*, 1996). Thus, under the political standard of a 'new beginning' for Northern Ireland, the party restated their commitment to Northern Ireland's position as an integral part of the United Kingdom, but defended the right of any group to seek constitutional change by democratic, legitimate and peaceful means. Elsewhere they recognise what they call the rights and aspirations of all law-abiding citizens, 'regardless of religious, cultural, national or political inclinations' (PUP, *Election Communication*, 1996).

Unlike the DUP, both the PUP and UDP have specifically sought to address the issues of those who have been involved in political violence, calling for an amnesty, the phased release of all political prisoners, and a comprehensive social reintegration programme for returning prisoners to the community. The Ulster Democratic Party Forum election campaign, for example, promised effective leadership which 'others' have denied the electorate. Under the slogan 'Look to the Future', Gary McMichael, the party leader, said the election was designed to lead to meaningful negotiations, and the party would:

> argue a political settlement which puts the people back into the driving seat. We will pursue an accountable democratic framework of government for Northern Ireland, a settlement in which the rights of the people are enshrined in their own constitution. Over the past 25 years loyalists have resisted all attempts by those who sought to force political change against the will of the people. We will not now allow them to do so by political coercion.
>
> (*The Irish Times*, 26 May 1996)

THE POLITICS OF THE 'SLIPPERY SLOPE'

The strength of the DUP's appeal, in contrast, rests upon a discourse specifically constructed around the peace process involving 'a final conflict for Ulster', which runs counter to the will of the democratic majority. Crucial is the belief that this process involves a pan-nationalist set agenda, and is a 'first step to Dublin Rule'. All of these clearly have resonance with large sections of unionism. The DUP effectively positions its members within loyalist culture and imposes specific meanings onto contemporary political events. Central to all of this is an idea that entering into negotiations is embarking upon a journey that leads to the 'slippery slope' and a spiral towards an all-Ireland.

The broad thrust of these perspectives can be seen in many recent statements by DUP representatives. The Rev. William McCrea, for example, recently challenged Ulster Unionist MPs to unite with the DUP against the talks process, accusing the 'defeated soldiers' of the UUP of surrendering to an entirely republican-driven process. For McCrea (and many others in the DUP), the major designation of British government policy is to introduce a united Ireland by steady graduation. As he put it:

> Step by step, unionists are being conditioned to become accustomed to Irishness rather than Britishness to prepare them for the government's intended destination. Anything and everything British must be removed from the province's daily life – the national anthem, the Union Jack, the Queen's portrait, Orange culture and unionist traditions become targets for extinction and demonisation. Wholesome unionist values taught by our

forefathers for generations are rendered sectarian, right-wing, old-fashioned, hardline and backward.

(*The Irish Times*, 1 December 1997)

There is evidence that wider unionist support is falling in line with the DUP position. In a poll organised by the leading unionist newspaper, the *News Letter*, on 27 October 1997,[2] respondents were asked to vote for the party leader they believed had the right strategy regarding contemporary negotiations. The responses were enlightening, with Ian Paisley (DUP), winning 47 per cent of the total vote; David Trimble (UUP), with 24 per cent; Robert McCartney (UKU), with 16 per cent; David Ervine (PUP), winning 5 per cent, and Gary McMichael (UDP) 3 per cent. These findings were mirrored in another survey organised by BBC Northern Ireland and presented in their 'Hearts and Minds' programme (*Belfast Telegraph*, 10 September 1997; *The Irish Times*, 11 September 1997). This involved 1561 respondents, and results showed a clear split within unionism. Just over half of the unionists who replied wanted their leaders to take part in face-to-face talks with Sinn Fein, with just under 50 per cent against such action. Overall, the UUP received 23 per cent of the poll, the DUP 16 per cent and the Social Democratic and Labour Party 22 per cent. Sinn Fein support stood at 15 per cent, the Alliance Party 11 per cent, the PUP 4 per cent and the UDP 3 per cent.

Following the publication of these results the DUP deputy leader, Mr Peter Robinson, claimed that the combined support of the DUP and the UK Unionists, standing at 63 per cent, showed that both parties now had 'the moral authority to speak on behalf of Unionism'. Further he argued, that the: 'process does not enjoy the support of the Unionist community, and it is clear that those within it no longer have the support of the Unionist people' (*The Irish Times*, 28 October 1997). Such events merely reinforce the frame set by the DUP. Thus the Party Leader, the Rev. Ian Paisley, has claimed that Northern Ireland is 'facing its gravest crisis' and that no unionist should be holding negotiations with the Government or the SDLP, let alone with Sinn Fein. As he put it, the 'Union is not negotiable, it is illegal to seek to negotiate it' (*The Irish Times*, 1 December 1997).

UNIONISM AND THE PEACE PROCESS

Unionism has responded to the peace process in a convoluted and sometimes contradictory fashion. For some this has simply led to a restating of unionist first principles, politically, intellectually and pragmatically. Politically there has been an attempt by key sections of unionism to reconstruct its core hegemony around leadership figures such as Ian Paisley and

Robert McCartney. Amongst those who desire to restate this traditional agenda, however, it is the DUP who have remained in the vanguard. Central to the continuing self-image, symbolism, iconography and political discourse of the DUP remains the claim that it is only they who will take all the actions necessary to defend Ulster.

New loyalism, as presented by the loyalist paramilitaries, offers the possibility of an alternative set of values and structure being created within unionism. For some this involves a less sectarian, more community-based expression of culture and pluralist politics within a unionist framework. However, many unionists still perceive the peace process as something deliberately designed and manufactured to undermine their 'British' identity and constitutional status. This position maintains the strength to reabsorb alternative arguments into the traditional unionist hegemony. This can be seen in the following statement issued by UDA/UFF prisoners in 1996 which indicated that, although not under the direct political control of the DUP, many had begun to accept the essential parameters of their analysis:

> Daily we have had to witness examples of erosion of our political and cultural identity from a united pan-nationalist front (Sinn Fein, SDLP and the Irish government) with their attitudes towards the banning of Orange Order parades and the boycotting of Protestant businesses.
>
> (*The Irish Times*, 3 October 1996)

CONCLUSION

Much of the dominant discourse within unionism suggests a restructuring of political hegemony around the DUP as a central voice of unionist opposition to the peace process. It is the ideology of the DUP that, for many, best expresses the continuities between past and existing unionist cultures. This can be thought of as that form of frame alignment by which the DUP assign a set of meanings to contemporary events that fit most directly with the meanings and discourse many unionists already hold. The emergence in party politics of the PUP and the UDP is part of a social process that represents a differing but still distinctive ideological force within the unionist political culture. Both the UDP and PUP have sought to some extent to realign the frame of unionism. These groupings have tried to link their frames, and their specific assignments of meaning, to existing frames, perhaps even at times to suggest a transforming frame within unionism. Whether or not new loyalism can continue to effectively compete with the DUP's ideological position remains central to the future shape and political direction of unionism.

NOTES

1.   What is involved in the 'peace process' is clearly a matter for much debate. At
      its minimum it can be thought of as that sequence of events which began with
      the talks between Gerry Adams, the Sinn Fein president, and John Hume, the
      leader of the SDLP, which resulted in a joint statement in April 1993. This was
      followed by the presentation of joint proposals to the Irish government.
      Following this, and partly in response to increasing political violence, the two
      governments sought to develop their own initiatives. In December 1993, and
      with the support of all the major political parties in the UK and Irish Republic,
      the two governments issued a joint declaration of principles, which was to
      become known as the 'Downing Street Declaration'. On 22 February 1995 the
      two governments published new proposals under the title of *Frameworks for
      the Future*. Since then, Northern Ireland has held elections to a new Forum in
      June 1996 and begun 'multi-party' talks, which have been boycotted by the
      Democratic Unionist Party and the United Kingdom Unionist Party. The publi-
      cation of the 'heads of agreement' document in January 1998 sought to clarify
      the position of the British and Irish governments, although both still regard the
      1995 Framework Documents as the basis for future negotiations. For detailed
      accounts of these events see Gilligan and Tonge (1997); Maille and McKittrick
      (1996); McKittrick (1994, 1996); Rowan (1995).
2.   This was a 'phone-in' telephone poll in which more than 13 000 readers took
      part. Because of this methodology the results must be treated with some scepti-
      cism. That said, it gives a reasonable indication of some of the main dynamics
      within contemporary Unionist politics.

REFERENCES

Anderson, B. (1991), *Imagined Communities* (London: Verso).
Aughey, A. (1994), 'Irish Kulturlampf', *Ulster Review*, no. 15 (October).
Aughey, A. (1995), 'The End of History, the End of the Union', in *Selling Unionism
    Home and Away* (Belfast: Ulster Young Unionist Council).
Aughey, A., Burnside, D., Harris, E., Adams, G. and Donaldson, J. (1995), *Selling
    Unionism: Home and Away* (Belfast: Ulster Review Publications).
Belfast Community Economic Conference (1995), *Conference Proceedings*, Island
    Pamphlets, 12 (Island Publications).
Bew, P., Gibbon, P. and Patterson, H. (1995), *Northern Ireland, 1921–1996: Political
    Forces and Social Classes* (London: Serif).
Billig, M. (1995), 'Rhetorical Psychology, Ideological Thinking, and Imagining
    Nationhood', in H. Johnston and B. Klandermas (eds), *Social Movements and
    Culture* (London: UCL Press).
Cardogan Group (1992), *Northern Limits, the Boundaries of the Attainable in Northern
    Ireland Politics* (Belfast).
Cardogan Group (1994), *Blurred Vision, Joint Authority and the Northern Ireland
    Problem* (Belfast).
Cardogan Group (1995), *Lost Accord: The 1995 Frameworks and the Search for a
    Settlement in Northern Ireland* (Belfast).
Cardogan Group (1996), *Square Circles, Round Tables and the Path to Peace in
    Northern Ireland* (Belfast).

Carroll, L. (1946), *Alice in Wonderland and Through the Looking Glass* (Kingsport, TN: Grosset & Dunlap).

Clayton, P. (1996), *Enemies and Passing Friends* (London: Pluto).

Coulter, C. (1994), 'Class, Ethnicity and Political Identity in Northern Ireland', *Irish Journal of Sociology*, 4.

Coulter, C. (1997), 'The Culture of Contentment: the Political Beliefs and Practice of the Unionist Middle Classes', in P. Shirlow and M. McGovern (eds), *Who Are the People?* (London: Pluto).

Democratic Dialogue (1997), *Report Number 4: Power, Politics, Positionings: Women in Northern Ireland* (Belfast: Democratic Dialogue).

English, R. and Walker, G. (1996), *Unionism in Modern Ireland* (Dublin: Gill & Macmillan).

Eriksen, T. H. (1993), *Ethnicity and Nationalism: Anthropological Perspectives* (London: Pluto).

Foster, J. W. (ed.) (1995), *The Idea of the Union: Statements and Critiques in Support of the Union of Great Britain and Northern Ireland* (Canada: Belcouver Press).

Gamson, W. (1992), 'The Social Psychology of Collective Action', in A. Morris and C. McClurg (eds), *Frontiers in Social Movement Theory* (New Haven, CT: Yale University Press).

Garner, R. (1996), *Contemporary Movements and Ideologies* (New York: McGraw-Hill).

Gellner, E. (1993), *Nations and Nationalism* (Oxford: Blackwell).

Gillespie, N., Lovett, T. and Garner, W. (1992), *Youth Work and Working Class Youth Culture: Rules and Resistance in West Belfast* (Milton Keynes: Open University Press).

Gilligan, C. and Tonge, J. (eds)(1997), *Peace and War? Understanding the Peace Process in Ireland* (Aldershot: Ashgate).

Gilroy, P. (1987), *There Ain't No Black in the Union Jack* (London: Hutchinson).

Hall, M. (1986), *Ulster – The Hidden History* (Belfast: Pretani Press).

Hall, M. (1994a), *The Cruthin Controversy* (Belfast: Island Pamphlets).

Hall, M. (1994b), *Ulster's Protestant Working Class: A Community Exploration* (Belfast: Island Pamphlets).

Hall, M. (1995), *Beyond the Fife and Drum* (Belfast: Island Pamphlets).

Hall, M. (1996), 'Ulster's Protestant Working Class: A Community Exploration', *Journal of Prisoners on Prisons*, 7(2).

Hall, M. (1997), *The Death of the 'Peace Process'? A Survey of Community Perceptions* (Belfast: Island Pamphlets).

Hall, S. (1985), 'Signification, Ideology and Representation: Althusser and the Post-Structuralist Debates', *Critical Studies in Mass Communication*, 2, 91–114.

Hall, S. (1990), 'Cultural Identity and the Diaspora', in J. Rutherford (ed.), *Identity* (London: Lawrence & Wishart).

Hall, S. (1993), 'Culture, Community, Nation', *Cultural Studies*, 7, 349–63.

Hall, S. (1996), 'Introduction: Who Needs "Identity"?' in S. Hall and P. duGay (eds), *Questions of Cultural Identity* (London: Sage).

Hobsbawm, E. and Ranger, T. (eds) (1983), *The Invention of Tradition* (Cambridge: Cambridge University Press).

Jackson, P. and Penrose, J. (eds) (1993), *Constructions of Race, Place and Nation* (London: UCL Press).

Jarman, N. (1997), *Material Conflicts: Parades and Visual Displays in Northern Ireland* (Oxford: Berg).

Johnston, H. (1995), 'A Methodology for Frame Analysis: From Discourse to Cognitive Schemata', in H. Johnston and B. Klandermas (eds), *Social Movements and Culture* (London: UCL Press).

McAdam, D. and Rucht, D. (1993), 'The Cross-National Diffusion of Movement Ideas', *Annals of the American Academy of Political and Social Sciences*, 528, 56–74.

McAuley, J. W. (1991a), 'Cuchulainn and an RPG-7: The Ideology and Politics of the UDA', in E. Hughes (ed.), *Culture and Politics in Northern Ireland* (Milton Keynes: Open University Press).

McAuley, J. W. (1991b), 'The Protestant Working Class and the State in Northern Ireland since 1930: a Problematic Relationship', in S. Hutton and P. Stewart (eds), *Ireland's Histories* (London: Routledge).

McAuley, J. W. (1994a), *The Politics of Identity: A Loyalist Community in Belfast* (Aldershot: Avebury).

McAuley, J. W. (1994b), 'Loyalists and their Cease-fire', *Parliamentary Brief*, 3(1).

McAuley, J. W. (1995), '"Not a Game of Cowboys and Indians" – the Ulster Defence Association in the 1990s', in A. O'Day (ed.), *Terrorism's Laboratory: The Case of Northern Ireland* (Aldershot: Dartmouth).

McAuley, J. W. (1996a), 'From Loyal Soldiers to Political Spokespersons: a Political History of a Loyalist Paramilitary Group in Northern Ireland', *Études Irlandaises*, 21, 1.

McAuley, J. W. (1996b), '(Re)Constructing Ulster Loyalism: Political Responses to the Peace Process', *Irish Journal of Sociology*, 6, 127–53.

McAuley, J. W. (1997a), 'Flying the One-Winged Bird: Ulster Unionism and the Peace Process', in P. Shirlow and M. McGovern (eds), *Who Are the People?* (London: Pluto).

McAuley, J. W. (1997b), 'Divided Loyalists, Divided Loyalties: Conflict and Continuities in Contemporary Unionist Ideology', in C. Gilligan and J. Tonge (eds), *Peace or War?* (1997).

McAuley, J. W. (1997c), 'The Ulster Loyalist Political Parties: Towards a New Respectability?', in P. Joannon (ed.), *Le Processus De Paix En Irlande Du Nord, Études Irlandaises*, 22, 2.

McAuley, J. W. and McCormick, P. J. (1989), 'The Protestant Working Class and the State in Northern Ireland: The Loosening Bond', *Social Studies: An Irish Journal of Sociology*, 10, 1(2), 32–44.

McAuley, J. W. and McCormick, P. J. (1990), 'Hounds of Ulster and the Re-writing of Irish History', *Études Irlandaises*, 15, 2.

McCartney, R. (n.d., a), *The McCartney Report on Consent* (Belfast).

McCartney, R. (n.d., b), *The McCartney Report on the Framework Documents* (Belfast).

McGarry, J. and O'Leary, B. (1995), *Explaining Northern Ireland* (Oxford: Blackwell).

McKittrick, D. (1994), *Endgame: the Search for Peace in Northern Ireland* (Belfast: Blackstaff Press).

McKittrick, D. (1996), *The Nervous Peace* (Belfast: Blackstaff Press).

Mallie, E. and McKittrick, D. (1996), *The Fight for Peace: The Secret Story Behind the Irish Peace Process* (London: Heinemann).

Morgan, V. (1995), 'Peacemakers? Peacekeepers? – Women in Northern Ireland 1969–1995', Professional Lecture, given at the University of Ulster, 25 October.

Morgan, V. and Fraser, G. (1995), 'Women and the Northern Ireland Conflict: Experiences and Responses', in S. Dunn (ed.), *Facets of the Conflict in Northern Ireland* (Basingstoke: Macmillan).

Nesbitt, D. (1995), *Unionism Restated: An Analysis of the Ulster Unionist Party's 'Statement of Aims'* (Belfast: Ulster Unionist Information Institute).

Northern Ireland Women's Coalition (1996), *Election Communication* (Forum Election).

O'Neil, C. (1971), 'The Social Function of Physical Violence in an Irish Urban Area', *Economic and Social Review*, 2, 481–93.

Paisley, I. R. K. (1997), 'DUP Rebuff Trimble Remarks', DUP Press Statement, 24 March.

Porter, N. (1996), *Rethinking Unionism: An Alternative Vision for Ireland* (Dundonald: Blackstaff Press).

Progressive Unionist Party (n.d.), *War or Peace: Conflict or Conference*, Policy Document of the Progressive Unionist Party, n.p.

Progressive Unionist Party (1996a), *Manifesto for the Forum Election* (Belfast: PUP).

Progressive Unionist Party (1996b), 'Submission to the Northern Ireland Office by the Progressive Unionist Party on the Question of Political Prisoners and Prisons', *Journal of Prisoners on Prisons*, 7(2), 11–24.

Progressive Unionist Party (n.d.), 'Support the Progressive Unionists', Election Communication (1996 Forum Election).

Robb, J. (1992), 'A Divided Community: the Effects of Cultural Divisions', in J. Lundy and A. Mac Póilin (eds), *Styles of Belonging: The Cultural Identities of Ulster* (Belfast: Lagan Press).

Robinson, P. (1985), *Ulster in Peril, an Exposure of the Dublin Summit* (Belfast: DUP).

Robinson, P. (1995), *The Union Under Fire: United Ireland Framework Revealed* (Belfast: published by the author).

Robinson, P. (1996), 'A Separate Identity: Understanding Northern Ireland – a Part of the United Kingdom' (Belfast: DUP Publicity Department).

Robinson, P. (1997), 'Speech to United Unionist Rally', DUP Press Release, 27 October.

Roche, P. J. and Birnie, J. E. (n.d.) 'An Economics Lesson for Irish Nationalists and Republicans' (Belfast: Ulster Unionist Information Institute).

Roche, P. J. and Birnie, J. E. (1996), 'Irish Nationalism – Politics of the Absurd', *Ulster Review*, Summer, No. 20.

Roman, B. (1995), *Behind the Lines: The Story of the IRA and Loyalist Ceasefires* (Belfast: Blackstaff Press).

Ruane, J. and Todd, J. (1996) *The Dynamics of Conflict in Northern Ireland: Power, Conflict and Emancipation* (Cambridge: Cambridge University Press).

Said, E. W. (1980), *The Question of Palestine* (New York: Vintage Books).

Said, E. W. (1985), *Orientalism* (Harmondsworth: Penguin).

Said, E. W. (1990), 'Narrative Geography and Interpretation', *New Left Review*, 180, 81–100.

Said, E. W. (1997), *Covering Islam* (London: Vintage Books).

Sales, R. (1997), *Women Divided: Gender, Religion and Politics in Northern Ireland* (London: Routledge).

Sarup, M. (1996), *Identity, Culture and the Postmodern World* (Edinburgh: Edinburgh University Press).

Shankill Think Tank (1995) *A New Beginning*, Island Pamphlets (13) (Newtownabbey: Island Publications).

Shirlow, P. and McGovern, M. (eds) (1997) *Who are the People? Unionism, Protestantism and Loyalism in Northern Ireland* (London: Pluto).

Snow, D. A. and Benford, R. D. (1992), 'Master Frames and Cycles of Protest', in A. D. Morris and C. McClurg Mueller (eds), *Frontiers in Social Movement Theory* (New Haven, Conn.: Yale University Press).

Tarrow, S. (1994), *Power in Movement: Social Movements, Collective Action and Politics* (Cambridge: Cambridge University Press).

Taylor, P. (1989), *Families at War: Voices from the Troubles* (London: BBC Books).

Trimble, D. (1997), 'Speech to the Annual General Meeting of the Ulster Unionist Council', UUP Press Statement, 22 March.

Ulster Defence Association (1979), *Beyond the Religious Divide* (Belfast: Discussion Papers).

Ulster Democratic Unionist Party (1996), 'Our Covenant with the Ulster People', Manifesto for the Forum Election (Belfast: DUP).

Ulster Democratic Unionist Party (n.d., a), *The Framework of Shame and Sham: Yes the Framework Document is a One-Way Road to Dublin* (Belfast: UDUP Headquarters).

Ulster Democratic Unionist Party (n.d., b), 'The Unionist Team You Can Trust', Election Communication (1996 Forum Election).

Ulster Democratic Unionist Party (n.d.,c), 'Election Special', Election Communication (1996 Forum Election).

Ulster Democratic Party (n.d.), 'Look to the Future', Election Communication (1996 Forum Election).

Ulster Democratic Party (1996) 'Look to the Future', Manifesto for the Forum Election (Belfast: UDP).

Ulster Unionist Party (1996) 'Building Your Future Within the Union', Manifesto for the Forum Election (Belfast: UUP).

Ulster Political Research Group (1987) *Common Sense* (Belfast: UPRG).

Walker, B. (1996), *Dancing to History's Tune: History, Myth and Politics in Ireland* (Belfast: Institute of Irish Studies, Queen's University of Belfast).

8 Resisting the Green: Political Culture and Environmental Activism
Beth Simpson and Brian Elliott

> *Towards the end of our interview, the senior pastor handed us a yellow sheet. It was a 'flyer', an advertisement for and invitation to 'The 7th Annual Mayor's Prayer Breakfast', to be held at his church in a few days time. For seven dollars we could join the company of business leaders, pastors and politicians, hear about some of the currently pressing economic issues preoccupying the Mayor and council, and have the pastor lead us in prayer for the success of the Mayor's strategies.*

(Field notes, April 1995)

INTRODUCTION

In every research project there are 'defining moments' when something is said or done that gives direction or focus to the whole investigation. Looking at that advertisement and listening to the pastor was one of them. We were both strangers to this town, but we knew enough of its reputation to believe that we would need to look closely at the role of the churches in the structuring of social relations and the exercise of power. We wanted to know about these matters because, in our wider project, we were attempting to explain the highly varied responses of different communities to some broadly similar environmental issues that they confronted. What we had learned so far, told us that, in this city of Abbotsford, environmental problems had been the focus of much public commentary but that efforts to mobilise citizens around these issues encountered not only apathy and indifference, but active resistance. Our intuition was that understanding the role of religion in the community would be vital for our analysis of almost any aspect of its collective life. That lunchtime interview turned the hunch into a conviction, for it made plain the intimate connection between religion, economics and politics. It opened up questions about networks and structures, but it hinted too at norms, perspectives and practices that we should try to grasp. Most of all, it

126

reinforced our determination to find ways in which we could examine the interface of 'culture' and 'politics', incorporate some of the interests in 'political culture' being explored by a number of our colleagues, but somehow surmount the limitations of the traditional uses of that concept. In essence, we needed to find out whether a distinctive form of conservative, Christian culture really served to structure political and all other aspects of social life in the town, as many insisted it did and, if so, to show how that worked. When it appeared a few months later, a paper by Margaret Somers (1995) pointed to a 'rejuvenated' concept of political culture that captured neatly much that we were struggling to articulate:

> rather than a collection of internalised expressions of subjective values or externalised expressions of social interests, a political culture is now defined as a configuration of representations and practices that exists as a contentious structural social phenomenon in its own right. ... By existing as something apart from either the economy or the state, a political culture, when *acted upon*, will shape the outcome, meaning, and the very course of political action and social processes.
>
> (Somers, 1995: 134)

A series of preliminary interviews, our reading about the history of the area and our efforts to monitor local elections convinced us that we were, indeed, dealing with a community that had a distinctive political history and a political culture that distinguished it from most of the other settlements in our research area. But before we plunge in to the details of our study we need to put it in the context of the much larger investigation and provide some description of the area in which the work is being carried out.

THE SETTING

The Lower Fraser Basin

The Fraser Valley in British Columbia is a triangle of land extending 150 kilometres inland from the Pacific shore, from the delta of the Fraser River and the city of Vancouver, to the town of Hope. It is a wedge of fertile floodplain, bounded by mountains to the north and south that converge at its eastern end. A century and half ago the area was populated almost exclusively by aboriginal people. The first sizeable migration of non-natives into the area was triggered by the 1858 Cariboo Gold Rush, and by the time of the first census in the province, in 1881, the population of the lower Fraser Basin was around 7000 (Galois and Cole, 1994). They were soon joined by Chinese and Japanese migrants alongside Sikhs who provided an important source of labour in the British Columbia forest industry. In the 1920s,

Mennonites – who had migrated to the Canadian prairies from the Ukraine and other parts of the Soviet Union – came further west and settled in the Abbotsford area in the central valley. After the Second World War many Dutch immigrants arrived, contributing their skills in the construction of dikes, flood control systems, dairy farming and bulb growing to the region.

Today there is a population of 1.9 million in the lower Fraser Valley and Vancouver, the cosmopolitan centre. In the past decade it has experienced immigration on such a scale that in the city core and some of the suburbs fewer than half of the students enrolled in elementary and high schools have English as their first language. One suburb – Richmond – now has a very substantial Chinese population. Vancouver has had a 'Chinatown' since its earliest days, but the inner-city area that carries that name is an urban space that mostly reflects European notions of 'Chineseness' (Anderson, 1991). By contrast, large parts of the city of Richmond have been shaped by recent immigrants, who are not subordinated in the way that earlier Chinese settlers were. They have shaped a space that reflects the tastes and styles of an affluent, sophisticated population – mainly from Hong Kong.

The region is now home to more than 250 000 Chinese-Canadians, around 200 000 IndoCanadians, many from other areas of the Pacific Rim, as well as immigrants from eastern and central Europe and the Islamic countries of the Middle East.

The City of Abbotsford

In the centre of the Lower Fraser Basin lies Abbotsford (since 1995, amalgamated with neighbouring Matsqui), a city with 106 000 inhabitants and the hub of a prosperous district that still derives the greatest part of its wealth from agriculture – from dairy and poultry and hog farming, from fruit farming and the food-processing industry. The city has become much more ethnically diverse of late, with constituent communities from Central America and Vietnam, as well as from Hong Kong, Taiwan and parts of the Chinese Diaspora. The Sikh population has grown considerably, and Sikhs are now prominent as the owners as well as the workers, on the soft-fruit farms, and as local entrepreneurs in real estate and construction.

As the largest settlement in the central part of the lower Fraser Valley, Abbotsford presents itself as a natural focus for some of our sociological enquiries about the impact of rapid demographic and economic growth on the health of the natural environment. Some of its environmental problems are very obvious and frequently discussed in the media. At various periods in the year it experiences serious air pollution, as temperature inversions trap the discharges from cars and trucks, and from oil refineries and power stations on both the Canadian and the US sides of the border. Water supplies too have been contaminated, and over the last few summers there have been several public health 'advisories', warning residents that they should boil their water. Water supplies are drawn from lakes and from a very large aquifer. There have been problems with both sources. There has been much publicity about these two issues in the Abbotsford area. There has been a constant monitoring of air pollution, and various public meetings have been convened with experts recruited to talk about its causes and consequences. The possibility that water supplies are being contaminated by agricultural chemicals and by the inadequate disposal of enormous quantities of animal manure was given prominence in the early 1990s, when a group was formed to represent the interests of several hundred people who believed that they were suffering from diverse environmentally induced ailments. But this kind of public exposure does not necessarily mean that these environmental issues have great 'social visibility' in the city. If we accept the findings of Gould's studies (Gould *et al.*, 1996), then social visibility requires high levels of community mobilisation and collective action, which in their turn seem to spring only from particular kinds of political history and political culture. Even with high levels of mobilisation, local grassroots groups seem often to need the assistance of national environmental organisations in order to have much real success.

Its prominent place in the valley, its high rate of growth, its experience of environmental problems, all recommend Abbotsford as a place to study. There are, though, particular features of this community that, we believe, will shape its response to environmental issues in discernible ways. Abbotsford stands at the centre of British Columbia's 'bible-belt', with 83 churches and very large congregations of Mennonites, Dutch Reform, Alliance and diverse evangelical Christians (Riggins and Walker, 1991; Klassen, 1992). The average size of a congregation in this city is 500, when across North America the average is little more than 100. The largest church has a congregation of 4000 and at least two churches have auditoria, capable of holding 2000 people at a time. This is the most deeply Christian community in all of Canada, set in the province which is the most secularised in the country. Moreover, the forms of Christianity which flourish here are of a decidedly conservative kinds – pietistic, evangelical and charismatic. There are also Roman Catholic and Anglican and United churches, but they do not have comparable salience.

One other matter deserves comment. Abbotsford and Matsqui stand out as having remarkably low educational levels. Agricultural areas traditionally have provided many forms of work that did not require much formal schooling. This no doubt explains the fact that in 1981 fewer than 26 per cent had anything more than grade 9 education in Abbotsford, and that figure was even lower in Matsqui. In 1991 there are clear signs of change. More students are graduating and more have obtained some form of post-secondary education (mostly college-level courses). At the same time the local occupational structure is changing, with far more people being employed outside the agricultural sector.

Previous studies in many parts of the world have shown that religion, political ideology and education seem to have some definite associations with environmental attitudes and activism. Lynn White (1967) detected a negative relationship between the 'dominion over nature' doctrine in Judeo-Christianity and environmental concern. With the surge of religious enthusiasm and Christian conservatism that swept the USA in the mid-1970s to mid-1980s the focus shifted to the likely significance of specifically fundamentalist religiosity for the environmental movement (Hand and Van Liere, 1984). It was not only President Reagan who was expressing antipathy towards environmentalism, environmentalists and environmental regulation: many fundamentalist Christians shared his views. More recent work qualifies both of these earlier attempts to link religious belief and practice to environmental attitudes and behaviour, but the importance of religion in relation to 'green' beliefs and behaviour continues to surface in current research.

In a similar way, sociologists and political scientists continue to explore the impact of particular political ideologies on environmental concerns and actions. Neo-conservative and neo-liberal ideas seem frequently to be negatively associated with 'green' attitudes and activities. Education too is very often shown to be linked – this time positively – with levels of environmental concern and a willingness to become involved in forms of green activism.

Some of our colleagues in the Fraser Basin research project have generated data about environmental concern and activism from a telephone survey of residents in all areas of British Columbia (Blake *et al.*, 1997). Their findings pointed to the fact that those with no religious affiliation were likely to show more sympathy for the environment when responding to Dunlap and Liere's (1978) statements that expressed their 'New Environmental Paradigm'. They found that preferences for particular political parties were linked to environmental concerns – with those intending to vote for the populist British Columbia Reform Party showing the lowest scores when asked about local environmental concerns, and (apart from the Green Party supporters) New Democrats showing the highest level of concern both for local and global issues. Exploring political values, and comparing 'Populists' with 'Post-Materialists' and 'Neo-Conservatives', they found that political ideology was clearly associated with levels of concern about local and global environmental concerns. Neo-Conservatives (predictably) were the least concerned.

Education is generally found to be positively associated with levels of environmental concern and, indeed, in this survey those with the highest scores do have the highest educational levels, but the authors point out that the differences are quite small and that it was the group with the middling level of education that had the lowest scores on the 'local concern' items, not those with least education.

According to Blake *et al.*, residents of the Lower Mainland (roughly our research area) are somewhat more concerned about environmental issues than people in other regions of the province, but setting their general findings alongside the overview that we have provided, we can see that there are several factors that will probably moderate environmental attitudes and constrain environmental activism.

METHODS AND RESEARCH DESIGN

The basic research design is that of a case study. Case studies characteristically involve relatively intensive analysis of a single instance of a phenomenon being investigated – here a particular political culture – which we believed might help explain the comparatively low level of mobilization around environmental issues. Our hope was that face-to-face interviews with a cross-section of those who held positions of some power and influence in the community would allow us to identify those factors that shaped the limited kinds of environmental activity that did exist, and that underlay resistance to any seriously challenging forms of environmentalism. We share the belief, expressed by Gould *et al.* (1996), that local mobilisations of 'citizen-workers' are vital to produce change in our currently profligate systems of production and consumption but, like them, we recognise that local groups frequently face opposition within their own communities. Some of that comes in very obvious attempts at repression, or co-optation by local authorities and local employers, but much of the control is embedded in cultural representations and practices – in what here we call 'political culture'. Getting at that is not easy, but some combination of highly structured questions, along with opportunities and prompts for more discursive answers, seemed the appropriate way to proceed.

Subjects were 'purposefully', rather than randomly sampled. Our goal was to have 25 respondents in each of four categories: local business leaders, local community service leaders and activists, local politicians and bureaucrats, and local church leaders. Of course, such a method, while it has the benefit of convenience, carries with it dangers of bias and the obvious disadvantage that one cannot analyse the data or generalise the findings in the ways made possible by more rigorous sampling. Our sample is undeniably, indeed, deliberately skewed in a number of ways that give us access to the experiences and viewpoints of a diverse array of community leaders.

Lists of potential respondents were drawn from local directories such as those compiled by the Chamber of Commerce, City Council, Community

Services, and the local Ministerial Association. The list provided by the Ministerial Association was in many ways the best, the most comprehensive, but such is the rate of geographical and occupational mobility among the pastors and ministers and priests, that even it was not as accurate as we hoped. The other sampling frames had all to be compiled from several sources in order to give adequate coverage of the political, business and community leadership. Contact letters were sent to 162 potential subjects. We were unable to contact 35 potential respondents (four political respondents, six bureaucrats, seven business leaders, and 18 church leaders), frequently because they had relocated outside the area, or were travelling elsewhere. Of the 127 we could contact 20 declined, 11 of whom were church leaders, primarily from the more conservative churches.

In the end 107 face-to-face structured interviews of community leaders who lived and/or worked in Abbotsford took place between March 1996 and 31 July 1996 (84 per cent response rate from those we could contact). Because men tend to dominate positions of influence, women were specifically targeted to ensure their representation. Although women form only 28 per cent of our sample, this almost certainly over-represents women community leaders in Abbotsford. Women were most likely to be community activists and least likely to be church leaders. This sample differs from a random sample of the general public in other important ways. The average age was 51.6 years, with a standard deviation of 8.95. Although the range was from 35 to 73 years, 50 per cent were between 46 and 56 years of age. Overall, these are also highly educated people. Fully 68 per cent have at least some university education, and 56.3 per cent have completed at least one degree. Clearly, these are higher than proportions for the general population of the area. The 1991 census found that in Abbotsford only 9 per cent had completed a degree, while in Matsqui it was slightly lower; only 7 per cent had finished a degree. The respondents also enjoy a higher than average household income; 35 per cent have an annual household income of $95 000 or more. More than 70 per cent have a household income of more than $55 000 (only 40 per cent of the Abbotsford population and 37 per cent of those in Matsqui had household income above $50 000 in the 1991 census). These, then, are people we should expect to be more than usually aware of environmental issues and, since they have the resources – material, social and intellectual – we might anticipate that environmental concerns will be reflected in their personal lives and in their involvement in various kinds of collective action (see Table 8.1).

Data were collected by means of an interview schedule containing 175 items, most of them employing Likert scales measuring agreement/disagreement on a series of seven-point scales. There were questions designed to examine the structural relations – the networks of organisational and personal connections between the various 'elites' and institutions in the city –

Table 8.1   *Bivariate Relationships of Variables Measuring Demographic Variables to Group Type (percentages)*

Demographic variables	Total (n = 107)	Business leaders (n = 24)	Community activists (n = 29)	Politicians, bureaucrats (n = 29)	Church leaders (n = 25)
Sex					
Male (n = 77)	72.0	75.0	79.0	79.0	96.0
Female (n = 30)	28.0	25.0	21.0	21.0	4.0
Household income[a]					
<$25 000	5.2	4.8	7.7	–	4.2
25 000–34 999	6.2	4.8	11.5	3.8	4.2
35 000–44 999	6.2	4.8	7.7	–	12.5
45 000–54 999	11.3	9.5	11.5	11.5	12.5
55 000–64 999	11.3	–	11.5	3.8	29.2
65 000–74 999	9.3	4.8	7.7	11.5	12.5
75 000–84 999	7.2	–	3.8	11.5	12.5
85 000–94 999	9.3	14.3	7.7	15.4	–
>94 999	35.0	57.1	30.8	34.6	12.5
Education					
Less than secondary school	4.9	4.2	6.9	3.4	4.0
Secondary graduation	0.9	–	3.4	–	–
Trade/technical[b]	12.6	16.7	6.9	24.1	–
Community college[b]	5.8	8.3	13.8	10.3	–
Some university	11.7	20.8	10.3	10.3	4.0
Undergraduate degree	27.2	33.3	24.1	27.6	20.0
Graduate/professional degree	29.1	15.7	34.5	24.1	72.0

[a] n = 97 (business leaders n = 21; community activists n = 26; politicians/bureaucrats n = 26; church leaders n = 24).
[b] Includes both those who completed a programme of study and those who did not.

and questions seeking the conventional information about social background, such as education level, personal and household income, and religious affiliation. Where permission was granted, as it was in most cases, the interview was tape-recorded so that pertinent qualitative data would not be lost. The following sets of variables were included in our analysis:[1]

1. *Local Environmental Concern.* A variety of indicators was used to examine environmental concern (see Table 8.2). In each case we distinguished four groups of respondents: business leaders, community activists, politicians/bureaucrats, and church leaders. The question 'How concerned are you about the local environment?' was used as both a dependent and independent variable.

2. *Environmental Activism*. This was examined from two aspects. *Environmental activism* was examined by asking respondents whether they had participated in any of 10 activities in the previous year (see Table 8.3). An index made of these responses was used both as a dependent and independent variable in regression analysis. *Awareness of local environmental activism* was examined by quantifying responses to open-ended questions regarding local environmental leadership and groups (see Table 8.4).

3. *Demographic Variables*. These include sex, education, household income and group type (see Table 8.1). Although other research has found that age is a significant factor affecting environmental concern (Jones and Dunlap, 1992) we did not find it to be the case in this instance and so did not include it in our analysis. Our sample has a marked preponderance of people of middle age.

4. *Political Culture*. *Business Ideology* is similar to Ronald Inglehart's (1990) concept of materialist values. Here, however, the emphasis is exclusively on economic factors. *Populism* was included because other research has indicated the importance of populist values in the politics of British Columbia (Blake *et al.*, 1997). However, populism turned out to be relatively unimportant for this sample, and was not included in the multiple-regression models. Part of the problem might lie in the low correlation between the variables that form the index, as indicated by an *alpha* of 0.4758. Yet by most definitions of populism these variables do capture its different attributes (McCormick, 1991: 350). *Socialism* was measured in some very limited ways – willingness to expand government spending and concern for quality of life. *Ethnic Tolerance* examined tolerance of others (especially those who might be making special social and economic claims against the government).

5. *New Environmental Paradigm Variables*. *DWW* measured attributes associated with the Dominant Western World-View as described by Dunlap and Van Liere (1978). Supporters of DWW assume the right of humanity to dominate non-human nature. *Limits to Growth* measures support for the alteration of current lifestyles and growth-oriented economics. We assume that those persons who support DWW and reject Limits to Growth will be less likely to engage in environmental activism.

RESULTS

We use both the quantitative material and the discursive responses to explore our respondents' 'green' attitudes and behaviour. First we describe the respondents' levels of local environmental concern, environmental activism, and awareness of local environmental activism. Next we try to explain why 'resisting the green' is so pervasive in this sample. Finally we use the responses to open-ended questions to explore characterisations of the structure and culture of the community provided by our respondents. From these, the lineaments of a distinctive and rather durable political culture emerge.

Local Environmental Concern

Table 8.2 presents our findings on the level of local environmental concern. More than one in five of the total sample indicate that they are 'very concerned' about the local environment. More than 84 per cent show at least some level of concern while only 2.8 per cent are 'unconcerned'. No-one claims to have 'no concerns at all'. Not surprisingly, community activists are most likely to be 'concerned' or 'very concerned'. Politicians and bureaucrats are the least likely to have serious concerns about local environmental quality and are the group most likely to be 'somewhat unconcerned' or 'unconcerned'. Business and church leaders were most likely to state they were 'somewhat concerned', while business leaders had the highest percentage that were neutral on the issue. These rates, indeed, suggest that these Abbotsford community leaders are a good deal more aware and somewhat anxious about environmental matters than others in British Columbia (Blake *et al.*, 1996).

In an open-ended question almost three out of four selected air pollution as a local environmental issue. Community leaders and politicians/bureaucrats were most likely to mention air pollution. Groundwater contamination was mentioned by 70.1 per cent of the sample. Business leaders and politicians/bureaucrats were most likely to mention this. The other most frequent responses were vehicle exhaust, which was most likely to be mentioned by business leaders, and land loss/overdevelopment, which was most likely to be mentioned by church leaders and politicians/bureaucrats.

When asked directly whether local air quality posed a serious health risk, almost 90 per cent of the sample agreed that at some level it did. Politicians and bureaucrats were the group most likely to disagree or be neutral on the issue. The group most likely to believe it was an issue were church leaders. Over all, 39 per cent 'strongly agree' that local air quality poses a serious health risk (not shown on Table 8.2). Community activists were most likely to believe this, followed by business leaders, and church leaders. Yet only 27.6 per cent of local politicians 'strongly agreed' that local air quality posed a serious health risk. When asked directly whether local water quality posed a serious health risk, over half agreed, though only 17 per cent 'strongly agreed'. Interestingly, church leaders were most likely to 'strongly agree', followed by business leaders, community activists, and politicians/bureaucrats. Politicians/bureaucrats were also most likely to disagree that the local water

Table 8.2 Bivariate Relationships of Variables Measuring Local Environmental Concern to Group Type (percentages)

Variables measuring local environmental concern	Total (n = 107)	Business leaders (n = 24)	Community activists (n = 29)	Politicians, bureaucrats (n = 29)	Church leaders (n = 25)
Local air quality poses a serious health risk[a]					
Mainly agree	89.7	95.8	89.7	79.3	96.0
Neutral	5.6	4.2	6.9	10.3	–
Mainly disagree	4.7	–	3.4	10.3	4.0
Local water quality poses a serious health risk[a,b]					
Mainly agree	55.7	66.7	65.5	37.9	54.2
Neutral	9.4	8.3	–	13.8	16.7
Mainly disagree	34.9	25.0	34.5	48.3	29.2
How concerned are you about the local environment?					
Very concerned	21.5	16.7	34.5	13.8	20.0
Concerned	28.0	25.0	31.0	31.0	24.0
Somewhat concerned	34.6	41.7	27.6	27.6	44.0
Neutral	7.5	12.5	3.4	10.3	4.0
Somewhat unconcerned	5.6	4.2	–	10.3	8.0
Unconcerned	2.8	–	3.4	6.9	–
Not at all concerned					
Who contributes more to the creation of local environmental problems?[c]					
Large industrial companies	7.9	–	13.8	7.4	9.1
Agriculture	26.7	21.7	20.7	33.3	31.8
Individual consumers	57.4	60.9	55.2	59.3	54.5
Combination/all	17.4	17.4	10.3	–	4.5

Table 8.2 (*Continued*)

Variables measuring local environmental concern	*Total* (*n* = 107)	*Business leaders* (*n* = 24)	*Community activists* (*n* = 29)	*Politicians, bureaucrats* (*n* = 29)	*Church leaders* (*n* = 25)
My behaviour as one individual really makes no difference in the fight against pollution[a]					
Mainly agree	7.5	12.5	6.9	3.4	8.0
Neutral	2.8	–	3.4	3.4	4.0
Mainly disagree	89.7	87.5	89.7	93.1	88.0
Open-ended Questions					
Are there any environmental issues or problems in Abbotsford?[d]					
Percentage stating air pollution	74.8	58.3	82.8	82.8	72.0
Percentage stating groundwater contamination	70.1	79.2	65.5	72.4	64.0
Percentage stating vehicle exhaust	27.1	41.7	24.1	20.7	24.0
Percentage stating land loss/overdevelopment	22.4	12.5	20.7	27.6	28.0

[a] Variables are Likert scales where 1 means 'strongly agree' and 7 means 'strongly disagree'. For this table only: responses 1–3 = 'mainly agree'; 4 = 'neutral'; responses 5–7 = 'mainly disagree'.

[b] *n* = 106 (church leaders 24).

[c] *n* = 101 (business leaders = 23; community activists = 29; politicians/bureaucrats = 27; church leaders = 22).

[d] These are the four most frequently stated environmental issues. Only 4.6 failed to mention or did not know of any local environmental problems.

quality posed serious health risks. Overall, 34.9 per cent did not believe that local water posed serious risks.

When asked who was responsible for local environmental problems, the majority of the respondents stated that individual consumers were. More than half of each group gave this response. The second most popular response was agriculture, selected by 26.7 per cent. Politicians/bureaucrats and church leaders were most likely to choose this response. Few respondents chose large industrial companies; however, 17.4 per cent did indicate that they felt some combination of individual consumer and agriculture and/or industry was responsible.

Finally, respondents were asked to agree or disagree with the statement that 'My behaviour as one individual makes no difference in the fight against pollution'. Differences in a sense of 'agency' or 'personal efficacy' might well have a bearing on a person's willingness to change behaviour, to turn concern into action. Almost 90 per cent disagreed at some level, while almost 44 per cent 'strongly disagreed' (not available on Table 8.2). Community activists were most likely to 'strongly disagree' that individual action made no difference, followed by church leaders and business leaders, while politicians/bureaucrats were least likely to 'strongly disagree'.

If such a large percentage of this sample has concerns about local environmental quality, particularly regarding local air and water quality, and if they largely agree that individual consumption is a main contributing factor, and if they believe that individual action can make a difference, we may ask 'How environmentally active are they?'

Local Environmental Activism

Table 8.3 reveals the responses given by the four groups to 10 measures of environmental activism. Certainly respondents were most likely to participate in the previous year in those activities that presented the least 'cost' in time or effort. Thus, 37.7 per cent had boycotted a product because of environmental concerns, 35.8 per cent had signed a petition, and 41.5 per cent had donated money to an environmental cause. For the most part these are 'anonymous' activities. Far fewer were willing publicly to declare their position by displaying a bumper sticker or wearing a pin in support of an environmental issue. Although politicians/bureaucrats are the least likely to have serious concerns regarding the local environment, they are the most likely to display bumper stickers or to wear pins – substantially more than community activists. In politics, cultivating the *appearance* of 'greenness' may be an intelligent electoral strategy. The business leaders of this sample had high levels of concern about local air quality, but were apparently unwilling to reveal that concern publicly, since none displayed bumper stickers or wore pins.

Declaring a position on a political issue might be bad for business – which fits what we know about the thinking, particularly of small entrepreneurs. Except in the matter of donating money, business leaders were less likely than other groups to engage in environmental activism. Although 29.3 per cent of the business leaders claim to have joined an environmental group, this should be viewed with caution. More often than not this refers to a non-environmental organisation that has shown some form of 'ecological' concern, such as the Chamber of Commerce. This organisation sponsors an 'Adopt-a-Block' anti-litter campaign, but considering the serious environmental issues facing the Central Fraser Valley, this hardly amounts to a major green commitment. Similarly, 25 per cent of church leaders claim to belong to an environmental group, but most of these are church organisations that may have participated in a one-time environmental project, but do not have environmental activism as their primary objective. When asked in an open-ended question to name organisations to which they belonged, only 4.2 per cent of business leaders and 8 per cent of church leaders mentioned an environmental organisation. Overall, only 9.3 per cent of the sample mentioned they were members of any environmental organisation, community activists being the most likely (20.7 per cent) to belong to such bodies. This is quite different from the 16 per cent of the whole sample who claimed to have joined an environmental group, when the question did not require them to name it. Compared with their responses to other elements of this question, surprisingly few of the community activists claim to have joined an environmental group. That is probably an artefact of the way we asked the question. The focus was on 'activities done in the past year?' Many of the activists may well have had memberships entered into longer ago than that.

Although one in five have worked on behalf of a candidate because of their environmental views, only 10.4 per cent have written a letter to the newspaper, and only 6.6 per cent have phoned either television or radio talk-shows about environmental issues. Only 6.6 per cent have participated in a demonstration or a protest. Although we expected community activists to be the most likely to have participated in these activities, church leaders were most likely to have written to a public official about environmental concerns, and were the second most likely to participate in demonstrations or protests, though admittedly very few do.

A scale measuring environmental activism was created from these 10 activities as described earlier. Not surprisingly, the highest levels of activism are to be found among community activists. While 12.3 per cent of the sample have participated in five or more of the activities in the past year, 17.2 per cent of community activists have done so, followed by 13.8 per cent of politicians/bureaucrats, 12.5 per cent of church leaders and 4.2 per cent of business leaders. Overall, it looks as though those most unwilling to

Table 8.3 *Bivariate Relationships of Variables Measuring Environmental Activism to Group Type (percentages)*

Variables measuring environmental activism	Total (n = 106)	Business leaders (n = 24)	Community activists (n = 29)	Politicians, bureaucrats (n = 29)	Church leaders (n = 25)
Environmental Activism (percentage stating yes):					
Signed a petition supporting a pro-environmental issue	35.8	25.0	41.4	41.4	33.3
Displayed a bumper sticker or wore a pin in support of an environmental issue	14.2	–	17.2	31.0	4.2
Boycotted a product because of environmental concerns	37.7	25.0	48.3	31.0	45.8
Joined an environmental group	16.0	29.2	17.2	6.9	25.0
Donated money to an environmental cause	41.5	50.0	48.3	41.4	25.0
Worked to elect someone because of their views on the environment	21.7	12.5	31.0	17.5	25.0
Written a letter about the environment to newspapers	10.4	8.3	17.2	3.4	12.5
Phoned TV/radio talk show about environmental issues	6.6	10.3	10.3	10.3	4.2
Written to a public official about environmental issues	23.6	12.5	24.1	27.6	29.2
Joined a protest or demonstration concerned with the environment	6.6	4.2	10.3	3.4	8.3
Level of environmental activism:					
No activism (does none of the above)	22.6	29.2	17.2	24.1	20.8
Minimal activism (does 1 or 2)	38.7	45.8	34.5	27.6	50.0
Some activism (does 3 or 4)	26.4	20.8	31.0	34.5	16.7
High levels of activism (does 5 or 6)	8.5	4.2	6.9	13.8	8.3
Highest levels of activism (7 or more)	3.8	–	10.3	–	4.2

[a] Chronbach's alpha = 0.6767.

engage in even these limited forms of environmental activism are business people and church leaders.

Table 8.4 reveals levels of awareness of local environmental activism. When asked to identify local environmental leaders, less than half could name a highly visible city councillor who campaigned specifically on environmental issues and is closely associated with several local environmental projects such as initiating a recycling programme. Only 5.6 per cent could name the local environmental planner, while 18.7 per cent named the mayor an environmental leader. More than 30 per cent named others, primarily colleagues and associates who had participated in a local environmental project, such as 'Adopt-a-Block' or cleaning a local salmon stream. Slightly less than 30 per cent were unable to name any environmental leaders, and only 7.5 per cent could identify the head of the Backyard Habitat environmental group, or the head of the Central Fraser Valley Naturalists, despite the fact that this wife-and-husband team has received a good deal of publicity, and the Backyard Habitat educational materials are now incorporated in a trio of well-produced instructional booklets published by the provincial government in its efforts to promote the very practical but quite sophisticated forms of environmentalism under its Naturescape programme. Clearly church leaders were the group most at a loss here. More than half could not name any environmental leaders. Business leaders were the least likely to state they did not know of any environmental leaders. However, 50 per cent provided a disparate array of names that had to be categorised as 'other', while fully 25 per cent mentioned the mayor. Surprisingly, although community activists have high levels of environmental concern and higher levels of environmental activism than most, almost one in four could not name any local environmental leader, and not one of this group mentioned the organiser of the local chapter of most 'established' and widely consulted environmental association in the province. Like business leaders, they were very likely to mention 'other' or the mayor. The group most successful in naming local environmental activists were politicians/bureaucrats, who presumably have had dealings with them in the past.

The three most-mentioned responses to 'what do environmental leaders do?' were 'raise awareness of local environmental issues', 'initiate projects' or 'don't know'. Again, church leaders are the least likely to know what local environmental activists do. Three out of five could not name any activity. Only 3.7 per cent mentioned environmental research, 7.5 per cent mentioned 'educate the public', 8.4 per cent said environmental leaders have a 'balanced view' (frequently used by those citing the mayor as an environmental leader), while 1.9 per cent stated that environmental leaders engage in 'protests' and 'demonstrations'. More than 11 per cent stated that environmental leaders 'lobby governments'. Politicians and bureaucrats were the most likely to give this response.

Table 8.4 Bivariate Relationships of Variables Measuring Awareness of Local Environmental Activism to Group Type (percentages)

Variables measuring awareness of local environmental activism	Total (n = 107)	Business leaders (n = 24)	Community activists (n = 29)	Politicians, bureaucrats (n = 29)	Church leaders (n = 29)
Open-ended Questions (percentage stating the following):					
Can you identify local environmental leaders?[a]					
P.R. – City council member	47.7	54.2	58.6	55.2	20.0
PA. – Municipal environment officer	5.6	–	3.4	13.8	4.0
G.F. – Mayor	18.7	25.0	24.1	10.3	16.0
S.P. – Local environmental activist	5.6	4.2	3.4	10.3	4.0
J.S. – Local environmental activist	1.9	–	–	6.9	–
Other	31.8	50.0	44.0	31.0	16.0
Don't know	29.0	16.7	24.1	24.1	52.0
None mentioned	3.7	4.2	–	3.4	8.0
What exactly have they (environmental leaders) done?[c]					
Raise awareness of environmental issues	47.7	54.2	44.8	55.2	24.0
Initiate projects	33.6	41.7	41.4	34.5	16.0
Don't know	34.6	20.8	34.5	24.1	60.0
Can you identify a local environmental group?[b]					
Names of a local environmental group[d]	18.7	12.5	17.2	37.9	4.0
Chamber of Commerce	10.3	29.2	3.4	6.9	4.0
City Council	18.7	16.7	24.1	17.2	16.0
Names of other groups that have shown some environmental concern	41.1	37.5	44.8	48.3	32.0
Don't know	33.6	25.0	31.0	27.6	52.0

Table 8.4 (Continued)

Variables measuring awareness of local environmental activism	Total (n = 107)	Business leaders (n = 24)	Community activists (n = 29)	Politicians, bureaucrats (n = 29)	Church leaders (n = 29)
What exactly have they done?[c]					
Raise awareness of environmental issues	26.2	29.2	24.1	34.5	16.0
Initiate projects	36.4	37.5	48.3	31.0	28.0
Don't know	29.2	27.6	27.6	27.6	60.0

[a] The question read: 'Can you identify leaders of the community who, in your opinion, have shown great concern for these issues?'

[b] The question read: 'Can you identify local groups of organisations (the college, the CFVEHG, etc.) that have played an active role in terms of these issues?'

[c] These are the top three responses.

[d] Local environmental groups included: Central Valley Naturalists, Central Fraser Valley Environmental Health Group, Sumas Mountain Conservation, Backyard Habitat, and Healthy Communities Project.

Similar questions were asked regarding local environmental groups, and what they did. It is surely a telling commentary on the representation of 'environmentalism' in this local political culture that respondents were just as likely to mention the City Council as they were to mention a local group whose primary purpose was environmental activism. Again, politicians and bureaucrats were more successful than others in naming such groups (37.9 per cent), more than twice the success rate of community activists (17.2 per cent). Business leaders were the most likely group to name the Chamber of Commerce as a local environmental group. Community activists were most likely to name 'other' groups, often groups they personally were involved in that conducted mainly rather small-scale, and strictly local environmental amelioration projects. Very surprisingly, community activists were second only to church leaders in their failure to name any group that had shown environmental concern. More than a third of the sample could not name any local group or organisation that had shown concern regarding environmental issues. As with environmental leaders, knowledge of environmental group activities was limited to 'raising awareness', 'initiating projects' or 'don't know'. Church leaders were more than twice as likely as other groups to be unaware of what local environmental groups do.

Why 'Resist the Green'?

Clearly there is widespread agreement among the members of this sample that there is reason to be concerned about the local environment, yet personal engagement in environmental activism is very limited and mostly takes forms that really do not challenge industry or government. There is also a surprising lack of awareness about local environmental groups and activists. It is surprising because these are mostly well-informed men and women, actively involved in leadership roles with, we thought, extensive social contacts across this community. What explains this paradox?

We have premised this research on the fact that political culture must be part of the explanation, and factors that influence this political culture include the historical presence of the Mennonite and Reform Churches and the more recent influence of the Alliance Church (a Pentecostal assembly).

Correlation matrices were produced, exploring the relationships between measures of political culture, church membership, group type, environmental concern, environmental activism, and measures of the New Ecological Paradigm. Among the measures of political culture, business ideology, populism, and socialism had the strongest relationships with environmental concern and environmental activism. Table 8.5 gives bivariate relationships between political culture and New Ecological Paradigm variables and group type.

Table 8.5 *Bivariate Relationships of Variables Measuring Political Culture and New Ecological Paradigm to Group Type (percentages)*

Variables measuring political culture	Total	Business leaders	Community activists	Politicians, bureaucrats	Church leaders
Support for business ideology					
Mainly support	72.0	87.5	63.0	77.8	60.0
Neutral	21.4	12.5	22.2	18.5	32.0
Mainly don't support	6.8	–	14.8	3.7	8.0
	(n = 105)	(n = 24)	(n = 28)	(n = 28)	(n = 25)
Support for populist ideals					
Mainly support	23.8	20.8	28.6	14.3	32.0
Neutral	38.1	29.2	32.1	35.7	56.0
Mainly don't support	38.1	50.0	39.3	50.0	12.0
	(n = 103)	(n = 24)	(n = 28)	(n = 28)	(n = 25)
Support for socialist values<sup>					
Mainly support	14.7	4.5	21.4	6.9	26.1
Neutral	31.4	9.1	53.6	34.5	21.7
Mainly don't support	53.9	86.4	25.0	58.6	52.0
	(n = 103)	(n = 22)	(n = 28)	(n = 29)	(n = 24)
Ethnic tolerance					
Mainly tolerant	52.9	31.8	65.5	55.6	54.2
Neutral	27.5	27.3	20.7	29.6	33.3
Mainly intolerant	19.6	40.9	13.8	14.8	12.5
	(n = 102)	(n = 22)	(n = 29)	(n = 27)	(n = 24)
Support for dominant Western World View (DWW)					
Mainly support	4.8	8.3	3.4	7.1	–
Neutral	26.7	29.2	13.8	32.1	33.3
Mainly do not support	68.6	62.5	82.8	82.8	66.7
	(n = 106)	(n = 24)	(n = 29)	(n = 29)	(n = 24)

146

Table 8.5 (*Continued*)

Variables measuring political culture	*Total*	*Business leaders*	*Community activists*	*Politicians, bureaucrats*	*Church leaders*
Support for limits to growth thesis**					
Mainly support	49.1	25.0	75.0	41.4	52.0
Neutral	24.5	37.5	10.3	17.2	28.0
Mainly do not support	26.4	37.5	7.1	41.4	20.0
	($n = 106$)	($n = 24$)	($n = 28$)	($n = 29$)	($n = 25$)

** Pearson chi-square probability < 0.01.
Note: Variables are Likert scales where 1 means 'strongly do not support' and 7 means 'strongly support'. For this table only: responses 1–3 = 'mainly don't support'; 4 = 'neutral'; responses 5–7 'mainly support'.

Almost three-quarters of the sample support business ideology as some level. Although only 9.3 per cent very strongly support business ideology, no-one strongly rejects it. Strength of support varies between groups with business leaders more likely to support very strongly, while community leaders are more likely to 'weakly support' business ideology. Church leaders are the individuals most likely to be neutral. Church leaders, however, are most likely to support populist ideals or to be neutral. Politicians/bureaucrats have the least sympathy for populist values, only 14.3 per cent offer any level of support. Half the politicians/bureaucrats and half the business leaders reject populist values. Community activists are second to church leaders in their support of populist values. Although 26 per cent of church leaders and 21.4 per cent of community activists support, at some level, socialist values, most of that support is weak, and no-one strongly supports such goals. On the other hand, only 2 per cent strongly reject socialist aspirations, although more than half reject at some level and another 31.4 per cent are neutral. Community activists are most likely to be neutral in their responses.

More than half of the respondents are ethnically tolerant and 7.8 per cent are very tolerant. Only 20 per cent could be considered intolerant. Business leaders are the most likely to express intolerant opinions while church leaders are the least likely to hold such views. Community activists were most likely to be ethnically tolerant. However, only 2 per cent of the sample could be considered very intolerant.

There was almost no support for the Dominant Western World-View. Only 4.8 per cent of the sample supported this view. No church leaders held the position that could be likened to Lynne White's (1967) concept of 'domination'. However, church leaders were the group most likely to be neutral on this issue. More than 80 per cent of both community activists and politicians/bureaucrats reject this position. Business leaders were the group most likely to accept the DWW and the least likely to reject it. The 'limits to growth' thesis was supported by three-quarters of the community activists but by slightly less than half the total sample. Not surprisingly business leaders were the least likely to support this concept. However, they were the most likely to be neutral. Politicians and bureaucrats were the most likely to reject the concept of limits to growth.

To summarise, there is widespread concern for the local environment, widespread agreement that individual consumers are at least partially responsible, and general agreement that individual action can make a difference. There is limited personal environmental activism by the members of this sample, and almost no knowledge of local environmental organisations, local environmental activists, or what they do. There is general widespread support for a business ideology that promotes economic expansion, limited and weak support for concepts such as government expansion and limited support for populist views. Business leaders and politicians/bureaucrats are the most likely to endorse business ideologies and to reject populist and socialist views. While almost no-one supports the DWW, community activists and politicians/bureaucrats are most likely to reject such a position. 'Limits to Growth' received widespread support only from community activists and, to a much lesser extent, church leaders. Politicians/bureaucrats and business leaders were more likely to reject such a position. Although most of the sample was ethnically tolerant at some level, the majority of business leaders (68.2 per cent) could not be described as ethnically tolerant.

Table 8.6 shows bivariate regressions of several independent variables on local environmental concern. Household income, level of education, and support for populist views were not significant predictors of environmental concern. Being female, a community activist, ethnically tolerant, having socialist values and high levels of environmental activism were all positive predictors of local environmental concern. On the other hand, support for business ideology, DWW, and membership in the Alliance, Mennonite, or Reform churches were negative predictors of local environmental concern. Table 8.7 shows the same variables regressed on local environmental activism. Interestingly, though gender and community activism were positive predictors of environmental concern, neither is significant in predicting environmental activism. Support for business ideology, DWW, and membership in the Alliance, Mennonite, or Reform churches were negative predictors of local environmental concern. Positive predictors of environmental activism include ethnic tolerance, concern for the local environment, and support for the limits to growth position.

To discover which variables had the most influence on local environmental concern and local environmental activism, multiple-regression models were developed, regressing independent variables in stages. Table 8.8 displays the regression models on local environmental concern. The first test involved respondents' characteristics. The second test added religion, the third added political culture variables, and the fourth included environment variables. As these tests show, gender (sex = female) remains highly influential in predicting local environmental concern, although in the final test environment variables are stronger predictors. Although significant, church affiliation does not make dramatic changes in the value of R^2 (adjusted) when it is entered into the model. Political culture variables have a greater impact. As test three reveals, church affiliation is a stronger negative predictor of environmental concern than is support for business ideology. On the other hand, at least for this sample, ethnic tolerance is a stronger positive predictor than is support for socialist values. The fourth test reveals the impact of each variable once all have been entered. The variables support for socialist values and support for limits to growth thesis were dropped from the final model because of high levels of multicollinearity. This last model reveals that, at least for this sample, lack of local environmental concern is best explained by

Table 8.6 *Bivariate Regressions, Dependent Variable = Local Environmental Concern*

Independent variables	r	r² (adjusted)	b	SEb	B	Durbin–Watson	Standard error
Sex (female = 1)**	0.28591	0.07300	0.779221	0.25467	0.285913	2.06636	1.18431
Household income	0.13708	0.00846	−0.052409	0.038856	−0.137078	2.04979	1.22474
Education (highest)	0.07405	−0.00399	0.38031	0.049982	0.074052	1.96324	1.23240
Type (1 = Community activist)*	0.21060	0.03525	0.580018	0.262749	0.210598	2.03087	1.20808
*Church affiliation**							
(1 = Alliance/Mennonite/Reform)	0.24275	0.04961	−0.653333	0.259797	−0.242746	1.84866	1.17308
Support for business ideology**	0.25044	0.05344	−0.281854	0.108416	−0.250440	2.08913	1.19664
Support for populist ideals	0.18086	0.2332	0.245254	0.131409	0.180864	2.01589	1.21553
Support for socialist values**	0.25773	0.05709	0.299238	0.112183	0.257730	1.95527	1.19433
Ethnic tolerance*	0.20640	0.03303	0.193736	0.091845	0.206396	1.97858	1.20947
Support for DWW***	0.45134	0.19597	−0.505561	0.098490	−0.310230	1.86491	1.10287
Support for limits to growth thesis***	0.46168	0.20559	0.432830	0.081546	0.461685	1.88585	1.09626
Level of environmental activism***	0.41257	0.16223	0.255282	0.055270	0.412569	1.79968	1.12577

* $p < 0.50$; ** $p < 0.01$; *** $p < 0.001$.

Table 8.7 Bivariate Regressions, Dependent Variable = Environmental Activism

Independent variables	r adjusted	r^2	b	SEb	B	Durbin–Watson	Standard error
Sex (female = 1)	0.00799	0.00953	0.035088	0.430640	0.007989	1.55121	1.99724
Household income	0.03588	-0.00934	0.022169	0.063690	0.035878	1.77223	1.99702
Education (highest level)	0.09421	-0.00066	0.078192	0.081027	0.094206	1.56309	1.98842
Type (1 = Community/activist)	0.15934	0.00810	0.182927	0.707120	0.159340	1.97178	1.43376
Church affiliation[*]							
(1 = Alliance/MennoniteI/Reform)	0.21705	0.03758	-0.968147	0.435419	-0.217048	1.63410	1.96246
Support for business ideology[*]	0.20320	0.03170	-0.369591	0.178090	-0.203200	1.56477	1.95600
Support for populist ideals	0.12376	0.00566	0.271214	0.215323	0.123757	1.66772	1.98213
Support for socialist values[*]	0.24380	0.04994	0.457477	0.182896	0.243804	1.58536	1.93750
Ethnic tolerance[**]	0.25394	0.05503	0.385221	0.147467	0.253935	1.49328	1.93229
Concern for local environment[***]	0.41257	0.16223	0.664016	0.143764	0.412569	1.39525	1.81939
Support for DWW[***]	0.38659	0.14112	-0.699850	0.165310	-0.386594	1.45089	1.84218
Supports limits to growth thesis[**]	0.31465	0.9026	0.476737	0.141707	0.314652	1.47168	1.89594

[*] $p < 0.05$; [**] $p < 0.01$; [***] $p < 0.001$.

Table 8.8 *Multiple Regression Models of Local Environmental Concern*

Independent variables	Test 1 (Beta)	Test 2 (Beta)	Test 3 (Beta)	Test 4 (Beta)
Respondent's characteristics				
Sex (female = 1)	0.238688	0.207055	0.219303	0.184400
Religion				
Church affiliation (Alliance/Mennonite/Reform = 1)		−0.182494	−0.144115	−0.091104
Political culture				
Support for business ideology			−0.113689	−0.039548
Support for socialist values			0.047824	[a]
Ethnic tolerance			0.117176	0.125920
Environment				
Support for DWW				−0.257163
Support for limits to growth thesis				[a]
Level of environmental activism				0.229843
	R^2adj. = 0.04601	R^2adj. = 0.06785	R^2adj. = 0.10568	R^2adj. = 0.26397
		Change = 0.02149	Change = 0.03783	Change = 0.15829
	$p = {} < 0.05$	$p = {\sim}0.05$	$p = {} < 0.05$	$p = {} < 0.0001$

[a] Removed from the final model because of high levels of multicollinearity.

support for DWW, followed by membership in the Alliance, Mennonite, or Reform church, and finally support for business ideology. Local environmental concern is best explained by level of environmental activism, being female, and being ethnically tolerant. The final model can explain 26 per cent of local environmental concern.

Table 8.9 shows the different regression models on environmental activism. As test one shows, church affiliation is statistically significant, but does not explain much of local environmental activism. In the second model, political culture variables were introduced, resulting in a significant change in the value of R^2 (adjusted), from 0.037 to 0.091. Church affiliation continues to exert more negative influence than does support for business ideology. Ethnic tolerance has greater positive influence than support for socialist views. The final model includes environment variables. Limits to Growth was not included in this model because of high levels of multicollinearity. The variable having the greatest explanatory power for local environmental activism was, not surprisingly, concern for the local environment, followed by ethnic tolerance, and support for socialist views. The variable having the greatest explanatory power for 'resisting the green' was support for DWW, followed by membership in the Alliance, Mennonite, or Reform church and support for business ideology. The final model can explain approximately 21 per cent of local environmental activism.

DISCUSSION

To state that the best predictor of 'resisting the green' is the belief that humanity has a special right and claim over non-human nature, and that any possible problems will be solved by science seems simply to reaffirm the importance of an element in Judeo-Christian tradition on the one hand and a persistent faith in a particular form of enquiry on the other – both of which have received much attention in the environmental literature. But does it constitute a good explanation for why men and women in this sample participate in so few environmental activities, and are so lacking in awareness of local environmental activism? Certainly not. Why? Because less than 5 per cent of our sample actually support, at any level, the Dominant Western World-View. Though it may be the best predictor, it only predicts the actions of a few. How can the actions of the rest be explained?

First, we must keep in mind that the regression models only explain a small amount of environmental concern or environmental activism. Obviously these are very complex issues and there are many other factors involved that were not examined in this research. The second-best predictor for 'resisting the green' was membership in one of the three traditional and highly influential church denominations in the area, namely the Alliance, the Mennonite, or

Table 8.9 *Multiple Regression Models of Environmental Activism*

Independent variables	Test 1 (Beta)	Test 2 (Beta)	Test 3 (Beta)
Religion			
Church affiliation (1 = Alliance/Mennonite/Reform)	−0.2170048	−0.181868	−0.091528
Political culture			
Support business ideology		−0.053538	−0.056361
Support socialist values		0.149698	0.101327
Ethnic tolerance		0.168278	0.150430
Environment			
Support for DWW			−0.237523
Support for limits to growth thesis			a
Concern for local environment			0.240100
	R^2adj. = 0.03708	R^2adj. = 0.09174	R^2adj. = 0.21301
		Change = 0.05466	Change = 0.12127
	$p = < 0.05$	$p = < 0.05$	$p = < 0.001$

[a] Removal from final model because of high levels of multicollinearity.

the Reform churches. Approximately 27 per cent of our sample belonged to one of these churches. Some were business people; others were politicians, bureaucrats, and community activists. Many were church leaders. While more respondents were members of established churches, only membership in the 'big three' was found significant in predicting a negative relationship for either environmental concern or environmental activism. Nevertheless, it is not a perfect predictor; in fact it actually explains only a small portion of either dependent variable. While the multiple-regression models show that support for business ideology is weaker as an explanation for a negative relationship for either environmental concern or environmental activism, it is a political ideology that has widespread support. Stated more simply, one could more accurately predict individual 'resistance to the green' based on high support for DWW than for support for business ideology, but it would be applicable to few of the sample. Support for business ideology does not have the same power of prediction. Persons could support business ideology and have concerns for the local environment and even have higher levels of environmental activism. But overall, business ideology has a negative relationship with both dependent variables *and* is widely shared by the members of this sample. Thus, we argue that the lack of environmental activism found in this case study can best be explained by a widespread acceptance of business ideology that values deficit reduction, increased industrial development, and free enterprise. Of course, it could be argued that this is not particularly revealing, that business ideology is widely supported throughout North America. However, in the case of Abbotsford such a business ideology is incorporated into a particular political culture that has been shaped by groups of aspiring immigrants who have sought material success as farmers, farm workers, artisans and small business people in what has become a highly productive and profitable agricultural region.

Their attachment to a 'business ideology' reflects, in part, their structural location in what for the past 30 years has been a rapidly expanding regional economy. Many have prospered; most in only relatively modest ways; a few mightily. Their economic values are those of men and women who have acquired a little property and are anxious to defend and nurture it. Recently, with large-scale immigration and with large in-flows of capital from countries of the Pacific Rim, towns such as Abbotsford have become caught up in rival quests for growth, their politicians, businessmen and farmers all powering a treadmill of expansion, a 'growth machine', as Logan and Molotch (1987) call it.

A further very important element is added to this when we consider that many of the immigrants came to the Fraser Valley as members of particular religious and ethnic groups. The valley offered them the opportunity to practise their faiths in a number of relatively independent communities. These communities of pious Mennonites, Dutch Calvinists and more recently-arrived evangelical Christians have given the valley, especially the central section, a distinctive structure of social relations and a distinctive set of beliefs and practices that have profoundly affected political culture and process.

To understand the political culture of this area, and to show how it inhibits and represses 'green' activism, we need to consider how class, ethnicity and religion have interacted. Some understanding of these matters comes from the insightful and often critical analyses supplied by a number of our respondents. Consider this passage from a Mennonite, one who was raised in the area but spent most of his life living elsewhere in Canada and the USA. Coming back home in his retirement, he reflects:

> I have seen a massive shift from the poor lower middle class to upper middle class – a shift in thinking. There's a kind of reflective conservatism politically which is, I think, rooted to a large degree in an economic status. To a lesser degree in traditional families, and also traditional religious beliefs. I differ from many of your analysts [who] attribute the conservatism mainly to religious allegiances. I think that at least as much is attributable to socio-economic features. People who have moved up the socio-economic ladder fairly recently and fairly rapidly are jealous of guarding their situation.

The Mennonites, especially, were attracted to what was, in the 1920s, the relative isolation of the Fraser Valley because it offered them a place where they could live as 'a people apart' (Redekop, 1989). Communities of believers, practising their pietistic religion, they grew numerous and prosperous but, according to some (and we heard this from those inside and outside the church), a degree of separation remains. A pastor in one of the smaller churches observes:

> We [local churches] tend to be isolationist. We tend to be very comfortable looking after our own. This can be a really vicious church community. There tends to be a lot of competition ... there is serious competition and pride. ... The Christian Reform Church stays together. The Mennonite community very much stays together.

A pastor of one of the largest evangelical congregations in the whole of Canada talked about 'A Nation Church' – one that was so large that it offered something close to 'institutional completeness' (to use Raymond Breton's phrase, coined to describe that situation where members of an ethnic group have achieved such size and density in an area that they can live virtually their entire lives within the confines of their ethnic group). In this case the church offered women's ministries, men's ministries, a 'foreign college kids' ministry, schools, colleges, a wide range of sports teams and sports facilities, an array of businesses owned by church members, with whom the faithful were encouraged to trade – all were there. The pastor of a 'nation church' instructed us:

> I think the churches are very, very strong value-based organisations. We have politicians, lawyers, business people, farmers and ordinary folks that come here and they lead and they impact the infrastructure of the community. That's probably an area, I would say, you should look into.

He seems to be talking not only about a structure, a network of believers in positions of leadership, but about a kind of 'embodied' culture. This is reminiscent of Bourdieu's sense of cultural capital existing in the very dispositions of individuals (Bourdieu, 1990). Another respondent also felt that we had not focused sufficient attention on religion (in fact we deliberately avoided asking leading questions that would steer respondent to talk about it).

> I'm surprised you didn't spend more time talking about religion, because there is a religious ethos out there that is very oppressive. The Sikhs have a very strong, visible presence in the community and they live pretty well to themselves. The Mennonites always have a very strong presence there, and a very strong political presence... . You talk to Mennonites and they are just aghast if you suggest ... if you say... . 'You people have so much control over the political process' and they don't know what you are talking about – because they see political process so differently, because they see that it is something they control, therefore it's okay. And there is a booklet put out about Christian businesses and it's called the Shepherd book, or something like that. So members are encouraged to buy and deal with those businesses... . So it's a bad place you know.

By the time we completed our interview survey we had compelling evidence from comparative studies that we were conducting, that Abbotsford, indeed, does have markedly fewer 'green' groups than other municipalities, that it lacks the networks of organisations and activists that make up local 'environmental public sphere' that we found elsewhere.

The material from our interviews with Abbotsford community leaders provides – from the open-ended and from the fixed-choice questions – two broad kinds of explanation for this. First, there is a structural explanation. Abbotsford is not really one community. More than most small towns, it is divided into a series of relatively distinct religious and ethnic collectivities with varying but substantial degrees of geographical, social and cultural insulation from one another. This finds its clearest expression in the largest church groups with their impressive arrays of confessionally separate organisations and networks, not only for worship but for education, leisure and recreation, business and politics. In their answers to the structured questions, church leaders gave clear evidence of that. Particularly in respect of green groups, leaders and activities, they were very 'unconnected'. But the evidence of social division came also from many discursive passages throughout the interviews. Time and again we were told how religious/ethnic groups 'kept to themselves'. Such division inhibits the building of community-wide organisations to address environmental issues. This is not to claim that there have been no attempts to start environmental groups within particular congregations, and occasionally on an ecumenical basis; but mostly they have enjoyed only a brief existence, partly because they appeared to be attacking wealthy members of their own congregations. The second kind of explanation relates to constellations of politico-economic ideas – specifically to the high levels of support for those kinds of values so commonly identified as 'neo-liberal'. In truth there is nothing very new about the suspicion of government, the belief in 'free' markets and conservative fiscal 'housekeeping', and strong commitments to forms of individualism. These are widespread in capitalist societies, but they have long enjoyed especially strong support among certain elements of the population – particularly the rural and (very often) the rural petite bourgeoisie. Again, both our fixed-choice and open-ended questions showed the importance of an economically conservative ideology. Given the history of settlement and the relative recency of the economic currents which have carried many Abbotsford area residents to higher levels of socioeconomic status, such a complex of economic views is readily intelligible. It is most unlikely to encourage forms of activism that challenge the appropriateness of 'growth' or put issues of sustainability before profit.

Here, as everywhere, 'structure' and 'culture' interact – producing groups, networks, parties, and other institutions that reflect and express distinctive economic and religious or moral beliefs. In their turn, patterned relationships and forms of association help to sustain, defend or disseminate particular notions of 'oughtness'. A more or less distinctive political culture grows up – establishing, among other things, the parameters of acceptable dissent. Such a culture exists in Abbotsford. Here, the 'green' lies, mostly beyond the moral boundary. It must be resisted.

ACKNOWLEDGEMENTS

The authors acknowledge the financial support of the Canadian Tri-Council for their funding of the multidisciplinary project on the Prospects for Sustainability in the Lower Fraser Basin.

NOTE

1.   An appendix detailing the variables and index construction was included in the original paper presented at the conference. Those interested can receive a copy of the variables list by writing to the authors at: Department of Anthropology

and Sociology, University of British Columbia, 6303 North West Marine Drive, Vancouver, British Columbia, Canada, V6T iZi.

REFERENCES

Anderson, K. (1991), *Vancouver's Chinatown* (Montreal and Kingston: McGill Queens University Press).

Blake, D. B., Guppy, N. and Urmetzer, P. (1997), 'Being Green in BC: Public Attitudes Towards Environmental Issues', *BC Studies*, 112, 41–61.

Bourdieu, P. (1990), *In Other Words* (Cambridge: Polity).

Breton, R. (1964), 'Institutional Completeness of Ethnic Communities and the Personal Relations of Immigrants', *American Journal of Sociology*, 70, 193–205.

Dunlap, R. B. and Van Liere, K. (1978), 'The New Environmental Paradigm', *Journal of Environmental Education*, 9, 10–19.

Galois, R. and Cole, H. (1994), 'Recalibrating Society: the Population Geography of British Columbia in 1881', *Canadian Geographer*, 38, 37–53.

Gould, K. A. and Schnaiberg, A. (1994), *Environment and Society* (New York: St Martin's Press).

Gould, K. A., Schnaiberg, A. and Weinberg, A. S. (1996), *Local Environmental Struggle: Citizen Activism in the Treadmill of Production* (Cambridge: Cambridge University Press).

Hand, C. M. and Van Liere, K. D. (1984), 'Religion, Mastery-over-Nature and Environmental Concern', *Social Forces*, 63, 555–70.

Inglehart, R. (1990), *Culture Shift in Advanced Industrial Society* (Princeton, NJ: Princeton University Press).

Jones, R. E. and Dunlap, R. B. (1992), 'The Social Bases of Environmental Concern: Have They Changed Over Time?', *Rural Sociology*, 7, 28–47.

Klassen, A. J. (1992), *The Church in the Heart of the Valley: 1892–1992* (Abbotsford: Matsqui-Abbotsford Ministerial Association).

Logan, J. R. and Molotch, H. (1987), *Urban Fortunes: The Political Economy of Place* (Berkeley, CA: University of California Press).

McClosky, H. (1964), 'Consensus and Ideology in American Politics', *American Political Science Review*, 58, 361–82.

McCormick, P. (1991), 'The Reform Party of Canada: New Beginning or Dead End?', in Hugh G. Thornburg (ed.), *Party Politics in Canada*, 6th edn (Scarborough, Ont.: Prentice-Hall Canada, 1991).

Koenig, D. J. (1973), *British Columbia Voting Patterns and Political Attitudes* (Vancouver: Province Newspaper).

Redekop, C. W. (1989), *Mennonite Society* (Baltimore: Johns Hopkins University Press).

Riggins, L. and Walker, L. (1991), *The Heart of the Fraser Valley: Mennonites of an Era Past* (Clearbrooke, BC: Matsquil Abbotsford Community Series, Matsqui Centennial Society).

Somers, M. R. (1995), 'What's Political or Cultural about Political Culture and the Public Sphere? Toward an Historical Sociology of Concept Formation', *Sociological Theory*, 13, 113–48.

White, L., Jr (1967), 'The Historic Roots of our Ecological Crisis', *Science*, 155, 1203–7.

Part III

Transforming the State and State Resistance

9 Re-Conceptualising Feminist Agency in the State: a Study of the Implementation of Women's Equal Opportunity Policy in British Local Government

Cinnamon Bennett

INTRODUCTION

The organisation of feminist agency in local state bureaucracies has broadly shifted from, in the 1980s, separate women's structures, such as women's policy units or women's working parties, to a mainstreamed approach in the 1990s which dispenses with dedicated staff. The agenda for 'mainstreaming equality' has been articulated most clearly at the European Union level. This discourse expressly embraces the economic and human resource arguments for equality outcomes. It has been praised by proponents as 'transformative' (Rees, 1996), while simultaneously provoking unease among women's activists. They feel that mainstreaming may represent 'male-streaming', the deradicalisation and eradication of feminist practice in the local state.

This chapter is based on qualitative data drawn from one British district council's experience of delivering equal opportunities for women. Using the experience of this case study I want to explore some of the practical and theoretical issues arising from the move to a mainstreamed approach. The chapter starts by outlining the background of local government women's equality initiatives, describing the differences which the new mainstreaming equality agenda envisages. I will then go on to introduce Connell's conceptualisation of organisational relationships, to explore local authority practice in terms of a 'gender order' composed of different structuring elements. The last section applies this analysis to my case study authority, identifying how women's officers have acted

161

to change elements of the authority's gender order, where and why their efforts at implementation have fallen down, and consequently why the move to main-streamed equality has not been as transformative as promised.

LOCAL GOVERNMENT WOMEN'S INITIATIVES

Feminist women councillors in local Labour parties were the key actors in the creation of formal committees for women's equality within local government (Halford, 1988: 401). Their intention was to support women within and through local government. The establishment of separate structures and practices was seen as a way of building up women's confidence and skills, protected from an environment they identified as male-dominated and unsympathetic. The administrative support units, which accompanied the committees, were often more radical in their outlook, since the staff tended to be 'political' appointees, often women who had a proven track record of campaigning for women's rights (Goss, 1984: 109). These women brought with them agendas for greater participation of local women in the process of deciding where and in what form local resources should be used.

Local political history and economic circumstances were also important factors in determining the status of the council structures established, and the orientation of their policies. For example, Susan Halford and Simon Duncan's research, conducted between 1986 and 1988, demonstrated the links between non-unionised, industrially mixed urban labour markets and the existence of a large number of politically active single women, and progressive party memberships who were predisposed to setting up women's initiatives (Halford and Duncan, 1991: 7). They showed how women's committees were not a universal or coherent strategy of socialist councils. Even at the height of the women's committee movement in 1988 there were only 68 Labour councils with a structural initiative, which represented 13 per cent of all councils (Halford and Duncan, 1991: 4).[1] With this caveat a distinct set of equality practices were undertaken, to varying extents, by all women's committees. The most common of these was to target the council's record as an equal opportunities employer. The second was to ensure the appropriateness and adequacy of existing services to women. Indeed, service provision had been a long-standing focus of local women's campaigns (Gelb, 1986: 117). Units responded by funding women's groups and projects to fill the gaps in public provision and by highlighting the hidden stereotyping and discrimination in existing allocation strategies. Lastly, reflecting a concern that women were under-represented in 'formal' politics, consultation mechanisms and co-option onto committees were attempted to introduce women's perspectives into the policy-making process.

Working within broadly similar parameters and political circumstances, it comes as no surprise that members of women's committees and those employed in administrative support are remarkably consistent in their identification of the barriers to their practice. They have felt themselves held back by the legal framework on sex equality, which defines their work as dis-cretionary and therefore an addition to the statutory duties of the council.[2] This has not been helped by the paucity of guidelines from central govern-ment, acting in the guise of the under-funded Equal Opportunities Commission[3] (Edwards, 1988: 44). The definition and legitimisation of women's equality work has therefore typically depended on the patronage of local leaders, the majority of whom are men.[4] Consequently women's com-mittees have been faced with a constant process of negotiation and justification of their actions (Edwards, 1988: 42). The policy influence which units attempted to bring to bear over service departments aroused profes-sional jealousies and resistance. Often this resistance hid deep-seated sexism (Perrigo, 1986: 105) although a misunderstanding and lack of clarity of the issues themselves has been a major problem (Riley, 1990: 54–5).

The new equal opportunities agenda that has emerged since the early 1990s attempts to get to grips with the issue of legitimisation by insisting on both corporate *and* individual levels of responsibility for equality work. To this end it proposes the abolition of specialist workers. This approach reasons that universal ownership will simultaneously remove the administra-tive resistance to implementation of women's equality that strategies have so far produced. The mainstreaming equality agenda has been adopted by many councils on this simple premise. It has resulted in the merger of women's committees into generic equal opportunities structures covering all categories of discrimination, or their abolition and the substitution of corpor-ate mission statements which are intended to affect every officer's working brief. Women's officers have reacted sceptically to this trend. They generally support dedicated, named provision as the only way to sustain progress. They are also suspicious of the agenda's concerns for more efficient human resource management of a changing workforce. They claim that buried beneath this rhetoric is a neo-liberal agenda of individualism and public sector cost-cutting which proponents of the concept have failed to problematise.

INTRODUCING MAINSTREAMING EQUALITY: ITS ORIGINS AND INTENTIONS

Mainstreaming equality as an approach to equality practice was first described in the European Commission's Third Community Action Programme for Equal Opportunities as: 'the integration of equality into mainstream policy formation and implementation' (EOC, 1996). Since then the features of the concept have been expanded by the Fourth Action Programme, the UN Fourth Conference on Women in Beijing in 1995 and most recently in Britain by the Department for Education and Employment. Mainstreaming tacitly recognises the need for the state itself to take action within its existing remits to promote the public equality policy established in law (EOC, 1996). More recently the arguments of the business cases for equality has been added to the definition. This reflects the concerns of global business to manage diverse workforces, to benefit from quality gains in goods and service provision and lastly to avoid the economic costs of inequality (from legal penalties to inefficient use of human capital).

The concept's originality has been to articulate the need to tackle organisational cultures in the workplace, such as the hidden barriers (or 'glass ceilings'), which limit individuals' performances and promotions. Targeting organisational cultures gives scope for strategies which are gender-inclusive, since these cultures inhibit men as well as women. An inclusive approach to equality work circumvents the antagonism which women-only approaches are alleged to incite, and encourages broad ownership. By making mainstreaming an organisational rather than a political or human-rights concern, the concept is reflecting the increasing precedence given to corporate imperatives. Mainstreaming equality is shaped to resemble any other organisational task that can be quantified, delegated and measured. The difficulty facing local authorities wishing to apply the approach on the ground is in defining the priorities that should follow, since an overemphasis on the organisational and business advantages holds serious implications for the understanding of equality being promoted.

CONNELL'S THEORY OF GENDER ORDER

R. W. Connell (1987) conceptualises the gender relations (or in his term the gender order) operating in a social organisation as constituted by interacting social structures. These social structures are not only visible physical arrangements but also refer to unspoken cultural and emotional rules. They cause human agents to limit their behaviour and actions, while providing them with a framework through which they can produce results beyond their individual capacity. Agency (practice) and structures in Connell's gender order are inseparable. The influence of structures is present in everyday actions; consequently structures are vulnerable to change in the event of major shifts in practice. By giving practice a role in constituting structure, Connell moves away from a systematic view of male power, where male authority is fundamental and can be reversed only by an extreme revolution of gender relations. A duality of agency and structure (after Giddens, 1979) suggests that piecemeal action can affect and reverse underlying social structures over time. Connell emphasises the historicity of this interaction. Unlike Giddens he considers that the context in which agency takes place does not derive from the alternatives offered by the underlying structures. Instead he sees a situation (a historical period of time) providing the context for agency where underlying social structures frame its precise action: 'Since the consequence of practice is a transformed situation which is the object of new practice, "structure" specifies the way practice (over time) constrains practice' (1987: 95)

Connell's gender order combines three discrete social structures. These structures have been identified in recent academic research. They are structures concerned with the sexual division of labour, those concerned with power through control and coercion, and those which fashion emotional or personal interaction (cathexis). More specifically, the structure of sexual division of labour includes elements such as the gendered segregation of labour market, the tradition of labelling jobs as 'women's' and 'men's' work and the gendered design of machinery, hours and career paths. Power structures serve to legitimise male authority, and consist of the effort and resources needed to maintain men's priviledged position, the hierarchical arrangement of men and women within the male hegemony and its demonstration through organisational cultures. Cathexis details the many levels of emotional behaviour, visible, covert and frequently ambivalent, that are expressed and experienced by members of the gender order, and the cultural fashioning of these behaviours into acceptable relationship patterns.

The concept of a gender order is a helpful way of describing the social organisation of a local authority. In my case study the women's officers have identified the hidden and overt social structures in the bureaucracy that limited their agency, but have failed to link them into one whole picture. Their perception of themselves as facilitators to encourage ownership for equality policies acknowledges the duality of agency and structure. Their practice over time, with varying momentum, in different milieux, has changed the way things were done and perceived. Historicity is represented by the external events initiated by central government (for example, rate capping, compulsory competitive tendering, media campaigns) and internal decisions (for example, decentralisation) which fundamentally changed the context in which the dynamic of agency and structures operate.

THE CASE STUDY DISTRICT AUTHORITY

The case study district council, which I will refer to using the pseudonym Houghton DC, has many of the features common to women's initiatives set up in the 1980s as identified by Halford (1988). It is an urban council, with a long-standing Labour majority. The demand for a women's initiative was led by feminist councillors in the local Labour party, who had strong associations with the local women's movement, in this case focused on women's health and women's refuges. Two equality structures were established, an Equal Opportunities Committee and a Women's Committee.

Starting with one women's officer based in the Personnel Department, the equality initiative was promoted to committee level in 1986. An Equal Opportunities Subcommittee was attached to the Policy and Resource Committee, served by an equality unit. The women's officer was transferred across to this unit. Part of her brief was to draw up plans for a women's committee, which was created in 1988 as a full standing committee of the council with a support unit alongside that of equality in the chief executive's department. The women's committee was equal in status to a recognisable set of service and strategic committees, such as Leisure, Housing and Works. In 1991, in response to financial constraints, the two committees (and their units) were briefly merged into one full standing committee – Women and Equalities. In 1993 this committee was abolished and its responsibilities mainstreamed to a newly implemented, council-wide, decentralised structure of neighbourhood committees.

In this chapter I will focus on feminist agency in the local authority arena. I have used the term feminist agency to include the work of the women's officer in the equality unit up to 1988, the women's officers in the women's unit and the women's officers in the women's and equality unit. As there was considerable overlap of staff in all three structures and a common purpose, I refer to them indiscriminately as 'women's officers' and the 'women's unit'.

APPLYING CONNELL'S FRAMEWORK TO EQUALITY PRACTICE IN HOUGHTON DC, 1986–92

Of the three social structures which combined to make up the gender order in Houghton DC up to 1992, the sexual division of labour was the most visible because it was founded in managerial arrangements. Table 9.1 outlines the situation and the actions which women's officers took to remedy it. The unit's initial target was the authority's recruitment and employment practices. It was widely known that male service heads recruited people they liked, and saw nothing wrong in doing so. Discrimination was reinforced by the form of employment offered. Contracts made no allowances for women staff's domestic and child-care responsibilities. The women's unit was instrumental in detailing job-share arrangements and writing guidelines on maternity and adoption leave. To the same end it heavily promoted women's training and career development with an emphasis on transferable skills and non-traditional areas of work. The impact of this work on the number and

Table 9.1 *Sexual Division of Labour*

Elements of structure	Situation: new women councillors; pro-active Labour authority	Equality practice – specialist unit
Gendered segregation of labour market	Service heads all men – controlling recruitment	Personnel procedures re-drawn
Labelling jobs as women's and men's	Gendered jobs with women at the bottom	Women trained/retained in manual trades and management
Gendered design of machinery, hours, career paths	No inclusive policies to account for women's domestic responsibilities	Procedures for maternity, adoption leave and job share

status of women in the organisation was increased by the high retention of women in the authority. During this period the personnel practices of Houghton DC were permanently reformed. They catered for women's family role and instilled a tradition of women in senior managerial roles.

Alongside employment policy, another of the unit's tasks, from its inception, was to tackle service delivery issues. This brief brought women's officers into direct conflict with the underlying power structures of the departments. They described the resistance they faced in terms of a front-line culture of professionalism and autonomy from the executive, combined with 'laddish' obstruction. I have interpreted the tradition of front-line exclusivity in terms of Connell's power structures and the laddish 'locker-room' culture as a cathexis structure of behavioural rules.

The local authority's power structure was based on a certain understanding of the departmental role in relation to other service and executive hierarchies and to the community. Staff distinguished between front-line departments who delivered statutory services and had direct contact with customers, and back-line departments which supported front-line actions. The latter included the strategic policy-making areas, such as the women's unit, even though their policy input affected how services were quantitatively and qualitatively delivered. Service heads ran their departments with a 'Greek temple' mentality which discouraged communication between the service 'pillars', sometimes even labelling it as treacherous. The autocratic nature of different departmental 'empires' was reinforced by an emphasis on their unique expertise. The deference accorded to professionals served to divide staff and keep them at arms' length from the community.

The women's unit had clear strategies to infiltrate the front-line (shown in Table 9.2). To encourage broad ownership of equality goals it introduced a system of link officers nominated by their departments, to meet with women's officers to discuss their department's equality initiatives. This had the advantage of formalising regular close contact. However, the strategy failed because it expected too much of the link. One women's officer described how, when link officers were with her, they could see things through her eyes, but they quickly reverted back to their department's general outlook when they were back behind their desks. It was too much to expect them to pursue uncomfortable policies with the colleagues with whom they worked closely on a daily basis. A second approach to service heads who refused or avoided complying with the unit was to rely on the system of annual action plans for equality, rubber-stamped by politicians. Each department had to design a 12-month programme of actions and submit these, along with the past year's results, before their committee. Unfortunately it was often the case that the chair of the committee colluded with the service head, limiting even this low-key attempt to incorporate equality objectives into service delivery.

Table 9.2 *Power/Authority*

Elements of structure	Situation: new women councillors; pro-active Labour authority	Equality practice – specialist unit
Masculine authority is legitimated power	Strict front-line/back-line conception	Link officers from departments – work with women's unit
Effort and resources needed to maintain male hegemony	Endemic professionalism, 'expert' culture	Developmental approach to pass on skills and responsibility
Hierarchies of men/women within male hegemony	Territorialisation, empire building between service heads	Alternative ideology: officers as facilitators not experts, community knowledge valued
Power enacted via the medium of culture	Collusion between male councillors and officers against women's issues	Action plans for equality progress monitoring

As a direct challenge to the authority's reliance on professional expertise women's officers gave precedence to community knowledge. To find more imaginative and apt solutions they extensively consulted with constituents and invested time to train a number of local women who had been nominated to sit and vote on the women's committee. While the departments were largely untouched by these new models of practice, the unit had pioneered important consultation mechanisms which were more widely adopted after decentralisation.

Taken as a whole the unit's strategies (link officers, action plans, etc.) were a challenge to underlying power structures. They were attempting to bring a back-line influence to bear on front-line departments, which saw this influence as usurping their rightful responsibility. More particularly, liaison with the unit threatened to diminish the validity and integrity of departmental power arrangements by setting up alternative loyalties among the staff. The unit's close connection with local women's community groups derided officers' expert knowledge. This community know-how challenged the status of many individuals in their department hierarchies and in terms of their own personal esteem and identity. The extent to which the departments saw the unit as a threat was apparent in a petition signed by officers, against the chief officer grade accorded to the head of the women's unit.

The second form of resistance which women's officers identified was the 'locker-room' behaviour of officers.[5] Across the authority there was resentment of the prioritisation given to women's issues and the high grades given to the unit's staff. Jokes and innuendoes that the unit was an 'add-on' 'policing unit' served to undermine its serious equality purpose. The leader of the council gave the most striking example of one individual's attempt to exclude the unit from the 'male-stream'. He stopped the debate on the formation of the women's committee. By silencing supporters, and allowing sexist opposition to go unchallenged, he gave a clear message to the authority that the initiative had been set up to fail.

Acknowledging the impact of single actors on organisational culture has been missing from previous analysis of feminist practice in local state. Cathexis is a particular strength of Connell's framework and one which I am pursuing in my research. Women's officers adopted personal strategies to counter laddish behaviour, and to break through the neutral veneer of professionalism which prevented staff members from making emotional commitments to equality. Firstly, by astutely managing their personal relationships, women's officers secured more progressive results. One former women's officer described how she saw her role as coming into a meeting 'all sparky', ready to say the unthinkable while maintaining an engaging and warm relationship with the person she was challenging. This unconventional behaviour lessened people's resistance, either because they enjoyed the jovial sparring or because they were flummoxed and felt unable to use their accustomed put-downs. Those officers

Table 9.3 *Cathexis/Emotions*

Elements of structure	Situation: new women councillors; pro-active Labour authority	Equality practice – specialist unit
Many levels of emotional behaviour – visible and shadow	Grading determined behaviour towards colleagues	Ignoring grades, saying the unthinkable
Emotional experience characterised by ambivalence	Locker-room mentality; resistance on a personal level	Female-stream: mutual support of all-women units
Patterning of acceptable social relationships can change		Importance of personal attributes to success of strategy

in the women's unit who were successful at facilitating change in others, appeared to consciously rely on the added factor of their appealing personality and social intuition to aid progress.

Secondly, women in Houghton DC had created what I have called a 'female-stream': a network of friendships which overstepped the formal distance characterising relationships between colleagues. The incoming women's chief officer described how the central management team had expected a 'cat fight' to erupt between her and the principal officer of the equality unit. They were shocked when the two women got on immediately without professional competitiveness. The beleaguered atmosphere in which the women's unit operated encouraged women's officers to develop a deep level of intimacy with each other. It also compelled them to identify strategic external allies. One ally of the unit was the Economic Development Unit, significantly an all-woman team. The friendships formed between women across the authority were meaningful and held potential openings for the development of further work. Table 9.3 details the authority's cathexis structures.

To summarize the effects of the unit's agency in the period 1986–92 in terms of Connell's framework: the unit was successful in altering the sexual division of labour for women employees in the authority. This social structure was the most visible of the three and easiest to counter. Changes to the employment practices could be effectively implemented via existing personnel training mechanisms. The effect of women's agency on the departmental power structures was less effective and provoked a defensive reaction. The 'Greek temple' arrangement of service departments made it relatively easy for them to resist the unit's work. In attempting to alter cathexis structures the unit was helped by the introduction of more women to the authority workforce. Pockets of good practice were established in departments where individuals were allies of the unit. Those women's officers who were adept at managing their personal relationships achieved considerable results.

THE GENDER ORDER OF MAINSTREAMING: 1992 ONWARDS

There are two important observations to make about the strategy to mainstream equality in Houghton DC. Firstly, the reorganisation of the unit was not designed as a discrete policy; secondly, it did not happen in a political or economic vacuum. Mainstreaming equality was one small part of two larger overlapping projects: down-sizing employee numbers and decentralising service delivery. Both projects were a response to the considerable financial constraints imposed on Houghton DC by central government through consecutive years of rate capping. They were justified in terms of increased efficiency and quality in service provision which would secure the council's electoral mandate in the long term. Mainstreaming equality was consequently tarred with the brush of financial necessity and market orientation.

Down-sizing, initiated by a new chief executive officer, aimed to flatten the management structures to produce streamlined departments. His motives were two-fold. Firstly, he aimed to remove 'dead wood', the service heads whose 'cradle to grave' mentality made them unable to accept the new financial and political environment. Secondly, the need to progressively reduce the authority's budget demanded staff cuts and a more efficient deployment of the remaining resources. Decentralisation was sponsored and carried through by the elected members. It broke up the service departments into local neighbourhood administrations, leaving a strategic policy-making core, to ensure a town-wide perspective was maintained. It was hoped that democratisation would spring from the greater interface between the service staff and the community. This project echoed similar experiments being carried out by other Labour councils and promoted by the Local Government Management Board in the early 1990s.

The women's unit had been created in part out of the members' long-standing commitment to greater democracy and accountability. As I have already described, it had pioneered mechanisms for community involvement. Decentralisation legitimised this practice across the authority. For the supporters of decentralisation and mainstreaming, a new stage in equality delivery had been reached where the staff would take collective responsibility for equality work. Keeping a central women's unit in a decentralised authority was an anomaly, as it would be split off from the now-dispersed service functions. The unit was therefore closed. Its staff were encouraged to apply for service department posts within the authority, so their expertise (if not their function) was retained. An equality brief was given to one of three new neighbourhood chief officers in the central management team. The procedures of assessing equality implications were standardised on all reports and policy documents, and raised to the status of one of the authority's business objectives.

In theory, the benefits of mainstreaming responsibility for equal opportunities work were clear and the reporting mechanism for achieving them logical and straightforward. However, there were so many changes happening to staff at once that the mainstreaming message became confused. Mainstreaming equality suffered from the problem of all equality work; it was hijacked by other priorities, such as maintaining statutory service delivery. Crucially, one of its main proponents in the management left the authority soon after the process was complete, depriving an already overworked core of a strong articulation of mainstreaming's goals. Similarly, women councillors were burnt out or too preoccupied with smoothing the administration in their neighbourhoods to reassert where equality was going.

While mainstreaming equality failed to impact on the new cultures being set up in the authority there were unintentional benefits for some women in the decentralisation and down-sizing process. The mechanism which the chief executive used to shake out obstructive service heads was a training session run by independent consultants away from the town hall. Second-tier managers were deliberately invited to this session. There were many younger, able women at this grade. The effect of juxtaposing these two levels of management was to demonstrate to existing heads the quality of young talent competing for their jobs. For women who attended, the message they received was that they should see themselves as part of the management team, capable of applying for more senior positions. Two out of the six newly appointed chief officers were women. These women managers had a heightened awareness of how they had been helped as women, which in turn influenced their view of women below them, and the working cultures they established around them.

The response to mainstreaming of the former women's officers whom I interviewed was negative. They rejected the claim that mainstreaming was a positive development of their work. The consensus was that the unit had lost its way by antagonising politicians and management, who consequently had used mainstreaming as an excuse to get rid of it. Their reasons for believing mainstreaming to be a token gesture were based on some of the following observations: proponents had to fight to keep the name 'equalities' on one of the central briefs. The decentralisation project team had not consulted women's officers in the mainstreaming design. The project team was close to the local Labour group which was perceived to be hostile to the unit. This view was reinforced by the evident relief among some leading politicians when the unit was abolished.

In a situation of complacency, of the authority resting on its laurels, of sprawling structures where equality initiatives are invisible, former women's officers continue to advocate the need for dedicated provision to provide a focus for future work. In effect they want to return to the former situation, but working with the lessons of hindsight. What has been lost and what gained in the new situation? How has the move to mainstreaming and decentralisation altered the context of the gender order in Houghton DC, and therefore of the form of each of its component structures? I will start with the positive changes.

Changes to the sexual division of labour are summarized in Table 9.4. Decentralisation has removed the former service heads and replaced them with a greater proportion of women, in a flatter management hierarchy. The personnel practices and women's training have been carried over to the new structures. They are actively promoted by those women at the top who personally benefited from them. There is now visible gender diversity in the authority's workforce.

The power structures of the former departments have been reformed by the process of fragmenting the service departments into neighbourhood areas (Table 9.5). While the tendency exists for smaller 'Greek temples' to form, the stranglehold of the power structures has been minimised by the flatter management arrangements. The emphasis of decentralisation for customer-led service delivery formalises the acceptance of local knowledge by the expert culture. The ideological policing of the women's unit and

Table 9.4 *Changes to the Sexual Division of Labour*

Elements of structure	Situation 1993 onwards: Decentralisation/democratisation of authority structures; central government capping; media attack on loony left	Equality practice – mainstreaming
Gendered segregation of labour market	Male service heads ejected, women recruited to replace them	Visible gender diversity in top management
Labelling jobs as women's and men's		Women role models
Gendered design of machinery, hours, career paths		Career progression and training for women formalised but on hold due to financial cuts

176

Table 9.5 *Changes in Power and Authority*

Elements of structure	Situation 1993 onwards: Decentralisation/ democratisation of authority structures; central government capping; media attack on loony left	Equality practice – mainstreaming
Masculine authority is legitimated power	Customer/provider model promoted	Community consultation widely used
Effort and resources needed to maintain male hegemony	No unit: equality everybody's responsibility	Equality underwriting some departments' daily practice
Hierarchies of men/women within male hegemony		Antagonism of unit's policing removed, Central Management Team has responsibility for overview
Power enacted via the medium of culture		Action reports on every policy document to ensure routine consideration of gender implications

Table 9.6   *Changes in Cathexis/Emotions*

Elements of structure	Situation 1993 onwards: Decentralisation/ democratisation of authority structures; central government capping; media attack on loony left	Equality practice – mainstreaming
Many levels of emotional behaviour – visible and shadow	Women officers and councillors 'burnt out'	Women within the authority have scope to act creatively around equality issues
Emotional experience characterised by ambivalence	Unit staff dispersed/made redundant	
Social patterning of acceptable relationships can change	Networked organisation encourages communication	
	Authority has many more learning edges/ interfaces with the local community	

women's committee has been removed, and with it the fear and defensiveness it provoked. Action reports are a routine requirement of every policy proposal, with ultimate responsibility resting with one of the six chief officers of the central management team.

The new managerial shape of the authority as a networked organisation, in which different services talk to one another in a neighbourhood context, has given greater incentive for staff interaction. The new personal relations (cathexis structures) are summarized in Table 9.6. One former officer of the authority described the changes as they appeared to her on the ground. She no longer found people sitting behind their desks for all of the working day, they were freely moving around to communicate. Coupled with more points of contact with the community, the authority has many more 'learning edges'. This potentially allows for a more imaginative, sensitive development of piecemeal equality initiatives by different groups of women on the inside and the outside.

Although former women's officers are negative in the face of these changes their disapproval to a mainstreamed approach contains some telling contradictions. While they insist there is a need for dedicated equality staff, none would want their former job back; it was too stressful. They support the reinstatement of the women's unit but can identify no obvious place for it to go in the new neighbourhood structure. In describing a complacent situation where very little is now happening around equality, all still feel able to work creatively on equality in their new positions. Their reaction appears to reflect a recognition of two losses rather than blanket rejection of the new state of affairs.

The first lies with feminist practice in the area of power structures. The articulated commitment at the top level of the authority for gender equality has been lost. As one officer said, dedicated provision gave feminist practice an unspoken edge in the authority power struggles. As the women's unit proved, the symbol of political commitment to equality does not need to be popular or generally accepted, but it does need to be there to label feminist practice as a legitimate endeavour in the authority. Without the physical structure of a women's unit to symbolise this legitimacy the importance of spoken or written discussion of the issues becomes of paramount importance. It is this message that has got lost in Houghton DC, and for this reason women in the authority feel unable to act or reorganise as women.

The second loss relates to cathexis structures. While the scope for meaningful relations has increased, former officers recognise that there is no-one left to take up the equality debate. They themselves are unwilling or unready to fight again, and recognise this exhaustion in the women they worked with through the 1980s. They can see there are not enough gender-aware women to maximise on the opportunities offered by the new neighbourhood arrangements. The limitations on feminist agency of the post-1992 gender order are summarized in Table 9.7.

Table 9.7 *Importance of Organisational Arrangement of Authority in Perpetuating the Social Structures of the Gender Order*

Structure	Equality practice – mainstreaming	Requirements
Sexual division of labour	Visible gender diversity in top management	
	Women role models	
	Career progression and training for women formalised but on hold due to financial cuts	
Power/authority	Community consultation widely used	Clear articulation of the organic development of the equality agenda from units to mainstreaming – strong central equality committee. Legitimisation of feminist agency as a valid endeavour
	Equality underwriting some departments' daily practice	
	Antagonism of unit's policing removed, CMT has responsibility for overview	
	Action reports on every policy document to ensure routine consideration of gender implications	
Cathexis/emotions	Women within the authority have scope to act creatively around equality issues	Gender-aware agents to maximise new opportunities

CONCLUSION

There are three general conclusions to draw from the experience of main-streaming equality in Houghton DC. Firstly, the organisational cultures identified by women's officers were underpinned by the physical organisation of the authority into separate central service departments. This encouraged a front-line/back-line split and entrenched masculine professionalism. The women's unit's strategies were finely tuned to tackle the cultures but could do nothing to change the structure. It was not until the move to decentralisation that the cultures were open to discussion and change. The accepted definition of mainstreaming equality puts changing organisational cultures at the centre of its methodology. However, attempts to change cultures may not be successful if those cultures are rooted in organisational arrangements.

Secondly, for mainstreaming to move the equality agenda forward it needs to be explicit about where it has come from. In Houghton the common agenda for women's rights of dedicated provision and mainstreamed approaches was left unsaid. Mainstreaming was perceived as an unrelated development which had more in common with cuts and down-sizing than in tackling social inequality. The ways of ensuring that mainstreaming retains a critical vantage point still need to be worked out.

Thirdly, successful mainstreaming in Houghton required key proponents in the centre to explain the way equality was developing, and agents in the authority to hear and respond to the call. Neither type of agent was present. The result was an impression that nothing was happening and nothing was achievable. Mainstreaming may not be possible without the presence of gender-aware women at every level in the organisation. If this is the case, we need to ask how this situation can be brought about. It may be that without a preliminary rehearsal of the positive action debate, using the catalyst of a women's unit or dedicated officers, the gender-aware agents, needed to make a success of a mainstreamed situation, will not be present.

My final point concerns the usefulness of Connell's 'gender order' as a conceptual model for auditing the strengths and weaknesses of different forms of equality implementation strategies. A gender order helped me to analyse the complex historical situations in the lifetime of Houghton's equality initiative, which had been produced by competing material and social structures and human agency. It demonstrates all too plainly the difficulty and chance involved in achieving consensus on an organisational scale for a political idea. The model's articulation of the key role which individual feminists play in maximising opportunities is one which I intend to pursue. In particular, the ways in which the construction of a feminist identity may turn out to be a significant element of the cathexis structure. This issue is relevant not only to academics who have largely ignored the individual's hand in political action, but also for practitioners. Women's officers who have been in post since the 1980s will in time hand their positions to women who were too young to experience their unique political initiation into local government. What is being done to shape future women's understanding and enactment of feminist agency will be critical for the success of women's initiatives in the state arena over the next decade.

ACKNOWLEDGEMENTS

I thank all the people from the case study local authority discussed in this paper for being so enthusiastic about my research, and generous with their time. I am also very grateful to Bharat, who made my field visits so enjoyable. The conclusions and views expressed here are my sole responsibility.

NOTES

1. Excluding Northern Ireland.
2. The Sexual Discrimination Act of 1976 confers anti-discrimination responsibilities on local education and housing authorities, exempting all other activities.
3. EOC is the non-government organisation established by the Sexual Discrimination Act 1976, charged with its implementation.
4. Male councillors outnumbered women four to one, and not all women councillors supported the changes to women's traditional roles which many committees espoused.
5. Di Parkin and Sue Maddock's (1994) typography of gender cultures in organisations suggests that a 'locker-room' culture is an exclusive, laddish culture, based around out-of-work-time interaction.

REFERENCES

Connell, R. W. (1987), *Gender and Power: Society, the Person and Sexual Politics* (Cambridge: Polity).

Edwards, J. (1988), 'Local Government Women's Committees', *Critical Social Policy*, 24, 50–64.

EOC (Equal Opportunities Commission) (1996), 'Briefing on Mainstreaming', paper given to seminar 'From Equal Opportunities to Mainstreaming Equality', SPS University of Bristol.

Gelb, J. (1986), 'Feminism in Britain: Politics Without Power', in D. Dahlerup (ed.), *The New Women's Movement* (London: Sage).

Giddens, A. (1979), *Central Problems in Social Theory* (Basingstoke: Macmillan).

Goss, S. (1984), 'Women's Initiatives in Local Government', in Boddy, M. and Fudge, C. (eds), *Local Socialism* (Basingstoke: Macmillan).

Goss, S. (1989), 'Making Space – Bring Feminism into the Town Hall', in S. Goss, L. Stewart and C. Wolmar (eds), *Councils in Conflict: The Rise and Fall of the Municipal Left* (Basingstoke: Macmillan).

Halford, S. (1988), 'Women's Initiatives in Local Government: Where Do They Come From and Where Are They Going?', *Policy and Politics*, 16(4), 251–9.

Halford, S. and Duncan, S. (1991), *Implementing Feminist Policies in British Local Government?*, Centre for Urban and Regional Research, University of Sussex. Working paper 78.

Parkin, D. and Maddock, S. (1994) 'Gender Cultures Determine Women's Choices and Strategies at Work', in M. J. Davidson, and R. T. Burke (eds), *Women in Management* (London: Paul Chapman Publishing).

Perrigo, S. (1986) 'Socialist Feminism and the Labour Party': some Experiences from Leeds', *Feminist Review*, 23.

Rees T. (1996), Paper given to seminar 'From Equal Opportunities to Mainstreaming Equality', SPS University of Bristol.

Riley, K. (1990), 'Equality for Women: the Role of Local Authorities', *Local Government Studies*, January/February.

10 Social Movements and Equal Opportunities Work

Elizabeth Lawrence and Nicholas Turner

INTRODUCTION

Social movements of the 1960s and later have radically challenged the existing situation of Black people, women, lesbians and gay men, and disabled people. These movements had their impact on many areas of society. The enactment of equal opportunities legislation, such as, in the UK case, the 1975 Sex Discrimination Act, the 1976 Race Relations Act and the 1995 Disability Discrimination Act,[1] arose to a large extent because of these social movements. Similarly, within many organisations the development of equal opportunities policies and the establishment of specialist services for particular groups in society owe their origins to these radical social movements. Nonetheless the link between equal opportunities policies and social movements is often not acknowledged, particularly when equal opportunities as an issue becomes sanitised as 'good personal practice' or 'the management of diversity'. However, Halford's work (Halford and Durcan, 1991; Halford, 1992) explored the extent to which the local state could be used to implement feminist policies. Halford charted the growth of women's initiatives in local government, using 'women's initiatives' as an umbrella term to include the adoption of policies, the establishment of women's committees, the appointment of women's officers and the creation of women's units. Her work indicates that women's initiatives were more likely to occur in Labour-controlled councils, in urban areas, especially London, and in parts of the country with a higher than average proportion of single women and women in full-time work, suggesting an influential feminist presence in the local community.

This chapter is drawn from an ongoing study of equal opportunities officers in a variety of organisations. It discusses the significance of participation (past and present) in social movements for this group of workers. Involvement in social movements, such as the women's liberation movement, anti-racist movements, disability organisations, lesbian and gay groups and trade unions, can provide individuals with knowledge of areas of oppression and political organising skills. This experience, and the expertise gained through it, can both enable people to obtain employment as equal opportunities officers and assist in performance of their work. Interview material also explores the continuing significance of the social movements for those now employed to implement equal opportunities policies.

The role of new social movements in creating equal opportunities officer posts and departments within organisations should be recognised. This is necessary for an adequate sociological understanding of the origins and development of this work. It is also the case that the contribution of social movements should be honoured in respect of what they have achieved in terms of social change, both structurally and ideologically. This process of the development of a layer of equal opportunities personnel represents a professionalisation of campaign work and political activism. This chapter focuses on the contribution of social movements to the development of equal opportunities work within organisations, their impact on individuals working in the field and the continuing links between this work and the social movements. It reports research findings from interviews with equal opportunities officers.[2]

Work in the equal opportunities field involves a combination of 'radical' and 'conventional' skills. Equal opportunities officers need a knowledge of relevant equality legislation, personnel and other organisational procedures, together with highly developed skills in the management of organisational change. In this respect they resemble other staff with policy development and managerial responsibilities. However, they also need an understanding of the nature of oppression and discrimination, an ability to relate to those who believe they have suffered injustice, and a commitment to working for change. It is often through participation in social movements and related campaigning and lobbying work that individuals have developed this particular mix of skills.

Employment as an equal opportunities officer provides the chance to do, on a paid and full-time basis, work that many equality activists had previously performed in a voluntary capacity, in addition to their paid work or domestic responsibilities. It also, in a period in which some social movements, particularly feminist and anti-racist movements, are less visible and less structured in terms of public campaigns, offers scope for continued activism, through attempting to introduce equality changes within organisations. In this sense these posts may play a role similar to the 'abeyance structures' identified by Taylor (1989) to examine the continuity of the women's movement. Thus it is reasonable to expect that among equal opportunities personnel a substantial proportion will have a background within radical social movements, and this has been the case with those interviewed so far.

The chapter is organised in eight sections. The first two contain a brief discussion of social movements and the current state of the four main social movements relevant to the field of equal opportunities work: Black people's organisations and anti-racist movements, the women's liberation movement, the lesbian and gay movement, and the disability rights movement. (The selection of these movements for discussion in this chapter is not intended to down-grade the importance of other dimensions of the equal opportunities agenda or other social movements, such as those challenging divisions on the basis of age or religion.) The next three sections of the chapter discuss what interviewees learned from participation in social movements, how far they identified with these movements and how this contributed to their employment as equal opportunities officers. The last three sections examine the successes and tensions for equality activists who have become professionalised as equal opportunities officers, in terms of the continuing relationship with the social movements and the advantages and dangers of 'mainstreaming' on equal opportunities.

SOCIAL MOVEMENTS – OLD AND NEW

Scott (1990) explores the distinction between 'old' and 'new' social movements. The term 'old social movements' refers most especially to the workers' movement (both political parties and trade unions). 'Old' social movements were characterised by their ability to make demands on the state, or to organise around the issue of state power, their claims for political and economic rights, and their formal organisational structures. By contrast 'new' social movements were located in the realm of civil society. They organised around issues of identity and lifestyle and rejected formal and hierarchical organisational structures in favour of looser, semi-autonomous networks. While Scott (1990) to some degree considers the women's liberation movement of the 1970s and Black liberation movements in this framework, particularly in terms of their concerns with identity and culture, he recognises that they also have some continuity with earlier social movements. Similarly in the case of feminism, Taylor (1989) has identified continuities in the US women's movement through tracing the lives of a layer of feminist activists who kept feminist ideals and organising alive through unfavourable times.

While the distinction between 'old' and 'new' social movements is useful in directing attention to some important features of social movements, and highlights the way the social movements of the 1970s challenged and redefined the identities of their participants, this latter point also may apply to older social movements when they affirmed the democratic right to the franchise and concepts of citizenship or the case for human dignity and decent treatment in the workplace. For interviewees in our study, when they reflected on their past and present activism, there was no rigid distinction between the two types of social movement.

'Old' social movements were organised around political projects such as democracy or socialism (Scott, 1990; Hobsbawm, 1996). While advocating the interests of certain groups of society, such as the disenfranchised or the working class, they had as their goal the emancipation of the whole of humanity. Thus their agenda went beyond that of movements based on identity politics. For some interviewees in the research on equal opportunities officers, these political principles were still important. They talked about the object of equal opportunities policies being to establish a level playing field, reflecting the liberal approach to equal opportunities (Jewson and Mason, 1986). Some also stated that socialism was still important to them, and that inequalities based on social class needed to be part of the equal opportunities agenda. Thus, while they had in varying degrees added issues of identity politics to their concerns, they were aware of the inter-relation of different forms of social inequality. Consequently, in a number of ways there is much from 'old' social movements which is relevant to equal opportunities work within organisations. Moreover, some equal opportunities officers had acquired negotiating skills from trade union activism, which they found relevant and necessary in their work as equal opportunities officers. What the new social movements, around race, gender, sexuality and disability, have added is an appreciation of the importance of redefining personal identity and addressing issues of culture and representation, as well as social structure. Thus participation in new social movements, particularly, may make activists aware of how they have changed as people and redefined their identity. Colgan and Ledwith (1996), for instance, in their discussion of the impact of feminism on society, identify a category of women in transition from more traditional attitudes to gender towards feminism, whom they define as holding a 'women-aware' position. Such women, while not identifying themselves as feminists, have an awareness of gender inequalities in society and of their position as women, which they employ in understanding what happens to women within organisations and in acting as change agents.

This development of a layer of 'women-aware' women is evidence both of the impact of feminism as a social movement and of its partial absorption into the mainstream of society. This can be viewed, depending upon one's perspective, as evidence either of the success or failure of a social movement (a point which will be explored in relation to the concept of mainstreaming later in this chapter). Much of the literature on social movements (Banks, 1972; Scott, 1990) suggests that social movements, if successful, will be absorbed within social institutions and disappear as distinct social movements.

THE CURRENT STATE OF THE SOCIAL MOVEMENTS

In terms of the development of affirmative action and equal opportunities programmes within organisations, the Civil Rights Movement in the United

States was one of the earliest movements to place these issues on the political agenda. The development of the concept of affirmative action was important in achieving an awareness that the problems and disadvantages of particular groups in society could not be addressed simply by removing formal barriers and establishing non-discriminatory procedures at the point of selection for education and employment. Affirmative action approaches contained a recognition that the effects of both past discrimination and social structural inequalities had to be taken into account and addressed. Affirmative action in the USA was established following Executive Order 11246 in 1965 and Executive Order 11375 in 1968, building upon the 1964 Civil Rights Act. The operation of contract compliance meant that in the late 1960s around 40 per cent of the American workforce and around 300 000 companies were covered by affirmative action programmes (Stamp and Robarts, 1986).

Affirmative action has been under attack and legal challenge since at least the late 1970s. Critics of affirmative action argue that it is 'affirmative discrimination' or 'reverse discrimination', and that it violates individual rights in the name of group rights (Glazer, 1983). The extent of progress made by women and minorities under affirmative action has been debated. Pinkney (1984) and Small (1994) argue that, despite affirmative action and equal opportunities policies, Black workers still experience substantial inequality and discrimination in both the USA and Britain.

Controversies over affirmative action have continued in the USA, most recently around Proposition 209 in California, the so-called California Civil Rights Initiative, which aimed to end all affirmative action programmes in California. As in earlier controversies over affirmative action, Proposition 209 also activated many supporters of affirmative action to campaign for its retention. In the event Proposition 209 was carried by a very narrow majority.

The history of Black people's struggles in Britain (Fryer, 1984; Ramdin, 1987; Sivanandan, 1986) demonstrates continued resistance to racism and colonialism. Black people have organised against discrimination in housing, employment and the trades unions. They have formed their own educational, cultural, political and religious associations, which have enabled them to maintain a positive Black identity in a racist society. These structures have also provided a base from which to organise against various forms of discrimination, oppression and injustice. Their history and achievements are relatively under-acknowledged.

In Britain anti-racist political activism has in recent years addressed a number of issues, including racial violence, immigration and anti-deportation cases, and school exclusions (Searle, 1996). The TUC organised two national demonstrations against racism, in 1994 and 1995. Much work has also been carried on by Black community groups, by activists within work organisations and by the CRE (Commission for Racial Equality). Much of this work, however, receives limited press attention. Thus social movement activism often continues, but not in a way in which the mass media identify the presence of a social movement, especially if the activism occurs via a large number of groups rather than one central campaign organisation. Within local government in recent decades Black political activists have made concerted attempts to address issues of racial inequality at the level of the local state and community (Ball and Solomos, 1990; Solomos and Black, 1995).

Ian Law's chapter in this volume discusses the growth of 'ethnic manageri-alism' in which the CRE has used management tools, such as a concern with quality, to promote racial equality. One of the key features of ethnic man-agerialism in the public sector is that it distances local authorities from Black-led activism. Thus like all mainstreaming strategies it risks shifting the ownership of movements for change from oppressed layers of society to managers. This type of change strategy is less likely to attract media report-ing than riots, street demonstrations and similar events, but it should equally be recognised and studied as an area of equal opportunities work.

Similarly Griffin (1995) argues that feminist activism has continued in the 1990s, but in a way which appears fragmented because there is no over-arching women's liberation movement, with regular conferences and similar events. To some extent the logic of identity politics means that there is more attention to diversity among women and that feminist campaign groups focus on particular issues and specific groups of women, for example Southall Black Sisters. Nonetheless many of these groups network with other groups and subscribe to a feminist analysis which goes well beyond the concerns of the particular constituency they represent. Griffin also discusses the institu-tionalisation and professionalisation of feminism. This is a process with both benefits and detriments. The benefits include: 'the possibility of impacting directly at sites where change is needed such as the law, education, or the labour market' (Griffin, 1995: 4).

Detriments include the charges of compromise and 'selling out' and poss-ible deradicalisation. Social movements sometimes appear to have difficulties in coming to terms with their own successes. Many social movements, which sought to represent groups who suffered social exclusion and discrimination, argued for the concerns of these groups to be brought into the mainstream of the work of organisations and the political system. The question for the movement and its activists is how to continue the work, once partial integra-tion into powerful institutions has been achieved.

If we examine the history of feminism in Britain, we can see the partial successes of a social movement. In 1971 a national women's liberation demonstration took place in London. Participants on the demonstration marched under the banner of four demands. These were for 'equal pay', 'equal educational and job opportunity', '24-hour nurseries' and 'free contraception and abortion on demand'. Since then the 1970 Equal Pay Act and the 1984 Equal Pay Amendment Act have removed the discriminatory situation in which women did the same work as men and received a lower rate of pay, and have enabled women (and men) to bring equal value claims. While women's average earnings are still lower than men's, this arises from occupational segregation rather than directly unequal pay. The demand for 'equal educational and job opportunity' was formally endorsed in the 1975 Sex Discrimination Act. While there are continuing inequalities in education, these are not supported by the law. Thus in the areas of pay, education and employment legal changes have given legitimacy to feminist demands and few public commentators seriously argue that women and men should not have equal rights in these areas. Substantial inequalities do remain, but some of the major formal barriers to equality have been removed. Hence feminist activity in these areas has moved from street demonstrations and a focus on achieving major pieces of equal rights legislation, to work inside organisations to promote equality. Colgan and Ledwith (1996) have documented the efforts and achievements of women as change agents within organisations, together with their disappointments at the slow rate of change.

In respect of child care social progress has been far more limited. The absence of good-quality, affordable child care is a major barrier to employment for many women. Access to contraception and abortion is subject to constraints of income and variations in local provision, although the women's movement in Britain, under the leadership of the National Abortion Campaign, has successfully fought off four attempts (in 1975, 1977, 1979 and 1984) to restrict the operation of the 1967 Abortion Act.

Since the early 1970s the organised women's liberation movement added new demands to its programme in respect of equal rights for lesbians, ending violence against women, and affirming women's rights to legal and financial independence. As Lovenduski and Randall (1993) argue, feminism has substantially changed the political agenda of society, in that matters such as domestic violence and abortion rights have become public issues.

The lesbian and gay rights movement came about after the 1969 Stonewall riots in the USA and spread to Europe soon afterwards. In England specifically there have been a number of issues that have stimulated social action. In the early 1970s there were demonstrations about the unequal age of consent for gay men. These have continued up until the present day, and even when a bill was carried in parliament to change the age of consent to 18, this was seen as an unacceptable compromise and the campaign continues for an equal age of consent. There have been a number of other issues that have mobilised the lesbian and gay movement. Clause 28, which bans the promotion of homosexuality, has been used to justify the lack of sex education in schools and colleges, has had many challenges made to it and has been the target of many campaigns. Other inequalities which are being campaigned against are the removal of victimless crimes, such as gross indecency, from the legal system, employment and housing rights for lesbians and gay men, an end to the ban on lesbians and gay men in the military, immigration rights, partnership rights and many other issues.

There are large campaigning organisations such as Stonewall coordinating many different projects, from mass lobbying of parliament to sponsoring challenges to the legal system. There are also groups working in other ways, such as Outrage who are using more direct action to emphasise the problems that are being faced by lesbians and gay men within British society. Paul Reynolds, in his chapter in this volume, explores the role of outing as a means of challenging entrenched homophobia. Also the lesbian and gay community has to face irrational prejudice with no legal redress. The lack of any legal protection has forced the lesbian and gay movement to develop quickly and use many different methods to bring about change. It has also forced people within the movement to strengthen their resolve, as many could lose their jobs, homes, family and friends through openly admitting their sexuality. In a recent survey carried out by Social and Community Planning Research (SCPR) of 600 heterosexuals, one in three said that they would be less likely to hire a gay or lesbian job applicant (Stonewall, 1995). These problems make the lesbian and gay movement one of the most active at the present time, as unlike many other groups they have almost no equality within the British legal system. The recent (1997) case of Lisa Grant, against South West Trains for equal partnership rights in respect of free and concessionary rail travel, may open the way to wider legal protection for lesbians and gay men in employment rights (Labour Research Department, 1997). Nonetheless, political parties have tended to see lesbian and gay issues as a vote loser. While many Labour MPs and local Labour Party branches have supported many lesbian and gay campaigns, some of our interviewees working in local government openly acknowledged that directives came from Walworth Road (Labour Party headquarters), around the time of general elections, to Labour councils not to touch lesbian and gay issues.

The disability rights movement is probably the newest of the social movements. Like lesbians and gay men, disabled people have, until recently, been openly discriminated against and excluded from certain areas of life. The movement has a clear demand for civil rights legislation, like the 1992 Americans with Disabilities Act. In the UK there has been the 1995 Disability Discrimination Act, but many campaigners think that it is too little, too late, and feel that they have been let down, again, by the legislators. Many disability activists would still wish to see the DDA replaced by comprehensive civil rights legislation, since the DDA, while giving disabled people some protection against discrimination, also permits discrimination where the costs of disability adjustments can be defined as unreasonable.

The movement is currently at the stage where it is raising its profile through direct action. The new legislation is being used to mount legal challenges against discrimination. Disability rights trainers are also working to bring about a clear understanding of the distinction between medical and social models of disability in a similar way perhaps to the sex/gender distinction used by feminists to argue for equality. The development and publicising of the social model of disability (Oliver, 1990, 1996) has been central to the growth of the disability rights movement. The definition of the problem in terms of social barriers (both physical and attitudinal), rather than the incapacity of the individual, has facilitated the making of demands on institutions, as well as a redefinition of identity. One problem that the disability rights movement had was the lack of media interest in the cause, which led it to have a low profile. Many people were not aware of the years of direct action against inaccessible facilities and public transport. Morris, in *Pride Against Prejudice* (1991), reports an inspiring demonstration of disabled people against charity fund-raising, but there is still little public appreciation of the case against charity and for its replacement with disability benefits financed through taxation. This relatively low profile made the task of bringing about change more difficult, as the general public were not aware of the problems faced by disabled people, and therefore politicians felt that it was not an issue that was fully worthy of their attention. But this is changing as public attitudes become more sympathetic to the cause. The profile of disabled issues is moving more into the mainstream with television programmes such as 'From the Edge', and coverage of the Paralympics. Nonetheless, the fact that the main television programme on disability issues is tellingly titled 'From the Edge' indicates how far disabled people define their problems in terms of social exclusion and the extent of change they regard as necessary to be in the mainstream of society.

LEARNING FROM ACTIVISM IN SOCIAL MOVEMENTS

New social movements were concerned not only with traditional equal rights demands, such as equality in education and employment; they also addressed issues of identity, definition and re-definition of the self. For instance, one form of feminist organizing, the consciousness-raising group, was developed to enable women to identify and recognise their oppression in the area of personal relationships and family life, as well as inequalities in the workplace and the wider society. Moreover, unlike 'first-wave' feminism of the 19th and early 20th centuries, whose political programme was largely concerned with establishing that women could perform equally to men in the public sphere (and so focused on issues such as the franchise and equal citizenship, educational, employment and legal rights), second-wave feminism was equally concerned to establish that men could undertake the domestic and emotional labour traditionally done by women. Second-wave feminism was about changing men's as well as women's identities. Thus there was both continuity and development within a social movement. The focus on 'coming out' in the gay liberation movement challenged social assumptions of heterosexuality. The slogan that 'the personal is political' advocated a closer connection between lifestyle and political beliefs.

The importance of personal experience and activism to work in the field of equal opportunities was expressed by several interviewees. For instance one stated:

> You have to experience being a woman, being disabled, and being Black, and to experience the indirect discrimination that you've had, to be able to understand what the issues are.
>
> (Asian woman working as a women's officer in local government)

Another interviewee, who had been involved in Women Against Pit Closures, also emphasised the importance of learning about other women's experiences, and found this important for her current work as a local authority women's officer:

> I think it [the women's movement] helped to educate me, probably in a way that I would not have been if I had not been involved in those organizations, because you meet women from all walks of life, involved in political struggle, community work, things about their own lives, and you get a lot of different perspectives. Whereas if you just constantly worked in a local authority, and never had any involvement with women's organizations outside of work, I think your knowledge would be incredibly limited.
>
> (Female equal opportunities officer in local government)

Thus this interviewee suggests that social movement activism brings a general educational benefit for participants in terms of wider knowledge of society. Some interviewees were also conscious of learning from social movements in which they were not themselves participants. Several made reference to recent campaigns around disability.

> I think we certainly wouldn't even have the disability debate or the Act [Disability Discrimination Act 1995] if it hadn't been for protests by disabled people.
>
> (Asian female equal opportunities officer in a university)

Some white women spoke about being on a steep learning curve with respect to race issues, since they recognised that work for the rights of women had to encompass all women. One head of a council women's unit commented:

> I learned loads about race issues. As a white woman, having lived mostly in small towns for the previous twelve years, I had had very little exposure to race issues, so my learning curve on that was very steep. I also learned a lot about disability issues. I think if I am honest at the outset I would have taken a rather patronising attitude towards disabled people. They should get decent services, but I suppose I had been sucked in by all the medical models, so my awareness on that grew enormously.
>
> (Head of women's unit in local government)

There was also a recognition that, without the social movements, equal opportunities policies were unlikely to exist and equal opportunities officers would not be employed by organisations.

> I don't think we'd have equal opportunities if you hadn't had social movements, like the feminist movement, or campaigns for racial equality, or disabled people putting pressure for changes. I think equality work, equal opportunities work, is down the line from activism.
>
> (Female equal opportunities officer in a university)

Some of the skills which individuals learned through political activism were ones that they may not have recognised at the time. This included basic skills of political organising, advocacy skills and the ability to stand up for your rights and those of other people. As one interviewee stated:

> You learn, you pick up skills that you don't actually realise you are picking up at the time. It certainly helped, like organising a meeting. I think a lot of people struggle with things like organising a meeting, whereas it comes second nature to me, because I've had to do it in my political work.
>
> (Female equal opportunities officer in local government)

Nonetheless these skills were highly relevant to their employment. For those not already in managerial jobs, particularly, these skills may have been important in acquiring both the confidence and the expertise to tackle the challenge of implementing equal opportunities within an organisation. Thus participation in social movements, and learning from those movements, even if not directly involved oneself as an activist, had developed both knowledge and understanding of different forms of oppression and general political organising skills. It had also led to some appreciation of the unfolding nature and depth of equal opportunities issues, so that interviewees referred to being on a learning curve and were aware that new issues could be added over time to the equal opportunities agenda. Thus equal opportunities officers had a much deeper awareness of the range and extent of equal opportunities issues than many of their work colleagues not specialising in equal opportunities. In this sense most tended to possess a long agenda (Cockburn, 1991) in their understanding of what equal opportunities was about and in recognising the need for organisational transformation.

ACTIVISM AS AN OCCUPATIONAL QUALIFICATION

Interviews also indicated how participation in social movements helped interviewees get jobs as equal opportunities officers. Participation provided useful contacts plus evidence of relevant skills. Some interviewees had used experience of voluntary work, such as working with disability organisations, running women's studies courses and work in a women's refuge as evidence of relevant experience. Political and trade union involvement (older social movements) had also been important in establishing credentials for work in formal organisations. For instance one interviewee, who had gone from being a single (divorced) parent without an income, had found employment as head of a local authority women's unit. One of the items on her curriculum vitae which helped her obtain the post was that she had been on the conference arrangements committee for the regional Labour Party women's conference. This provided excellent evidence of ability to deal with bureaucratic structures and procedures and so established credibility with councillors. Another interviewee stated:

> I would say that being involved in the union and in women's groups generally has been very relevant; I mean that forms part of the CV in my opinion for being an equal opportunities officer.
>
>   (Female equal opportunities officer in local government)

This interviewee had been involved in Women Against Pit Closures and in her trade union. Her emphasis on union involvement was echoed by another interviewee, who had held a number of posts within her union, including responsibilities for negotiating, training shop stewards and equal opportunities:

> I was very involved in NALGO [National and Local Government Officers' Association, one of the predecessor unions of UNISON], and in NALGO I did a fair amount of equal opportunities work. I also had a lot of experience campaigning on women's issues. I'd been involved in women's liberation since the seventies, but in terms of the specific requirements of this particular job, it was really through the trade union movement that I gained the necessary skills.
>
>   (Women's officer in local government)

Another interviewee, who was working as an equality officer in a local authority, commented:

> I've worked on a lot of women's issues. I've worked in the Asian women's refuge for a few years. I've done community development work, and it's almost like a natural progression from working in the voluntary sector.
>
> (Asian woman working as a women's officer in local government)

The reference to a 'natural progression' indicates how the interviewee saw a continuity in the type of work. Another explained her motivation for working in equal opportunities as a way of bringing together her political interests and her working life. She stated:

> I think it is to do with wanting to be employed in the areas of my main interest. Previously in the 1970s I had felt vaguely schizophrenic. I had felt that I had one kind of identity outside work as a political activist and then I had a job which was rather marginal to my political activity, and I wanted to bring the two things together. I wanted to focus on issues that I was committed to and that was the main focus of it.
>
> (Head of women's unit in local government)

Thus for this equal opportunities officer her political activism had been an important factor in choice of career.

IDENTIFICATION WITH THE SOCIAL MOVEMENTS

Interview material indicated the importance of social movement involvement for many in both their route into their current employment and their motivation to continue their work. One explained how she drew optimism from the women's movement and believed that she could achieve changes as a women's equality officer in local government:

> What I like particularly, and I think it is particularly true of working on women's issues, is that there is a feeling that history is on our side. So a lot of things that I would have campaigned on twenty years ago are now accepted as what every reasonable person, certainly every reasonable woman, thinks.
>
> (Women's officer in local government)

For many people a political and emotional commitment to the issues provided much of the raw material for continued activism. One interviewee stated about equal opportunities work: 'It's something very personal to me' (Asian woman working as a women's officer in local government). Another Black woman emphasised the importance of not becoming too professionalised, but of still being able to feel the pain of injustice and discrimination:

> I'm 46 years old now, and even now things can still hurt me. I haven't become emotionally dead to the issues that I'm dealing with every day, and I don't want to be. I think that's really important to keep me going and feeling so strongly about the issues.
>
> (Asian female equal opportunities officer in a university)

Personal commitment to the issues was also vital for this interviewee in terms of work motivation:

> I remind myself that if I didn't do it I wouldn't be true to me. It's because I believe it so passionately and I don't think you can do this job without a passionate belief, and it's good to have a nice salary and all the income. But I think I do it because I believe in it so passionately.
>
> (Asian female equal opportunities officer in a university)

Thus this interviewee, while appreciating and honestly acknowledging the benefits of white-collar employment, still had a strong activist identity. Another interviewee similarly showed identification with the social movements. When asked whether the disability movement had influenced his views, he stated:

> It's difficult to say whether they've affected my views, or whether I just felt that those were my views.
>
> (Male head of equal opportunities unit in local government)

Nonetheless, some interviewees also emphasised a need to place personal experience and anger within a wider context, in order to focus on achievable goals and be able to prioritise work, and not be overwhelmed by personal involvement in the issues.

> All the people I know who are in equal opportunities I think come in with an awareness of their personal history, and very often personal battles against oppression, but if they don't move beyond that, they don't really become very effective.
>
> (Women's officer in local government)

This interviewee, who had worked for many years in equal opportunities, further stated:

> I'm also an Equal Opportunities Manager, and I have recruited excellent staff who have left after a year because they cannot bear that process where you actually professionalise in a sense really deep-seated beliefs.
>
> (Women's officer in local government)

She also discussed when to bring in personal experience, for instance as useful illustrative material in training events, and when it was better to distance oneself from it, in order to be an effective change agent. Thus for some experienced equal opportunities officers a degree of professional detachment was seen as necessary in order to succeed. This is not to imply that these individuals were less committed to the issues; it was rather that they had found that they needed to contain and channel personal feelings of anger and compassion, if they were to achieve changes in the organisations they worked in.

'INSIDERS' AND 'OUTSIDERS'

Interviews also provided evidence about how equal opportunities officers relate to present-day social movements. For those working in local government there was a general belief in accountability to the local community, as well as to councillors. Thus there was an appreciation of the usefulness of social movements in articulating the demands of particular groups in society and bringing outside pressure to bear to support change. There were also at times tensions when chief officers wanted answers from within the council and the equal opportunities officer wanted to bring in the social movements.

> I also learned that it was absolutely crucial to work very closely and directly with the community one was working for. So that it was not my job to set agendas, but it was my job to enable and empower organizations to be able to take control for themselves, and there were a lot of instances where the chief officers would be trying to negotiate directly with me about things, when I was saying 'Look there is a women's organization here which is involved in the project', for example Southall Black Sisters got involved in a project, and I would say to the chief officers 'I can't make the decision. You need to engage in direct dialogue with these women's organizations.'
>
> (Head of women's unit in local government)

This statement shows how some equal opportunities officers saw bringing the outsiders in to the organisation as part of their job. For those working in universities and colleges links with groups of students were similarly important. Student groups and informal groupings of staff could play a similar role in articulating issues and bringing pressure for change. One interviewee in a university mentioned as one of the good things about working as an equal opportunities officer: 'the support I got from the grassroots activists' (Female equal opportunities officer in university).

Thus, even in the absence of outside social movements, it may be possible within some organisations for equal opportunities personnel to identify a layer of activists who are supportive of the changes they are trying to bring about. Some interviewees were aware of a women's voice within the local community. As one equal opportunities officer, working in local government, put it:

I can see a lot of angry women out there who are outraged by the low representation of women artists in the art gallery, about the state of the women's changing areas in the swimming pools, about the sexism in schools, and they are growing. I do feel women speak up much more for themselves, and are prepared to make demands as women.

(Women's officer in local government)

The increased ability of women to make demands 'as women' indicates the pervasive influence of feminism. However, despite the supportive links there were also tensions, with some equal opportunities officers believing that they were seen as not radical enough, because outside campaign groups wanted change to occur at a very much quicker rate than occurred within large-scale organisations. As one interviewee commented:

There is a lot of conflict around because of the nature of the work. We get caught in conflict between the expectations of women and the slowness of the organization to respond, and often women will project their anger on to you, 'What are *you* doing about it?'

(Women's officer in local government)

Moreover those with professional jobs could easily be characterised as 'sell-outs'. One interviewee commented on the relative privileges of the insiders, compared with some social movement activists: 'If you've got a senior job within a council, you have quite a lot of privileges' (Male head of equal opportunities unit in local government). This would particularly be the case in relation to some social movement activists, who may not have any job at all and hence might regard anyone with a permanent job as privileged.

One interviewee, a principal equal opportunities officer in a local authority, expressed the view that 'insiders' and 'outsiders' have complementary roles in achieving the aims of the social movements through equal opportunities work in organisations. He argued that the two groups need each other, particularly because the 'insiders' have knowledge, not only of how changes can be made to happen, but also of how they can be blocked.

You have to have the double approach, there has to be some sort of a social movement, a wish for change, ... a political movement for change, there also have to be people on the inside, because it's when you are on the inside, you can see how easy it is to stop, or to confuse, that demand for change, very easy to frustrate from within. Without there being motivated people from within to actually generate that change, then the frustration just continues until you get things like riots. We need each other, the inside people need the outside people and the outside people need the inside people.

(Male head of equal opportunities unit in local government)

Being identified with the social movements did, however, sometimes also create difficulties in their work for equal opportunities officers.

> I am known in the city as a difficult woman. The leader of the council used to describe me in that way. So I've done things like I've picketed, I've stood outside with banners, I've written to 'Right to Reply', when I've seen something wrong on the television' ... I do things like that, and unfortunately it gets me in a lot of trouble, because the danger with being seen to be associated with that sort of thing is that people marginalise you.
>
> (Asian woman equal opportunities officer in a university)

Some interviewees indicated tensions between the activist and the professional self, while others suggested a feeling of confidence and balance. Some had secure professional identities and felt comfortable with the organisations they were employed in. For instance one described herself as essentially 'a local government officer', because she believed that the ideals and culture of local government were compatible with what she was trying to achieve as a women's equality adviser. Another (male) equal opportunities officer saw equal opportunities work as part of a wider managerial field.

> In local government it [equal opportunities] is still quite an important area of management, and it's an area that gives you access to senior levels of management and senior decision-making processes, and it is one of the central policy areas of the council.
>
> (Male head of equal opportunities unit in local government)

Clearly this man did not feel marginalised in equal opportunities work and saw himself as having a developing career whether he stayed in equal opportunities work or moved into other areas of management.

Others felt a continuing tension between their professional and their activist selves. As professionals they were aware that changes could take many years to introduce, but as activists they wanted to see these changes happen immediately. Moreover they were aware that without some people demanding changes now, then changes would never happen, but they also knew the time-scale it took for large bureaucracies to change. One interviewee, speaking with some frustration, used the metaphor of turning round a tanker to describe the time it took to get any changes through the structures of local government. One equal opportunities manager commented on the problems some activists from social movements had encountered when recruited to work in equality units in local government. They found it difficult to accept the structures of local government, particularly the authority of councillors. She said:

> Because maybe their commitment and their involvement and their experience of the issues would be much greater than, say, the chair of their committee, they found it really difficult to understand why the person who

knows less and who has less of a track record calls the shots. It's just something some people never quite crack.

(Women's officer in local government)

Thus these staff had not been able to manage the transition from being 'outsiders' to becoming 'insiders'.

A DISAPPOINTED GENERATION?

In recent years there has been debate around the notion of a backlash to equal opportunities (Faludi, 1992). One interviewee criticised the notion of a backlash, because it implied there had been one period in history in which there had been overwhelming support for equal opportunities, which was not the case. For some of the women interviewed there was, however, the sense of the absence of a social movement around women's rights. They were aware that the 'insiders' could push for change more easily if they could point to groups outside actively campaigning for change. While some positive changes have come about in women's situation, the changes are much less than those envisaged by feminists in the early 1970s. Thus for women who had participated in the women's liberation movement in its early days, they missed the radical edge and the sense that profound social change was possible. Weeks has referred to the 'heroic period' of the gay liberation movement and the women's liberation movement (Weeks, 1991).

In their 'heroic period' these movements displayed a creative energy and an ability to pose fundamental challenges to the way people lived and the way society was organised. They had links with the commune movement and explored ways of collective living. As these movements have achieved a degree of acceptance and legitimacy, and some of their ideas entered the mainstream of society, the presentation of their goals has shifted. Thus for instance feminists are more often found talking about family-friendly employment policies, than the abolition of the family. The vision these movements had of the replacement of the family by non-possessive and more emancipated arrangements regarding human sexuality and personal life, has been downplayed in favour of legal reforms, such as gay marriage, and more progressive employment policies, which include provision of child care and career breaks.

Similarly one interviewee commented on the loss of the idealism of the 1960s and early 1970s. She compared a recent visit to the USA with her experiences in 1970:

Last time I was in the States was in 1970, it was a very optimistic time, cultures were in a melting pot, there was a gentleness and a determination to do right by everyone. When I went to the States for this couple of months, back in the summer, I kind of anticipated that that was all going to come to fruition. I was so wrong. Far from becoming more of a melting pot, each culture and each race had pulled further and further apart.

(Female equal opportunities officer in a university)

Thus some of our interviewees, who had experienced the idealism of the late 1960s and 1970s, were aware of a sense of disappointment that their visions of a better world had not been achieved. They recognised growing social inequality and polarisation, despite the achievements of the social movements. Another interviewee described her feelings about working as an equal opportunities officer within a formal organisation as a sense of 'being underground' because there were aspects of her personal beliefs and feelings which she believed she could not show too publicly in her job.

MAINSTREAMING

While interviewees wanted to see equal opportunities within the mainstream of the organisation, they were also fearful of deradicalisation. Tensions were attached to being part of the mainstream. For instance, one interviewee commented:

In this university we did have a very, very strong culture of activism... . Once equal opportunities becomes part of the mainstream, it can lose a lot of that power, a lot of that force for change, it can start to become bland, just part of the furniture, and then people can feel that their vision has not been achieved and they've been betrayed by what has actually happened.

(Female equal opportunities officer in a university)

Thus she both appreciated the importance of social movement activism, and also recognised the problems of becoming part of the establishment. The phrase 'part of the furniture' nicely catches the problem of losing a radical edge to the issue. Cockburn refers to the same problem when she writes:

Equal opportunities is widely seen as a tool of management that has sanitised and contained the struggle for equality.

(Cockburn, 1991: 213)

One interviewee mentioned dangers of tokenism and dilution. Equal opportunities can become lost in the mainstream. Mainstreaming can also mean getting rid of the equal opportunities officer post.

I think they are going to get rid of my post, in the next year or so, and they will talk about it in terms of mainstreaming.

(Asian female equal opportunities officer in a university)

Cinnamon Bennett's chapter in this volume also reports the use of the argument for mainstreaming as a means of abolishing specific women's officer posts. Moreover, mainstreaming led to a loss of emphasis on equalities work and a subsequent delegitimation and downgrading of its importance. However, some women working in equal opportunities believed that the women's movement had continued, but in different forms:

> If you don't have International Women's Week, people don't talk about the issue, don't think it exists. I find that with movements like that [the women's movement], although nowadays it's not in the same format. In the 60s, 70s and even in the 80s, you had mass demonstrations. All of that has died down now to a new phase, where there's work that needs to be done, and it's being done at a different level, where it's sitting down and talking. We have seen some women who have been able to get into really powerful positions. It's more sort of sitting down, talking and trying to get into organizations to make changes.
>
> (Asian woman working as a women's officer in local government)

Sitting down, talking and trying to make changes are necessary to progress the goals of social movements. Some interviewees believed that equal opportunities were well established in their organisations and were being seen as increasingly central to their work. For others, however, talk about mainstreaming had in effect led to deprioritisation of equal opportunities and removal of specialist posts. Thus while mainstreaming may be a principle to which all subscribe, its implementation in organisations had taken many different forms and had different consequences for equal opportunities. One interviewee, while strongly committed to a strategy of mainstreaming, also recognised the potential problems:

> I think that where we are going now is we're going through management channels, we're going through working with senior people and with elected members, and I'm sure that's what we will do. What remains to be seen is whether – the risk with that strategy is – it all becomes very diluted and that people learn the language of equal opportunities without really making changes of any substance. The old model, which was much more in vogue here when I started, it was really about being a bridge between oppressed people in the community and the organization. There was a feeling that the dissatisfaction of the different interests in the community could be channelled through the committees and through the equal opportunities officers, and that that would create change. Now I think it created some change, but I hope the way we are going to do it will ultimately be more effective, but it will all come out in the wash.
>
> (Women's officer in local government)

This summary is similar to the trends identified by Ian Law as 'ethnic managerialism'. The emphasis is clearly on working to educate managers to incorporate equal opportunities considerations in the mainstream of their work, rather than acting as a tribune for oppressed groups outside the organisation. The question here is who defines what the problems are and whether the solutions achieved are acceptable. Furthermore there is the risk that the managers will see the oppressed group or the issue (such as ethnicity, disability, sexuality or gender) as a problem to be managed. Indeed those equal opportunities officers who rejected the 'management of diversity' approach did so because they disliked its implication that diversity was an issue or problem that needed managing. In the case of the disability rights movement there has been and is a continual struggle against non-disabled professionals who seek to define what is best for disabled people, and an insistence that disabled people themselves must be recognised as the experts on disability. So if mainstreaming means that oppressed groups lose control over the definition of their oppression and the strategies to overcome it, there are real dangers in the mainstreaming of equal opportunities.

CONCLUSION

Interviews with equal opportunities practitioners indicate the importance of new social movements. Many of these personnel are activists who have become (semi-)professionalised. Their roots in the social movements are still often significant for them. Working within large-scale bureaucracies they have to pursue social change at a different pace from their 'street-fighting' and demonstrating years. Nonetheless they still draw strength from both their past involvement in social movements, and their present contacts. They also appreciate complementary roles for 'insiders' and 'outsiders' as change agents.

The questions of mainstreaming and incorporation both reflect the partial successes of social movements, in that they have forced their issues on to the agenda, and also demonstrate the impact of cuts and redundancies in local government, and some stalling of movements for equality. Interviewees were in general sensitive to the dilemmas of mainstreaming. They did not view it as a legitimate reason for abolishing specific posts and departments dealing with equal opportunities. While they wished to see equal opportunities mainstreamed, in that they wanted everyone to be committed to equal opportunities and to take responsibility for it, they were concerned that mainstreaming could lead to a dilution of the impetus for change, so that no-one took any specific responsibility for, or initiative on, equal opportunities, since it had become defined as everyone's responsibility. Given the significance of the new social movements in establishing equality initiatives, including equal opportunities officer posts and departments within organisations, the question arises as to how far their continued existence and vitality depends upon the impetus provided by the social movements. The prospect for the future of equal opportunities work in organisations is uncertain at the time of writing. Within parts of the public sector, especially local government, cutbacks, redundancies and 'mainstreaming' have led to the abolition of designated equal opportunities officer posts and units, or a reduction in their number. Within the private sector there has been some growth in the number of equal opportunities officer posts, but the organisational culture does not easily favour acknowledging links with radical social movements in the same way as occurred in local government.

NOTES

1.   While the 1995 Disability Discrimination Act owes its origin to the pressure of a social movement, it is not the civil rights legislation on disability sought by disabled people and their organisations. Thus it should not be viewed as a companion piece of legislation to the 1975 Sex Discrimination Act or the 1976 Race Relations Act.

2.   The data reported in this chapter were collected through semi-structured interviews with equal opportunities officers, conducted by Nicholas Turner and Elizabeth Lawrence. Nicholas Turner carried out the greater part of the data collection and Elizabeth Lawrence of the writing. Interviewees were obtained through CUCO (Commission on University Career Opportunities), via a flyer circulated in a mailing of the Equality Exchange (a network for equal opportunities officers established by the Equal Opportunities Commission) and through personal contacts. Interviewees were predominantly female, white, non-disabled and working in local government or universities. Of the 27 interviewees, on whose views this chapter is based, 10 worked in local government, 10 in universities and seven in other organisations (trade union, retail, police, fire service and a further education college). Five had a disability, 23 were white, one African–Caribbean and three Asian. Twenty-four were female. Interview questions explored the links between equal opportunities officers and social movements in a number of respects, including what individuals had learned through participation in social movements and how this had contributed items on their curriculum vitae which helped them to gain employment as equal opportunities officers. A question was asked about whether personal experiences of oppression had influenced their work, in order to identify how identity and life experience had impacted upon careers. The current links with social movements emerged as a topic in a number of questions about how work was performed, how interviewees understood equal opportunities and how they viewed the future for equal opportunities.

REFERENCES

Ball, W. and Solomos, J. (eds) (1990), *Race and Local Politics* (Basingstoke: Macmillan).

Banks, J. A. (1972), *The Sociology of Social Movements* (Basingstoke: Macmillan).

Cockburn, C. (1991), *In the Way of Women* (Basingstoke: Macmillan).
Colgan, F. and Ledwith, S. (eds) (1996), *Women in Organizations: Challenging Gender Politics* (Basingstoke: Macmillan).
Faludi, S. (1992), *Backlash: The Undeclared War Against Women* (London: Vintage).
Fryer, P. (1984), *Staying Power: The History of Black People in Britain* (London: Pluto).
Glazer, N. (1983), *Ethnic Dilemmas, 1964–1982* (Cambridge, MA: Harvard University Press).
Griffin, G. (ed.) (1995), *Feminist Activism in the 1990s* (Basingstoke: Taylor & Francis).
Halford, S. and Durcan, S. (1991), *Implementing Feminist Policies in British Local Government*, Centre for Urban and Regional Research, University of Sussex, Brighton, Working paper 78.
Halford, S. (1992), 'Feminist Change in a Patriarchal Organization: the Experience of Women's Initiatives in Local Government and Implications for Feminist Perspectives on State Institutions', in M. Savage and A. Witz (eds), *Gender and Bureaucracy* (Oxford: Blackwell).
Hobsbawm, E. (1996) 'Identity Politics and the Left', *New Left Review*, 217, 38–47.
Jewson, N. and Mason, D. (1986), 'The Theory and Practice of Equal Opportunities Policies: Liberal and Radical Approaches', *Sociological Review*, 34, 307–334.
Labour Research Department (1997), 'Sexuality Bias: On its Way Out?', *Labour Research*, December, 17–18.
Lovenduski, J. and Randall, V. (1993), *Contemporary Feminist Politics: Women and Power in Britain* (Oxford: Oxford University Press).
Morris, J. (1991), *Pride Against Prejudice: A Personal Politics of Disability* (London: Virago).
Oliver, M. (1990), *The Politics of Disablement* (Basingstoke: Macmillan).
Oliver, M. (1996), *Understanding Disability: From Theory to Practice* (Basingstoke: Macmillan).
Pinkney, A. (1984), *The Myth of Black Progress* (Cambridge: Cambridge University Press).
Ramdin, R. (1987), *The Making of the Black Working Class in Britain* (London: Gower).
Scott, A. (1990), *Ideology and the New Social Movements* (London: Unwin Hyman).
Searle, C. (1996), '"OFSTEADed, Blunketted and Permanently Excluded": an Experience of English Education', *Race and Class*, 38, 21–38.
Sivanandan, A. (1986), *From Resistance to Rebellion: Asian and Afro-Caribbean Struggles in Britain* (London: Institute of Race Relations).
Small, S. (1994), *Racialised Barriers: The Black Experience in the United States and England in the 1980s* (London: Routledge).
Solomos, J. and Black L. (1995), *Race, Politics and Social Change* (London: Routledge).
Stamp, P. and Robarts, S. (1986), *Positive Action for Women: Changing the Workplace* (London: NCCL).
Stonewall (1995), *Fact Sheet: Discrimination in the Workplace*.
Taylor, V. (1989), 'Social Movement Continuity: the Women's Movement in Abeyance', *American Sociological Review*, 54, 761–75.
Weeks, J. (1991), *Against Nature: Essays on History, Sexuality and Identity* (London: Rivers Oram Press).

11 Modernity, Anti-Racism and Ethnic Managerialism
Ian Law

INTRODUCTION

Tensions within the modernist themes of science, rational bureaucracy, civilisation and liberal democracy underlie many of the strategic responses to racism and the formulation of ethnic boundaries. Evidence of the persistence of racism, revival of ethnic conflict and embedded patterns of racial and ethnic discimination have challenged modernist conceptions of emancipatory progress. There is not only a need for critical reflection and re-assessment of our understanding of the processes of racism and ethnicity, there is a related search for new ways to construct and frame policies, strategies and initiatives in response to social problems associated with these processes. An example of the latter is illustrated by the Commission for Racial Equality's (CRE) new approach, turning to the use of management tools such as quality/equality assurance and citizens' charters in search of the means for effective policy intervention. This reflects the pervasive influence of the 'new managerialism' (Pollitt, 1993) whose effects on the construction of 'race'-related policies are likely to be far-reaching. This is not to deny, however, that there is an immense managerial and technocratic task involved in reducing racial and ethnic inequalities in the provision of employment and services, particularly in large organisations. The weakness of legal enforcement in the UK, compared to the USA for example, has encouraged this turn to managerial solutions which are often perceived as quicker and more productive. This chapter proposes the concept of 'ethnic managerialism' and examines its application to two public service organisations: the Benefits Agency and the NHS Ethnic Health Unit.

MODERNIST THEMES, ANTI-RACISM AND STRATEGIES FOR CHANGE

Despite controversies over the conceptualisation of 'modernity', it is useful to highlight the legacy of the European Enlightenment in emphasising the capacity of science and rationality, which, combined with faith in unilinear progress and liberal democracy, would lead towards the ideals of civilisation and the emancipation of humanity (Giddens, 1990; Hall, 1992). The economic foundation of Western European modernity depended in part on the institution of plantation slavery and paradoxically critiques of slavery influenced modernist thought. Gilroy (1993) demonstrates that the critiques of injustice which informed European arguments for liberal democracy and universal suffrage were influenced by slave resistance and abolition movements, for example in the work of Hegel. In that sense the mutually defining relationship between Europe and Africa helped create what we know as modernity (Lipsitz, 1995). The utilisation of the capacities and ideas of modernity have facilitated both racism and anti-racism. Slaves, free blacks and many other groups have developed emancipatory strategies based on appeals to *reason and rights*. Yet reason and rights have also been articulated in strategies of colonialism, imperialism and institutional racism. Science provided a discursive context for both the elaboration of racism and for the most thorough rational rebuttal of the 'race' idea. *Science, technology and rational bureaucracy* have provided the means for both the implementation of the holocaust (Bauman, 1991) and implementation of policies and strategies to analyse and challenge racial and ethnic inequalities. The political and social project of *civilisation* in Europe is documented by Elias (1978). Here, the feudal aristocracy developed codes of manners and behaviour as processes whereby they attempted to civilise themselves, and subsequently impose their civilisation on other classes inside Europe. This process involved the racialisation of both 'superior' and 'inferior' classes, and also export of the civilising mission became a theme for European colonialism. But such ideas have also provided a moral foundation for notions of civilised treatment and international human rights. Arblaster (1984) has documented the history of western *liberalism* and common themes here are a belief in freedom and liberty underlain by minimal state regulation to achieve the conditions for the exercise of such rights. The belief in the rule of law and the universality of human capacities provide potentially strong arguments in challenging racism. Yet conceptions of individual liberty can also provide the basis for challenging attempts to tackle the structural sources of social inequality where there is a concern for group inequalities (Parekh, 1997a). It is possible to trace these themes of rationalism and a belief in the inherent (individual) 'fairness' of the law and Western democracies in the construction and development of British 'race' relations policy (see Law, 1996). Such dualistic tensions within these modernist themes of science, rational bureaucracy, civilisation and liberal democracy underlie many of the policy approaches to racism and ethnicity, and have often been ignored in policy analysis.

The problem of *rationality* and racism has been highlighted in recent debates reflecting on the effectiveness of two counter-posed strategies of intervention in the field of education:

> there are fundamental similarities in conceptualisation and prescription
> between multi-culturalism and anti-racism which are flawed ... their
> frameworks and policies share significant and disabling weaknesses.
>
> (Rattansi, 1992: 24)

One of these similarities and weaknesses is the assumption that racism operates somehow rationally and that it is systematic and unchanging from
context to context. For example, in education a rational 'facts and empathy'
set of prescriptions often characterises anti-racist or multicultural classroom
practice (Nixon, 1985). This has been challenged by many writers (Billig,
1978; Jenkins, 1986; Cohen, 1988; Rattansi, 1992) who stress the contradictory, ambivalent and contextual characteristics of racist attitudes, discourses
and behaviour. This means that racism, as a complex phenomenon, is much
less amenable to change, particularly through rationalist pedagogues or
policy interventions, than has been anticipated. People express their racism
in different forms in different places, and are often notoriously difficult to
pin down and challenge. Also, the internal rationalism of racist discourses in
adequately 'making sense' of the world, for some people, through the
grounding of such ideas in real social experience, may make it impervious to
counter-arguments or alternative interpretations, however 'rational' they
may seem in comparison. Racists ideas frequently interact with notions of
sexual and class difference while at the same time articulating with discourses about equal treatment, fairness, merit and citizenship.

An explicit belief in the effectiveness of law in tackling racism pervades
British and European 'race' relations policies. In response to continuing violence and forms of exclusionary practice many practitioners and activists
have not fundamentally questioned their assumptions, goals and methods
and instead have argued that what is required are stronger 'race' relations
law and more vigorous policy implementation. The critique of liberal legal-
ism has particularly developed from within feminism (O'Donovan and
Szyszczak, 1988; Mackinnon, 1989), and has only recently been drawn on in
critiques of racism (Lacey, 1992; Fredman and Szyszczak, 1992). The construction of liberal rights theory and the liberal legal world as 'colour-blind',
as racially neutral, as one where decisions are made and enforced in a
neutral and formally equal way, has been particularly criticised. In addition,
the general critique of the discourse of rights as inherently individualistic
and essentially competitive has led to an assertion that, far from undermining racial inequalities, the establishment of formally equal rights will
entrench inequalities still further through racial, gender and class differentials in access to legal forums. This line of argument opens up a series of
related questions.

The deconstruction, or analysis of the underlying meanings and assumptions, of the supposedly gender- and culture-neutral legal subject against

whom comparisons of equal treatment are made reveals a subject which is white and male. Here the racialised and ethnocentric values and assumptions built into legal rules and principles become a focus of attention. Therefore, the extent to which this legal world, which underlies a 'rights' approach, is operating in a racialised manner becomes crucial in the assessment of the effectiveness of using law, rather than other means, in anti-racist strategy. The establishment of a legal process which requires the individualisation of conflict between specific parties indicates the limits of 'rights-based' law as attention to group inequality or disadvantage cannot then be adequately addressed. This then leads to consideration of how 'group distribution equality' or some form of group based rights can be advocated, for example the attempts in the US to construct black women as a legal group (Fredman and Szyszczak, 1992). This leads to potential conflict with values of equity and fairness as regards treatment of individuals which are deeply rooted in British culture and is evident in public support for anti-discrimination legislation. Therefore, to abandon or minimise that goal would be 'politically suicidal' as Lustgarten warns (1992: 456). The hysterical attacks on the notion of quotas, for example Simon Jenkins' article in *The Sunday Times* (quoted in Runnymede Trust, 1994: 3), are evidence of hostility to arguments for group equality and support for liberal notions of free and fair competition between individuals.

The fundamental comparative flaw in the concept of racial discrimination, where the treatment of those subject to discrimination and exclusion is assessed against the treatment of the 'white majority' requires a substantial transformation in policy assumptions and strategy. The assessment of equality of treatment against the 'white norm' is a prevalent assumption in discussion of racial inequalities in, for example, housing allocations, educational achievement, benefit take-up or the labour market. Indeed the methodology of researching racial discrimination in many of these sectors, and the practice of many of the CRE's investigations, rests on such an assumption. How far is this appropriate? The problem of assessing the nature of racial or ethnic equality in provision of public services stems from the difficulties of reconciling differences in needs with notions of formal equality. Secondly, resistance to recognising issues of racism and ethnic difference and the resulting colour-blind construction of political, policy and professional discourses has been an ongoing object of criticism (Ben-Tovim *et al.*, 1986). This reflects a preference for universalist racially neutral approaches, or in other words a 'we treat them all the same' attitude, and this has frequently been identified as a barrier in equal opportunity policy development and racial equality campaigns. This unwillingness to move beyond an assumed 'racial neutrality', for example in primary-school classroom teaching, is identified as masking a white, ethnocentric curriculum. This position is compounded by the 'discursive de-racialisation' (Reeves, 1983) evident in the use of coded language. In other words where references to 'race' or black people are not made, but where the context allows racial or cultural stereotypes to be invoked. The emphasis to put 'race' explicitly on the policy agenda is then often set up as the appropriate radical response and the task is then seen to be one of constructing a racial equality strategy. Fitzgerald (1993) highlights an ironic contrast in racist and anti-racist approaches to social policy. In some policy areas, such as education and housing, there can be strong resistance to anti-racist demands for the recognition of material differences and inequalities between racialised groups; whereas in the field of crime, such differences are seen to have been amplified through the use of statistics to stereotype minority groups and the explicit and inappropriate use of 'race'. In response to this, anti-racist demands are to take 'race' off the agenda, removing unjustified references and attempting to explain away racial differences. However, the irony of this contrast exists only when racist and anti-racist discourse is assumed to operate in a rational and systematic form from context to context. This assumption of rationalism is a crucial mistake in the conceptual understanding of racism and, as noted earlier, this has been a frequent mistake in anti-racist work.

MODERNISM AND ETHNIC MANAGERIALISM

The 'modernist' approach to issues of racism and ethnicity, with all its pitfalls, is particularly evident in governance strategies in the 1990s with an emphasis on finding managerial solutions to complex political and social questions. The ambiguous and contested conceptualisations of 'racial equality' and the failure to adequately construct the idea of 'difference' within the idea of 'equality' characterises such strategies. Allied to these issues is an unjustified faith in rational bureaucratic procedures which fail to take into account relative positions of power and powerlessness across ethnic groups and within public services. The prevalence of organisational and managerial approaches to ethnic difference has been recently celebrated by Herman Ouseley, the Chief Executive of the CRE:

> Managing diversity is already a reality in most aspects of our society, in schools, at work, in leisure and in the arts. Many private sector employers recognise that their markets and customers are diverse and their workforces need to reflect cultural diversity.
>
> (CRE, 1993: 5)

Acknowledgment of progress is important; but the extent to which the 'reality' of the 'management of ethnic diversity' should be applauded requires critical interrogation.

The concept of ethnic managerialism is used, more specifically, in this chapter to refer to the application of 'new public management techniques' (Farnham and Horton, 1996; Hughes, 1994; Pollitt, 1993; Massey, 1993) to issues of ethnicity in public services. The general key features of such an approach include firstly, giving organisational legitimacy and authority to managers and hence challenging professionalism, syndicalism and black-led activism; secondly, developing a rational approach to 'ethnic' issues through strategic management and objective setting with respect to ethnicity and devolving managerial responsibility, for example, for target setting; thirdly, replacing any participative relationships with black-led and minority ethnic organisations with contractual ones; fourthly, measuring organisational achievements in terms of economy, efficiency and effectiveness and quality with consideration of ethnicity subsumed under these categories where it appears; fifthly, changing organisational cultures with an emphasis on market and entrepreneurial values and a focus on 'public-service orientation' and the public as clients, customers and citizens and minority ethnic groups; and sixthly, separating policy and administration, and creating executive units within the new administrative structures which have a particular brief to address questions of ethnicity.

The crisis in public expenditure and rising demand for public services gave the opportunity, the election of four Conservative governments provided the means, and ideas drawn from scientific management theory and the New Right provided the motive: as a result a wave of managerialism has systematically transformed public services since the early 1980s. At the same time, political and administrative hostility to anti-racism and racial justice, due in particular to the growing influence in public services, produced a situation in which, in varying contexts, only a narrow focus on addressing issues of racism and ethnicity though new managerial language became politically expedient. This accorded with a wider shift in material conditions and political agendas which gave voice to issues of difference, diversity, cultural hybridity and multiple subjectivities, which cannot be fully addressed in this chapter (Gilroy, 1990; Bonnett, 1993; Gillborn, 1995; Modood, 1996; Mirza, 1997). Some of the key factors here include the increasing divergence of material conditions across ethnic minority groups, the exhaustion of municipal anti-racism, critiques of black homogeneity, and renewed political and professional pressure for the recognition of ethnic difference from minority groups themselves. The resurgence of ethnicity as a totem in social and political movements, combined with the rapidly shifting construction of new forms of hybrid cultural identity and theoretical reflection on the re-working and renewal of concepts of culture, ethnicity and ethnic identity, have impacted unevenly across social policy arenas.

The privileging of ethnicity and ethnic diversity has been identified as the dominant theme in social policy responses in the 1990s (Law, 1996). It has established an important place in Benefits Agency policy, child care policy, community care policy and health policy amongst others. The attempt to construct 'consociationalism' (Lijphart, 1977), where the liberal democratic state accommodates ethnic pluralism, simulataneously as attempts are being made to construct more ethnically exclusive criteria in the specification of citizenship in Britain and Europe, characterises not only the 'liberal settlement' of the 1960s, but the appeal of the 'management of ethnic diversity' in the 1990s (Parekh, 1997b). Poulter (1986, 1992) has analysed the accommodation of ethnic minority customs and cultural pluralism in English law. In the context of law governing marriage and divorce, choice of school, court sentencing and prisoners' rights there is evidence of both separate and distinctive treatment being given to minority ethnic or religious groups, and regulation in situations where there is a refusal to recognise ethnic diversity. Poulter notes that English judges have emphasised that ethnic tolerance is bounded by notions of reasonableness and public policy, and that minority customs and laws will not be recognised if they are considered repugnant or otherwise offend the conscience of the court (1992: 176). The adaptation of English law on an *ad-hoc* basis leaves open the question as to where the limits of ethnic diversity, for example, on public policy grounds, are to be set. Poulter sets out a 'human rights' approach to such questions. The European Convention on Human Rights and the International Covenant on Civil and Political Rights provide frameworks to assess whether demands for legal or public policy recognition of particular cultural practices are supported by an emphasis on general human rights, or whether such practices constitute a violation of human rights. The operation of Islamic personal law would then be resisted because of the risk that the rights of women would be violated through such practices as *talaq* divorces and forced marriages, whereas the unequal treatment of Muslim religion by blasphemy law could not be justified. International human rights law, it is argued provides a basis for establishing the principles of both non-discrimination and differential treatment in that the latter can be justified by reference to genuine equality in the form of equal respect for religious and cultural values. Poulter recognises some of the problems with this approach, including the level of generality which leads to difficulties in prescribing the limits of ethnic pluralism in practice, and the vulnerability to criticism of ethnocentric bias from either those who favour assimilation or those who emphasise cultural relativity.

In the political arena, 'strong' management and political rhetoric in relation to immigration policy stands in marked contrast to 'weak' management and rhetoric in relation to addressing ethnicity in public service policy and provision (Law, 1995). The universalism which is strong in policy discourse and professional ideologies frequently turns out to be concealing racial and ethnic particularism in the operation of structures of service provision and markets. In these ways the increasing dominance of ethnic managerialism is continually subject to the persistence and renewal of both racist and anti-racist discourse.

ETHNIC MANAGERIALISM IN THE BENEFITS AGENCY

The Benefits Agency provides a particularly good example of a public service organisation which has pursued an ethnic managerialist approach. This section provides some background and provides an initial assessment of policy development between 1994 and 1997. There has been widespread concern at the general quality of benefit provision (Towerwatch, 1991; Social Security Committee, 1991; Ditch, 1993), and particularly at that provided to black minority ethnic claimants. A number of issues have been identified in the existing literature, including: the inadequate provision of multilingual facilities (NACAB, 1991), the extent to which racist attitudes and erroneous cultural assumptions lead to direct discrimination by Benefits Agency staff (CRE, 1985; NACAB, 1991), and the extent to which residence tests and the contributory basis of some benefits resulted in indirect discrimination. The provision of benefits to refugees and asylum seekers, and the impact of the Job Seekers Allowance on minority ethnic groups, are two more recent areas of concern. In 1994 the lack of an effective racial equality strategy was also identified (Law *et al.*, 1994, 1995) as activities were restricted to the following: a twice-yearly forum, a focus on racial discrimination in the processing of benefits assisted by a Commission for Racial Equality survey, the issue of guidelines for 'Bridging the Language Barrier' and sporadic staff training (Benefits Agency, 1993, 1994; Bichard, 1993). These are welcome moves but they do not in themselves amount to a coherent strategy. These activities were seen as being the key implementation features of policy to improve 'services to ethnic minority customers'. The attention to needs of minorities was also incorporated in the new 'quality framework' for service review of local offices in the Benefit Agency. The focus on ethnicity and needs, the emphasis on service to individual customers, the devolvement of policy development to managers and the linking of 'ethnic needs' to quality assurance mechanisms indicate the firm placement of policy in the Benefits Agency within the framework of ethnic managerialism.

> Since 1994, the impact of 'new public management' on the Benefits Agency has generally increased and has highlighted tensions through its specific impact on policy concerned with improving the provision of benefits to minority ethnic groups. In responding to criticism of a lack of co-ordinated policy development, a central Equality team has been formed to pursue policy operating with a 'weak' conception of individual equality, where: 'Equality means providing all our customers with an accessible service which takes into account individual needs.'
>
> (Benefits Agency, 1997b: 1)

Pursuit of equality in service delivery is explicitly justified in ethnic manageri-alist terms as reference is made to valuing (ethnic) diversity amongst cus-tomers which is seen as making sound business sense, as responding to customers' needs is seen as leading to improvements in customers satisfac-tion, which meets Agency objectives. In this way equality policy is seen as providing general support for the Benefit Agency's core service values. The formal emphasis on equality is, however, operationalised as ethnicity rather than 'race', through the guidelines for service delivery which show that policy implementation involves a combination of meeting language needs, by use of interpreters, translated information, language skills points cards, community liaison and provision of 'the same standard of professional, fair, efficient service' (1997a; para 2.18). But mandatory service requirements for local offices with respect to equality issues generally have been reduced from about 12 to six in recent years, and the only requirement that relates to eth-nicity is that arrangements must be made for the provision of interpreters within 24 hours of the need for an interview being established (Benefits Agency, 1996). Local office equality action plans are optional and there is no requirement that equality issues should be actively addressed in local busi-ness plans or local strategic plans. The devolvement of financial control and determination of priorities to managers is seen as increasingly producing negative effects: firstly, problems in how local needs are identified, avoid-ance of stereotypical and fixed cultural notions of need, how needs of differ-ent ethnic minority groups in local areas will be prioritised and the formulation of how needs can be best responded to remain contentious; sec-ondly, service variations between the innovative and responsive offices and those who takes no action in this field appear to be increasing; and thirdly, the increased assertiveness of local managers in a context of tight constraints on staffing and budgets, combined with some negative perceptions of the value of 'equality' policy, may be producing an increasing resistance to manage ethnicity in any shape at all. A further source of central/local conflict is over the extent to which ethnicity is seen as racialised. At the centre, eth-nicity is conceived as referring to all minority groups, including the Irish (see Patterson, 1994), whereas local managers are much more likely to see ethnic-ity as racialised and implying application and attention to service provision for black minorities only.

The pursuit of ethnic monitoring which would potentially strengthen a centralised approach, as has happened in personnel policy in the benefits Agency, has yet to be implemented. Concerns about benefit provision to par-ticular minority ethnic groups have not been linked in any way to key man-agement performance indicators, such as those on clearance times. Indeed, this would require ethnic monitoring of claimants cases for this to be imple-mented. Approval of monitoring of 'customers' in principle has been agreed by senior management, but due to the priority given to the introduction of the Job Seekers' Allowance, and the cost of changing management information systems, this has not been implemented. The lack of ethnic monitoring is seen as an important constraint on policy development because the consequent lack of data often leads to *ad hoc* and piecemeal initiatives to improve service delivery. Craig (1996) also emphasises the central importance of ethnic monitoring to basic research in this field as examination of the extent, nature and consequences of low benefit take-up amongst minority groups cannot take place without it. In 1994/5 equal opportunity initiatives seemed generally to be marginal to service delivery in the local offices according to both the perceptions of black minority ethnic claimants and local office plans. An internal review of equality and service delivery is at present taking place and will shortly provide data as to the impact of policy change in the past two years.

Ethnic managerialism may, as a result, be providing a cover for declining quality of services to minority ethnic claimants. Local managerial decision-making in a climate of financial constraint is leading to reductions in community liaison and outreach work across benefits Agency offices, which is of significant importance in promoting benefit take up amongst ethnic minority groups. The value put on community-based advice work by black and minority ethnic claimants and eligible non-claimants indicates their importance in reducing racial differentials in benefit take-up (Law *et al.*, 1994, 1995). For example, the need to improve the perceptions and knowledge of benefit and employment rights amongst Chinese households is vital as such perceptions are particularly weak, and as many of these households are linguistically and socially isolated. Targeted take-up initiatives and campaigns which are particularly sensitive to traditional notions, such as vicarious family pride, a dislike of state dependency and a sense of shame involved in claiming benefit, as well as to language, have been developed in a number of local areas. Research findings supported those of Bloch (1993) in pointing to productive joint work carried out by Chinese Advice and Community centres and liaison staff from the Benefits Agency and local authorities, for example, with eligible Chinese and Bangladeshi non-claimants. There does appear to be evidence that such welfare rights advocacy work, through emphasising needs and rights, can, over two or three years, start to overcome prevailing community-based perceptions of stigma attached to claiming and lead to an accumulating pool of knowledge amongst informal community networks and advisers, thereby improving levels of take-up (Law *et al.*, 1994, 1995). The value of this work is recognised by the Equality team and is disseminated and promoted in the Benefits Agency's *Good Practice Guide* (1997c). However, it appears not to be adequately recognised by local managers. The congruence between the views of Agency local managers and the Department of Social Security is, however, much closer, given the political and bureaucratic insulation of social security policy from notions of racial equality and anti-racism. (Such insulation is strongly paralleled within the NHS; Law, 1996.)

The Benefits Agency does provide an example of an organisational attempt to operationalise a strategy which addresses some of the modernist tensions previously identified, although in a very limited and constrained manner. It seeks to incorporate ideas of ethnicity and equality in policy, but the failure to conceptualise and adequately operationalise ethnic inequality in managerialist terms appears to produce a minimal outcome. The rejection of bureaucratic monitoring in favour of local responsiveness to articulated needs delegates power to local managers. Such power, combined with the strength of liberal individualism, contrasts starkly with the powerlessness of minority claimants and community organisations. This indicates that the adverse effects of ethnic managerialism are likely to be amplified.

ETHNIC MANAGERIALISM IN THE NATIONAL HEALTH SERVICE

The NHS in 1994 set up an ethnic Health Unit to take the lead in policy development; it has not set up a Racial Equality Unit or an Anti-Racist Unit to spearhead organisational change. This reflects the long tradition of opposition to more radical conceptions of the health experiences of black minority ethnic groups and racial and ethnic inequalities in health status in Britain, both within the NHS and within government. The dominance of the concept of ethnicity in health policy is also reflected in health research. The loose and dangerous operationalisation of ethnicity in health research is becoming increasingly common, and this has increasingly become the object of criticism (Sheldon and Parker, 1992; Smaje 1995). The lack of consistency in the use of ethnic categories has been critised, particularly given the multiplicity of dimensions that are frequently collapsed into ethnic categories, including notions of colour, country of birth or geographical origin and nationality, as can be seen in 1991 Census definitions. Ethnicity is a problematic and contested concept. There may frequently be a difference between the externally imposed categories used in data collection and research, and the perceptions of identity held by those defined into a particularly category. The boundaries of ethnic groups are inevitably unclear, and caution is required in assessing the extent to which external categories accurately reflect social meanings, social roles and wider social inequalities. Blakemore and Boneham (1994: 4–8) have used the concept of ethnicity to identify a range of distinct minority ethnic groups in their study of the health experiences of Afro-Caribbean, Indian Punjabi, Indian Gujerati, Pakistani Punjabi, Pakistani Mirpuri, Bangladeshi and 'East African' Asian elderly. But what actually is being described when ethnic categories are employed, and how are differences being explained? The danger of the construction or implication of genetic or biological bases for ethnic categories is of particular concern in the health context. Sheldon and Parker (1992) identify four problems with the interpretation and examination of ethnicity. Firstly, descriptive ethnic inequalities in health outcomes tend to be explained by implication or reference to 'ethnicity' as the primary cause. Secondly, failure to examine the structural determination of socioeconomic conditions and racism on health outcomes is common. Thirdly, improving health amongst minority ethnic groups then becomes a question of identifying deviant or deficient cultural practices, for example diet, highlighting 'special' health needs and changing behaviour. Fourthly, in guidance for health professionals, ethnicity tends to become commodified as lifestyle and reduced to static stereotypical generalisations.

In this way it is easy to see how the failure to understand and thus adequately operationalise ethnicity leads to severe shortcomings in the construction of health policy. Strong demands for 'cultural awareness' training by health professionals to improve 'ethnically sensitive' service provision are one common example of the privileging of ethnicity in explanations of the health experiences and outcomes of black minorities, which are comparable to social work perspectives two decades ago, in the 1970s. This critical analysis points to the need to look beyond 'ethnic' differences and seek to establish complex multi-factor explanations. It is also necessary to constantly review and assess the 'fit' between externally imposed ethnic categories and the inter-subjective construction of ethnic identities as the dynamic processes of ethnic formation and cultural hybridity may leave bureaucratic categories as inappropriate or misleading. Establishing the diversity of health experiences and outcomes within specific ethnic groups, with particular attention to gender and socioeconomic position, is a task that should undermine production of stereotypes. Lastly, rejecting the mechanical implementation of 'ethnically' driven health policy and seeking to disaggregate racist ideologies and health needs will facilitate more effective intervention.

The NHS Ethnic Health Unit (EHU), under the leadership of Professor Chan, has sought to embrace an ethnic managerialist approach with a pragmatic recognition that 'ethnicity' was the only politically expedient theme under which policy development on issues of racial justice, racial and ethnic equality and anti-racism in the NHS could take place. Formally, the importance of an ethnically-centred approach is emphasised in the NHS and Community Care Act 1990, which recognises the 'particular needs and problems' of ethnic minorities, and more recently in the joint Department of Health/Department of Environment/Social Services Inspectorate guidance for stakeholders in establishing community care plans and commissioning (1996). The EHU has a remit to work with NHS bodies to secure improvements in NHS services for black and minority ethnic people from the development of purchasing, the internal market and the primary care led NHS

(NHS, 1996b). This framework focuses decision making on patient care with general practitioners (GP) through fundholding and through a stronger partnership between GP and health authorities. The importance of establishing performance and quality indicators in primary health care for minority ethnic groups and the importance of delegating policy development to local health 'managers' are commonly stressed. For example, the appointment of an 'ethnicity and consumer consultation' manager by North West Anglia Health Authority is given as a model of best leadership practice in a recent briefing (NAHAT, 1996). The dissemination of such best practice, together with commissioning new evidence, is one of four key areas to work for the EHU. The stress on the value of a managerial solution to racial and ethnic inequalities in health care is made most strongly in a recent document on quality indicators in primary health care (NHS, 1996b). These indicators for primary health care providers comprise a series of rather general questions and are not specific, quantified or concerned with measuring output; for example, 'what mechanisms do you have to determine that the population you serve know when and how to access your services?' (NHS, 1996b: 23). The available research data show geographical access problems particularly for Bangladeshis, raised levels of diagnostic difficulties for GPs when consulted by Asian and African–Caribbean patients (McCormick *et al.*, 1995) and significantly longer waiting times for these patients in GP surgeries (NHS, 1996b). The concrete ways in which ethnic managerialism impacts on these inequalities has yet to be demonstrated or evaluated.

A key difference in the implementation of ethnicity policy between the NHS and the Benefits Agency is an emphasis on minority ethnic empowerment in the former. The Benefits Agency set up national liaison arrangements with NACAB and other agencies, primarily as a result of the publication of *Barriers to Benefit* in 1991, and there is also a national forum on Refugee and Asylum Seeker issues. These provide a channel of communication leading to some amendments in benefit administration, but do not in any sense empower minority organisations and users. Full evaluation of the perceptions of participants and the impact of the forums is required. The EHU has, however, explicitly sought to go beyond the limitations of a narrow ethnicity-based approach, despite operating under this banner, and address issues of professional hostility and inclusion of minority ethnic groups in policy development. The primary objective of the EHU is the promotion of the voice of local minority ethnic people in decision-making and quality delivery of health care services. This was implemented through provision of project funding being tied to participation of minority ethnic groups in project management. Monitoring of projects has been closely pursued by the EHU and assessment of the impact of this 'empowerment' approach is under way (NHS, 1996c,d). The temporary nature of previous local health and ethnicity projects, combined with a tendency for such marginal funding to lead to evasion of changes in mainstream provision, provides a sceptical perspective on the impact of these projects. Further research is required to assess this strategy. The closure of the EHU in May 1997, after its three-year funding came to an end, is indicative of these problems. As with the Benefits Agency, the glimmers of hope in policy innovation are to be found in those elements which seek to directly address underlying thematic tensions and move beyond liberal egalitarianism.

PRIVILEGING ETHNICITY

Privileging the idea of ethnicity in public service management has a series of detrimental consequences. Firstly, increased insularity to the development of interventions to challenge racist ideas, beliefs and values and their determination of specific policies and practices may result. The strength of anti-racist traditions varies significantly across public services and professions, and such a strategy is likely to increase the variation in the permeation of racist ideas. Secondly, the new language of managing ethnicity in public services may carry with it and reproduced racialised coding. The NHS Ethnic Health Unit, for example, sees its remit as being to address the concerns of purely black minorities. In this sense ethnicity is being used in the 'old' meaning to refer to Others. The term ethnicity is derived from the Greek word *ethnos* (previously *ethnikos*), meaning pagan or heathen. To be ethnic was to be heathen, to be different, foreign, marginal, 'not one of us' and outside the nation (Eriksen, 1993; Hutchinson and Smith, 1996). The concept was used in this sense in English from the middle of the 14th century through to the mid-19th century, after which it was combined with notions of 'race' in the anthropological classification of groups of people. To be 'ethnic', to dress in 'ethnic' fashion today carries overtones of these earlier meanings. 'Ethnic' here means something different from 'us'. This concern with 'Others' which the term 'ethnic' carries reflects the racialised coding of language, like immigrant.

In practice in the NHS, ethnicity may still encompass the notion of racialised biological causation. For example, a patient self-assessment questionnaire used by a breast clinic in Airedale Health Authority, West Yorkshire (November 1995) used the categories of 'Caucasoid', 'Mongoloid', Negroid' and Other, in requesting information o ethnic group. This was accepted as regular and appropriate by consultants, doctors, nurses and administrators, and had been in use since the early 1990s. The author challenged this usage and met with a reaction of tremendous surprise and defensiveness. The practice was subsequently changed when Department of Health advice was circulated to the clinic, which had previously been obtained from the Ethnic Health Unit itself.

When the concept does not carry a particular racialised code it has generally been extended, or inflated, to include the varied ways in which groups of people differentiate themselves from others. Physical or phenotypical difference is here seen as just one of the characteristics used in this process of differentiation. Apart from skin colour, distinctions have also drawn on language, religion, historical or territorial identity as well as more diffuse notions or 'symbolic identifications', such as dress, diet and kinship systems and other 'ethnic boundary markers'. Particular 'markers' chosen may be arbitrary and there may be no reason why they should inevitably become strong 'ethnic markers' with exclusionary implications – particularly in the case of physical difference.

The common usage of ethnicity in public service policy is a simplistic reference to difference cultural groups and it is assumed that there is little difference between culture and ethnicity. Culture can be seen as an inappropriate term in public policy discourse, however, particularly due to its wider meaning and lack of racial coding. Barth (1969), following Edmund Leach and the earlier Chicago School, stressed that the focus of study should be on the construction, maintenance and consequences of boundaries between ethnic groups rather than the 'cultural stuff' they enclose. There is a focus here on what is socially effective in inter-ethnic relations, and Barth defines ethnicity as categorical ascription of the 'basic most general identity determined by origin and background'. So, a group's culture may change while boundaries are maintained and groups may become culturally and socially more similar with little change in boundary maintenance. Barth's view of ethnicity has been called 'primordialist' by Cohen (1993; 1994; 1995), and others, as it tends to see ethnic identity as a more or less immutable or fixed aspect of the social person. Cohen goes further than Barth in severing the tie between ethnicity and culture, in adopting an 'instrumentalist' view where ethnic identities develop in response to specific political and historical contexts. Here, ethnic boundaries are invoked through political organisation to secure the group's resources. Ethnicity then is an indicator of the complex process by which people create and maintain a sense of group identity in relation to others. Ethnic identity is also conceptually problematic. Firstly, there is the question of the conceptualisation of social identity in general, how it is constructed and how different elements of identity operate and interact. Secondly, grasping the dynamic construction of ethnicity and the triggers to change in both identities and boundaries is an important challenge. Thirdly, the level at which ethnic identity and ethnicity are aggregated and categorised remains problematic. The treatment of ethnicity in public service management frequently and routinely ignores these questions.

> The world of culture and medicine in relation to monitority ethnic communities is largely the world of these lifeless, limp, cellophane and neatly tagged cultures, rather than one of living and lived in cultures.
>
> (Ahmad, 1996: 199)

Although such anti-essentialism is a predominant academic criticism, much less attention has been given to addressing how linkages can fruitfully established between such criticism and policy itself. Public policy that develops by addressing ethnic boundaries and dynamic ethnic identities is likely to be completely different from that which concerns itself purely with the generalised needs of homogenous cultural groups. It is also one that would complement rather than conflict with the aim of anti racism.

PRIVILEGING MANAGERIALISM

Farnham and Horton (1996) have evaluated the advantages and disadvantages of the new public managerialism, and these have either general or specific implications when applied to the issue of ethnicity. There are a variety of positive outcomes in the use of ethnic managerialism that may accrue to minority ethnic users. The shift to 'consumer' values may produce increasing responsiveness to those users. Reduction of waste and increased value for money in public services through budgetary decentralisation would provide general rather than specific benefits, crucially dependent on participation of minority ethnic groups as managers, professionals and as service users. Greater clarity about organisational objectives, performance and quality of services may produce significant benefits in the explicit focus upon ethnic inequalities. Curbing professional and union power may lead to improved continuity and realiability of services and greater accountability to users. This may be of particular significance where such power has been used to obstruct and divert previous policy intervention. Greater organisational flexibility which leads to improved managerial and professional innovation provides much greater scope for the development of interventions that are responsive to the major spatial variations in ethnic boundaries and location of ethnic groups.

Negative consequences include, firstly, increasing variations in standards of provision and quality of service due to devolved management and fragmented services, with responsiveness to ethnicity dependent particularly on the local manager. This is particularly evident in the Benefits Agency, and may be common across health, education and personal social services. This may be accompanied by an emphasis on the 'right to manage', which makes managerialist ideology directive, authoritarian and elitist and leads to increased managerial staffing costs. This process may frequently involve a move from 'neutral' to more potilicised public managers as they drive through political reform in the name of managerial competence, fashion policy on the way and receive handsome rewards. Increased job insecurity, lower staff morale, deterioration in employment conditions and deterioration in working conditions have resulted from more aggressive management and will have significant implications given the occupational location and job levels of minority ethnic staff. failures in financial management due to mis-management, waste, corruption, abuse through a lack of political account-ability and a 'fractionalised and balkanised' system of contracting may have a general negative impact on public service provision. The introduction of internal markets in public services may have a similar effect as it has pro-duced transaction costs (implementing contracting) and a series of problems due to information deficiencies, asymmetry of information between costs and prices and contentious quality measures. Lastly, ethnic managerialism may provide a cover for reduced real levels of expenditure, investment and staffing so that issues of ethnicity are being addressed in the context of increasing social inequalities.

CONCLUSION

The extent to which an approach which privileges ethnicity can provide the best basis for public policy agenda is questionable. This position is becoming a dominant one in policy discourse across many public services, but it is not the approach which has necessarily reaped the greatest rewards. However vague and problematic, calls for – and policy built upon the objective of – racial equality have been more significant in achieving improvements in the quality and quantity of provision of public services to black and minority ethnic groups. Evidence which bears out this assertion in one service context can be found in an assessment of the Housing Corporation's 10-year programme for black and minority ethnic housing associations (Harrison *et al.*, 1996) where an emphasis on providing capital and property to be owned by black-led organisa-tions has led to real improvements in the housing conditions of black house-holds nationally. The undermining of this programme, and its replacement in 1997 with a policy which emphasises differentiation in local housing needs, pushes this programme away from its equality objectives and towards ethnic managerialism. This move carries with it the implication that new authentic communities are being sought, which in turn may generate new constituencies with often rival claims for priority in the allocation of public resources.

Key problems remain, reflecting again fundamental modernist tensions inherent in liberal egalitarianism: the comparison of outcomes against the white norm, faith in bureaucratic monitoring to achieve change, and a failure to engage with changing ethnicities. The positions of power and powerlessness through an explicit focus on empowerment through ownership is, however, innovatory. Attention to empowerment issues was found in the work of the NHS Ethnic Health Unit, but not of the Benefits Agency. Ethnic managerial-ism, as noted above, may have three particularly adverse effects, Firstly, it may provide a cover for a decline in real levels of service provision. Secondly, it may provide a cover for inaction and reduce innovation and change dependent on the whim of local managers. Thirdly, it may provide a terrain for the renewal of racist discourse and fail to engage with the challenge of anti-racism.

The benefits of ethnic managerialism (recognition of the need to respond to ethnic diversity in social policy and opportunity to establish real improvements in rights and the provision of services) need to be carefully weighed against its disadvantages (increased bureaucracy, stereotypical and pathological constructions of 'special' needs and a tendency to ignore racial and socioeconomic inequalities). The promise of a more diversified, positional and pluralised notion of identity, the building around this of a new politics of ethnicity, its mobilisation and subsequent translation into changes in public policy and service provision remains unfulfilled. This is not 'the only game left on the table' as Stuart Hall put it (1996: 135); public service managers are, however badly, pursuing strategies which logically entangle ethnicity with ideas of racial equality, often, as in the case of the Benefits Agency, with precious little involvement from minority communities and organisations. Avoiding the issues of voice and empowerment is likely to increase the adverse effects of 'ethnic' managerialist' approaches. In conclusion, the distance between policy and theorisation indicates the increasing importance of both seeking ways of resolving and managing these tensions, and rejecting the 'tragic anti-intellectualism' (Gilroy, 1994) which can often characterise policy debates over issues of racism and ethnicity.

ACKNOWLEDGEMENTS

This chapter draws upon findings from a programme of research into racism, ethnicity and social welfare conducted in the 'Race' and Public Policy Research Unit at the University of Leeds (see Law, 1996). This material is supplemented by interviews carried out with staff from the Benefits Agency and the NHS Ethnic Health Unit in Spring 1997 which reviewed changes and developments in comparison to evidence from fieldwork carried out in 1994/5. An earlier version of this chapter was published in *Policy Studies*, vol. 18 (3/4) December 1997.

REFERENCES

Ahmad, W. I. U. (1996), 'The Trouble with Culture', in D. Kellerher and S. Hillier (eds), *Researching Cultural Differences in Health* (London: Rouledge).
Arblaster, A. (1984), *The Rise and Decline of Western Liberalism* (Oxford: Blackwell).
Barth, F. (1969), *Ethnic Groups and Boundaries* (London: George Allen & Unwin).
Bauman, Z. (1991), *Modernity and Ambivalence* (Cambridge: Polity).

Benefits Agency (1993), *Equal Opportunities Action Plan 1993/94* (Leeds: Benefits Agency).

Benefits Agency (1994), *Quality Framework* (Leeds: Benefits Agency).

Benefits Agency (1996), *Services to Ethnic Communities* (Leeds: Benefits Agency).

Benefits Agency (1997a), *Code of Practice for Equality* (Draft) (Leeds: Benefits Agency).

Benefits Agency (1997b), *Equality Policy* (Draft) (Leeds: Benefits Agency).

Benefits Agency (1997c), *Good Practice Guide* (Leeds: Benefits Agency).

Ben-Tovim, G., Gabriel, J., Law, I. and Sredder, K. (1986), *The Local Politics of Race* (London: Macmillan).

Bichard, M. (1993), 'Presentation to Welfare Rights Workers', University of Bradford, July 1993.

Billig, M. (1978), *Fascists: A Social Psychological View of the National Front* (London: Harcourt Brace Jovanovich).

Blakemore, K. and Boneham, M. (1994), *Age, Race and Ethnicity: A Comparative Approach* (Milton Keynes: Open University Press).

Bloch, A. (1993), *Access to Benefits: The Information Needs of Minority Ethnic Groups* (London: Policy Studies Institute).

Bonnett, A. (1993), *Radicalism, Anti-Racism and Representation* (London: Routledge).

Cohen, P. (1988), 'The Perversions of Inheritance: Studies in the Making of Multiracist Britain', in P. Cohen and H. Bains (eds), *Multi-Racist Britain* (London: Macmillan).

Cohen, P. (1993), *Home Rules: Some Reflections on Racism and Nationalism in Everyday Life* (London: New Ethnicities Unit, University of East London).

Cohen, R. (1994), *Frontiers of Identity: The British and the Others* (Harlow: Longman).

Cohen, R. (1995), 'Fuzzy Frontiers of Identity: the British Case', *Social Identities*, 1 35–62.

Committee for Non-Racist Benefits (1993), *Charter for Non-Racist Benefits* (London: CNRB).

Commission for Racial Equality (1985), *Submission in Response to the Green Paper on Reform of Social Security* (London: CRE).

Commission for Racial Equality (1993), *Annual Report* (London: CRE).

Craig, G. (1996), '"Race", Social Security and Poverty', unpublished paper to Racism and Welfare Conference, University of Central Lancashire.

Department of Health/Department of Environment/Social Services Inspectorate (1996), *Race, Culture and Community Care: A Common Agenda for Action*.

Ditch, J. (1993), 'Reorganisation of the DSS', in N. Deakin and R. Page (eds), *The Costs of Welfare* (Aldershot: Avebury).

Elias, N. (1978), *The Civilising Process: The History of Manners* (Oxford: Blackwell).

Eriksen, T. H. (1993), *Ethnicity and Nationalism: Anthropological Perspectives* (London: Pluto).

Farnham, D. and Horton, S. (eds) (1996), *Managing the Public Services*, 2nd edn (London: Macmillan).

Fitzgerald, M. (1993), '"Racism": Establishing the Phenomenon', in D. Cook and B. Hudson (eds), *Racism and Criminology* (London: Sage).

Fredman, S. and Szyszczak, E. (1992), 'The Interaction of Race and Gender', in B. Hepple and E. Szyszczak (eds), *Discrimination: The Limits of Law* (London: Mansell).

Giddens, A. (1990), *The Consequences of Modernity* (Cambridge: Polity).

Gillborn, D. (1995), *Racism and Anti-Racism in Real Schools* (Milton Keynes: Open University Press).

Gilroy, P. (1990), 'The End of Anti-Racism', in W. Ball and J. Solomos (eds), *Race and Local Politics* (London: Macmillan).

Gilroy, P. (1993), *The Black Atlantic: Modernity and Double Consciousness* (London: Verso).

Gilroy, P. (1994), 'Foreword', in I. Gaber and J. Aldridge (eds), *Culture, Identity and Transracial Adoption: In the Best Interests of the Child* (London: Free Association Books).

Hall, S. (1992), 'The West and the Rest: Discourse and Power', in S. Hall and B. Gieben (eds), *Formations of Modernity* (Cambridge: Polity).

Hall, S. (1996), 'The Politics of Identity', in T. Ranger, Y. Samad and O. Stuart (eds), *Culture, Identity and Politics* (Aldershot: Avebury).

Harrison, M., Karmani, A., Law, I. Phillips, D. and Raretz, A. (1996b), *Evaluation of the Housing Corporation's Programmes for Black Housing Associations, 1986–1996* (London: Housing Corporation).

Hutchinson, J. and Smith, A. D. (eds) (1996), *Oxford Reader on Ethnicity* (Oxford: Oxford University Press).

Hughes, O. (1994), *Public Management and Administration* (New York: St Martin's Press).

Jenkins, R. (1986), *Racism and Recruitment* (Cambridge: Cambridge University Press).

Lacey, N. (1992), 'From Individual to Group', in B. Hepple and E. Szyszczak (eds), *Discrimination: The Limits of Law* (London: Mansell).

Law, I (1995), 'Immigration and the Politics of Ethnic Diversity', in M. Mullard (ed.), *Policy Challenges in the 1990s* (London: Routledge).

Law, I. (1996), *Racism, Ethnicity and Social Policy* (Hemel Hempstead: Harvester Wheatsheaf).

Law, I. and Harrison, M. (1997), 'Needs and Empowerment in Minority Ethnic Housing: Some Issues of Definition and Local Strategy', *Policy and Politics*, 25, 285–98.

Law, I., Deacon, A., Hylton, C. and Karmani, A. (1995), 'Black Families and Social Security', in J. Millar and H. Jones (eds), *The Politics of the Family* (Aldershot: Avery).

Law, I., Hylton, C., Karmani, A. and Deacon, A., (1994), 'The Effect of Ethnicity on Claiming Benefits: Evidence from Chinese and Bangladeshi Communities', *Benefits*, 9, 7–12.

Lijphart, A. (1977), *Democracy in Plural Societies: A Comparative Exploration* (New Haven, CT: Yale University Press).

Lipsitz, G. (1995), Review of *The Black Atlantic* by Gilroy, *Social Identities*, 1, 193–200.

Lustgarten, L. (1992), 'Racial Inequality, Public Policy and the Law', in B. Hepple and E. Szyszczak (eds), *Discrimination: The Limits of Law* (London: Mansell).

Mackinnon, C. (1989), *Towards a Feminist Theory of the State* (Cambridge, MA: Harvard University Pres).

Massey, A. (1993), *Managing the Public Sector* (Aldershot: Edward Elgar).

McCormick, A., Fleming, D. and Charlton, J. (1995), *Morbidity Statistics from General Practice: Fourth National Study* (London: HMSO).

Mirza, H. S. (ed.) (1997), *British Black Feminisms* (London: Routledge).

Modood, T. (1996), 'The Changing Context of "Race" in Britian: a Symposium on Anti-Racism', *Patterns of Prejudice*, 30, 3–13.

NACAB (1991), *Barriers to Benefit* (London: National Association of Citizens Advice Bureaux).

NAHAT (1996), *Health Care for Black and Minority Ethnic People* (Birmingham: National Association of Health Authorities and Trusts).

NHS Ethnic Heath Unit (1995), *Achievements 1994–95* (Leeds: NHS EHU).

NHS Ethnic Heath Unit (1996a), *Beyond the Boundary, an Action Guide for Health Service Purchasers – Consultation and Involvement* (Leeds: NHS EHU).

NHS Ethnic Heath Unit (1996b), *Good Practice Quality Indicators in Primary Health Care* (Leeds: NHS EHU).

NHS Ethnic Health Unit (1996c), *Project Funding Directory 1994/95* (Leeds: NHS EHU).

NHS Ethnic Health Unit (1996d), *Project Funding Directory 1995/96* (Leeds: NHS EHU).

Nixon, J. (1985), *A Teacher's Guide to Multicultural Education* (Oxford: Blackwell).

O'Donovan, K. and S. Szyszczak, E. (1988), *Equality and Sex Discrimination Law* (Oxford: Blackwell).

Parekh, B. (1997a), 'Equality in a Multicultural Society', in J. Franklin (ed.), *Equality* (London: IPPR).

Parekh, B. (1997b), 'National Culture and Multiculturalism', in K. Thompson (ed.), *Media and Cultural Regulation* (London: Sage).

Patterson, T. (1994), 'Irish Lessons: Irish Claimants in Britain in Context', *Benefits*, 9, 12–15.

Pollitt, C. (1993), *Managerialism and the Public Services*, 2nd edn (Oxford: Blackwell).

Poulter, S. (1986), *English Law and Ethnic Minority Customs* (London: Butterworths).

Poulter, S. (1992), 'The Limits of Legal, Cultural and Religious Pluralism', in B. Hepple and E. Szyszczak (eds), *Discrimination: the Limits of Law* (London: Mansell).

Rattansi, A. (1992), 'Changing the Subject? Racism, Culture and Education', in J. Donald and A. Rattansi (eds), *Race, Culture and Difference* (London: Sage/Open University),

Reeves, F. (1983) *British Racial Discourse* (Cambridge: Cambridge University Press).

Runnymede Trust (1994), *Runnymede Trust Briefing* (London: Runnymede Trust, March).

Sheldon, T. and Parker, H. (1992), 'The Use of "Ethnicity" and "Race" in Health Research; a Cautionary Note', in W. Ahmad (ed.), *The Politics of 'Race' and Health* (Bradford: University of Bradford/Bradford and Ilkley Community College).

Smaje, C. (1995), *Health, 'Race' and Ethnicity: Making Sense of the Evidence* (London: King's Fund Institute).

Social Security Committee (1991), *The Organisation and Administration of the Department of Social Security Minutes of Evidence*, 12 November, House of Commons Session 1991–2, H. C. 19-iii.

Towerwatch Advisory Claimants Action Group with Islington Council (1991), *Shame About the Service* (London: Towerwatch).

Part IV

Political Transformations and Social Theory

12 Reading the Community: a Critique of Some Postmodern Narratives of Citizenship and Community

Valerie Hey

THE CONTEXT OF CONTEMPORARY POLITICAL DISCOURSE: OLD AND NEW BOYS ON THE BLOCK

The 'community' has emerged as a potent theme in contemporary political and intellectual discourse. The construction of community supplied by the radical Right sets the dominant context for the ensuing discussion. The radical Right project has been the subject of a sustained left and feminist critique. Much of this work has focused upon the remaking of civil society in the form of markets in education and health (Arnot, 1992; Whitty, 1994; Epstein and Kenway, 1996; Hey, 1996). However, in the UK[1] there has been less feminist attention paid to the 'communitarian project', which itself has to be seen as an intervention in the politics of globalisation, community and civil society.

Intellectual evaluations of the radical Right as a social movement (Johnson, 1991) suggest some of the complex reasons why it has managed to establish itself as the dominant political formation. In this chapter, I cannot hope to review the range of analyses of the radical Right's political appeal. My aim is restricted to looking at an alternative analysis of the current (postmodern) community (Mulgan, 1997; Bauman, 1996). There is a certain editorial serendipity about my selection but it is not entirely random. This chapter looks at some of the effects of their 'take' on critical postmodernist ideas. Specifically, it takes issue with their shared lack of reflexivity about their (modern) standpoint. In that sense instead of disrupting the radical Right's hegemony, they are complicit with it.

229

In sum, I feel unease at the constructions of community that are being conjured here. I go on to suggest why these accounts fail to convince. Neither the optimistic ethico-technical new world order of Mulgan and his fellow 'connectors', or the bleak cityscape of Bauman's social isolates provides an adequate set of scenarios, let alone concepts, to think about some of the difficulties of contesting the prevalent discourses about contemporary urban communities. It is my general argument that there are overlapping tendencies in the radical Right, centre left and high modernity/Postmodernism that seek to erase/disperse or dispossess feminist conceptualisations. This is evident in the production of ideas and policies about civic society. My main concern in this chapter is thus to raise some objections to these repositionings. I argue that we cannot think through the complex of relations which make up the personal, private, public and political dimensions of community, civil society and citizenship (Griffiths and Sellers, 1996) *unless* we consider gender as one of the important power stratifications in play. That, put crudely, there are *at least* two versions of 'community' – his and hers (Bornat, 1993; Soper, 1994; Friedman, 1995).

The sort of civil society we want, and the type of social forms we should live within, are vital social, political and educational questions. I have a specific sociological and political interest in thinking through the notion of 'community' in terms of the material, cultural and social basis of friendship and other (neighbour) and affinity relations. In the final section I gloss what might be involved in taking these informal relations seriously as 'social capital' and as sources of identity. The purpose is to bring these social forms in from the 'private' to the domain of sociological analysis (Allan, 1993; Hey, 1997).

THE RADICAL RIGHT: COMMUNITY POLICING

The radical Right having reinvented *the parent–citizen* (as a necessary part of a logic about individual consumer choice) is heavily invested in retaining its hold on this privileged subject (Hey, 1996). Representations of the 'other' – the *parent–denizen* (black, single parent and unemployed) are now generated as the negative terms of what could be called *a discourse of proper parenting*. Within this discursive/material framework the state establishes itself as an exceptionally hostile place for 'the improper', *viz.* the elderly/disabled (chastised for being a 'burden'); the unemployed (accused of being 'slackers'); the poor (the undeserving feckless and reckless). A new political consensus has re-emerged. It is one that proposed two 'natural' parents as the best family arrangement (Etzioni, n.d.; Atkinson, 1994). The present social policy agenda of New Labour appears uncritically to support nostalgic, highly conservative family forms. This convergence of allegedly different political ideologies has to be seen as part of a wider rhetoric concerned with re-traditionalising sexual divisions. The 'boys' underachievement' movement is another related instance of what Jane Kenway has called 'the lads movement' (Kenway, 1995a).

The extent to which unease about 'communities' is a form of resistance by dominant groups and elites to economic, social and cultural gains made by women is suggested by how the *proper parenting discourse* is worked on through the same disciplinary logics that target those other community slackers – schools and school teachers (Miller, 1996). The parent-effectiveness movement, like its sister organisation (the school-effectiveness lobby), shares a common obsession with 'improvement' through mandating parental mission statements to bring recalcitrant workers/children into line through home–school contracts and homework reviews. This burgeoning disciplinarian interest in imposing 'standards' and with punishing 'failure' is instructive. One does not have to be Foucault to note how quickly we have witnessed the installation (quite literally at times) of invasive, intricate and private modalities of surveillance in the home. It is clear that the rush to control cuts across party and ideological lines. It is equally clear that there are gendered implications of different surveillance and control policies, if only because targeting practices are also split along the public/private lines: contracts for the home, video surveillance on the streets[2] and electronic tags on the offender.

Ann Oakley and Berry Mayall comment that the much-hyped home–school contract is redolent of a thousand initiatives that have set out to remedy a public ill (the shortfall in education expenditure) through a private presumption (the emotional and material unpaid labour of *women* – Oakley and Mayall, *The Guardian*, 1996). I have indicated elsewhere how deeply misogyny is imbricated in the state and civil society, and noted how potently it can rework *collective* responsibility into a specifically female one (Hey, 1994a, 1996). Such redistributions presume, and indeed seek to construct, an *'imagined community'* of the responsible (wage-earning/home-owning/caring) parents premised on women's invisible unpaid labour. Moreover, the rhetoric of blaming, shaming, punishing and thereby excluding variously gendered, racialised and classed improper 'others' is central to this binary tactic. It is in this sense only that one can speak of the radical Right's interest in ideas about community merely as an ideological extension of its fears about social indiscipline. It has an invested interest in constructing and policing a specific radical Right consensus. But this tendency to collapse accounts of communities of difference inside ideologically invested ideal/homogeneous ones is not confined to the right. There are similar tendencies inside other narratives. The next section locates the work of Demos as a partial counterpoint to the above.

DANCING ROUND THE MAYPOLE: THE ENTREPRENEURIAL COMMUNITY OF DEMOS

> ... a broad consensus has emerged among both experts and ordinary citizens that the quality of our public and civil life has declined alarmingly in recent decades.
>
> (Senator Nunn, quoted in *The Guardian*, 8 January 1997)

It is of course the case that the rush to privatisation has contributed in the form of *intensifying* the social divisions that make up the community (Whitty, 1994; Hey, 1996; Jonathan, 1990). Unsurprisingly civil renewal is *the* hot sponsorship bet in the USA. Funding bodies, charitable trusts and their respective patrons are falling over themselves to endorse work on preserving 'the community'. The ensuing initiatives have been variously shaped by different theoretical and moral positions from 'biblical republicanism' (Bellah *et al.*, 1985) to communitarianism (Etzioni, 1993). The US has many prestigious and well-financed think tank/foundations on civil society – like the Boston-based Institute for Civil Society with an endowment of 15 million dollars – and the UK has not been immune to these influences and trends.

The scope and size of the UK's Demos and the Institute of Public Policy Research (both with their distinctly communitarian inflections) seem modest in relation; but they too have grown – Demos exponentially since it was co-founded four years ago. Demos now has 18 staff and a turnover of £600 000. Recently it has become sufficiently visible to be parodied as Dildos in a Steve Bell cartoon! Certainly 'the bright young things' think tank[3] has made a bold bid to capture a specific left-of-centre agenda in relation both to the political project of community and to forecasting the state of sexual politics. Like all bright young things it has learnt how to market itself. It managed, in the space of a week, to promote the report on *Tomorrow's Women* in a well-publicised conference (Wilkinson and Howard, 1997) with lots of press coverage followed up by the launch of Geoff Mulgan's book *Connexity: How to Live in a Connected World*, which has also received media attention. Such synergy is daunting.

This self-promotional flair signals a new intensification of communitarian agenda setting and promises a differently situated citizenship critique; one that is more populist and politically interested than the academic critique provided by others (Turner, 1990; Ranson, 1993; Whitty, 1994). This latter strand has been subjected to a sustained feminist critique (Arnot, 1992; Young, 1995; Unterhalter, 1996; Hey, 1996), but far less feminist notice has been paid to the Demos project. This negligence is important since, from my reading, Demos' communitarianism seems to have found allegiance in the Labour Party's vision of community renewal. There is a new and well-connected kid on the block, and we[4] had better engage with his specific presence, not least because he is well organised, well intentioned and dense with quotable, portable and 'commonsensical' policies. Others have commented about loss of intellectual rigour in Demos' popularising impulses.[5] But that is not my concern here. I prefer to comment on the political repositioning sought by such popularising interventions. I want to offer a provisional feminist assessment of British communitarianism's bid to become the new common sense.

METAPHORS, MORALS AND MASCULINITY: HOW DEMOS CONSTRUCTS THE FUTURE

A recent publication by Demos (Atkinson, 1994) anticipates many of the ideas that are to be found in *Connexity*. The author takes the image of maypole dancing as metaphor of a post-industrial 'flat' entrepreneurial form. The maypole metaphor is recommended to us as a communitarian vision of a regenerated community – ribbon-holders (a.k.a. stakeholders), synergetically intertwining under a shared 'subjective vision' of local democratic/economic and moral renewal in a triumph of self-organisation and self-reliance.[6] Mulgan's preferred metaphors of synergy and interdependency are the formations of flying geese (sharing of leadership and team work) and improvised dance (see later).

I have (distant) sight of another metaphoric maypole. This one is called *An Offering for Mayday 1894 from Walter Crane* (unknown source). This is in its own way as romantic as the one above, but from the other direction. The engraving, in celebration of Mayday, is subtitled *The Worker's Maypole*. It calls up an altogether older, more heroic vision of socialist community and mutuality – its banners proclaim 'socialisation', 'solidarity' and 'humanity' – 'leisure for all'; 'a life worth living'; 'the land for the people'; 'abolition of privilege'; 'eight hours' and 'neither riches nor poverty'. Both visions code a relation between human agency and moral community, but here the resemblance ends. The socialist utopia of solidarity, leisure and equity has given ground to a new 'common sense' left of centre social realism. Whatever else is at stake in all this talk of stakeholding it is *not* the overthrow of Capitalism. The maypole dancers envisioned by communitarianism are as likely to be the moral rearmers of North London as the proletariat.

If Atkinson's pamphlet is a liberal plea for enlightened capitalism, Mulgan's model of connexity delivers a similar message, though the book represents a far denser engagement with late modernity and its multiple theoretical elaborations. Mulgan's reading is compendious. Unsurprisingly he references those sociologists whose upbeat views on late modernity he shares: Giddens and Beck. But he also selects from social anthropology, evolutionary biology, game and systems theory, symbolic interactionism and moral philosophy. The width of the reading and its recontextualisation is awesome. The result is a highly readable (high optimistic) account of a post-modern world transformed through global communications, time–space compressions and the intensification of global capitalism. However, it is a world that is not at ease with itself and so, according to Mulgan, we need to get some of these forces under human control. Yet, within this blueprint for a connected world, gender gets no mention (unless one counts Carol Gilligan as a metaphor of feminist scholarship perhaps?). Women get five mentions, including one under parenthood, whilst morality, exchange and order are densely indexed.

Mulgan is serious about restoring the moral orders, regulations and reci-procities of social life. To argue this case he posits a new understanding of the *interdependencies* of postmodern civil society. His concept of 'connexity' appears to capture two opposing trends. It represents both the consequence of globalisation (space–time compression, expansion in communication and transmission of information and knowledge) but it is precisely our inter-dependencies that warrant a moral recognition that the premise/promises of *the market's individual* freedoms are counterproductive in ensuring our col-lective welfare. On first sight it sounds just the sort of text to examine the systematic interdependencies of: men on women, capital on forms of gen-dered reproduction, the first world on the third. But the analysis – effec-tively a version of new age Gaia meets structural functionalism – has no sustained analysis of power and therefore no way of recognising global–local relations as gendered, racialised and classed. It also has hardly anything to say about material relations other than those produced by the excesses of global capitalist formations. It is not simply that ethical entrepreneurship is insufficient to bring down capital's relentless quest for new forms to conquer (Hall, 1988) but, as ever, another vision of a post-Tory utopia has failed to grasp that structures of power work *through each other* (Mercer, 1990; Hey, 1996).

To take one instance, Mulgan's ungendered account of the uneven distrib-ution of access to the new information technologies. Connell, for example, has suggested a powerful alliance between hegemonic forms of masculinity and 'mastery' over these new modalities of information flow (Connell, 1995). It would seem to me that the construction of global markets that has captiv-ated postmodern corporate men such as Murdoch, Black and Maxwell, owe aspects of their character and formation to their subjects' investment in forms of competitive individualism that has a distinctly masculinist gladiator-ial inflection. However, Mulgan's connected world is empty of social content beyond that of noting human beings' complicity with the market's capacity to render numerous individual choices. As others have argued elsewhere, markets are structured through divisions of power – of culture, class and gender (Cookson, 1992; Jonathan, 1990). Global capital is not amenable to demands for a better balance between what Mulgan calls 'guardians' and 'traders' – between yin and yang – between social/moral orders and the economic orders. Indeed it is the *presupposition of balance*[7] that is so wrong-headed. Indeed it is this presumption of a world not so much turned upside down, as out of true (through market forces) that skews the connexity analysis. The globalising imperatives of Coca-Cola cannot be down-sized through applying moral pressure concerning their 'unbalanced' pursuit of profits – this would be to ask a turkey to vote for Christmas! The extent to which the dominant corporate business elite take cognisance of government social or moral agendas is the extent to which they construe them as constraining their hunt for new markets and greater profitability.

If we shift to examine the communitarian 'remedy' for the crisis in the community – what Mulgan terms the thinning of the 'social glue' – we note that the privileging of stronger families and more invested neighbourliness tend to presume away all those processes which have *intensified* social divisions. Those divisions so lucidly noted by Mulgan in the form of the divisions between: those with time/those without; those with access to information/those without; those with mobility/those without. It is of course my argument that these stratifications are best understood as co-constructing divisions of power (class, gender and 'race') in communities (see Kenway and Epstein, 1996). In sum, the programme for 'connexity' assumes the ungendered citizen/subjects as the subject of 'communitarian' common sense (Atkinson, 1994; Mulgan, 1997). It is both paradoxical and problematic that this ambitious attempt to think through the relations of production and their social impacts (including moral consequences), simultaneously foregrounds and effectively forecloses the territory that would need to be interrogated if we want to see discussions about community and civil society that recognise their systemic features. The world changes but remains the same.

But connexity is not the only narrative of community on offer. What is so fascinating is that morally conscious entrepreneurial man envisaged (and presumed as the ideal subject of Mulgan's connected world) shares some features with fellow travellers from an opposing postmodern vision. Zygmunt Bauman (1996) provides an antithesis, a pessimistic disconnexity.

METAPHORS, IM/MORALITIES AND MASCULINITIES: HOW BAUMAN CONSTRUCTS THE FUTURE

In his latest writing Zygmunt Bauman returns to an earlier theme (Bauman, 1990): his key question being 'Is society dead?' His answer seems to confirm Mrs Thatcher's infamous dictum. However, in his account we are not even offered the consolation of a privatised domestic life. Bauman's dystopia configures an individualistic nightmare comprising four episodic 'mis/meetings' of late modernity. He represents postmodernity as moral collapse, in effect as already achieving the condition presaged in Mulgan's prognosis. Bauman's metropolis is *only* peopled by socially dysfunctional types: the flâneur (stroller), the game player, the vagabond and the tourist. Ironically his text produces its effects by performing in exactly the way he claims that late modernity regulates the social conditions of urban life. His use of four male archetypes (to characterise four different life strategies) reminds me of the fiction of Jack Kerouac, most obviously the player with his comprehensive lack of commitment.[8] The stroller is a particularly interesting icon. He is all surface, all consumption and style – gliding through the shopping mall like a spaced-out fashion victim besotted by the lure of the gifts on offer. 'Shopping malls make the world (or the carefully walled-off, electronically monitored and closely guarded part of it) safe for life-as-strolling. Or rather, shopping malls are the worlds made by bespoke designers to the measure of the stroller' (Bauman, 1996: 27). The vagabond cannot shop:

> ... factories vanish together with jobs, skills no longer find buyers, knowledge turns into ignorance, professional experience becomes liability, secure networks of relations fall apart and foul the place with putrid waste. Now the vagabond is a vagabond not because of the reluctance or difficulty of settling down, but because of the scarcity of settled places.
>
> (Bauman, 1996: 29)

Alienated even from the consolations of consumption, utterly bereft of locations in community, work and relationships – he is forever doomed to wander the globe like some over-conscientious Big Issue vendor. Addiction, repetition and compulsion seem to mark out the masculine postmodern: the tourist is an aesthetics junkie, while the player's single commitment is to the game of winner takes all. According to the account, all four life strategies emerge out of a power redistribution that stipulates/inscribes autonomy at the expense of moral accountability/responsibility (Bauman, 1996: 33). It is thus a shared concern with the im/moral dimensions of postmodernism that connects Bauman with Mulgan. Bauman asks bleakly 'What chance of morality? What chance of polity?' (1996: 32). Mulgan's answer is an optimistic one since he sees the proliferation of consensual relationships and longevity and lifestyle choice as enabling consensual self-organisation and participation. Bauman's pose is radically pessimistic, envisaging *no* redemptive possibilities – only a sort of perpetual gloom of alienated and alienating anti-sociality. He goes on to bemoan the lack of centredness, quoting Stuart Hall's assertion 'we have no notion of democratic citizenship', and Bauman notes:

> Or perhaps we may have – imagine – such a notion; what we cannot imagine, having no time left for exercising imagination, is a *network of relationships* that would accommodate and sustain such a notion. It is in the end the old truth all over again: each society sets limits to the life strategies that

can be imagined, and certainly to those which can be practised. But the kind of society we live in limits such strategy(ies) and may critically and militantly question its principles and thus open the way to new strategies, at present excluded because of their non-viability.

(Bauman, 1996: 35)

But is Bauman's depiction of delimited life strategies familiar to me? Are they convincing? Are they in effect archetypes at all?[9] My own work into the complex social nature of girls' lives shows, above all else, how powerfully *inter*dependency features to structure their struggles within personal, familial, community and affiliational ties (Hey, 1997). To pursue the point further, at the risk of appearing a bloody-minded empiricist I want to dress Bauman's abstractions in related but also different clothes. If I give a pram to 'the stroller' and call her a mother, she is outside the singularity presumed by Bauman; on the contrary she is positioned in a matrix of material, social and emotional obligations that constitute sources of work, pleasure, pain and identity.

She is pushing her baby, maybe stopping to chat to other female strollers. She is navigating not so much the urban wasteland, as all those shops with insufficiently wide enough doors. She might be meeting up with some of her friends for some welcome adult company. Whatever else these gendered 'adjustments' do to one's strolling capacities, they cast serious doubt on the ability to be absorbed by hedonistic mindless consumerism. Babies and small children do quite exceptional things to notions of *self* absorption. As for the other autonomous persona – how far do their life strategies reflect girls'/womens' realities? What would happen to this postmodern presumption of an individualised 'project of the self' to suggest that girls' and women's claims to autonomy are unstable, contested and insecure. Feminist critiques of citizenship have demolished the ungendered conceptualisation of its liberal autonomous subject (Yuval-Davis, 1996) and so women's positioning in un/employment (the vagabond) or as the consumer in free market economics (the stroller, tourist or player) cannot be read off unproblematically from men's. In other words postmodernism is different for girls.[10]

There is no further space here to engage with Bauman's interesting but infuriating article. His depiction of four life strategies can make sense only if read from a masculine position. There is simply no space within them to project a feminine subject, much less a feminist one. It is apparent to me that both connexity and disconnexity are incapable of rendering 'the community' in all its modalities – the private as well as public complexities within which we live. One serious consequence is that neither vision can articulate an appealing, not to mention an *inclusive*, politics of community. I indicate what might be central concerns of a feminist analytics of community and civil society in the following concluding section, which argues for a reinvestment in a feminist agenda about the personal and political, the communal and the civic.

'IT'S PERSONAL': FEMINISM AND 'THE PERSONAL WAS POLITICAL'

It is apparent that, despite their significant differences, the above accounts of 'community' all agree that there is something 'wrong'. My own questions arise out of the nature of the various (hegemonic and would-be hegemonic) positions that are being staked out here. As I have argued, I have serious reservations about aspects of the diagnosis as well as the cure! What should be our response?

Firstly, we need to acknowledge that the debate is being constructed on ground previously occupied by feminism(s). The fact that these male voices can collectively efface feminism(s) is cause and consequence of our partial demobilisation (Epstein and Steinberg, 1996). We need to get ourselves connected! We need to resist this silencing (Kenway, 1995c; Hey, 1996). After all, an insistence on challenging the 'male as norm' formulations of political and personal aspects of social life have been, historically, central preoccupations of various feminist campaigns and interventions (see Franklin *et al.*, 1991). Given that I consider ground has been ceded to what I term the 'community effectiveness' lobby (tighter parental control, home–school contacts, tagging, welfare to work or in a left inflection to the communitarian notions of socially responsible entrepreneurship) or has been occupied by the doomsday scenario of late modernity, I think we have no choice *but* to intervene.[11]

TOWARDS ANOTHER 'IMAGINED COMMUNITY': CONCLUSIONS – SPACES, PLACES AND FACES

A feminist agenda about community and civil life and notions of citizenship already exists, even if this is *not* evident from the new world ordering/ rendering of community. Feminist and post-colonial discussions of communities/diasporas has necessarily developed out of a complex double strategy; firstly, it has moved by disaggregating those cosy notions of 'families, communities and neighbourhoods' (Brah, 1996; Unterhalter, 1996; Yuval-Davis 1996) and the identities they propose. This critique has tended to retain a primary focus on the family as the site of women's specifically disadvantaged position in relation to their claim on citizenship.

My own specific investment in theorising civil society and community under conditions of intensifying marketisation arises out of work into non-institutionalised forms of affinity in other sites: firstly, girls' friendships in school (Hey, 1988, 1997) and secondly, the social networks of non-related carers involved in community care practices (unpaid work undertaken by neighbours/friends/professionals (Hey, 1994a,b). My own reading of 'community' is thus much more specific and located than the more abstract narratives. It emerges out of a political and intellectual desire to theorise the productivity of interpersonal relations as sites of identity production, negotiation and contestation as well as modalities of emotional and material labour.

I have argued elsewhere that the categories of class, gender and (hereto)-sexuality are taken up as positions within these 'communities' of girls' friendship through material practices and discursive conventions specific to girls' occupation of 'the private' (Hey, 1997). My exploration of the category of frailty, for example, offers another highly contextualised reading of how women and men are defined and define themselves in relation to the term. Taking up the identity of 'frailty' was very problematic for most elderly women since it left them bereft of their previous identity as coping and as a care-giver. This was not a contradiction experienced by the elderly men I spoke with (Hey, 1994b). Furthermore, frail elderly women asserted that they did not want either to become a 'burden' or dwell on their incapacities, since this might cut them off from the invaluable support of friends and neighbours. I can only suggest the complex manoeuvres undertaken by these elderly subjects. I have little space to indicate the range of the different 'life strategies' in play. But one thing is certain, the single most effective determinant of participants' capacity to remain 'in the community' was the extent to which they could command (the male strategy) or construct (the female strategy) sufficient social resources/social capital out of friends and neighbourhood social relationships.

It would pay us to develop a feminist analytics that takes forward the somewhat abstract feminist critique about citizenship by additional research into the social conditions of individuals in concrete social community situations. One strategy would be to extend our understanding of the gendered use of space and place in communities (Hey, 1986; Lofland, 1995; Friedman, 1995; Gordon, 1996), as well as far greater sensitivity to the gendered constructions of real and imagined communities. We also need to increase our awareness of age divisions as an important category in community analysis (Hey, 1994a). We could then be in a much stronger position to evaluate the degree, forms and types of 'social capital' provided within communities beyond that manifest in 'belonging' to the traditional markers of community participation – *viz*. church, schools and clubs.

There are (as I and others have argued) numerous other off-site spaces and places for the elaboration of communities – friendship and other informal non-institutionalised sets of relations (Allan, 1993; Jerrome, 1990; Hey, 1997; O'Connor, 1992). The work of Jeffrey Weeks and colleagues into non-heterosexual relationships is an exemplary instance (Weeks, 1999). We need to ask sociological and political questions about the nature of these networks. Are they implicated in redistribution, exclusion, censorship, policing? Do they offer other ways to be citizens? Do they offer forms of identity unavailable through other relationships and what role do they play in shelter-ing 'transgressive' identities and facilitating 'translations' or 'hybridity'? (Bhabba, 1990). If we recognise these social relations as important constitu-tive elements in the making of people's social and emotional ecologies of place, we might then be better able to site or include this recognition in com-munity dialogue in order to remake the community?

That the 'community is in crisis' is, as I suggested above, a key figure of contemporary political discourse. It arises in part out of the ideological and material assaults on the social fabric enacted under the zealotry of the Thatcherite 'modernisation' project, but it would be wrong to limit our expla-nations to this intervention. After all, the intervention was itself a *response* to wider social and economic dislocations of globalisation. These sociocultural forces have wrought their own locally inflected but important shifts in indi-vidual and collective identities, in how people come to think of themselves. The fracturing of identities around the relations of production and their re-articulation around those of consumption have installed what have been called, by some, postmodern markets (Arnold-Costa, 1994; Kenway, 1995b). These new relations of ruling/consuming have construed and in their turn been construed by new dreams, desires and discontents (Coward, 1984; cited in Kenway, 1995b). All this work converges on fathoming those processes in which the cultural is factored into subjects' lives (and to misquote Marx yet again!) 'but not necessarily in conditions of their own making'.

I have suggested that this rush to the postmodern market has not dis-placed sociality, intimacy and friendship as sites for the circulation of desires, dreams and discontents – for solidarity, diversity, difference *and* community. If we want to retain any analytical and political purchase upon the *contradic-tory, multiple* and uneven power relations in play (within social life, including those of our community/ies) we need to take on the abstract human (i.e. male) subject(s) proposed by what I have termed optimistic communitarian-ism (Atkinson, 1994; Mulgan, 1997) and 'pessimistic postmodernism' (Bauman, 1996). This chapter has thus sought to reposition this interest in 'the community' from a feminist post-postmodernist perspective (Holland, 1995; Kenway, 1995c). Whatever its limitations it *is* premised on notions of difference and contestation (Mercer, 1990) because it presumes that it is simply better theory, let alone more effective politics to work with rather than against the idea of difference and power.

ACKNOWLEDGEMENTS

I thank Elaine Unterhalter and Parlo Singh for their comments on an earlier version of this chapter, and for their continuing support and interest in my work.

NOTES

1. There is a lot of American feminist work that takes issue with the 'founding fathers' of communitarian ideas; see, for example, Weiss and Friedman (1995). A great deal of this work is being done within the philosophical paradigm.
2. I have recently learnt of a new domestic video surveillance device now being tested in the US. This is specifically seen as a mechanism to be marketed to the affluent so that they can monitor their nannies/au pairs and domestics. This development clearly shows who is watching who and has both class, gender and possibly 'race' implications.
3. *The Independent*, 3 March 1997.
4. Yes, I know the problems with invoking this term, but it will have to stand for now.
5. See Dahrendorf's comments cited in Catherine Pepinster's report (*The Independent on Sunday*, 3 March 1997).
6. Cf. the proposal of Lord Young for the School of Social Enterprise (*The Guardian*, 12 March 1997).
7. The reliance upon, and fascination with, science as the source of explanatory accounts (or metaphors) for social relations is redolent in the book – the metaphors of balance – and are shored up by reference to homeostasis as in steady-state physics. The author argues that systems theory avoids the bogus linearity of causal uni-directional explanations in its more organic forms of analysis – which I take to be just another (slightly more poetic) rendering of a structural functionalist view of the world.
8. Sheila Rowbotham's account of 'the ultimate man' captures the type perfectly (Rowbotham, 1973: 15).
9. It is clearly not one that Helen Wilkinson and Melanie Howard (1997) accept. See their 1990s archetypal women – Networking Naomi, Back to Basics Barbara, Frustrated Fran, New Age Angela and Mannish Mel – it is quite certain that these inhabit a different planet from Bauman's 1990s men! (Bauman, 1996).
10. I rather like the depiction of the female shopper as a 'frenzied coper'. Apparently she 'treats shopping like a tactical raid – in and out as fast as possible with minimal damage' (preview of 'Shop Till You Drop', Channel 4: *The Guardian*, 20 March 1997).

REFERENCES

Allan, G. (1993), 'Friends; Who Needs Them? Friendship and Sociological Issues', *Sociology Review*, September, pp. 17–20.

Arnold-Costa, J. (1994), *Gender Issues and Consumer Behaviour* (Sage).

Arnot, M. (1992), 'Feminism, Education and the New Right', in M. Arnot and L. Barton (eds), *Voicing Concerns: Sociological Perspective on Contemporary Education Reforms* (Wallingford: Triangle Books).

Atkinson, D. (1994), *The Common Sense of Community* (London: Demos).

Bauman, Z. (1990), 'Effacing the Face: On the Social Management of Moral Proximity', *Theory, Culture and Society*, 7, 5–38.

Bauman, Z. (1996), 'From Pilgrims to Tourist – or a Short History of Identity', in S. Hall and P. Du Gay (eds), *Questions of Cultural Identity* (London: Sage).

Bellah, R. *et al.* (1985), *The Habits of the Heart* (Berkeley, CA: University of California Press).

Bhabha, H. (1990), 'Interview with Homi Bhabha: The Third Space', in J. Rutherford (ed.), *Identity, Commmunity, Culture, Difference* (London: Lawrence & Wishart).

Bornat, J. (1993), 'Representations of Community', in J. Bornat, C. Pereira, D. Pilgrim and F. Williams (eds), *Community Care: A Reader* (Basingstoke: Macmillian, in association with the Open University).

Brah, A. (1996), *Cartographies of Diaspora* (London: Routledge).

Connell, R. W. (1995), *Masculinities* (Cambridge: Polity).

Cookson, P. W. (1992), 'The Ideology of Consumership and the Coming Deregulation of the Public School System', *Journal of Education Policy*, 7, 301–11.

Coward, R. (1984), *Female Desire* (London: Paladin).

Epstein, D. and Kenway, J. (eds) (1996), 'Feminist Perspectives on the Marketisation of Education'; Special Edition: *Discourse: Studies in the Cultural Politics of Education*, 17(3).

Epstein, D. and Steinberg, D. L. (1996), 'No Fixed Abode: Feminism in the 1990s', *Parallax*, 3, 1–6.

Etzioni, A. (n.d.) *The Parenting Deficit* (London: Demos).

Etzioni, A. (1993), *The Spirit of Community* (New York: Crown).

Franklin, S., Lury, C. and Stacey, J. (1991), 'Feminism and Cultural Studies: Pasts, Presents and Futures', in P. Scannell, P. Sclesinger and C. Sparks (eds), *Culture and Power: Media, Culture and Society Reader* (London: Sage).

Friedman, M. (1995), 'Feminism and Modern Friendship: Dislocating the Community', in P. A. Weiss and M. Friedman (eds), *Feminism and Community* (Philadelphia, PA: Temple University Press).

Gordon, T. (1996), 'Citizenship, Difference and Marginality in Schools: Spatial and Embodied Aspects of Gender Construction', in P. F. Murphy and C. Gipps (eds), *Equity in the Classroom: Towards Effective Pedagogy for Girls and Boys* (London: Falmer Press/Unesco Publishing).

Griffiths, M. and Sellers, A. (1996), 'Hannah Arendt and the World of Schoolgirls: Rethinking the Public, Private, Political and Personal'. Paper presented to the Re/Thinking Identities Conference, Nene College, 11 May.

Hall, S. (1988), *Thatcherism and the Crisis of the Left: the Hard Road to Renewal* (London: Verso).

Hall, S. (1993), 'Thatcherism Today', *New Statesman and Society*, 29 November, p. 16.

Hey, V. (1986), *Patriarchy and Pub Culture* (London: Tavistock).

Hey, V. (1988), 'The Company She Keeps: The Social and Interpersonal Construction of Girls' Same-sex Friendships', PhD thesis, University of Kent, Canterbury.

Hey, V. (1994a), *Elderly People, Choice and Community Care: a Report of a Research Project* (London: Social Science Research Unit, Institute of Education, University of London).

Hey, V. (1994b), ' "Surrogate Mothers" and "Good Wives": Gendered Interactions Between Community Care Workers and Elderly Frail Men'. Paper presented at the British Medical Sociology Conference, 23–25 September.

Hey, V. (1996), 'A Game of Two Halves' – A Critique of Some Complicities: Between Hegemonic and Counter-hegemonic Discourses Concerning Marketisation and Education', *Discourse: Studies in the Cultural Politics of Education*, 17: 351–62.

Hey, V. (1997), *The Company She Keeps: An Ethnography of Girls' Friendship* (Buckingham: Open University Press).

Holland, J. (1995), *Proposal for a Nuffield Research Fellowship* (London: Social Science Research Unit, Institute of Education, University of London).

Jerrome, D. (1990), 'Frailty and Friendship', *Journal of Cross-Cultural Gerontology*, 5, 51–64.

Johnson, R. (1991), 'My New Right Education', in Education Group II (eds), *Education Limited: Schooling, Training and the New Right since 1979* (London: Hyman).

Jonathan, R. (1990), 'State Education Service or Prisoner's Dilemma: the "Hidden Hand" as Source of Education Policy', *British Journal of Educational Studies*, XXXVIII(2), 116 – 32.

Kenway, J. (1995a), *Marketing Education: Some Critical Issues* (Malvern, Victoria: Deakin University Press).

Kenway, J. (1995b), 'The Marketisation of Education: Mapping the Contours of a Feminist Perspective'. Paper presented at ECER Conference, University of Bath, 14–17 September.

Kenway, J. (1995c), 'Having a Postmodernist Turn or Postmodernist Angst: a Disorder Experienced by an Author Who is Not Yet Dead or Even Close to It', in R. Smith and P. Wexler (eds), *After Post-Modernism, Education, Politics and Identity* (Brighton: Falmer Press).

Kenway, J. (1996), *Draft Proposal for a Feminist Research Programme on Marketisation and Education* (Deakin: Deakin Centre for Education and Change).

Kenway, J. and Epstein, D. (1996), 'Introduction: the Marketisation of School Education, Feminist Studies and Perspectives', *Discourse: Studies in the Cultural Politics of Education*, 17(3) 301–14.

Lofland, L. (1995), 'Observation and Observers in Conflict: Field Research in the Public Realm', in S. Canhill and L. Lofland (eds), *The Community of the Streets* (Greenwich, JAL).

Mercer, K. (1990), 'Welcome to the Jungle: Identity and Diversity in Postmodern Politics', in J. Rutherford (ed.), *Identity, Community, Culture, Difference* (London: Lawrence & Wishart).

Miller, J. (1996), *School for Women* (London: Virago).

Mulgan, G. (1997), *Connexity: How to Live in a Connected World* (London: Chatto & Windus).

O'Connor, P. (1992), *Friendships Between Women: a Critical Reader* (London: Harvester Wheatsheaf).

Ranson, S. (1993), 'Markets or Democracy for Education', *British Journal of Educational Studies*, 41, 333–52.

Rowbotham, S. (1973), *Women's Consciousness, Man's World* (Harmondsworth: Penguin).

Soper, K. (1994), 'Humanism and Postmodernism', in M. Evans (ed.), *The Woman Question*, 2nd edn (London: Sage).

Turner, B. (1990), 'Outline of a Theory of Citizenship', *Sociology*, 24, 189–217.

Unterhalter, E. (1996), 'Gender, Citizenship and Education: Two Readings of South African Education and Training Policy in the 1990s'. Paper presented at the Conference on Women and Citizenship, University of Greenwich, July, undated.

Weeks, J., Heaphy, B. and Donovan, C. (1999), 'Partnership Rites: Commitment and Ritual in Non-Heteroesexual Relationships', in J. Seymour and P. Bagguley (eds), *Relating Intimacies: Power and Resistance* (London: Macmillan).

Weiss, P. A. and Friedman, M. (eds), (1995), *Feminism and Community* (Philadelphia, PA: Temple University Press).

Whitty, G. (1994), 'Consumer Rights Versus Citizens' Rights in Contemporary Society'. Draft of a paper presented to a conference on Education, Democracy and Reform, University of Auckland, 13–14 August.

Wilkinson, H. and Howard, M. (1997), *Tomorrow's Women* (London: Demos).

Young, I. M. (1995), 'The Ideal of Community and the Politics of Difference', in P. A. Weiss and M. Friedman (eds), *Feminism and Community* (Philadelphia, PA: Temple University Press).

Yuval-Davis, N. (1996), 'Women: Citizenship and Difference'. Background paper for the conference on Women and Citizenship, University of Greenwich, London, July.

13 Will Hutton: Closet Durkheimian?
Ruth Levitas

INTRODUCTION

The language of contemporary political debate recalls Durkheim. The terms 'social cohesion', 'social integration' and 'solidarity' have become commonplace. This is the language of European Union policy documents; it has also become increasingly current in British politics, where there is a sometimes disturbing emphasis on moral integration. But if the words are to a sociologist strikingly Durkheimian, whether the discourse in which they are embedded is equally so is another question. If it is, might the underlying model of social process embedded in contemporary political discourse constitute a new Durkheimian hegemony? This paper examines the Durkheimian underpinnings of one major element in this discourse, the work of Will Hutton.

Hutton's *The State We're In* was published in January 1995 (Hutton, 1995a). By July 1997 it had sold 235 000 copies, while *The State To Come*, published in March 1997, sold nearly 40 000 in its first four months. It was 77th in the ranking of books first published in paperback in 1996, selling nearly 140 000 and grossing £1.1 million; no other work of politics, economics or sociology was in the top 100 (*Guardian*, 9 January 1997). Hutton's already considerable role as an opinion-former – through writing for six years for the *Guardian*, and from 1996 as editor of the *Observer* – expanded to guru dimensions. David Marquand and Anthony Seldon argued that Hutton's 'influence on the next fifty years may yet prove to be as seminal as that of Keynes and Beveridge on the last fifty' (1996: 3).

I first heard Will Hutton speak in a series of three lectures early in 1995, just as his book was published; my notes include the observation 'pure Durkheim'. There are, of course, different possible readings of Durkheim (Fenton, 1984; Giddens, 1978; Lukes, 1973; Pearce, 1989). Willie Watts Miller (1996) has explored Durkheim's arguments and their implications in terms of morality, identity and the self in ways which go beyond the issues dealt with here, where my interest is primarily in Durkheim's political economy rather than its ethical underpinnings. A careful reading of Hutton against Durkheim's main themes leads to a more qualified, and more interesting, conclusion than straightforward correspondence. Of course there are myriad differences between the two, but what is at issue here is the fundamental model of social process which is implied. In this respect there are some important areas of coincidence between Hutton and Durkheim which will be elaborated in this paper.

Firstly, both emphasise social integration through participation in paid work. Consequently both give inadequate recognition to the role of unpaid work in sustaining social life, and are correspondingly poor on questions of gender. To be fair, Hutton is not as bad in this respect as Durkheim; but then the context in which he writes gives him rather less excuse. The contemporary emphasis on paid work as the primary means of social integration is not confined to Hutton: it is visible in European Union documents, the Borrie commission and the Labour Party's welfare-to-work strategy (Levitas, 1996, 1998).

Secondly, both are concerned with social cohesion. Indeed, this is an over-riding concern of much contemporary political writing, which is redolent with images of social disintegration, breakdown and decay. However, there is a related point of divergence. Although both Durkheim and Hutton emphasise the importance of moral integration as the basis of social cohesion, for Hutton this arises from values. For Durkheim, values and moral integration are (at least in part) emergent properties of social structures. This sociological understanding is less visible in the predominantly idealist discourse of contemporary British politics and its strong tendency to moralism.

Thirdly, both regard the conflicts and inequities which actually surround them as the product of a pathological form of capitalism, rather than endemic in it. The resolution of these problem entails quite radical reforms, but these are perceived as possible within a capitalist economy. Hutton's diagnosis is more radical than Durkheim's, his prescription less so; but both are wrestling here with the same contradiction, and the same enemies of *laissez-faire* capitalism and state socialism. This is perhaps the most revealing point in relation to contemporary political thinking more generally, for it points to the constraints in which it is placed, and the effects of these. In conclusion then, I shall argue that the similarities between Durkheim and Hutton arise less from the fact that they address similar problems, than from the fact that they address these problems under similar ideological constraints. These explain not just the contradictions in Durkheim and in Hutton, and the parallels between the two, but the broader problems faced, or evaded, by contemporary political discourse.

WILL HUTTON: THE ARGUMENT OUTLINED

One of the most attractive features of Hutton's writing, both in the book and in his often pithier journalism, is his palpable anger at the state of British society, and at rising inequality, poverty and insecurity. He is uncompromising about the immorality of the current situation. But he is not fatalistic. Recovery is possible because the fracturing, decay and disintegration which he identifies are not necessary outcomes of a capitalist system, but the product of the particular pathological character of the political economy of Britain. There are different models of capitalism, and Britain is cursed with a system which is both inefficient and peculiarly socially divisive.

Hutton's account of the pathology of the British economy focuses on 'gentlemanly capitalism', inadequate investment, and short-termism. 'Gentlemanly capitalism' has both a structural and an ideological dimension, both deriving from the peculiarities of early industrial development. It has long been argued that the amalgamation of the rising bourgeoisie with the aristocracy in the 19th century led to a dominance of aristocratic values in the British ruling class, and the emulation of the lifestyle of the landed aristocracy by the bourgeoisie, to the long-term detriment of investment and industrial development. Hutton's argument, drawing on Cain and Hopkins (Hutton, 1995a), is similar. 'Gentlemanly capitalism' privileges the financial sector over the productive sector. Its value system 'places particularly high social status on the less risky, invisible sources of income generated in trading and financial activity rather than production' (Hutton, 1995a: 21–2). 'Generations of Englishmen' have thus been 'driven by the social goal of becoming gentlemen, apeing the lifestyle of the English aristocrat'. Although the ideal of gentlemanliness is hard to define, Hutton gives it his best shot. Among other things, 'A gentleman ... keeps his distance from those below him. [He] is a human island, simultaneously aware of the nuances of rank while recognising the importance of integrity and reputation in his dealings with his peers. The civilisation fostered by such values is extraordinary favourable to finance, commerce and administration – but not to industry' (1995a: 114). The value system of gentlemanly capitalism is deeply entrenched in the British elite, and sustains the institutions which result in deep inequalities and social divisions. Indeed, Hutton attributes the easy resurgence of conservatism in 1979 to the 'political innocence of the Labour Party and the poverty of its strategic thinking', whereby it tried to alter the economic balance of power through public ownership, trade unionism and the welfare state, but 'left the wider social and political order intact, together with its value system' (1995a: 46). And the central mechanism for the transmission of this value system, as well as for establishing the networks of trust on which the resulting economic and social processes depend, is the public school system. For this reason the relationship between private and state schooling must be a central area for reform.

The values of gentlemanly capitalism have institutional consequences. It is because of these that British companies are expected to generate a high rate of return and short-term profits for largely institutional shareholders, whose sole interest in those companies is the extraction of dividends. Notably, retained profits in 1993 were 0.5 per cent lower than at the bottom of the recession (*Guardian*, 15 November 1993). Hutton contrasts this situation with Germany, and with Japan, where there is more cross-shareholding between companies, and a higher level of commitment. European, Japanese and other Asian economies are, says Hutton, all characterised by a higher degree of trust and of long-term commitment on the part of shareholders than are Britain or America, where investors are chiefly interested in a fast buck. This is not conducive to industrial success, which requires committed investors. Moreover, the whole complex of legal, financial and political institutions has developed in a way which reinforces the problem of short-termism. It is these which are the root cause of poverty and inequality. Other varieties of capitalism, embedded in value systems and social structures characterised by a long-termism, stability and trust, are both more economically efficient and more socially cohesive.

It is the values espoused and institutions developed by what used to be called the ruling class which are responsible both for the weakness of the economy and the disintegration of society. Hutton's characterisation of Britain as a 30/30/40 society is now well known, although the basis of the distinctions is frequently misunderstood. The 30/30/40 division refers to adults of working age, differentiated according to economic activity and employment status, with the key variable being security of employment (Hutton, 1995b). Mysteriously, the ruling elite or owing class identified in the discussion of gentlemanly capitalism becomes invisible in this analysis. Moreover, the bottom 30 per cent does not correspond to the 30 per cent identified in other arguments as the excluded poor, although there is considerable overlap; for these are usually based on measures of household income, and include many pensioners as well as the working poor (Rowntree, 1995). Hutton's bottom 30 per cent are those potential workers who are not in paid employment, being either unemployed or 'economically inactive'. The next 30 per cent are the insecurely employed. This group includes those in part-time jobs of less than five years duration, those on short-term contracts, those self-employed for two years or less, and those in full-time work for less than two years or on less than half median earnings (Hutton, 1995b: 2). They have poorer employment rights and little access to occupational pension schemes, bearing the risks of sickness and unemployment themselves. Some of this group may be better paid than those in the most privileged (but shrinking) group, the 40 per cent in secure full-time employment; but 'predictability and security of income are as important as its absolute level' (Hutton, 1995a: 993).

Insecurity afflicts the (growing) middle 30 per cent. It also affects many in the 'secure' 40 per cent, who may be moderately paid and thus dependent on myriad forms of public provision. In this group are all those in full-time jobs for over two years (31 per cent), excluding those receiving less than half median wages; those self-employed for over two years; and those in part-time jobs for over five years. This covers a huge income range; in so far as the rich work, they will disappear into this group. It includes 'fat cats', news-paper editors, and nurses (with men disproportionately in the higher paid positions). But they are put together because they have better employment conditions and employment rights, including sickness benefit, pensions schemes and paid holidays, as well as more security of employment, than the rest of the workforce. Hutton argues that 'by the year 2000, full-time tenured employment, around which stable family life has been constructed along with the capacity to service 25 year mortgages, will be a minority form of work' (Hutton, 1996b: 3). Increased insecurity in the labour market is mirrored by marketisation in society, in pensions, housing, health care, education, trans-port, television and the privatisation of space itself, creating a collapse of the public sphere and 'an increase in anxiety, dread of the future and communal breakdown' (Hutton, 1995a: 197). 'Risk has grown, but the protections have shrunk' (Hutton, 1995b: 3), while 'social cohesion is deteriorating year by year' (Hutton, 1995a: 323).

STAKEHOLDING

Hutton's alternative to the present requires extensive economic, social and political reform. He describes it as a stakeholder society. Stakeholding, however, can mean many different things. Leaving aside proposals for 'stake-holder welfare' (Field, 1996) and 'stakeholder pensions' (Labour Party, 1996), two main strands can be identified, differing in the extent to which they support regulation, and exemplified by John Kay and Will Hutton. They do, however, share a number of assumptions, some of which have been set out in a joint article (Hutton and Kay, 1996). One of these is that the firm is a social, rather than a purely economic, institution; that, in fact, exchange relationships are an inadequate basis for a society based on a market economy. Kay (1993, 1996) develops the idea of the firm as a network of social relationships. Part of the point of this is to argue that contracts alone are an insufficient basis for economic and therefore social life. The relation-ships between different groups of actors, or stakeholders, are the context in which contracts are made and can be enforced, not simply through legal sanctions, but common moral assumptions. As Durkheim said, not every-thing in the contract is contractual.

What John Lloyd (1997) has called 'soft stakeholding' is little more than the elaboration of a business ethics agenda, which has been present in man-agement literature for decades. Some versions of stakeholding, however, require regulation. The TUC (1996) prescribes cooperation between employers and employees to promote their mutual interests in company success; but it also supports more wide-ranging regulatory changes in corpo-rate governance, company law and, crucially, employment rights, as well as formal limitations to property rights such that shareholder interests would cease to override all others. Hutton's proposals would involve regulation, and not just at the level of the firm. He is quite clear that reliance on volun-tary codes is inadequate. Like Durkheim, who was scathing about the efficacy of business ethics (1964: 2), Hutton refers to the 'gap between the rhetoric about leading British managers maintaining high ethical standards and the grubby reality' (Hutton, 1996a: 330). There must be changes in 'the workplace, the welfare state, the firm and the City, the constitution, and econ-omic policy more generally', as well as the extension of employment rights (*Guardian*, 17 January 1996).

Stakeholding is an attempt to 'recast the way we think about wealth cre-ation', which depends on 'building institutions, systems and values that allow co-operative relationships to flourish within capitalism' (Hutton and Kay, 1996). Although he recognises that behind the currently 'fashionable buzz-words' of globalisation and flexibility there 'stand some very old-fashioned power relations'(*Guardian*, 19 February 1996), Hutton's goal is an efficient and socially cohesive capitalism and he does not see this combination as intrinsically contradictory. Rather, social cohesion and economic efficiency are mutually reinforcing goals: 'the dynamism of capitalism is to be har-nessed to the common good' (Hutton, 1995a: 326), in order to 'build a just society and moral community that is congruent with private property, the pursuit of the profit motive and decentralised decision-making in markets' (*Guardian*, 17 January 1996).

INTEGRATION THROUGH PAID WORK

The move from stakeholding firms to a stakeholding society is simplified by Hutton's view of work as both the primary source of identity and the primary source of integration in contemporary society. Hutton argues that '[t]he basic actor in a market economy is the firm' (Hutton, 1995a: 111), and thus makes specific recommendations about corporate governance. But not only is 'the ultimate stake for most adults ... a job' (*Guardian*, 17 January 1996), work – meaning paid work – is the defining element in identity. 'The firm is not only at the heart of the economy; it is at the heart of society. It is where people work and define their lives; it delivers wages, occupation and status' (Hutton, 1995a: 111). The assumed centrality of work to identity is summed up in the phrase 'to work is to be' (Hutton and Kay, 1996). There is no con-sideration in Hutton's argument of informal, voluntary, or domestic work, and a presumption that the distribution of the social product properly takes place through the wage relation except for those above working age.

Hutton challenges the assumption that work is a 'disutility'. In free market economics, he says 'work is supposed to be a commodity like any other and obey exactly the same rules'. But this is not so:

> Work is not a 'disutility', even for those whose wages and conditions are poor, for the rhythm of work gives life meaning. The achievement of new tasks, the acquisition of skills and the social intercourse that is part and parcel of the work experience is not something human beings want to avoid; they want and need it ... Work, in short, is a utility.
>
> (Hutton, 1995a: 99)

One is tempted to ask, if this 'work' is so wonderful, why the rich often choose not to do it; and why teachers, for example, have been taking early retirement in such numbers that the Conservative government stepped in to change the rules and stop them. Work may be 'a supremely social act', but it is not necessarily 'a means of acting and interacting with the world that fulfils an individual's humanity' (Hutton, 1995a: 231). Socialists have long argued that work could and should be just this, but only under relations of production more radically transformed than is suggested by stakeholding. Paid work, for Hutton, is important to individual identity. It is also the prime means of social integration.

> Above all, work offers a sense of place in a hierarchy of social relations, both within the organisation and beyond it, and men and women are after all, social beings. Inevitably some work is demeaning and poorly paid, but the same need is there. Those who work belong; those who do not are excluded.
>
> (Hutton, 1995a: 99–100)

Thus participation is paid work delivers inclusion in society, rather conservatively construed as a place in a hierarchy, virtually irrespective of pay and conditions. Social exclusion and exclusion from paid work are synonymous. Not only does Hutton argue the employment is 'the most effective instrument for the social objective of bringing the marginalised back into the fold' (Hutton, 1995a: 24), and assume that those outside the labour market are unemployed or 'economically inactive' (Hutton, 1996a: 340). A stakeholding society can be built upon stakeholding firms because the workplace is the primary means of social integration.

How does this compare with Durkheim? It would be absurd to suggest that Durkheim's views coincide with Hutton's absolutely. After all, Durkheim says 'let us not forget ... that work is still for most men a punishment and a scourge' (Durkheim, 1964: 242). Nevertheless, there are significant parallels. *The Division of Labour in Society* of course sees the integration and cohesion of the whole society as brought about through the interdependence of all in the sphere of social production. More than that, the integration of individuals into the whole, both institutionally and morally, is primarily through their occupational roles. Durkheim both predicts and prescribes the development of 'corporations' or 'occupational groups', intermediate groups between the individual and the state. These are meant to be bastions against the excesses of the market and the potential excesses of a hypertrophied state. Their functions, as Sorel suggests for syndicates (Stanley, 1976), may extend beyond the workplace to the provision of welfare and leisure services. But they are occupationally based, indeed in some sense 'the heir of the family', since 'man passes a notable part of his existence far from all domestic influence' (Durkheim, 1964: 17). Although the 'sphere of influence of a corporation is ... more restricted' than that of the family, 'we must not lose sight of the increasingly important position the occupation takes in life as work becomes more specialised, for the field of each individual activity tends steadily to become delimited by the functions with which the individual is particularly charged' (Durkheim, 1964: 16).

This returns us to the question of identity. It is occupational specialisation which limits the scope of shared beliefs and sentiments as mechanical solidarity recedes; and these differences are constituted by differences in occupational role. So while commitment to individualism and thus the importance of individual identity arise from the increasingly abstract nature of the *conscience collective*, specific individual identities are largely constituted by occupational roles and the network of roles in society. For Hutton, then, individual identity as well as individual integration into society are primarily constituted through work.

But for Durkheim, as for Hutton, work means paid work in the public sphere, and the workers integrated by the division of labour are primarily men. So where does this leave women? Durkheim argues – as does Gilman, writing almost at the same time – that the division of labour itself has been partly responsible for the evolution of physical and psychological differences between the sexes. Unlike Gilman (1898) he does not develop this into a critique of the sexual division of labour. This is, argues Watts-Miller, because Durkheim's insistence on the importance of real attachments rather than abstract contractual relationships leads him to place a high value on the family as a locus of such particular attachments. Durkheim therefore foresees a great difficulty: 'the equality of the two sexes cannot increase unless woman becomes more involved in public life; but then how will the family have to be transformed? Profound changes will be necessary, which we perhaps cannot avoid, but must anticipate.' Durkheim is alarmed at the prospect of 'the weakening of the organic unity of the family and marriage' which are likely to come about if the roles of men and women become more similar (cited in Watts Miller, 1996: 75–6). As Lehmann (1994) points out, 'conjugal solidarity' complements the organic solidarity in the public sphere, both being based on difference.

Hutton, in contrast, subscribes to the now-dominant view that women should, like men, be integrated into society through paid work in a labour market characterised by equal opportunities. In this respect his position is diametrically opposed to Durkheim's. He too has some worries about the impact on the family of women's greater participation in the public sphere. But what the two have in common is that neither of them addresses this question in terms of the organisation or reorganisation of work currently done in the domestic sphere, because it is not fully recognised as work. Lehmann (1994: 147) picks up this point in relation to the translation of *'travail social'* as 'social labour' or 'labour in society'. Durkheim, she points out, sees women's labour as biological, not social, and his concern is with social labour, men's work, not with labour in society. He is thus not addressing what Miriam Glucksman (1995) has called the total social organisation of labour. Hutton, in a rare comment on domestic labour and parenting, sees it as part of a separate 'economy of regard', rather than a form of economic activity. Thus both Hutton and Durkheim see work as a vehicle of integration and identity only in relation to the public sphere. This is bizarrely characteristic of the broader political discourse – bizarrely, because central to concerns about the collapse of social cohesion is a panic about community and family breakdown and the 'parenting deficit' which is portrayed as a negative effect of paid work, with the emphasis usually on paid work by women.

SOCIAL COHESION

Social cohesion is, of course, the central theme in Durkheim's work. As the division of labour develops, organic solidarity replaces mechanical solidarity. Whereas undifferentiated societies are held together by a commonality of beliefs and sentiments, as society becomes more complex, so too do the ties that bind. The division of labour means that society is held together by the functional interdependence of its members. But this does not involve the disappearance of the *conscience collective*, rather a change in its character, whereby the shared elements become increasingly abstract and the concrete, specific beliefs more differentiated and specific to particular social and occupational groups. That abstract element includes a complex body of assumptions about obligations and justice in which contractual and exchange relationships are embedded, so that 'everything in the contract is not contractual' (Durkheim, 1964: 211). It also, crucially, involves a commitment to individualism (in the sense of respect for the rights of individual persons rather than self-interest). So much any properly taught undergraduate could tell you. Watts-Miller develops the implications of this for a global ethic, in which specific and different national ideals all involve 'a recognisable regard for everyone as a person, in a society of persons, as a core value and belief' (Watts Miller, 1996: 246).

Such ideas are clearly not alien to contemporary discourse. Compare them, for example, with the description of the cohesive role of commitment to the open society by George Soros in 1997:

> There has to be a common interest to hold a community together, but the open society is not a community in the traditional sense of the word. It is an abstract idea, a universal concept. Admittedly there is such a thing as a global community; there are common interests on a global level. ... But these interests are relatively weak in comparison with special interests. ... Moreover, the open society as a universal concept transcends all boundaries. Societies derive their cohesion from share values. These values are rooted in culture, religion, history and tradition. When a society does not have boundaries, where are the shared values to be found? I believe there is only one possible source: the concept of the open society itself.
>
> (*Guardian*, 18 January 1997)

The following day, Hutton devoted his entire column to Soros' argument, which is discussed further below. That his only point of disagreement was that Soros was, apart from advocating a degree of redistribution, a bit light on prescription, is perhaps negative evidence of his endorsement of this clearly Durkheimian position. A stronger positive case can be made for Hutton's concern with social cohesion, and his emphasis on the role of values in generating this. Hutton shares Kay's view of the firm as a social rather than a purely economic organisation. But he deliberately uses the term 'stakeholding' loosely and more widely to 'represent a different political economy of capitalism', involving 'an active participatory democracy' and 'underpinning social cohesion' (*Guardian*, 9 January 1996). He is, as we have seen, concerned about the caste-like separation of the upper echelons of society, and specifically the role of private education in fostering this separation. More specifically, social cohesion requires the inclusion of 'the top third of our society into a system that embodies a morality of citizenship' (Hutton, 1995a: 309). This entails binding them back into society, both in terms of participation in shared provision in health, transport and above all education, and by fostering their commitment to necessary social expenditure.

There is a gap between diagnosis and prescription, illustrated by his views on education. As we have seen, the values of 'gentlemanly capitalism', transmitted by the public school system, play a central role in Hutton's overall argument. What is wrong with Britain is precisely the network of values and attitudes in which economic life is embedded. Public schools are deeply implicated in the reproduction of 'gentlemanly capitalism' and the social division between the ruling elite and the rest of us. Indeed, Hutton says that 'the dominance of the public school system is a long-standing offence to any notion of democracy or meritocracy in our society' (Hutton, 1995a: 214). It is the principal mechanism through which the values which produce Britain's particular form of capitalism are transmitted. For this reason it is more important to address the divide between the state and private sectors than to insist on a comprehensive structure within the state sector. He is not sanguine about the possibilities of transforming the public school system. It 'remains the rock on which all education reform ultimately founders – and as it will never change, the fundamental reason for continued pessimism about Britain's educational prospects' (*Guardian*, 2 August 1995). This is especially so, since any change must be voluntary. Hutton therefore struggles in vain to find a strategy which will address the problem without infringing the rights of the rich: 'Rich parents may have the right to educate their children privately, but only if private schools discharge an obligation to educate equal numbers of the disadvantaged who need the resources supplied by private schools' (*Guardian*, 27 March 1995).

Indeed, since Hutton advocates reform through persuasion, it depends upon a transformation of the values held by the elite. True, values are produced by those institutions; but they are also called upon to produce a transformation of those institutions. Trade unions are called upon to abandon their adversarial stance, as if this were simply as matter of having the wrong attitude, rather than a product of an actual social relationship. The rich are expected to appreciate the folly of short-termism and stop trying to profit from it. Although Hutton is hostile to the new moral agenda, and is more inclined to be tough on the causes of crime than tough on crime, the necessity for changing values remains paramount. To be sure Hutton is inconsistent on this point, and might well agree with Durkheim that one role of the state is to sustain a 'sentiment of common solidarity' (Watts Miller, 1996: 90). It could be argued that Hutton places considerable emphasis upon the institutions and structures which reproduce values and thus, like Durkheim, understands perfectly well that moral cohesion is an emergent property of social structure. On the other hand, if this is so, there are profound problems in appealing to values or moral cohesion to transform the very structures of their own making. As Durkheim said, 'to will a morality other than that implied by the nature of society is to deny the latter' (cited in Watts Miller, 1996: 254).

PATHOLOGICAL CAPITALISM AND THE WAY OUT

This ambiguity – even inconsistency – in Hutton derives from the last, and most important, point of correspondence between Hutton and Durkheim, and that is the claim that a capitalism which gives rise to deep divisions, even class conflict, is in some sense pathological. Durkheim's discussion of 'abnormal forms' includes the anomic division of labour, where there is too little regulation; the forced division of labour, where there are the wrong rules rather than simply too few; and a failure of coordination which leads to insufficient economic activity. It is in the context of abnormal or pathological forms of the division of labour that Durkheim addresses inequality – except in so far as it is an expression of natural inequality – as something which compromises organic solidarity. He suggests that inherited wealth introduces a differential power and thus an inherent injustice into contractual relationships.

Hutton also abhors excessive inequality, although he does not suggest that this means all inequality which does not derive from individual talent. He does not suggest that inherited wealth necessarily undermines social cohesion. He suggests increasing inheritance tax, but on grounds which also constitute a defence of hereditary wealth. The rich 'depend upon he wider society's acknowledgement of their property rights if they are to enjoy them; indeed, without social order their rights are meaningless – and they have a greater stake in the social order holding together than the rest. A down payment, by way of inheritance tax at the time of assuming ownership of wealth, is that contribution' (*Guardian*, 8 November 1995). Oddly, this is one of the rare occasions on which Hutton acknowledges that the question of social cohesion may not be a neutral one, in that some groups have a greater interest in sustaining the social order of capitalism than do others.

Both Durkheim and Hutton observe around them an unacceptable state of affairs. Both have to square this with opposition both to the free market and to 'collectivism', and with a belief that capitalism is fundamentally compatible with social cohesion. In both cases there is a gap between analysis and prescription. Durkheim recognises that the real world is more unjust and exploitative than a model of organic solidarity suggests that it should be; the gap between *is* and *ought* is bridged by the idea of 'abnormal forms'. A similar gap exists for Hutton, bridged in a similar way, by reference to the peculiarities of British capitalism. In Durkheim's case one might argue that the prescription is more radical than the diagnosis. In Hutton's case the diagnosis is more radical and far-reaching than the prescription. In both cases the gap between diagnosis and prescription can be understood in terms of the limits both writers place upon possible ways out of the current crisis. These limits involve the simultaneous rejection of the visible effects of the 'free' market and *laissez-faire*, and of any form of state intervention which might smack of socialism or collectivism.

I referred earlier to George Soros' article, with its profoundly Durkheimian use of Karl Popper's idea of the open society. The central theme of the article was, in fact, that Soros has noticed that the consequences of the collapse of the Soviet block have not been wholly positive for those living in previously socialist societies. The 'free' market has not delivered utopia any more – indeed in many respects strikingly less – than the previous regimes. Soros argues that, in his view, capitalism now posits at least as much of a threat to a decent life for the majority of humankind as communism or socialism ever did. 'Before arguments of this weight', says Hutton, 'conservative responses are becoming ever less confident' (*The Observer*, 19 January 1997). Hutton, indeed, complains about New Labour making too many concessions to free market ideologues, but wishes Soros had embraced 'the new agenda stressing the regulation of finance, reinventing welfare and restructuring the institutions of democracy', in other words, the agenda of stakeholding.

Although Hutton believes that 'capitalism is definitionally unstable and its workings inequitable' (*Guardian*, 29 May 1995), his is emphatically not a socialist agenda: he is quite explicit that stakeholding is an alternative to public ownership and to 'collectivism'. He says:

> I would dispute that public ownership is necessary. ... If you can structure a firm well, you do not need public ownership. A stakeholder firm incorporates the social partnership and dialogue that you are trying to achieve. ... I hope stakeholding can reawaken the liberal tradition and escape collectivism.
>
> (Hutton, 1996b: 305)

Hutton refers to Labour's old Clause IV as 'the infamous clause that celebrates public ownership of the means of production'. Its defenders 'have rightly condemned the operation of contemporary British capitalism, with its inbuilt drive to casualise and marginalise employment', but have wrongly continued to support social ownership despite the fact that 'nationalisation ... promoted neither efficiency nor the common good' (*Guardian*, 24 April 1995). But he sees the New Right's narrow concept of efficiency (see also Levitas, 1986) as itself undermining of the social stability on which that efficiency depends, so that 'the promotion of uncertainty, risk, and insecurity has made the ... economy as a *system* less efficient' (Hutton, 1995b: 3).

The essence of Hutton's argument, however, is that one cannot talk about capitalism, only capitalisms. The pragmatic reason for this is that, post-1989, capitalism is the only game in town; there is perceived to be no alternative. Any way forward must be within a capitalist framework, and if capitalism itself is blamed, there are no grounds for optimism. Within these constraints, what then becomes important is to identify the pathological features of the British model, contrasted with the more socially cohesive varieties to be found in Germany or Japan – a position which Hutton defends despite recent pressures on social spending in Germany and elsewhere in Europe (*The Observer*, 26 January 1997). Stakeholding is, in effect, an attempt to find a way forward which will solve the problems of capitalism without advocating socialism, which will temper the power of property without challenging property rights beyond the point that the propertied can be persuaded to accept. Hutton's diagnosis of the problem is more radical than his proposed cure; but the limitations of apparently possible solution also restrict the possibilities of diagnosis. As Ernst Bloch (1986) suggests, a lack can be identified only in terms of its potential fulfilment; or as Marx said, humankind only sets itself such problems as it can solve. This disjunction between diagnosis and prescription is most apparent in Hutton's ambivalence towards property rights and the owning class, and the oscillation between emphasising material relations and values.

Durkheim was also trying to negotiate a route between the two routes of free market capitalism and state socialism, both deemed unacceptable. He was trying to avoid the Scylla and Charybdis of a 'conflict of unfettered egoisms', and 'despotic socialism' (Watts Miller, 1996: 4). He was adamantly opposed to Spencer's view that social cohesion could arise from the pursuit of self-interest. He too was thus forced to the view that the social consequences of capitalism that were actually visible to him were pathological and potentially avoidable.

It seems to me that almost all current political discussion is operating within this framework – and in that sense we are in the grip of a new Durkheimian hegemony, rather than merely subjected to a lot of verbiage about social cohesion and integration. It is a framework which renders it extremely difficult to confront the possibility that the interests of capital and labour may be fundamentally opposed, since to do so appears to be a counsel of despair. The characteristics Hutton and Durkheim share, therefore, are symptomatic of the straitjacket in which contemporary political thinking is placed. To some extent this straitjacket may be seen as ideological, and also as self-imposed. It has, of course, some important institutional supports at global and national level. But somehow these constraints need sloughing off, and a wider range of possibilities reinstated.

ACKNOWLEDGEMENT

The research on which this paper is based is part of a wider project supported by the ESRC, 'Discourses of Social Exclusion and Integration in Emergent Labour Party Policy' (R000222106).

REFERENCES

Bloch, E. (1986), *The Principle of Hope* (Oxford: Blackwell).
Durkheim, E. (1962), *Socialism* (New York: Collier).

Durkheim, E. (1964), *The Division of Labour in Society* (New York: Free Press).
Fenton, S. (1984), *Durkheim and Modern Sociology* (Cambridge: Cambridge University Press).
Field, F. (1996), *Stakeholder Welfare* (London: Institute of Economic Affairs).
Gane, M. (1992), 'Durkheim: Woman as Outsider', in M. Gane (ed.), *The Radical Sociology of Durkheim and Mauss* (London: Routledge), pp. 85–134.
Giddens, A. (1978), *Emile Durkheim* (London: Fontana).
Gilman, C. P. (1966), *Women and Economics* (New York: Harper Torchbooks) [1898].
Glucksmann, M. (1995), 'Why Work?', *Gender, Work and Organization* 2(2).
Hutton, W. (1995a), *The State We're In* (London: Jonathan Cape).
Hutton, W. (1995b), 'High Risk Strategy', *Guardian*, 30 October: 2–3.
Hutton, W. (1996a), *The State We're In* (London: Vintage).
Hutton, W. (1996b), 'The Stakeholder Society', in D. Marquand and A. Seldon (eds), *The Ideas that Shaped Post-War Britain* (London: New Statesman/Fontana), pp. 290–308.
Hutton, W. (1997), *The State To Come* (London: Vintage).
Hutton, W. and Kay, J. (1996), 'Only Working Together Will Save the Economy', *The Observer*, 13 October: 26.
Kay, J. (1993), *Foundations of Corporate Success* (Oxford: Oxford University Press).
Kay, J. (1996), *The Business of Economics* (Oxford: Oxford University Press).
Labour Party (1996), *Security in Retirement* (London: Labour Party).
Lehmann, J. (1994), *Durkheim and Women* (Nebraska: University of Nebraska Press).
Levitas, R. (ed.) (1986), *The Ideology of the New Right* (Cambridge: Polity).
Levitas, R. (1996), 'The Concept of Social Exclusion and the New "Durkheimian" Hegemony', *Critical Society Policy*, 16, 5–20.
Levitas, R. (1998), *The Inclusive Society? Social Exclusion and New Labour* (London: Macmillan).
Lloyd, J. (1997), 'Interview: Clive Hollick', *New Statesman*, 24 January: 18–19.
Lukes, S. (1973), *Emile Durkheim: His Life and Work* (London: Allen Lane).
Marquand, D. and Seldon, A. (1996), *The Ideas that Shaped Post-War Britain* (London: New Statesman/Fontana).
Pearce, F. (1989), *The Radical Durkheim* (London: Unwin Hyman).
Rowntree (1995), *Inquiry into Income and Wealth* (2 vols) (York: Joseph Rowntree Foundation).
Stanley, J. L. (ed.) (1976), *From Georges Sorel* (Oxford: Oxford University Press).
TUC (1996), *Your Stake at Work: TUC Proposals for a Stakeholding Economy* (London: Trades Union Congress).
Watts Miller, W. (1996), *Durkheim, Morals and Modernity* (London: UCL Press).

14 In Defence of Outing
Paul Reynolds

INTRODUCTION*

It has been described as 'homosexual terrorism', denounced as an affront to human dignity and labelled as a cause of misery and even suicide. Even those who defend it regret the need for its use, and those who use it target only those working in and supporting institutions which propagate homophobia. To defend Outing is to think the unthinkable and defend the indefensible. It strikes against notions of an individual's rights to privacy and personal liberty that are central to western societies.

To label Outing as indefensible renders it little more than the last resort of 'queer self-defence': another example of extreme counter-reactions to existing oppressions. It has been criticised as tactically inopportune at a time when legal and legislative changes appear to be moving gradually towards formal legal equality for gays and lesbians, and urban 'safe spaces' are emerging within modern societies. It is undoubtedly destructive in the negative outcomes it can have for those who have been 'Outed', and those outcomes are also seen as alienating support for gay and lesbian rights. These concerns, however, deflect attention from a deeper analysis of what Outing is and what it does as a political strategy. Such an analysis yields a different argument: that Outing is a credible, defensible and essential feature of any struggle to affirm the rights and liberties of – and equality and equity for – gays, lesbians and others of diverse, non-heterosexual sexualities.[1] Outing focuses on the core constituents of homophobic oppression and directly challenges us to critically engage with them. Whilst it is not without reproach, it is a sustainable and critical part of any politics that seeks to break down homophobic prejudice, discrimination and oppression.

This argument first clarifies the 'fictions' about Outing as a form of gay politics in Britain in the 190s, and about the politics of OutRage itself. It will place Outing within the specific context of gay politics in reaction to the homophobic 'New Right' moral agenda in the 1980s. It will then discuss the *idea* of Outing in more detail, aligning it with critical analyses of the nature and basis of gay and lesbian sexual oppression, which forms the basis for a defence of Outing as a political strategy. The ethical and political weaknesses of Outing will be explored, and finally the implications of Outing as a legitimate political strategy will be considered. The argument here is that ethical and political concerns about Outing are outweighed by its potential value as part of a political strategy which rejects the persistence of homophobic prejudice, discrimination and oppression.

I

'Outing' is an American export that has become injudiciously synonymous with the political activities of OutRage, the London-based gay collective. Whilst it has moved them onto the national stage in campaigning for gay and lesbian rights, it has equally saddled them with a disingenuously sloganised identity: *that OutRage are a group of zealous gay fanatics who forcibly expose 'closet homosexuals' who will not openly support gay and lesbian rights and work in public institutions which are homophobic.* Outing, by definition, is what OutRage does. This allows for the pathological representation of both activity and group: OutRage's politics breach the fundamental right of individuals to privacy and subject individuals to pain and suffering as a feature of their political agenda. The following press comment by Jean Rook (1991) is typical:

> ('outers') ... the dreariest, most vindictive people in the world. ... They have no self-respect, esteem or confidence to proudly live out their sexuality without crudely flaunting it. They're not in the same class as the good old homosexual Joneses who just get on with it, and shut up about it, between their private sheets which the rest of us have no desire to ... examine.

Even a cursory analysis undermines this representation. OutRage (1997) are, by their own definition:

> A radical action group with radical objectives. We believe that genuine queer liberation involves more than law reform and equality. ... We must challenge cultural attitudes, social structures and institutions which perpetuate homophobia. We have a revolutionary potential as we believe that conformity to masculinity and traditional gender roles denies choice, crushes individuality and sustains homophobia and misogyny.

OutRage's stated objectives are 'to campaign against all forms of homophobia and to work for he emancipation of all queers'. They are part of a growing community of gay and lesbian groups in Britain – OutRight in Scotland, similar OutRage and Lesbian Avengers groups around British cities – who take a proactive view to the recognition of their rights and liberties. OutRage offer support to emerging and established groups, but there are no formal structures that organise this 'network'. What links them is a common willingness to engage in direct participatory action to place their grievances in the public domain and on political agendas. They feel that the restricting of political agitation to legislative, legal or policy channels fails to address wider ideological, moral, legal and medical pathologies. It also ties progress towards equality to an attitude of tolerance and grudging accept- ance that mocks the notion of rights and liberties – producing change to the timetable and in the form designated by reluctant reformers and homo- phobes. Direct action compels public response and catalyses debate.

Outrage's direct action is heavily centred around individual casework and around highly public demonstrations against homophobia within and without institutional politics, such as 'zaps' and analogously, the Avengers 'kiss-ins'.[2] They also produce both scholarly and publicity materials and maintain a World Wide Web page. Peter Tatchell (1992, 1994, 1996a,b), their best-known member, has written on the contradictions in the campaigns for gays and les- bians to serve in the military, on the European context of gay and lesbian rights and struggles, and on homophobia in contemporary society as 'sexual apartheid'. They have also co-operated with other organisations such as Stonewall and Liberty in campaigns for gay and lesbian equality, and in the production of critiques of the role of the state in reinforcing sexual oppression (Foley, 1994). Their promotional activity is principally based around gay rights, but extends to larger issues of sexuality in contemporary society, such as their call on Valentine's Day of 1996 for a common age of consent of 14. OutRage is best known for their use of 'Outing', which they advocate as follows:

> ... We see Outing as queer self defence. We have a right and a duty to expose hypocrites and homophobes. ... Those people that have passed law to deny freedom or use a religious position to damn homosexuality have caused untold human misery to thousands of people. ... By not Outing (people in the public eye) such as gay bishops who publicly endorse homo- phobia but are privately gay themselves, we are protecting people that cause untold suffering to many gay people.
>
> (OutRage, 1997)

Outing is used more rarely than is assumed and only after deliberative meet- ings of members and substantial research to confirm the veracity of particu- lar cases. It is directed only against those whose public stance – within or outside homophobic institutions – is homophobic, and has principally been used against the church. Deliberations include considering the implications raised by the particular case in point, as well a broader consideration of the contribution this will make to gay rights and liberties. Hence, Outing gay politicians – even senior ministers in the cabinet – is considered counterpro- ductive because of the poor possibilities of a constructive reaction and because of the hostility it might create amongst those networks of politicians, civil servants and the judiciary who produce and apply the law.

Outing does not always begin with a public act. It is usually initiated by private correspondence that encourages the individuals concerned to reflect on their hypocrisy. This was the case with David Hope, the Bishop of London, in March 1995, who made a public statement about his 'ambiguous sexuality' after receiving a letter from, and then meeting, Tatchell. In his letter, Tatchell's approach to Hope was: 'It is our clear hope you will find the inner conviction to realise the importance of voluntarily coming out as gay and of speaking up in defence of lesbian and gay human rights' (Schwartz, 1995). Typical of a more public Outing was the storming of the enthrone-ment of the Bishop of Durham, Michael Turnbull, in October 1994. Peter Tatchell was arrested after shouting that Turnbull was a hypocrite and unfurling a banner which read 'He's Had Gay Sex But He Won't Allow Gay Clergy' (Malone, 1994). Turnbull had been conditionally discharged for an act of gross indecency in a public toilet 30 years earlier.

Whilst OutRage are typically associated with Outing, public disclosure is more often a product of the actions of the individual concerned or those well-meaning or otherwise who are close to them, or the press. Outing is commonly regarded as having its origins with *Time* magazine in 1990, when gay activist and publisher Michelangelo Signorile revealed that the recently deceased millionaire Malcolm Forbes had been gay. Signorile's justification for Outing was to rectify a homophobic and heterosexual history and acknowledge gay achievement and presence, and Signorile's magazine *Outweek* subsequently published weekly lists of openly gay people with those who were inferred as being gay. Most Outing in Britain has been done by the newspapers. The *Sun* Outed Peter Tatchell when he was Labour Parliamentary Prospective Candidate for Bermondsey in the 1983 by-elec-tion. It also Outed media presenter Russell Harty and hounded musician Elton John. Its sister paper, the *News of the World,* Outed actor Roy Barraclough and another actor, Gordon Kaye, came out in the *Daily Mirror* to pre-empt a *News of the World* story. Indeed, the first use of Outing in Britain, by FROCS (Faggots Rooting Out Closet Sexuality) in 1991, was an opportunist attempt to exploit newspaper homophobia. It is notable that, despite the condemnation of Outing from newspapers, they are happy to cover OutRage's activities, or any form of sexual disclosure, in great detail and sensational style (Sanderson, 1995).

The position of OutRage is that Outing is 'queer self-defence', judiciously and selectively applied. The 'fiction' of their zealotry is disabused by an examination of the breadth of their activities and the comparative sensitivity with which they use the tool of struggle in comparison with the media. The argument pursued here moves beyond that position to a point that neither represents the position of OutRage nor would necessarily be endorsed by them as a collective. It is that Outing is not only an essential element in the political struggle against homophobia, but takes gay and lesbian politics beyond the limited concessions of legal judgements or partly legitimated space created by legislative reform. Such an argument requires the exploration of the roots of homophobia in contemporary society and an understanding of the recent history of the struggle for gay and lesbian rights.

II

Outing can be quite specifically associated with the resurgence of gay and lesbian politics in 1988. It emerged from disillusionment with the continued, persistent and ingrained homophobia in Britain. The road to 1988 was one of gradual post-war change, first through passive lobbying of the legislature and media, then through a growing public concern about the spectacle of the state persecution of individuals for their private, victimless behaviour and, finally, *toleration* for the difference of a 'minority' (Cant and Hemmings, 1988; Weeks, 1990, Jeffrey-Poulter, 1991).

The legislative route led to the 1967 Sexual Offences Act (SOA). It had a long gestation from the 1957 Wolfenden Report, which formally questioned the role of the state in matters of private morality and advocated an end to the legal persecution of homosexual love. It was motivated by toleration, not acceptance. Hence Lord Arran, a key mover in the Act, on why his Bill only sought to decriminalise homosexuality: 'No single noble Lord or ... Lady has ever said homosexuality is a right or good thing. It has been universally condemned from start to finish' (Jeffrey-Poulter, 1991: 82).

Despite its shortcomings the 1967 SOA created a limited public space through the partial legitimisation – decriminalisation – of gay sexuality over the age of 21 (Weeks, 1990; Poulter, 1991). It also catalysed the formation of the Gay Liberation Front (GLF) which, as with the Stonewall riots and subsequent gay activism in the US, moved gay politics swiftly from toleration to *rights and liberties* (Weeks, 1990; Poulter, 1991). Public and visible collective action by gay activists replaced quiet advocacy and low visibility beneath the arguments of legislators. Gay politics acquired an identity and specificity, engaging critically with prejudice and arguing for the legitimacy of gay rights in a pathological homophobic society. OutRage claims the GLF and this form of collective direct action politics as its roots. As high-profile demonstrations subsided in the 1970s, gay and lesbian political gains were *consolidated* as public services, primarily through gradual gains within local government and municipal socialist politics, particularly through the Labour-controlled Greater London Council (GLC) in the late 1970s and early 1980s (GLC (Gay and Lesbian Working Party), 1985; Cooper, 1994).

Since 1988, however, gay and lesbian politics have enjoyed a renaissance in Britain, which can be attributed to three factors. First, the Conservative government's attack on 'permissiveness' and diversity from traditional family values and morality after 1979 was inherently *hostile* to gays and lesbians

(Durham, 1991). The substitution of tolerance with *bigotry* promoted negative images of gay and lesbian sexuality in law, culture and media, with the pathologising of HIV/AIDS sufferers a suitable conduit for such images. This social exclusion created the context for a growing politicisation of gays and lesbians.

Secondly, the inadequacy of state responses to the spread of HIV/AIDS, and the public pathologising of gay men through the conception of HIV and AIDS as a 'gay plague', which galvanised gay and lesbian 'communities' and 'straight' constituencies of support (Mort, 1987; Aggleton and Homans, 1988; Garfield, 1994). Those who suffered from HIV and AIDS – particularly in the public psyche, celebrities such as Rock Hudson – became people rather than the 'demonised'. The contrast between the hysterical moral frenzy and hostility of homophobes with the dignity and pain of those who suffered only served to further open wider debate over public representations of gay and lesbian people.

Finally the 1988 Local Government Act (LGA), Section 28 gave gay and lesbian protest a tangible focus. It set out legal constraints to the equal representation of heterosexuals and homosexuals:

> A local authority shall not –
> (a) intentionally promote homosexuality or publish material with the intention of promoting homosexuality;
> (b) promote the teaching in any maintained school of the acceptability of homosexuality as a pretended family relationship.
> (Weeks, 1990: 240)[3]

The 1988 LGA catalysed a resurgence of gay and lesbian rights groups, being easier to organise against than the less corporeal nature of discourses of homophobic prejudice and discrimination. It demonstrated that gays and lesbians had no basis of rights other than a narrowly drawn and strictly prescribed legitimisation of gay sex for those over 21 and no protection against homophobic political whim. It is not surprising that they were radicalised by the experience. OutRage were formed in 1990, a few weeks after, and perhaps modelled on, Queer Nation in the US.

The 1990s saw a reassertion of government tolerance with a more vigorous gay and lesbian politics, centred on equal rights and positive representations. The 1994 Criminal Justice Act reduced the age of consent for gay men from 21 to 18 and an equal age of consent is anticipated as coming through the European Courts.[4] There have also been constructive legal precedents, such as the judgement to make a joint residence order to a lesbian couple, giving them equal parental responsibility for their child, in the High Court in Manchester in 1994 (Beresford, 1994). There has not yet been a Sexual Orientations Discrimination Act, although Stonewall have a Bill in draft and are actively recruiting MPs to sponsor it.[5]

In the 1990s, Stonewall have continued the tradition of 'moderate' politics, by lobby, publicity and legal challenge, with a focus on law reform as a central feature of gay and lesbian protest. Gay individuals and groups have followed this lead. Herman (1993: 247) has observed: 'In the late 1980s lesbians and gay men have began increasingly to make 'Charter Challenges'; in other words, to litigate their exclusion from social benefits schemes, or to challenge discriminatory criminal law (for example, the age of consent), and so on.'

The 'legal' route to equality, however, has its limitations. It requires repeated micro-level challenges to precedent as well as macro-level legislative change. The absence of a written constitution weakens these precedents in defining rights and liberties, rendering them transient and vulnerable to political challenge (Fine, 1977; Crane, 1983; Robertson, 1989). They divert attention from embedded moral and political discourses which pathologise gays and lesbians and the prospects of wider political and ideological rejections of homophobia. The gradualism of working within the formal legal and political systems, whatever it has achieved, has assumed education and information will change attitudes and give impetus to equality – homophobia can be reformed away.

For those who support OutRage and other radical alternatives, there are three significant rejections to be applied to gradualism. First, it subordinates gay and lesbian change to the vagaries of homophobic political and legal institutions. However successful Stonewall's lobby of Parliament when the age of consent was reduced to 18 in 1994, it was still a campaign that worked with and took a lead from legislators – reminiscent in approach to the campaigning for the 1967 Act. Stonewall restricted grassroots gay and lesbian activism to passive, sympathetic rallies. The counterargument that OutRage offer is that gays and lesbians should not be grateful for concessions given, but indignant at rights withheld. The struggle for rights and liberties should be *public* and *participatory*.

Second, it minimises and restricts the scope of gay and lesbian politics, with an emphasis on campaigns that inform and educate rather than politically challenge. It presupposes that arguments will dissemble homophobia by force of egalitarian reason. Nothing in the history of the homophobic oppression of gays and lesbians supports that assumption. More radical and consciousness-raising approaches to gay and lesbian politics extend debate into public consciousness. A lesbian screen kiss or prominent gays and lesbians in the media and entertainment arguing for equal rights, or the challenge of Outing, are all every bit as important as legal change.

Finally, there is the argument that the focus on law and legislative politics fails to critically conceive of the nature of homophobic oppression. The law is not the root of homophobia. It represents the codification in precedent and statute of moral and scientific discourses that underpin 'compulsory heterosexuality', or more exactly a heterosexually norm-referenced ideological basis to society (Mort, 1987; Weeks, 1989; Caplan, 1987; Foucault, 1976;

1984a,b; Rich, 1991; Fout, 1992). The ingrainedness of these discourses of prejudice and oppression demand a more profound, ideological response, in which Outing plays a part.

III

The defence of Outing starts with a conceptual reappraisal of what Outing is. Outing, for want of any conclusive definition, is *the forced exposure of a person's sexuality into the public domain, where that sexuality diverges from the norm.* The term is applied exclusively to lesbians and gays, but could be similarly applied to other sexualities, for example 'sub-dom' or 'regressive'. It is distinct from 'coming out', which has an intrinsic element of voluntarism about it.

Outing is aimed at 'closet' gay men who work in institutions or occupations which are publicly visible and propagate homophobic views and values. The private practices of these individuals are in contradiction to their public behaviour or their acquiescence to the public behaviour of their institutions/associations. The outcomes of Outing will be that they confront the very intolerance and hostility which they contribute to – individual catharsis – whilst the act of Outing undermines the position propagated by their occupation or institution – social catharsis. They are commonly, therefore, people of public visibility and seniority – bishops in the church are typical targets.

Outing has three immediate political objectives. It is cathartic, in that it bares the contradiction between the public status and respect for a person or institution and the pathology that surrounds homosexuality. To expose gay bishops, celebrities, politicians, professionals, etc., is to counter two important myths and pathologies in the construction of homophobia: that gays are a minority, and have a deviant identity. The news that Rock Hudson, heterosexual matinee idol, was gay was cathartic because Rock Hudson did not fit the pathologies of gay sexuality – hence the pathologies themselves are questioned.[6] Outing directly strikes at hypocrisy amongst those whose concealment of their own sexuality is accompanied by a willingness to participate in homophobic behaviour or support homophobic pronouncements.

Secondly, as a form of participative politics, it promotes collective solidarity amongst gays and lesbians. It empowers activists to be pro-active in their struggles for equality and equity. It moves the rights and liberties agenda beyond the focus of individual experience or pathology and misfortune to a broader recognition of the injustice of homophobic society. This is asserted as reinforcing respect, dignity and recognition of community amongst gays and lesbians.

Finally, Outing contributes to a form of politics that challenges public consciousness and pathologies and propagates gay and lesbian rights and liberties. Outing actively disturbs the *status quo* of heterosexual power. It may provoke hostile responses but it uncovers the prejudice and hatred behind 'toleration' and so contributes to a collective politics and societal analysis to rally around for those who are 'Out' and dissatisfied at the 'progress' of gay law reform. It demonstrates and underlines the power of homophobia in society and the *transformative* nature of political strategies that seek to effect more than cosmetic, formal legal change. There are weaknesses with this argument, in that other forms of radical protest would seem to be as congruent without attracting as extreme negative responses. Watney (1994) goes further in claiming that the construction of 'gay' and 'queer' men is positive and the action of Outing represents a negative postulation of gay identity – the closet homosexual. This point is pursued below, but it does not detract from the assertion that Outing is one of a small number of political tactics that meet the range of aims of activists themselves, however problematic the outcomes.

Beneath these objectives, the defence of Outing arises from a number of general interwoven arguments: the legitimacy of direct action by the oppressed; the congruency of Outing as a weapon which strikes at the centre of the constituents of homophobic oppression and prejudice, and particularly the public/private divide; Outing as raising the strategic issue of reconstructing sexuality in society; and the impact of Outing on institutional sites of homophobic oppression.

First, Outing gains its legitimacy from the persistence of homophobia and prejudice in the institutions and ideologies of western societies. Where an oppressed people do not have the basis to redress the oppression exercised upon them or defend their rights and liberties within a political system, they can claim to be no longer bound by the precepts of legitimate politics that that political system propagates. The act of exposing hypocrisy and challenging oppressive utterances with truth would normally be regarded as socially valuable, and is only rejected because it stresses the limitations of the political system and its foundations in prejudice and oppression rather than liberty and democracy. Outing turns scrutiny back onto the nature of homophobic condemnation from homosexual love itself.

The argument of Outing as a 'queer self-defence' is extended here to justifying Outing as a legitimate response to homophobic oppression. The struggle against homophobic oppression acquires an honourable and dignified character in which the fight is for freedom, liberty and rights, the struggle is against doctrinaire hatred reinforced by a antipathetic state, and the attack is upon 'fifth columnism' by hostile closet gays and lesbians.

Second, Outing is an apposite form of rebutal of homophobic prejudice, since it attacks a fulcrum point of gay and lesbian oppression – the social construction of sexuality within the private domain. It creates a *public* struggle for meanings within a hitherto suppressed and shrouded *private* realm (Connell, 1987). The historical suppression of sexuality from public discourse, and its present fetishised and uncritical representation in the public domain, encourages acceptance rather than critical scrutiny of moral and scientific precepts. Prejudices pregivens about the body, virtue and cleanliness in sexual behaviour are concealed by a sanitised and heterosexually norm-referenced public realm or secreted behind notions of sex as a private subject of private individuals. Privacy has been a convenient mask for the containment of sexual freedom, obscuring dual standards in sexual attitudes and attributions of licentiousness, and supporting the pathologising of sexual diversity.

Critically, the *private* is conflated with *personal*, and the right to have personal, confidential intimate relations is conflated with the notion of a private realm where categories of knowledge and relations should be denied public scrutiny and beyond public redress. Outing challenges the private/public divide and makes a distinction between sexuality as a subject of personal intimacy and sexuality as a subject of the private realm. It removes sexuality from the private, though it does not challenge individuals' rights to have confidential and discreet relationships. Sexuality becomes a subject of public discourse, and self-identification or public identification of sexual preferences or relations becomes part of the public dialogue by which lines are drawn and issues debated – constructing democratic sexual law and regulation. Nevertheless, people, however they conform or move between forms of sexual behaviour, retain rights over the intimacy of their particular sexual relations with others.

Outing constructs this public discourse in a hostile environment and challenges that hostility. It does not dwell on *who* relations are with and *how* they are expressed sexually, but on the *contradiction* between a person's sexuality and his/her utterances on sexuality in public. As such, it unravels the roots of homophobia in moral and scientific discourses and challenges their rectitude by stimulating public debate and engaging public scrutiny. If gays and lesbians are appreciated and equal in contemporary society, what can be harmful about identifying someone's sexuality? Outing challenges hostile people to explain their hostility and knocks away the 'props' of pathologies or difference. If a bishop whose life work has been respected in the church is 'Outed' as gay, how can the church continue to sustain their prejudice and reconcile it with their previous attribution of value?

Outing and the attendant project of breaking down the conflation of private and personal is a strategy which has constructive applications for all forms of sexuality. Pathological representations of sexual ignorance, sexual diseases and safe sex, sexual ambiguity and shifting sexualities and sexual diversity could all be challenged with sex firmly but not fetishistically subjected to public discourse. Those who wish to apply pathologies or an oppressive privacy to sex might themselves be useful subjects of scrutiny. Outing as part of a *transformative* project becomes a tool for the breaking down of sexual oppressions and catalyses a more positive emancipation which involves the movement of sexual discourses in the public realm. Further, Outing gives those who support homophobia in their public statements the sense of pain they cause. If gays and lesbians are confronted by prejudice, violence and hostility, one counter is to use the same weapon of personal violence and alienation upon them. Outing may have persuaded some not to give vent to homophobic statements. 'An eye for an eye' might not be a sustainable weapon in a transformative politics, but it demonstrates publicly the sorts of pain that those who suffer homophobia have to bear. Those who feel compassion for the 'Outed' should consistently have to address the reasons *why* being 'Outed' has such negative outcomes – homophobic values and beliefs.

Outing is, therefore, a feature of a transformative politics of sexuality. It is not tactical in the way that lobbies or demonstrations for changes in the law or legislation are in contributing to attempts to impact upon individual parts of the legal, political, moral and scientific basis of homophobia. It is more *strategic*, in adopting a more holistic, societal critique of homophobia and in linking a means of pursuing sexual equality and social inclusion with the ends of what features a 'sexualised' society would have. Hence the second argument for Outing becomes a support for the third – the construction of a strategic and transformative politics which seeks to effect a paradigm shift in sexual beliefs and politics from working to reform a homophobic society to reconstructing a 'sexualised' society. As yet, this transformative politics and the idea of 'sexualising' society are relatively new, but Outing is a form of politics which has a greater 'reach' from the limited gains of legislative change to the goals of social transformation (Evans, 1993; Weeks, 1995; Plummer, 1995; Wilson, 1995; Reynolds, 1996; Whisman, 1996; Kaplan, 1997; Phelan, 1997).

Finally, Outing does have an impact upon those sites where public representations of gay and lesbian sexuality have been pathologised. David Hope, Bishop of London, in declaring his 'ambiguous sexuality' rather than risk Outing, admitted that however much he rejected Outing, the exposure of 10 bishops as gay, in November 1994, had catalysed debate in the Church of England as to the status of actively gay priests (Schwartz, 1995). Hence it may strike not only at the discourses of homophobic oppression, but at the institutional propagators of this prejudice – and with some constructive outcomes. Outing can be portrayed as an effective and legitimate weapon against homophobia, but it is not without its criticisms.

IV

The most often cited criticism of Outing is that it creates personal suffering. Rather than being a dignified act of truth, it is a violent act against the vulnerable which leaves them in misery and suffering. Undoubtedly, many of those who are 'Outed' suffer, although some have claimed a sense of release from the loss of a 'guilty secret' and the public freedom to express their sexuality. In western liberal democracies the suffering of the individual through an act of protest is seen to infringe upon individual rights and liberties, and would appear to contradict any constructive claims for Outing. The argument for Outing clearly involves the claims that it is justified through the rectitude of its objectives and that the strategy used is necessary. All struggles have victims who suffer as a consequence of those struggles. Whilst the victim's pain is real and appreciable, a greater good – changes away from homophobic discourses in society – may be served by the act. It is possible to approach this argument from both a utilitarian and a socialist position.

How the negative consequences of individual suffering are balanced against alleviating the negative consequences of homophobic society is difficult to calculate. Bill Halstead (1994), in a letter to the *Guardian* otherwise condemning Outing as a political strategy, represents the counter-argument that:

> ... it must be admitted that a proportion of the hierarchy of all the churches, and a proportion of legislators in any land have always been actively and clandestinely homosexual. When such people pass laws that punish homosexuality, or deny it freedom, or use their religious position to claim homosexuality is sinful, they are guilty of a form of hypocrisy which defies belief. They have caused more suicides and more human misery than the 'outers' by condemning a sexuality that they practise.

The question of whether the suffering caused by Outing is justified by its value as a political tool is not easily answered in liberal democratic societies. Much depends on how much the arguments against the ingrainedness of homophobic oppression are accepted. A further argument offered against Outing is that it uses pathologies and creates victims through the use of terror: it uses the very tools that homophobia itself uses. This is the alternative interpretation of using the methods of oppression upon oppressors themselves. Again, on the basis of liberal democratic ethics, this position is difficult to justify. The counter-arguments are two-fold. First, liberal democracy has allowed and even reinforced the historical persistence of homophobia and illustrates the hollow nature of its ethics and politics. This argument is one which is used by gay left radicals to associate collectivist struggle against homophobia with collective struggle against liberal capitalism (Reiche, 1971; Gay Left Collective, 1980). The second argument is that the means by which struggle is waged can only be considered within the context of the objectives and nature of the conflict – which again returns the argument to the legitimacy of violence by the oppressed. Outing is a politics of liberation – it does not create positive images by its action within contemporary society, which it is in opposition to. It does, however, retain its strength of argument as a strategic tool by which sexual liberation is progressed, and it becomes obsolete as a 'sexualised', egalitarian society is achieved. Its utility and efficacy lie in proportion to the hostility that is shown to gays and lesbians – in a more equal society its impact and meaning would diminish and wither.

In addition, it may be argued that Outing focuses on 'closet' homophobes and does nothing to direct struggle against 'straight' homophobes. This argument is accurate in its application to individuals, but less so when applied to homophobic discourses and institutions. The politics of Outing is effective because it challenges the institutional bases of homophobia and homophobic ideas themselves. It acts upon 'closet' homophobes but challenges the attitudes of those who support the homophobic positions of the institutions or organisations they belong to, and the larger population who support or acquiesce to homophobia as a feature of their norms or socialisation. It will never constructively challenge straight bigots. It may not necessarily carry the agreement of all those in the 'closet', who have some empathy with those who are 'Outed'. As a political tool, however, its functions as catharsis, direct action and as a strategic act give it sufficient reach in its challenge to validate its use.

A further argument is 'where do you draw the line on legitimate targets for Outing?'. Is it with a bishop or a priest, a national politician or a local councillor? What about entertainers in an industry more sympathetic to gay and lesbian rights? Outing has been aimed at people with positions in homophobic institutions where their support for homophobia perpetuates its prejudice. Is there a case for Outing beyond that political category? Theoretically there is; and at a point where significant challenges are being made against homophobic values – a transformative moment – its application can be argued to be more valid for all those who do not explicitly denounce homophobia in society. Even at present the Outing of all homophobes in the public eye is justifiable. Critics seek to establish a 'quantum of solace' for the individual – at what point does an individual become a legitimate target – without recognising that much of the argument for Outing is not at an individual level but at a political – and social – level, where the act upon the individual(s) has social effects. An entertainer's hypocrisy is as public and influential as a bishop's or an MP's.

Watney (1994) raises a more conceptual criticism, that Outing contradicts the notion of choice which is central to progressive sexual politics. Watney argues that the liberating diversity offered by gay theory is dispersed as Outing presupposes sexual identity within the value context of heterosexual society:

'Outing' ... pictures an immediate and exact fit between hidden, secret sexual *behaviour* and gay *identity* ... the entire political significance of the word 'gay' is eradicated, and its use as a term of identity is equated with 'homosexual'. 'Outing' presupposes that there is a simple, uniform 'truth' of homosexuality, and that everyone is equally aware of this private 'truth' of their nature.... The major problem with 'Outing' remains that its vision of supposedly 'rescuing' people from the closet ignores both the personal and the political significance of *choice* in 'coming out', as well as leaving the closet itself intact at the end of the day. (Watney, 1994: 21–2)

His concern is that Outing conflates an empowering gay identity with an unhappy homosexual one, and offers nothing positive to gay liberation. Thus, Outing departs from 'queer theory', where 'queer theory' demands a more positively constructed direct action than Outing offers (Fuss, 1991).

This is a cogent critique until one is again reminded that Outing as a political strategy is only part of a politics of transformation, and specifically that part of the politics of transformation which catalyses transformation. Its intrinsic value lies not with its representation of gays or lesbians, but its representation of the hypocrisy of those who deny that positive representation of themselves. That is not to say that all gays and lesbians have to emphasise their sexuality as the defining feature of their identity – but to argue that those who support gay and lesbian oppression do not represent gay and lesbian identity either. The important value of Outing is that it challenges assimilation, servitude and public denial and homophobia as features of gay and lesbian experience and life, as well as challenging the ideas and institutions which created the context within which these features characterise some gay and lesbian lives. Challenging oppression is not exclusively achieved by singularly positive means.

This argument could be aligned to the argument that any form of political strategy which emphasises gay and lesbian sexuality contradicts the objective of breaking down the representation of sexuality from identity and self. Tatchell (1996a) deals with the paradox that 'queer liberation eradicates queers'. He also argues, however, that this again is only a relevant paradox at a moment of transformation. The danger of not keeping sexuality on the political agenda is that invisibility has been a feature of maintaining homophobic prejudice. As a politics which moves towards liberation, Outing is effective in avoiding the vagaries of reformism.

A final weakness is more difficult to contest: that Outing is tactically weak because it may alienate potential support for gays and lesbians. This is typified by the distancing of Stonewall's politics from OutRage by its Director Angela Mason after the 1994 Age of Consent Amendment was passed at 18 and not 16, and the press assertion that Conservative MPs who moved from being persuaded by Stonewall's lobby campaign to ill-feeling at the demonstration which blockaded Westminster on the night of the debate (White and Weale, 1994). Does Outing create hostility rather than provoke debate? Does it alienate those in and out of power from supporting gay and lesbian rights?

Undoubtedly, Outing has provoked antagonism in the media, in the institutions which it has been aimed at and in the public understanding of Outing from these sources. Here, there is certainly a constructive point to be taken on board. Outing as more than queer self-defence – reaction – but as a political strategy for catharsis, direct action to gain rights and liberties and as a strategic tool against homophobia in contemporary society – pro-active – requires a clearer representation of its meaning and value than it is presently given. Outing will not help to catalyse debate unless that debate is primed and the message carefully marketed. Hopefully, this chapter in part fulfils this function.

V

This defence argues that as a political tool to catalyse debate and move gay and lesbian politics towards a social transformation to a more equitable position, Outing is a legitimate activity. Its cathartic, participatory action and strategic value makes it particularly potent in undermining homophobic institutions and the discursive roots of homophobia itself. It sits uneasily within liberal democratic politics – but then so should prejudice, discrimination, violence and oppression.

At present Outing is used in a limited sense, but this defence also argues its value as a tool which can be used extensively and centrally to the emancipatory project of gay and lesbian rights, liberties and equality. This more extensive use, accompanied by a clear representation of its meaning as an emancipatory tool and accompanied by the range of affirmatory and participatory public demonstrations of gay and lesbian sexuality, might well be critical in moving from the tolerance and gradualism of sexual politics in the late 20th century to a 21st-century politics of equality, equity and transformation.

ACKNOWLEDGEMENTS

The author thanks the following for their advice and discussion on previous drafts of this paper: Karen Corteen, Tony Fagan and others at the Edge Hill University College seminar; Bob Brecher and the Philosophy Society at Brighton University; participants at the Critical Lawyers Conference in Keele in 1996, and the BSA Annual Conference on the theme 'Power and Resistance' at the University of York in 1997, and the editors of this volume.

NOTES

*   Please note that this paper was written before the recent controversy over political 'Outings' – notably Peter Mandelson and Nick Brown – in the Labour Government. However, these events would not alter the argument presented.

1. This chapter frequently discusses the issue of Outing and sexual politics in relation to gay or gay and lesbian politics, but it is a politics which clearly has a broader impact upon the range of non-heterosexual sexualities, and this broader constituency should be kept in mind.
2. This account is partly based on a group interview with OutRage members (April 1995) and perusal of their public statements and literature.
3. See Weeks (1990) and Jeffrey-Poulter (1991).
4. Notably in the case of Euan Sutherland, who argued that the unequal age of consent is in breach the European Convention of Human Rights, claiming that it is in breach of his privacy (article 8) and right to protection of the Convention without discrimination on any grounds (article 14). The case has been referred to the European Court of Human Rights. See *Stonewall News*, June 1996. Also, more generally, see Tatchell (1992).
5. This is currently at the centre of a campaign by Stonewall, see *Stonewall News* 1994/5/6, *passim*.
6. Hudson was not Outed. His development of AIDS made the concealing of his sexuality problematic, and amongst his peers his sexual preferences were well known. Revealing sexuality, as many have found out, gives some control over the media agenda, whereas being exposed does not.

REFERENCES

Aggleton, P. and Homans, H. (eds) (1988), *Social Aspects of AIDS* (Brighton: Falmer Press).

Beresford, S. (1994), 'Lesbian in Residence and Parental Responsibility Cases', *Family Law*, November.

Cant, B. and Hemmings, S. (eds) (1988), *Radical Records: Thirty Years of Lesbian and Gay Experience* (London: Routledge).

Caplan, C. (ed.) (1987), *The Cultural Construction of Sexuality* (London: Tavistock).

Connell, R. W. (1987), *Gender and Power* (Cambridge: Polity).

Cooper, D. (1994), *Sexing the City: Lesbian and Gay Politics Within the Activist State* (London: Rivers Oram).

Crane, P. (1983), *Gays and the Law* (London: Pluto).

Durham, M. (1991), *Sex and Politics* (London: Macmillan).

Evans, D. (1993), *Sexual Citizenship: the Material Construction of Sexualities* (London: Routledge).

Fine, B. (1977), *Democracy and the Rule of Law* (London: Penguin).

Foley, C. (1994), *Sexuality and the State* (London: Liberty/Stonewall/OutRage).

Foucault, M. (1976), *The History of Sexuality*, vol. 1: *An Introduction* (London: Penguin).

Foucault, M. (1984a), *The History of Sexuality*, vol. 2: *The Uses of Pleasure* (London: Penguin).

Foucault, M. (1984b), *The History of Sexuality*, vol. 3: *The Care of the Self* (London: Penguin).

Fout, J. (ed.) (1992), *Forbidden History* (University of Chicago).

Fuss, D. (1991), *Inside Out: Lesbian Theories, Gay Theories* (London: Routledge).

Garfield, S. (1994), *The End of Innocence: Britain in the Time of AIDS* (London: Faber & Faber).

Gay Left Collective (1980), *Homosexuality, Power and Politics* (London: Allison & Busby).

GLC (Gay and Lesbian Working Party) (1985), *Changing the World: A London Charter for Gay and Lesbian Rights* (London: GLC).

Halsted, B. (1994), 'The Right To Stay In the Closet', letter to the *Guardian*, 6 December.

Herman, D. (1993), 'The Politics of Law Reform: Lesbian and Gay Rights Struggles into the 1990s', in J. Bristow and A. Wilson (eds), *Activating Theory: Lesbian, Gay, Bisexual Politics* (London: Lawrence & Wishart).

Kaplan, M. (1997), *Sexual Justice: Democratic Citizenship and the Politics of Desire* (London: Routledge).

Jeffrey-Poulter, S. (1991), *Peers, Queers and Commands* (London: Routledge).

Malone, A. (1994), 'Bishop Outed by Gay Crusader', in *The Sunday Times*, 23 December.

Mort, F. (1987), *Dangerous Sexualities* (London: Macmillan).

OutRage web.site 1997: *http://www.OutRage.cygnet.co.uk.*

Phelan, S. (ed.) (1997), *Playing with Fire: Queer Politics, Queer Theories* (London: Routledge).

Plummer, K. (1995), *Telling Sexual Stories: Power, Change and Social Worlds* (London: Routledge).

Reiche, R. (1971), *Sexuality and Class Struggle* (London: Praeger).

Reynolds, P. (1996), 'Between Equal Rights and Appreciating Diversity: Conceiving Sexualised Citizenship', Paper for the BSA Sexual Divisions Study Group One Day Conference on Saturday 16 November 1996, entitled 'Creating Spaces: Rethinking the Politics of Sexual Divisions'.

Rich, A. (1991), 'Compulsory Heterosexuality and Lesbian Existence', in H. Abelove *et al.* (eds), *The Lesbian and Gay Studies Reader* (London: Routledge).

Robertson, G. (1989), *Freedom, the Individual and the Law* (London: Penguin).

Rook, J. (1991), 'Shameful Revelations by a Bunch of Nasty Bullies', *Daily Express*, 30 September, cited in Watney (1994).

Sanderson, T. (1995), *Mediawatch: the Treatment of Male and Female Homosexuality in the British Media* (London: Cassell).

Schwartz, W. (1995), '"Outed" Bishop Attacks Tatchell', *Guardian*, 14 March.

Tatchell, P. (1992), *Europe in the Pink* (London: Gay Men's Press).

Tatchell, P. (1994), *We Don't Want to March Straight* (London: Gay Men's Press).

Tatchell, P. (1996a), 'It's Just a Phase: Why Homosexuality is Doomed', in M. Simpson (ed.), *Anti-Gay* (London: Cassell).

Tatchell, P. (1996b), 'Sexual Apartheid'. Paper given to the Critical Lawyers Conference, Keele University.

Watney, S. (1994), 'Queer Epistemology: Activism, "Outing" and the Politics of Sexual Identities', *Critical Quarterly*, 36, 20.

Weeks, J. (1989), *Sex, Politics and Society* (London: Longman).

Weeks, J. (1990), *Coming Out: Homosexual Politics in Britain from the 19th Century to the Present* (London: Quartet).

Weeks, J. (1995), *Invented Moralities: Sexual Values in an Age of Uncertainty* (Cambridge: Polity).

Whisman, V. (1996), *Queer by Choice: Lesbians, Gay Men and the Politics of Identity* (London: Routledge).

White, M. and Weale, S. (1994), 'Activists Threaten "Outing" of Gay MPs', *Guardian*, 23 February.

Wilson, A. (ed.) (1995), *A Simple Matter of Justice? Theorising Lesbian and Gay Politics* (London: Cassell).

15 Radical Sociology: What's Left?

John Holmwood

INTRODUCTION

The centrality of power to social relationships and, thus, as an explanatory category, to sociological theory, is one of the dominant themes of contemporary sociology.[1] This sensibility is of relatively recent origin, deriving from criticisms, in the 1960s and since, of what was held to be the 'orthodox consensus' of professional sociology, to which was counterposed a series of 'radical alternatives' (Atkinson, 1971). These alternatives were often linked to new social movements whose emergence challenged a post-war social and political settlement which had been hailed within 'professional' sociology as marking an 'end of ideology' (Bell, 1960). In these circumstances, radical critics sought to make power central to the understanding of social life, including the organisation of sociology itself. Against this new orthodoxy I shall argue that the radical project has been self-defeating. This claim is not an imposition upon current debates. Many recent commentators on the state of sociological theory also address a perceived crisis in social theory and sociology (see, for example, Seidman, 1994; Lemert, 1995; Turner and Turner, 1990). Despite their differences, each can agree that the current crisis began in the 1960s. Gouldner's *The Coming Crisis of Western Sociology* (1970) was, perhaps, the defining statement of the radical sensibility. 'It is no exaggeration to say that we theorize today within the sound of guns', he wrote, 'the old order has the picks of a hundred rebellions thrust into its hide' (1970: vii). In such circumstances, Gouldner argued, sociology must be 'reflexive', understanding its own partisan role in the reproduction of the crisis.

Several decades on, and the mood of hope and optimism among radical theorists has faded. This has a lot to do with changed social and political circumstances, but I shall suggest it is also to do with the character of the radical project itself. By seeking to make power all-pervasive, the specific, but limited, utility of the category has been lost such that power becomes continuous with the normal operation of any system of social relationships. Radical theorists try to avoid the potentially nihilistic and fatalistic consequences of the position by affirming 'resistance' as positive but, at the same time, any positive judgement about the outcome of resistance is withheld

277

precisely because the normal operation of any system – including any 'new' system – is understood to entail power. In this way the issue of power is effectively removed from judgements about different social arrangements. Since differentiation among social arrangements must be central to any wider public relevance that sociological argument might have, the consequence is the alienation of sociological argument from public debate, which is the opposite of what 'radical' theorists had sought to achieve. On a more positive note, I shall conclude by arguing that a 'non-radical' sociology can serve critical and public purposes more effectively.

SOCIOLOGY DISENCHANTED

Sociology begins by disenchanting the world, and it proceeds by disenchanting itself.

(Gouldner, 1973: 27)

With numerous assertions of crisis and imminent transformation of the discipline over the past few decades, any claim that current problems are especially acute may appear to be reassuring evidence of the opposite, that it is simply 'business as usual'. Certainly, crisis claims have become the normal currency of theoretical debate in sociology. For some this is the necessary condition of sociology. Habermas, for example, defines sociology precisely by its relation to crisis, writing that it 'became the science of crisis par excellence, it concerned itself above all with the anomic aspects of the dissolution of traditional social systems and the development of new ones' (1984: 4). With 'professionalisation', these features of the discipline had become attenuated. For Habermas, and many others writing under the influence of the new sensibility, the crisis of the 'orthodox consensus' and current society, alike, could be resolved by returning to the classics of the discipline, where issues of conflict and change were to the fore. For current writers, such as Lemert and Seidman, for example, this approach is already outmoded. For them, the underlying 'enlightenment' project of social theory – which motivated critics and advocates of the orthodox consensus, alike – has exhausted its potential for further insight and development. According to them, we are living in a period where the modern order, with its 'grand narratives' of social structural coherence and conflict, has itself given way to a fragmented and disordered postmodernity beyond the relevance of past – indeed, *any* – principles of 'order'.[2]

This cycle from optimism to pessimism is well illustrated in the development of Seidman's own position on the prospects for sociological theory. Initially, Seidman (1983) sought to reconstruct sociological theory via a new interpretation of classical social theory, showing how the professional orthodoxy had subverted its moral engagement and trivialised its concerns. In more recent work (Seidman 1991, 1994), he argues that current problems lie as much with the classical tradition as with its professional and routinised residue. The deficiencies of the latter – what he holds to be its arcane and specialised language, its isolation from public life, and the paucity of its results – he now regards as the logical outcome of a flawed project, that of a *science of society*. Seidman does not offer a renewal of classical social theory, but a line drawn under it.[3] He writes: 'if I am not mistaken, a scientific social theory that aims to establish the foundations for social knowledge and aspires to uncover a vocabulary mirroring the structure of society is collapsing under its own dead weight' (1994: 323). Seidman draws inspiration from C. W. Mills's (1958) call for a new 'sociological imagination' in a reinvigorated and publicly relevant sociology, but he seems to have abandoned Mills's conviction that it is from a general, empirical social science that any peculiar significance will derive; rather he wishes to ground inquiries in particular subject-positions, especially those associated with marginality and oppression.

A similar shift from a concern with the 'general' to the 'particular' is evident in Lemert's (1995) articulation of a 'post-crisis' sociological undertaking. Gouldner's 'coming crisis' in Western sociology Lemert accepts has finally arrived, but it will soon be over, he argues, because an appropriate way forward has at last been found in postmodern, poststructural approaches. On closer examination, however, what he offers is not a realised alternative, but the re-statement of a promise. Prior sociological approaches are argued to be irremediably flawed. Things cannot go on as before and 'whatever the dark secret of the present is, it is not what it once was. Sociologies, practical and professional, should begin anew, here and now' (1995: 195). Lemert contrasts the 'strong-self' of orthodox, 'universalist' theory with the 'weak-we' identity of marginalised lives whose concrete, fractured particularity is lost when inquiries are organised under the categories of 'strong selves' (which, as Seidman also argues, is itself really only another kind of particularism, the particularism of the privileged lives of white, Western, middle-class, heterosexual males).

On these arguments the transcendent 'hopes' that once inspired sociological argument are dismissed. Seidman, for example, regards them as 'naive' and as, at best, reflecting an 'age of innocence'. According to him the 'universalism' of scientific knowledge has been undermined in a fundamental way by the claims of those whose experiences do not fit its categories. Seemingly 'inclusive' claims of knowledge turn out to disguise a terrible 'exclusion', but one which has finally been unmasked by the 'return of the repressed'. He writes: 'the towering grandeur of scientific reason has all but crumbled under a barrage of assault from those who claim to be its victims: people of color, non-Westerners, women, lesbians and gay men, the disabled, and the poor and economically disempowered. Its promise of freedom has a dark side: a ruthless wish to control and order everything and an intolerance toward the unruly and deviant' (1994: 327). The paradigm of the 'strong self', as Lemert puts it, is also integral to the 'orthodox consensus' informing professional and expert attitudes to welfare and the resolution of social problems, which has diminished and marginalised those who do not fit its austere criteria.

Sociology, it seems, has indeed proceeded from the 'disenchantment of the world' to the 'disenchantment of itself'. Yet the character of much radical sociology is to offer itself as a promissory note drawn on the future. As Lemert says, whatever the present is, it is not what it was and whatever radical sociology might be is not to be found in what sociology has been. A partisan, radical sociology awaits to arise from the ashes. Notwithstanding, the arguments of Seidman and Lemert are remarkably similar to those of Gouldner, and there are at least two decades of development of a radical sociology in terms of which they might be judged. For example, Gouldner explicitly argued that a 'reflexive' sociology necessarily entails a sociology of sociology, and it is this turning in upon itself which brings about sociology's own disenchantment and a tragic sense of its enterprise.[4] Those who resist a reflexive sociology must, according to him:

> tacitly accept ... that there is a radical divorce between 'theory' and 'society'. This view mistakenly adopts an empiricistic/objectivistic position which wrongly assumes that 'society' exists apart from some theory about it. My own position, however, is that every society is a social reality in part constituted by a kind of everyday social theory, and that therefore the critique of society and of theory are inseparable. ... Every society is in part a product of social theory and every theory is in part a social product of the society.
>
> (Gouldner, 1973: 84)

Gouldner also linked the rise of 'reflexive sociology' to the moment of professionalism and its demise. The university, he argued, is a 'cleared space' for public debate, but it is 'immensely threatened' space, threatened by the very professional values it makes possible:

> the university's central problem is its failure as a *community* in which rational discourse about *social* worlds is possible. This is partly because rational discourse as such ceased to be its dominant value and was superseded by a quest for knowledge *products* and information *products* that could be sold or promised for funding, prestige and power – rewards bestowed by the state and the larger society that is most bent upon subverting rational discourse about itself.'
>
> (1973: 79)

In such a circumstances, sociology – radical, reflexive sociology – must seek new theoretical communities beyond those compromised within the university.[5] In line with this view of 'orthodox sociology' and its uncritical and unreflective absorption to the agencies of social control of welfare capitalism, radical critics sought to transform *social* problems into *political* problems (see, for example, Horowitz and Liebowitz, 1968). By attacking the professional and expert definition of social problems they criticised government welfare programmes in the name of a politicisation of deviance and radical, community-based movements of the marginal and the poor. The last decades have, indeed, witnessed the withdrawal of government welfare programmes, but this has not been accompanied by the success of these radical movements. With the politicisation of marginality and the assertion of 'deviant' lifestyles, social problems are, indeed, made matters of 'public debate', but there is no guarantee that the public will share the radical affirmation of the 'identities' being presented. Poverty has increased dramatically in many of the very groups whose marginality was the object of concern, and income differentials are wider than at any time in the century. The 'radical' affirmation of 'counter-cultural' values and 'expanded choices' is mirrored by a conservative politics of blaming those values (for conservatives, the values of an 'underclass') for the very conditions that require amelioration. Indeed, where the 'orthodox' approach to social problems regarded 'deviance' as a product of social circumstances and, therefore, favoured intervention to moderate those circumstances and favoured the rehabilitation of offenders, the politicisation of deviance, which makes it an expression of 'values' or 'resistance', renders 'deviants' responsible for their own actions, and therefore, potential objects of an 'appropriately' punitive response. Over the last decades the prison population in America and in Britain has grown dramatically, filled with the 'marginal' and the poor. Not only have social rights of citizenship been undermined, but political and civil rights too.[6]

Most current statements of a radical approach to social issues have followed Gouldner's proposal that sociology should be 'reflexive', applying its understandings to itself.[7] Rattansi, for example, offers a postmodern 'framing' of current social and political issues, which posits 'a *cultural politics of representation*, involving processes of 'self-identification' as well as formation by disciplinary agencies such as the state, including the involvement of the social sciences, given their incorporation in the categorization and redistributive activities of the state and campaigning organizations' (1994: 57–8). 'Reflexivity', it seems, has its limits. There is one practice of representation which is not addressed. What lies outside Rattansi's reflexive frame is the very postmodern and radical politics of representation itself. If other practices are shown to be 'incorporated', might not the same be the case for its practices? Indeed, the radical critique of the orthodox 'distributive' paradigm has echoes in conservative and 'new right' thinking. Elsewhere (Holmwood, 1992, 1996), I have drawn parallels between 'new left' and 'new right' critiques of the welfare state. Each presented welfare arrangements as mechanisms of social control and much new left writing was devoted to demonstrating failures of amelioration – for example, arguing that any redistributive impact on inequalities was minimal and could be assigned to external economic causes rather than to agencies.

At this point radical theorists often lay claim to a more conventional sociological argument of changing sociopolitical circumstances. The distributive problems described in the preceding paragraphs are seen to be consequences of a fundamental change in the nature of capitalism, *globalisation*, where new structures of global capitalism have driven down wages and undermined national welfare states. This is not the place to address such claims, except to note that the arguments are self-serving in that they remove any responsibility on the part of radical theorists for the circumstances they describe, which is not something they are prepared to concede to those sociologists they regard as orthodox. In any case, any proposed 'new dialectic' of the 'global' alongside the heterogeneous 'local' does nothing to establish the possibility of a politics that could reverse negative consequences since it involves a denial of the efficacy of those agencies which had been successful in the past. This has not diminished the radical rhetoric. As postmodern fragmentation is argued to progress under these global tendencies, it is held to produce a generalisation of 'weak-we', or 'hybrid', identities. These identities will become the norm and offer new possibilities of alliances. This resembles the quiet satisfaction of some orthodox Marxists predicting a process of proletarianisation, neglecting the immiserisation upon which it is predicated and, ultimately, preferring the future possibility, however remote, of revolutionary change to a present amelioration of conditions.[8] Meanwhile, those conditions worsen and radical theorists add their weight to right-wing criticisms of institutions that might ameliorate them.

At the same time, any proper analysis of those worsening conditions is compromised by the denial of a coherent sociological enterprise of explanation (or, at least, a denial of coherence as a condition of explanation). According to the new cultural politics of representation, globalisation is not so much a real phenomenon as *hyper-real*. In its hyper-reality it can be laid claim to, but not represented. Indeed, postmodern theorists argue that 'reduction to theoretical order', which is what any creative resolution of problems would entail, is 'oppressive', involving what Rattansi calls a 'fantasy of coherence' (1994: 34). In contrast:

> multidimensional analyses are intrinsic to a 'postmodern' frame, with no
> necessary connections assumed to exist between the forces involved, or
> any necessary logic of development presumed to inhere in any particular

driving force, whether this is said to be the economic, the political, the cultural or the geopolitical. Moreover, globalization is framed here as sets of uneven, contradictory, confused and uncertain processes which in their complexity and heterogeneity can make a mockery of the usual analytical binaries, such as universalization/particularization, homogenization/differentiation, centralization/decentralization and stability/instability, which are deployed in discussions of most global transformations.

(Rattansi, 1994: 27)

It is difficult to know what meaning to attribute to the idea of 'forces' without force, and 'global transformations' which need involve no transformation. Certainly, there is no way in which any claim about the nature of processes could be ruled out. By allowing that 'deviation' from what would be expected from the operation of any 'force' to be confirmation of the 'force' in its necessarily 'contradictory, confused and uncertain' character we are offered the possibility that the worse are our theories (in the sense of producing the maximum number of deviations from the 'order' of theoretical expectations), the more we will be able to confirm our postmodern condition![9] It is easy to agree with postmodern and radical theorists that we are confronted with pressing new social problems which cannot be accommodated to the current, substantive categories of sociological theory. It does not follow that 'incoherence' could be an appropriate condition of any new theoretical categories. Indeed, postmodern and radical theories involve the embrace of problems as their own solution; they are parasitic upon the 'orderliness' of previous claims for theoretical adequacy since they require the assumption of an order against which to identify a current, 'empirical', or 'found', disorder. The formulation has an immediate credibility – the 'reality' of our current problems – but it could bear no serious weight as a means of furthering understanding.

SOCIETY AS POWER

a deeper analysis of power relations is possible – an analysis that is at once value-laden, theoretical and empirical.

(Lukes, 1974: 57)

In this section of the chapter I shall consider how a conception of sociological knowledge as the operation of power is mirrored in arguments about society as power. In the process I shall show that the radical sociology's 'deeper' analysis fails precisely in what Lukes claims for it, the integration of ethics, theory and empirical analysis (the latter aspect, of course, is especially compromised in postmodern approaches).

For Lukes, and many others, Parsons's structural-functional theory exemplified the problematic features of the 'orthodox consensus' and the form of 'conservative' sociological theorising which must be displaced.[10] The main problem of his approach was seen to be his reliance upon a general scheme of sociological categories in which 'power' was identified as a phenomenon of the collectivity, serving collective interests and, therefore, as definitionally legitimate. For example, Lukes writes: 'Parsons's conceptualisation of power ties it to authority, consensus and the pursuit of collective goals, and dissociates it from conflicts of interest and, in particular, from coercion and force' (1974: 28). Yet, at the same time, Lukes also wishes to define those conflicts of interests as operating in terms of 'authority, consensus and the pursuit of collective interests', albeit *falsely represented* and *mis*understood interests. Thus, a 'radical' approach to power 'maintains that men's wants may themselves be a product of a system which works against their interests, and in such cases, relates the latter to what they would want and prefer, were they able to make the choice' (1974: 34).

It seems that, for Lukes (as for Habermas, Giddens, and many others, for that matter; see Holmwood and Stewart, 1991), the most fundamental operation of power is to have one's particular interests accepted as the measure of what is legitimate. But the issue must then become: how does the theorist distinguish those occasions when what is legitimate is 'truly' so, from those occasions when it is the operation of power and the creation of 'false wants'. As Lukes comments, any serious critical analysis must address the question: 'are social norms which claim legitimacy genuinely accepted by those *who follow and internalise them*, or do they merely stabilise relations of power?' (1982: 137). How are we ever to know when wants are 'false', given that those holding to them must do so as an expression of their 'truth'?[11]

While there can be little doubt that Parsons did not share the radical rhetoric or aspirations of many of his critics, there is a remarkable formal similarity in what he and his critics are proposing. Whatever Parsons's intentions, his theory is elaborated in terms of a division between 'the point of view of the system' and the 'point of view of the actor' (see Parsons, 1951; for discussion see Holmwood, 1996). The former is approached in terms of a concept of 'perfect integration', from which there is allowed the possibility of 'deviance' in concrete action. Now, it is precisely this feature of Parsons's writing which gave critics the space for their criticisms, but which also had the consequence of drawing them onto his terrain. For example, many critics took exception to the definition of fundamental aspects of power in terms of 'collectivity interests' within a model of perfect integration, and criticised him for neglecting conflictual aspects of power. At the same time, as with Lukes, they wished to argue that relations of power frequently do have a consensual form. Ultimately, Giddens argues, 'what slips away from sight almost completely in the Parsonian analysis is the fact that power, even as Parsons defines it, is always exercised *over* someone' (1968: 264). This is, indeed, a necessary feature of Parsons's analysis. From the point of view of the system, 'power' is defined in terms of 'collective interests', but, from the point of view of participants, it must be exercised in circumstances which include 'deviance' and it must, therefore, be exercised *over* someone.[12] This, it seems, might give a clue to the *illegitimacy* of (or latent conflict underlying) 'legitimate power'. At the same time, by making power a feature of all systems of interaction – *definitionally* – it must undermine the very possibility of *legitimate power*, at least from the point of view of the sociologist.[13]

Where Parsons was interpreted as addressing social issues from the perspective of the 'system', his radical critics identified with 'deviants' whose interests seemed to lie 'outside' it (see, for example, Becker, 1967; Gouldner, 1970). Parsons described the system in highly generalised terms and the generalisation of 'deviance' produces an equivalent abstraction. It is not any particular 'outsider' (to use Becker's phrase) whose behaviour is affirmed – though writers may begin from a personal identification with one particular group – but *any* behaviour which resists the 'normalising' processes of the system. The 'system' is argued to be repressive and its realisation would be 'totalitarian'. These arguments are familiar from Lyotard's (1984) declaration of war on the idea of 'totality', but they had their precursors in early criticisms of the 'orthodox consensus'. With an obvious allusion to Parsons, Horowitz and Liebowitz, for example, write that: 'the dilemma for those who consider social problems obstacles to be overcome is that any true overcoming of social problems implies a perfect social system. And this entails several goals: first, the total institutionalisation of all people; second, the thoroughgoing equilibrium between the parts of a system with respect to their functioning and the functioning of other sectors; third, the elimination of social change as either a fact or value. Thus, the resolution of social problems from the point of view of the social system would signify the totalitarian resolution of social life' (1968: 295). What is set against the 'totalitarian' realisation of the system is freedom as 'anti-system' behaviour. Put this way, the arguments of radical sociologists represent a simple inversion of the orthodox sociological position, rather than a break with it. Indeed, that this is so is demonstrated by the cyclical development in Foucauldian approaches to power, away from the emphasis upon 'resistance' and 'conflictual' aspects of power and back to an emphasis upon 'positive', or 'collective', aspects of power, in which power relations form subjectivities and are reproduced in those subjectivities (see Hindess, 1995; Barry *et al.*, 1996).[14]

It is evident in many commentaries upon radical social theory that the 'systemic' aspect of any theory gives rise to worries about its 'radicalism'.[15] The more an author gives substance to the possibility of a realised system, the more concerned commentators become until they find the 'anti-system' aspect and become reassured. But is 'anti-system' coherent as a radical position? At least in its initial formulation the 'system' is a general statement of resources and their deployment in the maintenance of order. Where the system is *general*, 'deviance' is always *particular* and represented as an instance of *difference*. It is easy to see why deviance might be regarded in a positive light because of an association with creativity and innovation which is set against conformity. However, although it is the case that innovation is always, in some sense, deviance, it does not follow that the reverse is true.[16] Moreover, the conception of 'deviance' as 'anti-system' assigns to any 'system' the logical possibility of 'closure' through the self-referential coherence of its categories. Thus, for many radical theorists, struggles against the 'system' are affirmed as intrinsically creative and positive, while the realisation of any new institutional forms is potentially negative, a new form of 'system'. Where deviance is *innovation*, rather than merely *resistance*, it produces new resources, but all resources are absorbed to systemic statements. It seems odd that sociological thought seeks to affirm human creativity, yet seems to withhold that affirmation from its products.

Seidman encapsulates the radical project as follows: 'postmodernism carries no promise of liberation – of a society free of domination. Postmodernism gives up the modernist idol of emancipation in favour of deconstructing false closure, prying open present and future social possibilities, detecting fluidity and porousness in forms of life where hegemonic discourses posit closure and a frozen order. The hope of a great transformation is replaced by the more modest aspiration of a relentless defence of immediate, local pleasures and struggles for justice' (1991: 131).[17] Certainly, freedom-as-becoming becomes a *relentless* business. Rattansi (1994: 57), for his part, proposes that postmodern politics will be a 'trench war' of political struggles, a metaphorical flourish that begs extension to ask for whom will the role of Generals be reserved, social theorists, perhaps? Such statements by Seidman and Rattansi affirm the truth of Ashley's observation (1994: 71) that postmodernism involves a 'Nietzschean valorisation of conflict'. Moreover, it is a valorisation where any victory turns to ashes; 'anti-system' is the struggle of Sisyphus.

Despite criticisms of the 'totalising' tendencies of prior forms of sociological thought, then, what we are offered is a 'totalising' of resistance, together with an unsubstantiated 'imagining'. At the same time as expressing these views of an essentially conflictual future, postmodern writers frequently also present an alternative scenario, where they are anxious to dispel the idea that the embrace of difference means irreconcilable conflict. The hopes embodied in this scenario seems no less 'utopian' or 'innocent' than those attributed to advocates of the 'Enlightenment' project. Thus, despite embracing a conception of knowledge as contested and as 'power', rather than 'truth', Seidman hopefully imagines 'a human habitat that is respectful of differences, values expanded choices, offers increased options for social bonding and community formation and encourages spirited efforts at negotiating just institutions and common social spaces' (1994: 327). Coming after all the imagery of warfare,[18] this sounds rather like Christmas in the trenches and a party in 'no-man's land'.

It would be hard not to sympathise with these hopes, but harder still to imagine what principles and agreed – that is, 'uncontested' – practices they might consist in which would not take us back on to the terrain of what has been denied; that is, some kind of inclusive theoretical statement. Social theorists may represent themselves as 'interpreters' engaged in a 'conversation', but what is the point of the conversation?[19] The role seems less arrogant than that of 'legislator', but where different points of view require not merely acknowledgement and recognition, but some kind of modification of previous practices, the moment of 'legislation' is necessary. It can be displaced from social theory, but not effaced as a requirement of social life. 'Legislation' must be an issue if, as Seidman avers, 'local struggles' are struggles for *justice*. But if they are *local* struggles then this implies judgements which would rule out an *a-priori* identification with any particular subject-position (see Holmwood, 1995).[20] Not all deviance or all resistance could be equally valid. If Seidman really means what he 'imagines', then, after the 'return of the repressed', we face a 'return of the super-ego'! Moreover, 'systems', too, must have particular institutional forms, as well as general representations of their resources and processes. Few – Parsons and Luhman, maybe, perhaps Alexander – would defend 'systems', in principle, but the evaluation of specific institutional forms would pose a different question, namely the evaluation of particular practices in the light of specific norms, their consistency and practical consequences. If not all deviance is valid, nor, then, could all sanctions or disciplines embodied in institutions be invalid. The problem from either a radical or an orthodox perspective lies with the generalised categories of 'system' and 'anti-system' that they share.

POWER: A REFORMIST RATHER THAN A RADICAL VIEW

to will a morality other than that implied by the nature of society is to deny the latter and, in consequence, oneself.

(Durkheim, 1974: 38)

In his *Power: A Radical View*, Lukes (1974) explicitly sets his approach against a 'reformist' approach, which he suggests rests upon an insufficiently deep and thoroughgoing approach to the problem of power and is timid in its approach to the powers that be. It is not merely that a 'radical' approach is out of favour in the current political climate that should cause us to question these claims, but the apparently self-defeating nature of the radical project itself. Just as I have suggested a convergence between 'new right' and 'new left' criticisms of the welfare state, so the general 'anti-system' rhetoric of the latter is close to the libertarianism of the former. Ultimately, then, it seems that the radical approach is 'anti-social', in just the ways implied by Durkheim.

If power is held to be a feature of all social relationships, as is frequently argued, then it is unlikely that an address to power can advance the critical purpose of differentiating among social relationships and contributing to the task of specifying 'just institutions'. Indeed, it is difficult to understand what the substance of *local* struggles for justice could be, except that what was 'just' was grounded in specific ways of life and their inter-relationships. Ultimately, the radical approach does 'will a morality other than that implied by the nature of society', but to accept that morality is not necessarily a conservative position. While the acceptance of a socially grounded morality could not be a 'radical' position, such acceptance would nonetheless be a necessary part of any 'reformist' approach, too. In contrast, 'radical' sociologists and 'critical' theorists have wished to produce a sociology that is 'radical' or 'critical', by virtue of *methodological* decision where the 'critical' attitude, apparently, can constitute inquiry, rather than be a *consequence* of sociological inquiry. As Watts-Miller (1996) has recently argued, to be concerned with the nature of society as the source of morality is to be engaged with a sociological task – in fact, *the* sociological task of an empirical science of morals – where the *real and its rationale* are issues of sociological argument which cannot be resolved by methodological fiat. Only a reformist sociology could secure the integration of empirical inquiry, theory and ethics that was the ambition of the radical view of power.

NOTES

1. This is evident, for example in the choice of 'Power and Resistance' as the theme of the conference from which this book is derived.
2. See Woodiwiss (1993) for a detailed discussion of the rise of postmodernism in American sociology.
3. In fact, Atkinson (1971) also argued that the classical tradition was implicated in the deficiencies of the 'orthodox consensus'.
4. As Gouldner further elaborated: 'the sociological enterprise, like others, becomes edged with a tragic sense when men suspect that they have wasted their lives. When they confine work to the demanding, misleading and unfulfillable paradigm of a value-free, high-science model, sociologists are wasting, indeed sacrificing, a part of themselves' (Gouldner, 1973: 77).
5. Gouldner's critique of the university oriented to 'knowledge products' and 'information products' is accepted by postmodern theorists such as Lyotard

(1984) as the current postmodern condition of knowledge and the 'pragmatics' of its production. At the same time, given the critique of the transcendent knowledge claims of a general social science offered by Lemert and Seidman, all that a 'new theoretical community' could consist in is a different 'pragmatic' operating alongside that of 'information production'.

6. The process has not been uniform. Not all 'deviant minorities' have fared badly. From Seidman's list, for example, women, lesbians and gay men appear to have experienced an improvement in their position despite the politics of backlash. However, to a significant degree that seems to be a consequence of being able to present past oppression as unjust in terms of the standard liberal principles of civil rights, rather than a wider public acceptance of a 'new' politics. Indeed, this would seem to be the basis of the suspicion of some feminists towards the postmodern critique of 'reason'. Hawkesworth, for example, writes: 'at a moment when the preponderance of rational and moral argument sustains prescriptions for women's equality, it is a bit too cruel a conclusion and too reactionary a political agenda to accept that reason is impotent, that equality is impossible' (1989: 557).

7. For a more formal treatment of 'reflexivity' see Giddens (1979). The 'reflexive turn' in radical sociology has led in some cases to an extreme solipsism. See, for example, Ashmore (1989), Woolgar (1993).

8. A number of writers cite Haraway's (1990) 'manifesto for cyborgs' as an example of the exciting new possibilities that the generalisation of 'hybrid' identities can bring. It is worth quoting in full: 'As robotics and related technologies put men out of work in "developed" countries and exacerbate failure to generate male jobs in third-world "development" and as the automated office becomes the rule in even labor-surplus countries, the feminization of work intensifies. Black women in the United States have long known what it looks like to face the structural underemployment ("feminization") of black men, as well as their own highly vulnerable position in the wage economy. It is no longer a secret that sexuality, reproduction, family, and community life are interwoven with this economic structure in myriad ways which have also differentiated the situations of white and black women. Many more women and men will contend with similar situations, which will make cross-gender and race alliances on issues of basic life support (with or without jobs) necessary, *not just nice*' (1990: 209–10, my emphasis). It is difficult to believe that the situation she describes will not, in fact, produce divisions and conflict, rather than a new solidarity. But what is 'not nice' is that she is describing conditions which Curtis (1985) describes as 'slow rioting' where racial uprisings against white authority 20 years previously have turned inward in internal social decay and fragmentation of 'ghetto' communities.

9. This would raise the question, 'how best to produce bad theory?' Not just any 'bad' theory will do, it must be plausibly bad. But 'plausibility' consists in the sense of its claims to 'order'. This is why postmodern theorists do not fully distinguish modernity and postmodernity. They claim the validity of the processes of modernity and the validity of their negation. Ultimately, this is an 'empiricism' of errors. The idea that 'deviations' are 'real' and 'immediate' (that is, have a meaning outside the particular schemes in which they occur as problems), gives rise to 'ethnographies' of 'contradictory particularities'. Just as statistical methods allowed a 'quantitative' empiricist research programme of diverse, 'significant' findings (see Turner and Turner, 1990: 174ff), so postmodernism produces an analogous 'qualitative' programme. Where mutually inconsistent 'differences' are held to be 'real', inconsistencies do not become a part of a process of checking and reflection upon 'findings'. Rather, the

'significance' of such found 'differences' is accepted, in principle, as a reflection of the 'truth' of a complex world. Ironically, given the critique of a 'science of society', it is as if 'self-evidence' has supplanted any evidential requirement for sociological theorising.

10.   Lukes is not only criticising Parsons's conception of power. He is also a critic of what he calls 'behaviorist', 'one-' and 'two-dimensional' approaches to power. These are associated with an emphasis upon processes of observed 'decision-making' by individuals and groups where power is defined in terms of one party able to affect another party in a manner contrary to their interests (see Lukes, 1974: 34). Lukes proposes a 'three-dimensional' view which is oriented to the systematic relationships in which individual decisions are located and which affects which issues become the objects of decision-making processes. This emphasis means that he must confront an approach to power, that of Parsons, which already occupies the space of the third dimension which he wishes to clear for the 'radical view'. If those committed to a 'one-' or 'two-'dimensional view of power are charged by Lukes with *unconsciously* accepting dominant power relations by failing to recognise the crucial significance of power in the third dimension (see Lukes, 1974: 37), Parsons stands accused of *self-consciously* accepting dominant power relations.

11.   The ambition of integrating theory, empirical analysis and ethics means that Lukes must be hostile to a Weberian 'decisionism' where critique merely consists in counterposing the theorist's values to those attributed to actors in the reproduction of their behaviour. An indication of this ambition and the difficulty in its realisation is that he finds such a decisionism to be the problematic of other radical approaches to criticism, such as that of Habermas (see Lukes, 1982). But his own version is hardly persuasive, arguing that some concrete indication of 'true' interests can be gained by considering the interests expressed in 'abnormal times' when 'submission and intellectual subordination are absent or diminished, when the apparatus of power is removed or relaxed' (1974: 47). At best, what we would have would be an *ex-post* demonstration based on *expressed interests*. How the apparatus of power comes to be removed or relaxed is unexplained. However, since 'abnormal' times must give way to 'normal' times, where any apparatus of overt power would seem to be diminished as actors 'follow and internalise norms', there could be no coherent justification of why the expressed interests of 'abnormal times' should be regarded as the guide to 'true' interests in normal times.

12.   Indeed, Giddens reproduces Parsons's distinction between points of view of system and participants and the form of his statement of the system directly, writing that: 'what from the structural point of view – where strategic conduct is bracketed – appears as *a normatively co-ordinated legitimate order*, in which rights and obligations are merely two aspects of norms, from the point of view of strategic conduct represents claims whose realisation is contingent upon the successful mobilisation of obligations through the medium of the responses of other actors' (Giddens, 1979: 86). Of course, the 'point of view of strategic conduct' and the 'bracketing' of structure is the actual operation of power in its 'observable' aspects, and thus involves a conception of power in its 'one-' or 'two'-dimensional aspects. Lukes also operates in terms of an unresolved dualism of structure and action, similar in form to that found in Parsons or Giddens. Thus, he refers to a 'dialectic' between two aspects of power which must not be reduced one to the other, writing that: 'any standpoint or methodology which reduces that dialectic to a one-sided consideration of agents without (internal and external) structural limits, or structures without agents, or

which does not address the problem of their interrelation, will be unsatisfactory' (Lukes, 1977: 29).

13.   Or, more precisely, the terms 'system' and 'legitimate power' become interchangeable, such that the 'systemness' becomes the meaning of legitimacy. Actors' subjective beliefs in legitimacy become all that is necessary to justify the sociologists' usage, just as it is the fact of the subjective 'disbelief' of (at least, some) actors – the fact that issue of legitimacy is constituted in *claims*, as Weber (1968) argues – that justifies the designation of systems of power as systems of *domination*. In other words, the 'tough-minded' realism of the Weberian empirical approach to power is formed in the very separation of theory and ethics – in ethical neutrality and value 'decisionism' – that Lukes seemingly deplores.

14.   In this development the 'radical' approach to power turns back on itself and becomes directly a contemporary form of the Weberian argument for 'ethical neutrality' and value-free sociological inquiry. Thus, there is a concern with 'enhancing the practices of freedom', at the same time as it is argued that modern political systems are governed through 'freedom'. From an apparently radical perspective it is enjoined that it is necessary to understand Thatcherism, for example, as 'positive', in the 'technical', rather than 'ethical' sense, 'that is, of an inventive and constructive alignment of interests, powers, objects, institutions and persons' (Barry *et al.*, 1996: 11). The issue is not to be *for* or *against*, but to undertake, the 'painstaking task of describing the consequences, the possibilities invented, as much as the limits imposed, of particular ways of subjectifying humans' (1996: 13). Since these techniques of government are *positive*, the issue of being against is a matter of *ethics* in the sense of elaborating a counterposing set of values, where the task of the 'Left', as Rose argues, is to 'articulate an alternative ethics and pedagogy of subjectivity that is as compelling as that inherent in the rationality of the market and the "valorization" of choice' (Rose, 1996: 61).

15.   This has been traced in detail in Holmwood and Stewart (1991) in criticisms of Habermas's critical theory and arguments that he converges upon Parsons. It is also a feature of discussions of Foucault's work. Mouzelis finds 'the methodological similarities between Foucault and Parsons ... quite striking. Both of them underemphasize agency, and as a result both of them have to resort to teleologically oriented functionalist explanations' (1995: 47). Best, for his part, is worried about Foucault's argument that power relationships 'constitute all social relationships' (1994: 45), but believes that while he could not have expected an end to power relationships he did 'seek an alternative set of power relationships that are more enabling' (1994: 45) since, after all, 'he clearly opposed the present form of society' (1994: 46).

16.   In fact, Foucault's emphasis upon 'resistance' implies that the sources of change (innovation) lie with the system and the expanded reproduction of its practices. This is what brings writers such as Barry, Osborne and Rose, and Hindess to emphasise those aspects of Foucault's work which give emphasis to the 'positive' and 'productive' aspects of power.

17.   Of course, implicit in the statement is the 'directionality' of general, systemic processes which are against pleasures and justice. Why else is defence *relentless*?

18.   Seidman, like Rattansi, uses the imagery of battles to describe the situation of contested knowledge – 'old orthodoxies, standard conventions, and established canons are being contested; local skirmishes quickly escalate into full-scale disciplinary warfare' (Seidman, 1994: 14).

19. See, for example, Rorty (1989) and Bauman (1987). The latter writes: 'the typically post-modern strategy of intellectual work is one characterized by the metaphor of the "interpreter" role. It consists of translating statements, made by one community based tradition, so that they can be understood within the system of knowledge based on another tradition. Instead of being oriented towards selecting the best social order, this strategy is aimed at facilitating communication between autonomous (sovereign) participants. It is concerned with preventing the distortion of meaning in the process of communication' (1987: 5).

20. Indeed, the very identification of a standpoint of the 'oppressed' becomes difficult to maintain once it is accepted, as Seidman does (in line with the arguments of Lukes), that there are general processes of 'legitimation', albeit 'false'. At least a significant proportion of those held to be oppressed will also be represented as accepting the dominant ideology as an expression of their (false) wants. The 'standpoint of the oppressed', then, is as much an 'observer's point of view' as that of the 'orthodox' approach to which it is opposed.

REFERENCES

Ashley, D. (1994), 'Postmodernism and Anti-Foundationalism', in D. R. Dickens and A. Fontana (eds), *Postmodernism and Social Inquiry* (London: UCL Press).

Ashmore, M. (1989), *The Reflexive Thesis: Wrighting the Sociology of Scientific Knowledge* (Chicago, IL: University of Chicago Press).

Atkinson, R. (1971), *Orthodox Consensus and Radical Alternative* (London: Heinemann).

Barry, A., Osborne, T. and Rose, N. (1996), 'Introduction', in Barry, T. Osborne and N. Rose (eds), *Foucault and Political Reason: Liberalism, Neo-Liberalism and Rationalities of Government* (London: UCL Press).

Bauman, Z. (1987), *Legislators and Interpreters: On Modernity, Post-Modernity and Intellectuals* (Cambridge: Polity).

Becker, H. (1967), 'Whose Side Are We On?, *Social Problems*, 14, 239–47.

Bell, D. (1960), *The End of Ideology: On the Exhaustion of Political Ideas in the Fifties* (New York: Free Press).

Curtis, L. A. (1985), *American Violence and Public Policy* (New Haven, CT: Yale University Press).

Durkheim, E. (1974), *Sociology and Philosophy* (New York: Free Press).

Giddens, A. (1968), '"Power" in the Recent Writings of Talcott Parsons', *Sociology*, 2(2), 257–72.

Giddens, A. (1979), *Central Problems in Social Theory: Action, Structure and Contradiction in Social Analysis* (London: Macmillan).

Gouldner, A. W. (1970), *The Coming Crisis of Western Sociology* (London: Heinemann).

Gouldner, A. W. (1973), 'The Sociologist as Partisan: Sociology and the Welfare State', in A. W. Gouldner (ed.), *For Sociology: Renewal and Critique in Sociology Today* (London: Allen Lane).

Habermas, J. (1984), *The Theory of Communicative Action*, vol. 1: *Reason and the Rationalization of Society* (London: Heinemann).

Haraway, D. (1990), 'A Manifesto for Cyborgs: Science, Technology, and Socialist Feminism in the 1980s', in L. Nicholson (ed.), *Feminism/Postmodernism* (London: Routledge).

Hawkesworth, M. E. (1989), 'Knower, Knowing, Known: Feminist Theory and Claims of Truth', *Signs*, 14, 533–57.

Hindess, B. (1995), *Discourses of Power: Hobbes to Foucault* (Oxford: Blackwell).

Holmwood, J. (1992), 'Citizenship and Welfare', in R. Bellamy (ed.), *Theories and Concepts of Politics* (Manchester: Manchester University Press).

Holmwood, J. (1995), 'Feminism and Epistemology: What Kind of Successor Science?', *Sociology*, 29, 411–28.

Holmwood, J. (1996), *Founding Sociology? Talcott Parsons and the Idea of General Theory* (London: Longman).

Holmwood, J. (1997), 'Citizenship and Inequality in Postmodern Social Theory', in P. Sulkunen, J. Holmwood, H. Radner and G. Schulze (eds), *Constructing the New Consumer Society* (London: Macmillan).

Holmwood, J. and Stewart, A. (1991), *Explanation and Social Theory* (London: Macmillan).

Holmwood, J. and Stewart, A. (1994), 'Synthesis and Fragmentation in Social Theory: a Progressive Solution', *Sociological Theory*, 12, 83–100.

Horowitz, I. L. and Liebowitz, M. (1968), 'Social Deviance and Marginality: Toward a Redefinition of the Relation Between Sociology and Politics', *Social Problems*, 15, 280–96.

Lemert, C. (1995), *Sociology After the Crisis* (Boulder, CO: Westview Press).

Lukes, S. (1974), *Power: A Radical View* (London: Macmillan).

Lukes, S. (1977), *Essays in Social Theory* (London: Macmillan).

Lukes, S. (1982), 'Of Gods and Demons: Habermas and Practical Reason', in D. Held and J. B. Thompson (eds), *Habermas: Critical Debates* (London: Macmillan).

Lyotard, J.-F. (1984), *The Postmodern Condition: A Report on Knowledge* (Manchester: Manchester University Press).

Mills, C. W. (1959), *The Sociological Imagination* (New York: Oxford University Press).

Mouzelis, N. (1995), *Sociological Theory: What Went Wrong? Diagnoses and Remedies* (London: Routledge).

Parsons, T. (1951), *The Social System* (London: Routledge & Kegan Paul).

Rattansi, A. (1994), '"Western" Racisms, Ethnicities and Identities in a "Post-Modern" Frame', in A. Rattansi and S. Westwood (eds), *Racism, Modernity and Identity on the Western Front* (Cambridge: Polity).

Rorty, R. (1989), *Contingency, Irony and Solidarity* (Cambridge: Cambridge University Press).

Rose, N. (1966), 'Governing "Advanced" Liberal Democracies', in A. Barry, T. Osborne and N. Rose (eds), *Foucault and Political Reason: Liberalism, Neo-Liberalism and Rationalities of Government* (London: UCL Press).

Seidman, S. A. (1983), *Liberalism and Modern Social Theory* (Oxford: Blackwell).

Seidman, S. A. (1991), 'The End of Sociological Theory: the Postmodern Hope', *Sociology Theory*, 9(2), 131–46.

Seidman, S. A. (1994), *Contested Knowledge: Social Theory in the Postmodern Era* (Oxford: Blackwell).

Turner, S. P. and Turner, J. H. (1990), *The Impossible Science: An Institutional Analysis of American Sociology* (Newbury Park, CA: Sage).

Watts-Miller, W. (1996), *Durkheim, Morals and Modernity* (London: UCL Press).

Weber, M. (1968), *Economy and Society*, 3 vols (New York: Bedminster Press).

Woodiwiss, A. (1993), *Postmodernity USA: The Crisis of Social Modernism in Postwar America* (London: Sage).

Woolgar, S. (1993), *Science: The Very Idea* (London: Routledge).

Index